Funk the Erotic

THE NEW BLACK STUDIES SERIES

Edited by Darlene Clark Hine
and Dwight A. McBride

A list of books in the series
appears at the end of this book.

Funk the Erotic

Transaesthetics and Black Sexual Cultures

L. H. STALLINGS

UNIVERSITY OF ILLINOIS PRESS

Urbana, Chicago, and Springfield

Support for this research was received from the Institute for
Advanced Study at Indiana University, a research center
for the Office of the Vice Provost for Research.

Library of Congress Cataloging-in-Publication Data
Horton-Stallings, LaMonda.
Funk the erotic : transaesthetics and black sexual cultures /
L.H. Stallings.
pages   cm. — (The new Black studies series)
Includes bibliographical references and index.
ISBN 978-0-252-03959-1 (cloth : alk. paper)
ISBN 978-0-252-08110-1 (pbk. : alk. paper)
ISBN 978-0-252-09768-3 (e-book)
1. African Americans. 2. African Americans—Sexual behavior. 3. Sex—
United States—Cross-cultural studies. 4. American literature—African
American authors—History and criticism.
I. Title.
E185.86.H775   2015
306.7089'96073—dc23   2015004611

For Paulette and Aaron Jr.
Children of Production/Clones of Dr. Funkenstein

But in the hold, in the undercommons of a new feel, another kind of feeling became common.

—Stefano Harney and Fred Moten

Contents

Preface

> Very often, however, the Negro's masking is motivated not
> so much by fear as by a profound rejection of the image
> created to usurp his identity. Sometimes it is for the sheer
> joy of the joke; sometimes to challenge those who presume,
> across the psychological distance created by race manners, to
> know his identity. . . . America is a land of joking maskers . . .
> the motives hidden behind the mask are as numerous as the
> ambiguities the mask conceals.
>
> —Ralph Ellison, "Change the Joke and Slip the Yoke"

> I never did anything where I wasn't in on it.
> Even if it was something I had to do, I would
> always find a way to be in on it.
>
> —Vanessa del Rio, *Fifty Years of Slightly Slutty Behavior*

Moral judgments about public sexual expression, as well as the art and culture divide, makes some people bristle at the idea that novelist Ralph Ellison and porn actress Vanessa del Rio perhaps shared similar philosophies about their creative writing and performances. Ellison wishes to legitimate the black novel as a form that should not be reduced to folklore alone, while del Rio intends that her performances in sex industries not be read as melodramatic narratives of coercion. Moreover, we have become accustomed to legitimating the trope of masking in matters of race and minstrelsy in ways that seldom pertain in studies on gender, sexuality, or desire.[1] Yet, Vanessa del Rio's performances in movies from the golden era of pornography are as laugh-out-loud funny as they are sexually evocative. Del Rio's comment about being in on the joke or con echoes Ellison's ideas about America and masks. Both refuse pacifist or patently violent strategies against oppressive establishments but rather inform us of guerilla tactics that can be employed in personal and political liberation struggles.

Funk the Erotic: Transaesthetics and Black Sexual Cultures presents sexual expressivity or explicitness in black literature and culture as a rejection of the Western will to truth, or the quest to produce a truth about sexuality, and underscores such truth as a con and joke. It demonstrates how some black cultural producers have strategized against the sexual con of white supremacist, capitalist patriarchy outside of politics. In lieu of singular truths about eroticism and sexuality, the writers, directors, and performers in this text offer multiple fictions of sex to slip the yoke of sexual terrorism, violence, and colonization. This book is not about pornography and women of color. I leave that in the capable hands of Mireille Miller-Young, Jennifer Nash, and Ariane Cruz. They are all scholars who have produced formidable work to fill in the gaps about black women and porn. *Funk the Erotic* is about what exists before, after, in the interim, and in the future of what has been called *sexuality, eroticism,* the *pornographic,* and *sex work* in black America. It intends to lay new foundations upon which we should think about how sexual cultures, including pornography, translate, produce, and reproduce black pleasure, pain, intimacy, relationality, individuality, and communality in the face of historical and ever-changing sexual terror and violence from white capitalist patriarchy and supremacist institutions that can neither comprehend nor regulate the diverse affective resistance of black bodies.

I reference Ellison and del Rio to underscore lineages that have been ignored or silenced in the quest for a sexual politics that includes pleasure and exhausting questions about agency: preexisting, affective, and personal genealogies of imagination that are themselves movements that cannot be made to do the work of political movements. How do these narratives, which may or may not include moralizing tendencies or sexual pathologies, recognize black women's and men's exchanges and consumption of sexual expressivity and strategies for dealing with pain and everyday survival among each other and outside of black communities? As we will see throughout *Funk the Erotic,* the question needs to be considered for black women, men, children, and transgender folk. And it needs to begin in home fictions, rather than home truths. When we go in search of our mothers' profane porn stashes, as well as their sacred gardens, we critique the very ways in which what is profane and obscene has been gendered as masculine and made violent and excessive in the West. We recover sacred-profane androgynies, or what I term *funky erotixxx,* that create identity and subjectivity anew and alter political and artistic movements.

Former prostitute, escort, and porn star Vanessa del Rio did not grow up wanting to be a porn star. As she tells interviewer Dian Hanson, watching movie star Isabel Sarli on-screen and witnessing her mother's unhappiness at home influenced why she became a professional slut instead of being a secretary.[2] Throughout that interview she colloquially captures the "change the joke and slip the yoke" sentiment of what it means to be a young Puerto Rican woman in the white, capitalist, heteropatriarchal society of the 1970s. Additionally, reading del Rio's interview with Hanson, as well as her interviews with others, in a transatlantic frame certainly links her with current ways that scholars such as Kamala Kempadoo and Mireille Miller-Young have asked us to reconsider sexual labor. Nonetheless, the implicit importance of imagination or ulterior play in del Rio's statement remains the central element that makes her a cultural theorist for the purpose of this preface. Del Rio is similar to the early woman writer or scholar, the female blues singer, the woman rapper, or the comedienne, but del Rio differs from those other cultural producers in that her field of interest and expression is sex.

Casting herself as a type of grifter, del Rio understands that the con or joke that means to ensure masculine privilege and power is not one she is meant to be a part of, be it in a career, job, or domestic pursuit. Del Rio's words corroborate that personal familial influences and popular culture representations influence who she becomes in the world. She accounts for her gaze upon her mother's normalized domestic situation as good wife and mother, neither tragic nor violent, but ordinarily unhappy. Feminists seldom turn to this type of gaze in feminist academic scholarship on porn. Were we ever able to correlate del Rio's individual performances of submission, dissatisfaction, anger, hostility, dejection, or dysphoria within her films to an emulation of her mother's affect throughout married life, would we admit that the basis of her exploitation or performance might as readily be the institution of marriage as it would be porn industries? If we were ever able to trace del Rio's individual performances of happiness, contentment, hunger, or pleasure in her many films to any of the campy performances of the Argentine actress she purports to emulate—Isabel Sarli, who starred in Argentine films dubbed *sexploitation flicks* by Western critics—would proporn and antiporn scholarship collapse into each other? In Sarli's films, sexual images and nudity derive from a cultural tradition with very different views about eros and sexuality than in the United States, one in which we might have to think of performances within sexual cultures as something other than pornographic or exploitative.

Despite the dominance of feminist and queer theory in this work, my initial motivation for completing this project arises from less institutional sources: radical gender and sexual philosophies traced to the two Vanessas in my life—my mother Vanessa and adult film star Vanessa del Rio. I became a Vanessa del Rio fan because my mother and her sisters were Vanessa del Rio fans. As my mother has noted, the porn she consumed came from her older and more risqué sisters. Del Rio only becomes a significant source to me because I have always read her through the iconic stature that I have given to my mother, her life, and her mysterious Scorpio charms. In her midtwenties to thirties, my mother was humble, funky, and fly. She liked wigs, dressing up, and dudes who could sing, drove sweet cars, and wore fly suits and gators. She was a Sunday-school teacher. She ushered on second Sundays, and she also sang in the choir on fourth Sundays. She started out as a single teenage mother working odd jobs who eventually would become a teacher's aide in the public school system for more than twenty years. She made sure her children read the Bible and spent copious amounts of their time at the library. She did all of this while keeping a secret stash of porn that stopped being a secret by the time my sisters and I were preadolescents in the 1980s.

After our initial discovery, we carried out thrilling covert operations to discover and rediscover my mother's stash of books, magazines, and videos while she was away from the house. These were epic counterintelligence adventures with lookouts, confirmation of work schedule changes that needed to be known, and technological inventions that shifted our access to other forms. There were also performances of innocence and ignorance. Never to be outsmarted, she somehow always knew when we found her stash, and we always knew when she knew that we knew because the stash would change locations. This parental secrecy and childhood curiosity around sexual cultures was not ours alone. Other cousins or friends did the same with their parents' stash. Though we never broached the issue until we were well into adulthood, the back-and-forth, hide-and-seek episodes were an unacknowledged agreement that none of us would ever be antipornography, and that we would always figure out how to traverse the limitations and boundaries of policing and privatization of sex through each other, in spite of demands to regulate or make illegal public forms of sex. Moreover, we would do so in ways shaped by work, society, technology, and black fundamentals of the ludic.

My mother was not a porn star or a sexual intellectual, but I have subsequently learned to read a porn star and sexual cultures through my mother and quite possibly through whatever my mother's relationship to her mother's life may have been: that is, against the American grain of racism and sexism that reads del Rio solely as representation and sign of Otherly human being. Instead of a male gaze, it is a third-eye perspective that reads del Rio as a porn star as well as a host of other potential subjects made absent by the one. As the daughter of a single mother, I cannot divorce my mother's unconditional love, her generosity, her laughter, her playfulness, and the tireless way she worked to make ends meet from the woman who found time to watch porn by herself or with company while her daughters were asleep or at sleepovers. I cannot see it as that stool-seating moment in Alice Walker's short story about heterosexual marriage and porn, "Coming Apart,"[3] because it is not that moment. It quite simply was something else for my mother, her sisters, and my sisters.

As a scholar of gender and sexuality and one of many heiresses to trickster traditions, I cannot omit or lessen the significance of these moments in which what is thrilling, erotic, obscene, pornographic, profane, or sexual intersects with what is feminine, sacred, spiritual, intellectual, and nurturing because they are still ongoing moments that inform how I read people, culture, communities, and political movements. I have instead theorized these exchanges as a funky erotixxx, an acknowledgment that what is profane or obscene has a lineage that exceeds its destructive imperialist mandates within Western patriarchy, and that is sacred. My study of a maternal profane imaginary remains very different from considerations of sexual scripts taken up in many scholarly fields and popular discourses ad nauseam. As I will show, funky erotixxx's emphasis on creativity and improvisation dictates that there are no scripts because what is profane changes over time depending on when and where it originates.

Funky erotixxx is unknowable and immeasurable, with transgenerational, affective, and psychic modalities that problematize the erotic and what it means to be human, and it can be made legible in sexual cultures rather than the biopolitics or necropolitics of asexual cultures. Funky erotixxx has multiple ongoing loops or exchanges across bodies, mediums, and persons that resist the historicity, linearity, and nationalism that come with sex as knowledge/power. In addition, these moments can create sexual guerillas among sexual pacifists and sexual terrorists for the reason that del Rio implicitly outlines—imagination, or *magic* as it is called in chapter 1. Imagination allows the sexual guerilla to change how she approaches and navigates sexual violence and terrorism.

In my previous book *Mutha' Is Half a Word: Intersections of Folklore, Vernacular, Myth and Queerness in Black Female Culture*, I relied on the trickster figure to stress that an unnaming of black women facilitates personal and communal revolutionary moments in black cultural traditions. I concluded that, for black cultural creators, it was not enough to poke, prod, and analyze gender and sexual scripts impressed upon black women, and that "instead of disregarding work that might be considered vulgar or profane, we should observe them for their strategies of creating radical black female sexual subjectivity and a discourse for that subjectivity" (294). Having created a space for my own unnaming as a black woman doing scholarship on black sexualities and sexual cultures that seem to have no use or function in black political machines (not movements), I now turn to creating strategies for inventing and revising research methodologies in black studies meant to examine race as it intersects with sexuality, gender, and class. Creating new readings of culture that have already been produced, and that have not been tied to past political movements, can form the basis of strategies of future movements instead of becoming nostalgic for outdated approaches. That is what I offer here.

By the end of *Funk the Erotic*, I hope to have provided evidence of how funk as a multisensory and multidimensional philosophy has been used in conjunction with the erotic, eroticism, and black erotica. Funk is the affect that shapes film, performance, sound, food, technology, drugs, energy, time, and the seeds of revolutionary ideas for various black movements. Thus, *Funk the Erotic* is a book that one should read as well as feel; hear as much as see, touch, and taste; and foresee as well as see. If publishing and financial acumen allowed it, this funky-ass text would have been encased in a hard cover made of feathers, cotton, or fur and printed with embossed letters in deep purple or red on silk paper scented with jasmine, patchouli, Egyptian night, or some other incense "real black" people love. If technology and copyright laws allowed it, some editions of *Funk the Erotic* would be holographic, scratch-and-sniff, sonic books with Chaka Khan, Betty Davis, Sugarfoot, Prince, Erykah Badu, and Van Hunt reading chapters as some of the greatest funk tracks of all time played in the background with enough bass to make readers feel the sounds knee-deep. Sadly, none of the aforementioned options are currently possible, which is why in each chapter I refer to funk's various modes and manifestations, using it as a lens to circumvent the disembodiment and cultural abstraction of text without sensation. I hope readers can get up, get down, get funky, and get loose[4] with what follows. I consider this a work of funk studies,[5] myself a funk studies scholar, and anyone reading this a superfreak.

Acknowledgments

Thank you, Vanessa Horton, mother-father, for all of your sacrifices. I continue to be in awe of the nurturing and unconditional love you gave me as a child. I truly picked the right one to come thru in you. I am so thankful for the relationship we continue to build, beyond mother-child, that allows us to laugh and criticize each other with love as friends and sisters now. I always write, think, and theorize from your love first. RaMonda and Latasha, your love and support sustained me as I continued to write and research. Jasmine, Rod Jr., Elijah, and Octavia: Thank you for letting me be an aunt to the funkiest, most superfly, and kind-hearted nieces and nephews on the planet. You are why I continue to think intergalatically.

The National Endowment for the Humanities (NEH)/Samuel I. Newhouse awarded me a Schomburg Fellowship that allowed me to begin researching for and thinking about this book. In our current era, it remains rare for institutions to recognize the importance of arts and humanities to sexuality, and sexuality's importance to arts and humanities, so I am especially grateful for the financial support and early recognition of this project. I amassed numerous materials and important contacts, and my time at the Schomburg Center for Research in Black Culture resulted in me meeting amazing people. Monica Miller, Kevin Mumford, and Dayo Gore: I learned so much of what I needed to bring to this project from reading your work for our fellows' meetings. Steve G. Fullwood and Herukhuti (a.k.a. Black Funk), our friendships have grounded my queries into funk. Thank you, Jeffrey Renard Allen, for your voice as a writer and for connecting me with Wanda Coleman during that time. Colin A. Palmer and Diana Lachatanere, your guidance and support were very much appreciated. The Institute for Advanced Study at Indiana University provided funding support for the publication of this book. Thank you Dawn Durante, Mary Reily, and Anne Rogers for your enthusiastic support and careful appraisal of various versions of this book.

I want to thank the two research and writing groups whose support also made the completion of this book possible. Members of the S.P.A.C.E. Collective: Marlon Moore, Marlo David, Angelique Nixon, Treva Lindsey, Darius Bost, Rachel Robinson, C. Riley Snorton, Sophia L. Buggs, and Nicky Banton; I appreciate all your thoughtful readings, suggestions, comments, signifying, and the moments that writing and studying blurred into partying and dancing and vice versa. I continue to be very grateful to have you all in my life. I also want to thank the Black Sexual Economies Research Group convened by Adrienne Davis and Mireille Miller-Young. Adrienne, you are a graceful and beautiful mentor. Mireille, thank you for your attention to detail, mean looks, laughter, and wonderful perspective on all things sexual. Marlon Bailey, Felice Blake, Xavier Limon, Jeffrey McCune, and Matt Richardson, thank you so much for reading my work and keeping me focused on the work of illuminating black sexual cultures. Outside of these groups, I continue to be appreciative of GAT—Greg Thomas and Michael Martin. Ariane Cruz, thanks for your astute and useful critique of chapter 3. Thank you Wanda Coleman, Miriam DeCosta-Willis, Fiona Zedde, Blake Aarens, and Zane for taking the time to speak with me about erotics, writing, and your life. What I learned in those interviews shaped this entire project in so many ways.

Finally, William, thank you for understanding the importance of autonomy, independence, and space for how I live, love, and write. Like little kids creating our own shortcuts, I am glad that we've stayed away from well-traveled paths. Thank you for ensuring a life-work balance and still playing. Thank you for a creative partnership bound by the aesthetics of funk.

Funk the Erotic

Introduction

Plato and Socrates, Freud and Jung, Bataille and de Sade, Afrekete and Audre Lorde, Sun-Ra and Parliament, and Prince and Sheila E have all contributed to our understanding of eros and eroticism and labor and leisure. However, only the last three cohorts have considered how to adapt eros to decolonizing efforts, or funk with the erotic. The musical history of funk has recorded its cultural significance in a number of ways. Rickey Vincent penned an award-winning popular study entitled *Funk*. Betty Davis spelled it out over some deep bass guitar licks, exclaiming, "F.U.N.K. / Funk. Funk y'all. Funk. . . . / I was born with it."[1] Parliament's philosophies on funk have offered a point of origin that explains, "In the days of the Funkapus / The concept of specially-designed Afronauts / Capable of funkatizing galaxies / Was first laid on man-child / But was later repossessed / And placed among the secrets of the pyramids / Until a more positive attitude / Towards this most sacred phenomenon / . . . / Could be acquired."[2] Likewise, Toni Morrison's *The Bluest Eye* also reminds us that funk is not merely a music genre or form, and that negative connotations associated with funk would persist for those interested in moral cleansing. Each delivers perspectives of funk as philosophy, epistemology, or ontology. But what does it mean to do as this text's title implores, to funk the erotic? Copulate with it, dismiss it, or make it stink? I privilege the multiple meanings of the demand over one meaning to link funk to creative endeavors and energies outside of music, to challenge the erotic as a concept that can be universally applied to various communities, and to uncover the way it distinguishes its observation of materiality away from eros and its role in developing the erotic as power.

Given the global dominance of hip-hop in popular culture and its relevance as a site of analysis in academic studies, a book that is about funk, but not funk music, could seem a little retro and old school. Yet every form of contemporary American music, past and present, has shown that funk is a resilient and revisionary force. Although this book is not a sonic text or a text explicitly about black music, *Funk the Erotic: Transaesthetics and Black Sexual Cultures* takes its inspiration from the interesting and unexpected places we find funk within and outside of the black music tradition. For example, an art exhibition created by Sanford Biggers, *Sweet Funk: An Introspective,* represents why it might be time to think about "funk studies" as an emerging branch of black studies that reorients our thinking about sexuality, gender, and agency away from dated notions of human being that are antiblack. From September 23, 2011, through January 8, 2012, Biggers's *Sweet Funk* was on display at the Brooklyn Art Museum. Biggers's mixed and multimedia exhibit engages numerous senses and aesthetics. For me, the exhibit challenged the dominant and historical discourses that view funk as situated solely in the sonic or musical sphere. One of the most imaginative pieces, *Blossom,* perfectly captures funk as a philosophy about being or (un)becoming human. Although Biggers had used *Blossom* in previous exhibits not related to funk, its inclusion in this one showcased how much of his art had engaged funk as a philosophy about what it means to be otherly human, inhuman, or nonhuman.

Blossom is a sculptural installation of a tree growing out of a baby grand piano converted into a MIDI system piano with a knocked-over piano bench lying in a circular patch of dirt in which the tree is rooted. The piece refuses either/or binaries of dividing nature from culture, nature from technology, and precolonial natural institutions from modern cultural institutions. *Blossom* produces multiple meanings based on viewers' perceptions of objectivity and subjectivity or privileging of the human and nonhuman. Some viewers might consider the tree as a historical site of death because the piano plays "Strange Fruit," a song explicitly about the lynching of black bodies. Conversely, the art piece represents the tree as a form of life since the tree can also be read as the player or musician of the song. In addition, the piano can be read as a sustainer of life for the tree as music has been crucial to the survival of black people in the New World. With *Blossom,* viewers come to understand the nonhuman as a living being capable of creating culture as well as serving as an inspiration for art. Biggers's perspective about human and nonhuman relationality and connection dictates his artistic representation of black experiences, music, and culture. Biggers does not privilege the human or disconnect it from nature, and therefore the aesthetics from which he draws do not derive from one singular cultural form or sensory experience. This piece, and the entire exhibit, showcases how funk allows us to understand black existence, creative production, and the imaginary outside of what it means to be human and alive in the West.

Such insights are of great use for moving past academic proclamations that seem more like epistemological cemeteries and graveyards in their call for new methods of analysis.[3] As *Funk the Erotic* consistently demonstrates, funk exists as a philosophy that usurps the divide between eros (life) and thanatos (death) since it is sustained by otherly human and nonhuman beliefs in the supernatural, afterlife, and reanimation. In addition to some of the creative endeavors outlined throughout this book, the contemporary critical examinations provided by Tony Bolden, Francesca Royster, Anne Danielsen, and Herukhuti build on the foundations established by Susan Willis, Toni Morrison, Robert Farris Thompson, and Rickey Vincent in preceding eras. Theorizing their works, and this one, as a field of funk studies will be especially useful to scholars who want to study joy, pleasure, race, and sexuality and navigate or avoid antiblackness discourses and necropolitics without losing sight of Afro-pessimism's careful annihilation of discursive analysis on being human and its critique of black social life.

Francesca Royster's *Sounding Like a No-No: Queer Sounds and Eccentric Acts in the Post-Soul Era* has been one of the few book-length studies to dynamically assess the importance of funk to African American discourses and histories of sexualities and genders. In her theorization of post-soul eccentricity,[4] Royster details how funk music challenged the edict of black power and civil rights strategies for the black body, as well as demonstrates how it fits into post-soul as an era and an aesthetic. She asserts that post-soul eccentrics ask, "What happens after the basic needs of family and community are met? What if the clothing of unity is too tight?" (9). She then suggests that post-soul eccentrics also inquire as to "where might blackness not only uplift us or feed our souls, but sometimes fail us, erasing our desires or constraining the ways we move in the world as sexual and sensual beings" (10). I add to her work by highlighting how funk creates new structures, myths, and points of origins for neoteric models of humanity that exceed soul and post-soul.

However, my work diverges from Royster's in that it understands funk as existing before and after post-soul and being more than sound. By looking at other black cultural products, we can glean funk as a philosophy about kinesthetics and being that critiques capitalism and the pathology of Western morality of the West while also possessing the wisdom to know and understand that the two are linked. Because funk sees the two as linked, it provides innovative strategies about work and sexuality that need to be highlighted. Black music scholarship has studied funk as a form that leads to dance and other music; I am examining funk as nonreproductive sex and transaesthetics of cultural art forms. Tony Bolden's "Theorizing the Funk" informs us that "funkativity invokes a reevaluation of the very notion of textuality" (18), and so I take him at his word and explore what funk does to the discursivity of sexuality. Comprehending funk's operation and existence outside of black music and within the African American literary, performative, and visual tradition means demonstrating how the black erotic and pornographic imaginary simultaneously addresses funk in its white, Eurocentric tenor, and funk as the indeterminacy of being it came to represent in black music and popular culture. *Funk the Erotic* acknowledges and further develops what Prince and George Clinton have been telling us all along—that sometimes *funk* and *fuck* are intertwined and interchangeable.[5] The interchangeability of *funk* and *fuck* relies on context and aesthetics.

The etymological triad for *funk*—nonvisual sensory perception (smell/odor), embodied movement (dance and sex), and force (mood and will)—shapes the readings and analysis of sexual cultures in this text. In tracing the etymology of *funk*, Robert Farris Thompson reveals its origins in West Africa:

> The slang term "funky" in black communities originally referred to strong body odor and not to "funk," meaning fear or panic. The Black nuance seems to derive from the Ki-Kongo *lu-fuki* "bad body odor" and is perhaps reinforced by contact with *fumet*, "aroma of food and wine" in French Louisiana. But the Ki-Kongo word is closer to the jazz word "funky" in form and meaning, as both jazzmen and Bakongo use "funky" and *lu-fuki* to praise persons for the integrity of their art, for having worked out to achieve their aims. . . . For in Kongo the smell of a hardworking elder carries luck. This Kongo sign of exertion is identified with the positive energy of a person.[6]

Although there is no specification about forms of art or aims, Thompson's charting the existence of funk outside the sonic did for the black-Atlantic visual tradition what had already been done with black language and music and the importance of improvisation and polyphonic sound in each: linked the cultures of various groups without depending on genealogy (a form of biopower). Moreover, funk becomes a philosophy about art in which the focus centers not on what is beautiful, but what is funky. Such a common orientation of aesthetics has been said to influence numerous facets of black life and culture, except when it comes to two dominant spheres for measuring Western development, expansion, and society: sex and work. Funk music recalls the Kongo ideology of corporeal exertion as positive force by using bass lines and guitar riffs to create "the one," an intense groove that distinguishes itself from other black music aesthetics, but other critics and I have theorized these definitions of *black funk* as an intersectional epistemology of knowledge about embodiment, aesthetics, sensory experience, and labor.

In each chapter, I bring to bear the triad of funk in my readings of black sexual cultures because it allows me to broach theories of eroticism and humanity that may differ from most theories of eroticism offered by Greek, Roman, and Eurocentric theorists of the past, as well as contemporary black feminist and queer theorists, even when I have to engage them. The triad of funk attends to what Rinaldo Walcott calls "the whatever of blackness": "The uncertainties and commonalities of blackness might be formulated in the face of some room for surprise, disappointment, and pleasure without recourse to disciplinary and punishing measures . . . a whatever that can tolerate the whatever of blackness without knowing meaning—black meaning, that is—in advance of its various utterances."[7] That *whatever* is funk. Given the number of scholarly and popular studies of black music and art that for more than a century have suggested the nature of improvisation in black lives, we cannot continue to believe that when the Greeks stole elements of African civilization, including its knowledge systems, that expressions of body and affect remained the same. Or that when Europe and the United States created categories and a history of sexuality during and after slavery, that these African people and their descendants who have improvised and creatively imagined everything else would not have done so with what modernity terms *eros,* and later *love, uses of the erotic, sexuality, sex,* and *work.* Rather than suggesting funk as a reactionary mechanism, as if it did not exist before Western eros, I see it as imperiocorporeal cognition or imperiocorporeal perception—a simultaneous creation of new knowledge and an acquisition of knowledge through the body to counter imperialist or colonial appropriation of bodies and cultures. Funk is force, not power.

Funk proposes a loop for desire that makes and unmakes objects outside of modernity and civilization. Using funk as a lens to read black sexual cultures offers us a way to answer Alexander Weheliye's important question asked in "After Man": "What different modalities of the human come to light if we do not take the liberal humanist figure of 'man' as the master-subject but focus on how humanity has been imagined and lived by those subjects excluded from this domain?" (321). Although Weheliye pursues the answer to what comes after man from a concern for technology and informational media, I am more interested in it for how it might lead to a recognition of what black sexual cultures mean to philosophies of being and life. Such an interruption attempts to do as Sylvia Wynter demands that any interruption of knowledge should do—remake man and knowledge:

> To sum up: this means that the epochal rupture that was set in motion by Western intellectuals, by means of which human knowledge of the physical cosmos would be freed from having to be known in the adaptive truth—for terms that had been hitherto indispensable to the instituting of all human orders and their respective modes/genres of being human—the rupture that was to lead to the gradual development of the physical sciences—had been made possible only by the no less epochal reinvention of Western Europe's matrix Judeo-Christian genre of the human, in its first secularizing if still hybridly religio-secular terms as Man as the Rational Self and political subject of the state, in the reoccupied place of the True

Christian Self, or mode of sociogeny, of Latin-Christian Europe; by the reinvention also of the secular entity of the West in the reoccupied place of the latter, with this reinvention being based on the model of Virgil's Roman imperial epic.[8]

Funk produces alternative orders of knowledge about the body and imagination that originate in a sensorium predating empires of knowledge. Scholarship on funk as a music genre downplays the significance of funk's philosophical link to the sense of smell and, consequently, the alternative mode of being that derives from sensus communis that prioritizes smell.

According to Alain Corbin's *The Foul and the Fragrant*, "abhorrence of smells produces its own form of social power" (5). Corbin contends that smell is also the sense least associated with intelligence and spirituality. A humanity envisioned by the West as civilized must not be funky. The only logical response is a repression and covering up of what stinks, which is the exact opposite of a culture that sees funk as a sign of good luck, artistic integrity, and hard work. The etymology of *black funk* emphasizes that funk is a rewriting of smell and scent away from nineteenth-century ordering and socialization of corporeal power that represses what stinks, but that does not mean it lacks intelligence or spirituality; rather, it provides other paradigms of intellect and spirit. Black funk enables artists and researchers to center our methodologies and readings on what Fred Moten and Stefano Harney have theorized as the touch of the undercommon, hapticality,[9] so that we come to understand why research aesthetics are as important as research methods and ethics. Funk remains an African diasporic philosophy about transition, movement, and embodiment as it relates to art, work, sex, gender, race, and national boundaries, but funk as a philosophy that debunks "the truth of sex" and its histories is the subject of this book. How one imagines and creates sexuality is just as important as how one produces knowledge about sexuality. Funk reminds us that there are aesthetics, or rather transaesthetics, of sexuality that can aid in the creation of neoteric modes of being human.

Cartesian dualism of a mind/body split has facilitated the need to create competing philosophies of rationality, labor, aesthetics, and imagination when it comes to art as an object of study. John Dewey's *Art as Experience* explains "that theories which isolate art and its appreciation by placing them in a realm of their own, disconnected from other modes of experiencing, . . . arise because of specifiable extraneous conditions" (9). Literary critic Russ Castronovo further explains of aesthetics:

> In their narrowest sense, aesthetics are purely about the discernment of formal criteria such as unity, proportion, and balance within the domain of art. If we trace the term's origins back to the German Romantic tradition of Immanuel Kant and Friedrich von Schiller, aesthetics appear as a philosophical topic rather than a cultural conjuncture.[10]

He concludes that when linked with the development of social ethics, aesthetics have proven pivotal in the democraticization of culture for numerous nations. The extraneous conditions and cultural conjecture, however, suggest that such democratization is for a specific genre of the human. Additionally, when concerns of aesthetics are also linked with theories of the imagination, we find a primary sensory experience governing most theories. The imagination, Dewey's *Art as Experience* expounds, "is a way of seeing and feeling things as they compose an integral whole. It is the large and general blending of interests at the point where the mind comes into contact with the world. When old and familiar things are made new in experience, there is imagination" (278). Leslie Stevenson theorized twelve conceptions of the imagination, defining it as "the ability to think of something not presently perceived, but spatio-temporally real" and "[t]he ability to think of whatever one acknowledges as possible in the spatio-temporal world."[11] From Kant and Hegel to current studies of cognition and imagination, two common threads remain in major Western philosophies about imagination and artistic inquiries: the human and image. Yet Nicole Fleetwood's *Troubling Vision* tells us that "blackness troubles vision in Western discourse" (6), and that includes visuality's imaging and the image. Michael Beaney also observes in *Imagination and Creativity* that traditional considerations of the imagination are limited. He asks, "Does 'imagination' really have a single sense or refer to a single faculty? Can any order at all be brought into the varieties of imaginative experience? What conceptions of imagination might be distinguished?" (3). Such critiques matter not only to how we think through art, culture, aesthetics, and the erotic, but also to how we theorize sex and sexuality.

These philosophies about aesthetics and imagination influence sexuality and the study of sexuality. Proclaiming historically that there are two strategies for producing the truth of sex, Michel Foucault argues that "on the one hand, the societies—and they are numerous: China, Japan, India, Rome, the Arabo-Moslem societies . . . endowed themselves with an ars erotica" but that "our civilization possesses no ars erotica. In return, it is undoubtedly the only civilization to practice a scientia sexualis."[12] How do we ignore Foucault's privileging of Cartesian dualisms and ways of being, in addition to specific social classes, in his proclamation about ars erotica/scientia sexualis as it relates to the history of sexuality? How do we not challenge his theories when we comprehend that what is called *sex work* has existed as long as these two strategies? Simply put, as is shown later, hoing and its politics reveal the Foucauldian binary as false. As this book notes, in all three volumes of *The History of Sexuality*, Foucault's refusal to acknowledge other sites of knowledge—fiction, the surreal, and the imagination—maintains a divide between work and labor and leisure and pleasure that we should not accept as fact for societies and cultures that might foster an understanding that truth, pleasure, and knowledge are not mutually exclusive or in opposition to each other. As Foucault has shown, sexuality has been written as an object of analysis rather than an object of imagination. Sexuality, he explains,

> appears . . . as an especially dense transfer point for relations of power: between men and women, young people and old people, parents and offspring, teachers and students, priests and laity, an administration and a population. Sexuality is not the most intractable element in power relations, but rather one of those endowed with the greatest instrumentality: useful for the greatest number of maneuvers and capable of serving as a point of support, as a linchpin, for the most varied strategies.[13]

Thus, we know what power does with sexuality and we understand the discourse of sex, but we understand less about what imagination does with sexuality and how imagination thwarts power's need to establish a knowledge-power of sex as either scientia sexualis or a truth-as-pleasure from ars erotica.[14] Turning to John Dewey's objection of a romanticist notion of imagination as power, it becomes clear why sexuality can exceed those two forms. Dewey explains, "[N]ot that imagination is the power that does certain things, but that an imaginative experience is what happens when varied materials of sense, quality, emotion, and meaning come together in a union that marks a new birth in the world" (279). When sexuality is theorized as imaginative experience, it becomes art as experience and less bound by capitalism's emphasis on production and biopower's reproductive ordering of time. It becomes embodied knowledge.

The human imagination requires a specific spatiotemporal world and being; funky being requires another. With funk, there is no definitive separation of mind and body that intends to disembody imagination or represent reality, even as there is art and lu-fuki. Unlike considerations of imagination and eros in the West, funk accounts for the time of thought. In theorizing time into thought, Elizabeth Grosz asks, "Is it possible to develop an understanding of thought that refuses to see thought as passivity, reflection, contemplation, or representation, and instead stresses its activity, how and what it performs, how it is a force that exists alongside of and in concert with other kinds of forces that are not conceptual? Can we deromanticize the construction of knowledges and discourses to see them as labor, production, doing?"[15] Funk's emphasis on embodied movement of dance and sex answers yes.

Imagination remains the major force that individuals can rely on to thwart or subvert power, but it is not solely an ocular force of the human mind as it has been defined. Imagination precedes, and proceeds from, power, power-knowledge, and power plays. Yet, the materiality of both creativity and imagination, outside of products produced by them and controlled by power, cannot be made evident as material within our current order of knowledge and its systems of discourse. Nevertheless, this text theorizes that elsewhere sexuality has been comprised from affective modalities, and sexuality demonstrates one way that imagination and creativity materialize despite our inability to manufacture evidence for such claims. *Funk the Erotic* argues that when we consider imperialism, colonization, and slavery, and the indigenous and displaced people they impacted, in this debate about the truth of sex, there might be more than two great procedures for producing the truth of sex.[16] Funk has produced knowledge about sex but it hails from an alternative order. By specifically nuancing its link with creativity, imagination, memory, and movement, these pages explore African diasporic funk as a possible avenue for producing many long-ignored truths, or competing fictions, of sex and the erotic as power.

Transaesthetics, Sexuality, and Uses of the Erotic

The erotic as power. I cannot say or think about it without remembering Audre Lorde's concept of the erotic. Lorde's "Uses of the Erotic" is a massive and communal theoretical dialogue that reimagines the erotic away from Western designs, spiritually reaffirming it for women and people of color especially. Although Lorde did not originate the term or theories of the erotic, her reimagining of them has been a central focal point for feminist studies and African American studies. For those of us who study black genders and sexualities, "Uses of the Erotic" is an introductory document that induces paralysis with the enormity of its expectations and goals and inspires awe with its discursive touch to symbolize the very thing that it speaks about: the erotic. It is a beautiful and delicious essay and tastes, *wm* for lack of a better parallel, like a lover well on the way to a climax. However, to fully implement the erotic as power, we must understand the magnitude of funk's role in the uses of the erotic. For example, how would comprehending "Uses of the Erotic" as foundationally situated in funk as mood change how that essay is read? Lorde begins writing the essay after she has been diagnosed with breast cancer. As Lorde notes, "The existence of that paper enabled me to pick up again and go to Houston and California, it enabled me to start working again. I don't know when I'd have been able to write again, if I hadn't had those words."[17] Lorde makes the connection between the essay, her cancer diagnosis, and her fighting spirit. *The Cancer Journals* confirms the link between funk and her revision of eros as a means for thwarting capitalism and Western science and medicine, as opposed to pornography alone.[18] Lorde's desire to reconsider her life and body away from the cancer cartel's treatment of the disease and not the person alerts her to the knowledge that the erotic can be a source of power.

Regarding the erotic, Lorde says it is not "a question only of what we do; it is a question of how acutely and fully we can feel in the doing" (54). Yet there remain two elements linked with the erotic that can hinder the latter mandate, what Achille Mbembe addresses as necropolitics and the economy of biopower composed by problematic definitions of being human.[19] Funk provides a reorganization of the senses to overcome necropolitics and biopower. Uses of the erotic may interrupt the economy of biopower, but these uses have not been able to counter necropolitics as Fred Wilderson's work has so dogmatically stated.[20] Yet, as my close readings and theoretical interventions of black cultural texts and performances explain, when funk is deployed alongside uses of the erotic, necropolitics can be avoided. I extend Lorde's concept of the erotic and honor her request to work fully to understand the diametrically opposite uses of the sexual ("pornography and eroticism") by insisting that this mission is as much a question about (colonizing) aesthetics as it is ethics. That is, what constitutes the ethical difference between pornography and eroticism is not and can never only be about gender hierarchies and oppression alone. We must first understand that the opposite uses of eros and the sexual demonstrate the dominant epistemologies that have produced sexuality before we can even consider debating the politics of those opposite uses. Is there really a difference between pornography and eroticism if the same systems of knowledge have produced or defined each artifact, form, and subject? No.

In order to subvert hierarchies of gender and sexuality and functions and form, I distinguish my study of sexual labor and sexual expression in literature and culture with what activist/theorist Susan Stryker explains as _transing_:

> Transing can function as a disciplinary tool when the stigma associated with the lack or loss of gender status threatens social unintelligibility, coercive normalization, or even bodily extermination. It can also function as an escape vector, line of flight, or pathway toward liberation. . . . What kinds of intellectual labor can we begin to perform through the critical deployment of "trans-" operations and movements? Those of us schooled in the humanities and social sciences have become familiar . . . with queering things; how might we likewise begin to trans our world?[21]

I trans black literary studies and sexuality studies to demonstrate how black communities' deployment of funk provides alternative knowledge about imagination and sexuality. Beginning with African American literature, as opposed to the end of it, provides a means of discerning this text's premise that funk produces fictions of sex to counter the truth of sex. Instead of downbeats and bass lines, writers and performers use sexually explicit expressions and unique ideas about sex and work to undo the coloniality of being/truth/freedom. I am calling this literary tradition _funky erotixxx_ rather than _black erotica_ because its texts form a black-Atlantic communal narrative on the fluid practice of what I theorize as "sacredly profane sexuality," as opposed to sexuality or sacred sexuality in other cultures. Sacredly profane sexuality ritualizes and makes sacred what is libidinous and blasphemous in Western humanism so as to unseat and criticize the inherent imperialistic aims within its social mores and sexual morality. I assert that cultural producers in this particular genre have been proposing a notably different understanding of sexual and erotic labor because they are also exploring new sensoriums and ways of being that cannot and do not align with Western traditions of humanism.

In Caroline Jones's edited collection *Sensorium,* the artists and authors in the collection allowed me to document the importance of black texts focused on sensation and the body to black movements, old and new. In the foundational essay of the collection, Jones explains that a sensorium acts as "the subject's way of coordinating all of the body's perceptual and proprioceptive signals as well as the changing sensory envelope of the self" (8). These modes of sensory organization, in turn, shape the social construct of race and any cultures that would be defined by the social construct of race. As Kenneth Warren's hyperbolic treatise "Does African-American Literature Exist?" indicates, black literature and culture cannot continue along such paths. Once we understand black literature as a multisensory and multidimensional text, we are no longer able to accept it as a form solely about race, racial uplift, and racial progress dependent upon sight and signs (discourses of race) or, as Warren notes, Jim Crow. The gift of what has been classified as an African American literary tradition, or more scholastically its signifying difference, originates in how writers in the tradition document that text and how narrative can be created using aesthetics and forms outside of written traditions.

What is now called African American literature existed as a transaesthetic tradition long before Jean Baudrillard's *The Transparency of Evil* dramatized transaesthetics as the end of Western civilization. For Baudrillard, transaesthetics mean a rejection of modernity and a negation of formal aesthetics where culture replaces what is formally known as art. With transaesthetics "there are no more fundamental rules, no more criteria of judgment or of pleasure . . . there is no gold standard of aesthetic judgment or pleasure" (14). However, these words are derived from an order of knowledge that seeks a divide between art and science or art and culture where aesthetics are created to make art as valuable as science. In order to determine aesthetics or aesthetic values, critics tend to value one sensory experience over another. Transaesthetics require a reorganization of senses and the sensorium, which funk offers. Although Baudrillard uses *transaesthetics* to discuss the medium of visual art, I am using it as a term applicable to all artistic forms, including sex as representative of art as experience. Because transaesthetics disturb forms, biological and otherwise, it derives from and produces causality and agency that does not privilege the human or one specific reality. Hence, transaesthetics provide a fresh line of inquiry for concerns about representation, agency, and sexuality.

Even as structural and poststructural critics circa the 1980s sought to theorize a valuable tradition pitting vernacular in accord or against the written, cultural producers of this written tradition in the early twentieth century had already been making transparent the evils of imperialism and colonialist aesthetics that would define art as separate and distinct from culture. They would distance their forms and aesthetics away from singular and binary sensory expressions in which objects could be easily commodified into a collectible artifact to reflect an empire or an empire's wealth. Transaesthetics made possible the survival of a posthuman imaginary over knowledge-power, the representation of black bodies, and the improvisational nature necessary for building black creative traditions. Further, if Caroline Jones is correct when she asserts that "modernism . . . organized the body in particular ways to colonize various sensory and bodily function (at least for American subjects)—working bureaucratically to enhance aesthetic relations to those functions, and to give them a commodity address,"[22] then I insist that African American writers, both cultural producers and commodities, conscious of such colonization of the senses, do the opposite.

Most notably this has already been remarked upon in critics' exploration of W. E. B. DuBois's use of occult discourses shaping his canonical sociological texts, Zora Neale Hurston's folk-ethnographic sensibilities influencing her literature, Bruce Nugent's skill as a visual artist influencing his writing, James Baldwin's gospel and ministry heritage shaping his oeuvre, and Ralph Ellison's musicianship influencing his writing. Because of the way senses have been ordered or colonized for commodification, each writer understood how to develop strategies necessary for shifting signs and signifiers into touch, hue, tenor, tone, performance, and emotion. The invention of printing presses, museums, theaters, or record companies did not make such labor intuitive. DuBois's, Hurston's, Nugent's, and Ellison's creativity attempts to configure a sensorium for a new humanity whose knowledge system would not require privileging one human sense over others, would not produce disciplines begging for interaction with each other or forms awaiting a validated deconstruction and reconstruction by capitalist endeavors and corporate institutions. DuBois's writings are as much sociological works as they are literary texts. Hurston's fiction is as much literature as it is a record of new ethnographic research methods. Nugent's writing is as much fiction as it is experimental visual art. Baldwin's polyform is as much fiction and essay as it is a gospel song and sermon. Samuel Delany's and Octavia Butler's science fiction is as much science as it is fiction. These transaesthetics are not only found in black literary texts but other cultural productions as well. More recently it has been seen in the way that transaesthetics disrupt the truths of politics—black, feminist, or otherwise. Fleetwood's attention to transaesthetics in *Troubling Vision,* specifically her development of concepts such as "non-iconicity" and "excess flesh" (9), tells us that some critics' attacks on the music and video art of Erykah Badu, Beyoncé, and Rihanna are not simply about proper feminist objects but also an unacknowledged discussion of what aesthetics and methods are best for critique: discursive, disembodied, or decorporealized forms versus others. Funk studies uses transaesthetics to demand that critics and scholars come up with research aesthetics that can overcome the science/art, politics/art, and art/culture divide still held in place by methods and ethics no matter how interdisciplinary. Funk serves as my research aesthetic for the study of black sexualities and black sexual cultures because sexual acts and desires are not monosensory experiences.

Funk the Erotic does more than engage African American literature or an African American literary tradition. Writing the obscene, the pornographic, and the erotic has been and always will be seen as a form of sex work, and so this book also explicates on work society, leisure, antiwork politics, and postwork imagination. It is about bodies in motion and texts that can adapt to such motion. It is about narratives invested in embodied movement, rather than disembodied movement. Disembodied movements are the foundation of recent conversations about blackness and cultural production, specifically literary, cultural, and political movements. In African American literary history, movements such as the new Negro movement, Harlem renaissance, black arts movement, postmodernism, black women's renaissance, post-soul aesthetics, and Afro-futurism have typically been defined by linear time periods, specific cultural aesthetics, or politics conducive of such time, fixed location, and geography, and essentially fixed genders and sexualities. Scholars who have focused on questions of postblackness or the end of the African American literary tradition have erroneously focused on the discourse of race used in the previously mentioned movements to validate their arguments and viewpoints.

The discourse of race is a text, and as a text, according to Caroline Jones: "[B]ecause it is visual and this shares visuality's claim on disembodied thought, text propels us into an abstract cultural realm. . . . [I]t can amalgamate sound or scent to coded image . . . to convey thought or experience. But this magic demands a quieting of the body's senses" (33). It would seem then that any attempt to translate the experiences of a particular body means erasing the body itself, magic, and, in the end, disembodying movement. Thus, the actual black body, which does change at micro- and macrolevels over time and wherever geographically located in ways that cannot be seen as much as felt, is displaced by the discourses of race and bodies that can be outdated or limited. As Kevin Quashie indicates in his assessment about interiority and the politics of representation:

> This is the politics of representation, where black subjectivity exists for its social and political meaningfulness rather than as a marker of the human individuality

of the person who is black. . . . The determination to see blackness only through a social public lens[,] as if there were no inner life, is racist. . . . [23]

The social or external forces can lead to stagnant movement. However, what happens when we focus on how black people inhabit their bodies outside of the designs of ocularity? Because kinetic energy and smell express interiority, they move us beyond the limits of what it means to be socially fabricated as black and human. Since everything we know of race and gender is socially constructed around what can and cannot be seen—pigmentation, gonads, cells, facial features—funk's move to reorder senses by privileging smell and internal kinetic energy in black communities leads us to other possibilities and configurations of bodies, psychically and affectively determined by how senses are ordered. Greek, European, and modern American sensoriums only consider five senses, whereas in the black sensorium, funk has revealed, as Western medicine is only now beginning to, that there are more than five senses. In funk, we might add to that list nociception, proprioception, temporal perception, interioception, and other extrasensory perceptions (knowledge gained and processed from the interior and exterior)—hence funk's futuristic implications.

Throughout *Funk the Erotic,* I explore how sexual expressivity and performance in black culture signals funk as a multisensory and multidimensional philosophy capable of dismantling systems of labor that organize race and sexuality for commercial profit (racial realism in African American literary studies and publishing, racial pride in black cultural nationalism, sexual identity in the history of sexuality/canons of gender and sex, and work ethics of capitalism) by simply interrupting and dismantling sensory regimes left over from the Enlightenment and modernist periods in black America that would fetishize written text and then orality. Toni Morrison's too-familiar philosophy on funk describes the women and girls of *The Bluest Eye*'s fictional town of Meridian. She writes of a black middle-class respectability haunted by historic trauma as well as influenced by present and future aspirations of belonging that echo the sentiments espoused by E. Franklin Frazier during the mid-twentieth century. As critic Susan Willis explored in her essay, "Eruptions of Funk," "Morrison translates the loss of history and culture into sexual terms and demonstrates the connection between bourgeois society and repression" (35). Yet in Morrison's work, there is only a dalliance with funk. Morrison's critically acclaimed *The Bluest Eye* was published four years after the lesser-praised work of one important writer under investigation in this text, Hal Bennett.

Bennett's *A Wilderness of Vines* and *Lord of Dark Places* showcase the full breadth and potential for funk to liberate black people from liberal humanism. As Bennett notes of his early oeuvre:

And I've come to understand that what I have been exploring in my earlier work . . . is the black American's obsession with filth. I think that once we live inside of a black grouping that is surrounded by white, right from slavery time until the present, we have a sense of being unclean. We feel unclean as a racial group. That might be a sense of physical filth.[24]

Bennett, like other writers, performers, and artists in this text, viewed his writing as a way to wallow in the physical filth of black America in order to present alternative visions of black futurity that move beyond bourgeois society, its expectations, and its repression. As we see later in this book, Bennett's artistic use of filth is black funk mobilized for those who would come to think of themselves as something more than man or woman. Following Robert Reid-Pharr's ideologies in *Conjugal Union* "that the blackness of Black American literature exists in a different, if parallel and often overlapping, historical trajectory from the blackness of Black American bodies" (4), part 1 of this text discusses *funky erotixxx* as the development of a literary tradition for freaks. Documenting this tradition's representation of black bodies in the sexual economy of slavery as that of freaks, this tradition separates itself from the foundation of what has properly been understood as black American literature and sexual representation and questions of agency—slave narratives and slavery. Explicating the ways funky erotixxx undoes or consumes the conjugal union, I analyze work by Paschal Beverly Randolph, Millie and Christine McKoy, Wanda Coleman, Miriam DeCosta-Willis, Zane, Chester Himes, Hal Bennett, Octavia Butler, and Fiona Zedde. I explore how these authors' challenges to Western man and notions of embodiment allow us to think differently about sexuality and eros in the lives of free black people doing sex work or what I refer to as *sex art as experience.*

Transing and Sex Work

Black sexual cultures are inextricably linked with what sex-work activists Margo St. James and Carol Leigh have coined as *sex work*, a term that numerous researchers have adopted to expand their own examinations of sexual labor. Black cultural transaesthetics and economies, however, suggest that the term and the practice may need to be transed beyond one of labor and economy. Transing research on sex work would make more discernible Martha Nussbaum's statement that "all of us, with the exception of [the] wealthy and unemployed, take money for the use of our body."[25] Fortunately, Kamala Kempadoo's book on transactional sex in *Sexing the Caribbean* and Gloria Wekker's ethnographic examination of mati work in *The Politics of Passion* have provided alternative models. Kempadoo defines *transactional sex* as "a term used to denote sexual-economic relationships and exchanges where gifts are given in exchange for sex, multiple partnerships may be maintained, and an upfront monetary transaction does not necessarily take place."[26] Like Nussbaum, Kempadoo, and Wekker, I am motivated to reimagine and reconsider the term *sex work* for the way it could contribute to potential antiwork politics and postwork imaginations. For what is the point of having a pimp/ho degree (PhD) in English if not to create a word hustle that can reimagine cultural and linguistic spaces in which laborers (those who trade sex acts), cultural producers (those who represent and depict sex), sexual intellectuals (those who critique one of the aforementioned or both), and the superfreaks (those who perform all of the work of the previously mentioned sex workers) can resist and riot against heteronormative, capitalist, and puritanical uses of sexuality and culture together, as opposed to in opposition to each other? And none of this is to make light of the economic and oppressive exploitation that may occur in the stigmatized commercial sex industry, or the moments when sexual labor becomes sexual slavery. The dangers of labor being exploited occur in every marketplace, and the trafficking of women and children is not a problem of the sex industry alone.[27] But we must reimagine and reconsider the terms and conditions because of the way the current connotations consistently separate and divide physical and intellectual sex labor and because of the way society hierarchically ranks and devalues the people who perform the physical labor while legitimizing the women who perform the intellectual and domestic labor, as if they could never be doing all three forms.

Although certain approaches to sex work, sociological and economic, have focused on the material circumstances, this book leans toward analyzing what has been termed *sex work* through the immaterial of creativity and imagination,[28] conceptualizing it as art as experience. Stevenson writes of imagination as the "non-rational operations of the mind, that is, those kinds of mental functioning which are explicable in terms of causes rather than reasons,"[29] and this is a component of imagination that has been utilized in sexual labor and sexual expression throughout the African diaspora. For example, what is less talked about in Kempadoo's and Wekker's analysis of sexuality and labor, which leads to their theories of transactional sex and mati work, is the role imagination plays in their theories as well as in the lives of the women trading sex. More than a term of economics, *transactional* alludes to fluid and liminal relationalities that refuse to be narrated by a singular universal narrative. Meanwhile, *mati* rebuffs capitalist understandings of sexual orientation, labor, and expression altogether. I insist that fuller analysis of narratives, authors, fantasy, and imagination in research on sex work and sexual cultures complicates basic questions about methodology, agency, and autonomy.

The initial use of literature and literary theory to further our understanding of human sexuality and eros is not an unheard-of intervention. After all, Plato's *The Symposium* establishes a textual discussion of eros that both explores the very meaning of eros and promotes critical thinking, argument, and rhetoric. Within *The Symposium,* we find theories of eros that define social justice in law and politics, the divine role of medicine and science, the importance of humanities and art, and basic configurations for various types of intimate, familial, and filial relationships. In addition, the entire field of psychoanalysis has somberly used literature to diagnose individual and social mental ills. Gilles Deleuze moves beyond Freud's and Jung's attention to the classic Greek texts and conjectures on sexual deviants' mental makeup: "What are the uses of literature? The names of Sade and Masoch have been used to denote two basic perversions, and as such they are outstanding examples of the efficiency of literature" (15). Most recently in African American literary studies, Aliyyah Abdur-Rahman's *Against the Closet* argues that "the generalized consensus among scholars of sexuality that sexual taxonomies emerged in the late nineteenth century should be reconsidered" (20). She goes on to show that "the era, institution, and literary representation of slavery helped to shape emergent models of sexual difference" (26). Examining the representation of sexual labor and sexual expressivity in noncanonical black literature and culture confronts traditional research paradigms about sexual difference equated as sexual deviance, which then fails to engage the affective experiences of racialized bodies.

The ways in which we have come to understand, regulate, and organize sexual labor and sexual expression in African American communities arises from very specific historical narratives. Narrativity, as Hayden White's "The Value of Narrativity in the Representation of Reality" informs us, has shaped not only fiction and nonfiction, but also the law and disciplinary knowledge and methods. It provides a fantasy "that real events are properly represented when they can be shown to display the formal coherency of a story" (8). White concludes that these narratives or stories have allegories, aesthetics, and plots, and that they moralize. Thus, transing the study of sex work with literary theory, black vernacular traditions, and African diasporic philosophies about sexuality, affect, and being offers a methodology that can resist embedded master narratives about sex work that depoliticize work, pathologize sexual morality, and continuitizes agency so as to maintain white supremacist capitalist patriarchy—narratives that consumers, laborers, and researchers may be reproducing to their own demise: narratives that they did not author.

As Foucault's "What Is an Author?" deconstructs both the function and subjectivity of the writer as well as the work, we understand that he means not only the fiction author when explaining certain assumptions made about writer and work, but critics, scholars, and laborers as well: "Using all the contrivances that he sets up between himself and what he writes[,] the writing subject cancels out the signs of his particular individuality" (102). In this case, that particular individual is the critic-person but also the particular discipline(s) with which the individual aligns him or herself and the function of her or his work on sex work and sex workers. Tragic moral narratives about family and nation are bound to ensue. In the introduction to her edited collection *Working Sex*, sex activist and educator Annie Oakley discusses the representation and narration of sex workers and sex work in American culture by arguing, "There are few different ways one's story is allowed to be entertaining: funny, sexy, tragic, scandalous. Repentance, marriage, college graduation, lurid death, or a piece of investigative journalism are the favored endings" (9). Oakley correctly observes that ethnographic autobiographies can often read as exceptional stories or tragedies of victimization that hardly capture the struggles for agency, empowerment, and survival. Current models of feminism incorporating social moral constraints convey that sex workers are only misguided, oppressed victims in need of saving or salvation. Yet, we note all too easily that the other sex industries, the ones based on the desexualization of bodies, profits from this rhetoric.

Elizabeth Bernstein's *Temporarily Yours* explains that most institutional discourses focused on sex work and sex workers cannot escape the impetus of human morality.

> Early twentieth-century sexological, psychoanalytic, and structural functionalist interventions around prostitution recast the Victorian "necessary evil" framework in a scientific guise, naturalizing the male desires that were seen to underpin the institution of sexual commerce. Such accounts rendered prostitution not only unproblematic but structurally integral to the institution of marriage. (22)

Bernstein's argument acknowledges the embedded agenda of sexual morality, and it also showcases why social scientific studies can rarely escape this pathology. Most analysis of sex work investigates the regulation or legalization of sex work, the gender inequities that precipitate participation, as well as the economic realities of the sexual market. As long as empirical data and quantitative and qualitative methodology shape the conversations, these fields will maintain a repetitive cycle of stigmatization and criminalization based on a pathology of sexual morality created by the buyer or market. Yet Cynthia Blair's *I've Got to Make My Livin'* argues that early black women who traded sex by participating in a "terrain that was increasingly associated with the everyday movements of black men and women, black sex workers redefined the relationship of prostitution to black urban leisure and to black community areas" (151). Narratives of sex work and sex workers can be created by numerous and varied authors. Yet, despite the writings of those doing antiwork activity that involves sex, research on sex work and sex workers has been predominantly narrated by and through the social sciences—psychology, sociology, criminology, political science, law, and anthropology—even when the person writing may have at one point been a sex worker.[30] These narratives have been so dominant across various eras that, like the medical discourse that Jay Prosser argues that transgender authors have to engage before they can write themselves into being,[31] the individual who performs antiwork activities involving sex must engage melodramatic narratives about sexual morality and/or embrace a capitalist work ethic for his or her work to have value—specifically redemptive value. Instead of the clinician's office and medical diagnosis, it is the church, the criminal justice system, and the threat of incarceration. Moreover, sex work and sex workers as constructed by authors in the aforementioned fields are no more real and authentic than the narratives of sex work and sex workers constructed in the narratives from various cultural sites that are examined throughout this text.

Historically and legislatively, writing, directing, and producing sexuality or representations of sexuality meant to arouse has been classified as a form of sex work. That is why *Funk the Erotic* also articulates funky erotixxx as a concept of art as experience instead of sex work to define why black men and women have used sexual expression to survive in the New World. Rather than building upon the pathology of sexual morality, I submit that antiwork activity involving sex authored by playwrights, musicians, novelists, filmmakers, and visual artists enables new knowledge about power, sexual violence, sexual terrorism, and sexual pacifism because they are utilizing a tradition in which there are no moral panics around sex or work. Roger Lancaster's important study *Sex Panic and the Punitive State* explains that "imagination plays a prominent role in panic mongering. The object of panic might be an imaginary threat (the devil, witches) or a real person or group portrayed in an imaginary manner (diabolized Jews, Negro satyrs, plotting homosexuals)" (37). Therefore, imagination in art, literature, culture, and sex might be just as useful in quelling moral panics as any political policy or news media outlet. The suggested use of African American literature and culture to trans research on sex work and sex workers makes us all the more aware of who the authors of these narratives are and what their function might be. Funky erotixxx does away with the moral and ethical claims of Western imperialism and capitalism that make sexual terrorism, sexual colonization, and human trafficking possible.

Transing of research on sex work allows a better approach to the revolutionary potential of this diverse, classed community charged with a radical potentiality to unmake Western humanity's overrepresentation of man, a spirit of rebellion that has survived centuries of Western religious morality, judicial criminalization, and scientific stigmatization. The current domestic and international sex workers' movement must resist dominant classifications of its effort as strictly a labor movement or a limited human rights issue about the human trafficking of women and children. In each case, both are connected to moral panics around sexuality and problematic discourse of rights. Thus, national and international policies meant to contain sex in general also explicitly end up policing racialized bodies in non-Western nations. Positioned solely as a sexual morality issue, none of these panics and policies ever fully confronts how the ethics of work society systemically organized around capitalism creates various industries, sexual or not, that factor into the problem of human trafficking. Current knowledge production and politics centered on sex work and sex workers means that some scholars and activists are contributing to the production of more machines. Capitalism may finally do what morality, stigma, and criminalization could not do. Nonetheless, these sexual guerrillas, currently defined as sex workers, represent a radical spirit of revolt against antierotic, sex-negative, and workcentric elements of society that get lost in the guise of survival rhetoric, individualism, moral and health panics, and capitalism's deadly recycling of a Protestant work ethic.

James Boggs's still-relevant and phenomenal examination of race, automation, and classless society, *The American Revolution: Pages from a Negro Worker's Notebook,* and Kathi Weeks's exceptional examination of gender, labor, and work society, *The Problem with Work: Feminism, Marxism, Antiwork Politics, and Postwork Imaginaries,* most convincingly provide the reason why research on sex work must be transed by the concept of art as experience. Common perceptions and scholarship on sex work theorize that sex work is something done out of necessity, desperation, and deprivation, and while this may certainly be true, the reality of this necessity is dictated by late twentieth-century sexual trade, which has more to do with automation and forces of production in US capitalism. As Boggs argued, the era of automation displaces post–civil rights and feminist persons and forces them to reconceptualize life and living.

> America today is headed toward an automated society, and it cannot be stopped by featherbedding, by refusal to work overtime, by sabotage, or by shortening the work week by a few hours. America today is rapidly reaching the point where, in order to defend the warfare state and the capitalist system, there will be automation on top of automation. The dilemma before the workers and the American people is: How can we have automation and still earn our livings? It is not simply a question of retraining or changing from one form of work to another. For automation definitely eliminates the need for a vast number of workers, including skilled, semiskilled, unskilled, and middle-class clerical workers. (101)

Boggs maintains that the right to life and therefore any articulations of human rights have been abominably tied to work. He implies that instead of simply changing jobs that there must be a reimagining of living in the United States. Like

Boggs's book, Weeks's entire project hinges on confronting the "depoliticization of work" in the United States. She convincingly differentiates her arguments in a manner particular to questions of gender:

> The workplace, like the household, is typically figured as a private space, the product of a series of individual contracts rather than a social structure, the province of human need and sphere of individual choice rather than a site for the exercise of political power. And because of this tethering of work to the figure of the individual, it is difficult to mount a critique of work that is not received as something wholly different: a criticism of workers. As a result of work's subordination to property rights, its reification, and its individualization, thinking about work as a social system—even with its arguably more tenuous private status—strangely becomes as difficult as it is for many to conceive marriage and the family in structural terms. (4)

Consistently showcasing how it is not enough to politically organize to change or improve work conditions, and that we must challenge the notion of work in general, Weeks advocates for the refusal to work as a form of work activism that might lead to a call for basic income and shorter hours for all Americans. Her arguments provide a new reading of agency, choice, and labor that uncovers the resistance of sex workers.

If, as Boggs and Weeks show, most of us have minimal choice and agency in choosing to work in the United States, as opposed to what jobs or careers we will work, then the decision to participate in nonwork or antiwork activities—sexual bartering before it became sex work—has political implications. It is not simply work as the pathologies, criminalization, and policies created around it show. These approaches to work in general enable me to advocate for the revolutionary and radical nature involved in the choice to take up sexual bartering. There are a number of illegal activities and legal jobs one could take up to survive and eat. The choice of sex hints at a specific way of being in the world. Whatever real and socially constructed tragedies exist in the lives of individuals consensually bartering in the nonwork sphere also exist for those who choose to do wage or professional work. The decision to trade sex has to be seen as not only a survival tactic like no other, but a radical reading and position against the current order of work society as well. The only way to understand the radical nature of the choice is to rewrite and reread that decision as one steeped in an everyday activism against a work society that seeks constant labor and production for capitalism. Such a reading provides the definitive marker to differentiate agency or nonagency in human trafficking and sexual bartering, while also highlighting work society's complicity with human trafficking. In a brief mention of the organized movement to recognize sexual activity for money as labor, and the shift in language from *prostitute* to *sex worker,* Weeks observes,

> For example, as a replacement for the label "prostitution," the category helps to shift the terms of discussion from the dilemmas posed by a social problem to questions of economic practice; rather than a character flaw that produces a moral crisis, sex work is reconceived as an employment option that can generate income and provide opportunity. Within the terms of the feminist debate about prostitution, for example, the vocabulary has been particularly important as a way to counter the aggressive sexual moralizing of some in the prohibitionist camp, as well as their disavowal of sex workers' agency and insistent reliance on the language and logics of victimization. The other side, however, has produced some comparably problematic representations of work as a site of voluntary choice and of the employment contract as a model of equitable exchange and individual agency. (67)

Current political mobilization of these persons across the globe will have a great impact on economic and class issues for women, people of color, and children. However, if the resistant spirit of this community is to survive, along with its potential to reorder the social constructs of gender and sexuality, the growing entanglement of the movement and its rebels with work society and work ethic must be broached. Long before the emergence of capitalism, the bartering of sexual favors for material goods allowed the wretched to both exist and survive in the margins without being consumed by the center and the majority.[32]

Rather than providing a romanticization of these individuals as lumpen proleteriats with a greater political purpose that surpasses the material needs of everyday people, or attempting to impede the activities that would provide safety and regulation to them, my transing of sex work research calls for greater clarity about a collective of people whose value and worth exceeds economics. As US society continued its automations, Boggs predicted that

> [t]his means that the new generation, the outsiders, the workless people, now have to turn their thoughts away from trying to outwit the machines and instead toward the organization and reorganization of society and of human relations inside society. The revolution within these people will have to be a revolution of their minds and hearts, directed not toward increasing production but toward the management and distribution of things and toward the control of relations among people, tasks that up to now have been left to chance or in the hands of an elite. (113)

Boggs sees the outsiders as needing to develop a postwork imagination. The black cultural producers in this text represent how trading sex and sexual culture in black communities had already been conceptualized as postwork imagination. In form and content, sexual cultures and the depiction of sexual cultures and labor accentuate a reorganization of society and human relations, and the revolution of hearts and minds happens as a result of how sexual morality, gender constructs, and identification with human ethics are destabilized.

As Georges Bataille argues, "[W]hat we call the human world is necessarily a world of work. . . . But labour does not only mean something painful. It is also the road to awareness that led man away from the beasts" (161). Bataille refers to rationality and its art form, science, while Foucault terms it *discursive eros*. So much time has been spent studying the sexual acts exchanged within sex industries that research on sex work has failed to think about the work done by and in the asexual sex industries of law, science, medicine, and technology. Hence, I also trans research on sex work to demonstrate how and why the science of sex and the order of law has managed to escape being classified as sex work when it appears to fit this paradigm more so than antiwork where sexual activity happens.

Instead of beginning from the position of the state, an entity that implicitly gets to authorize and define what constitutes sex work, even as the term was created by prostitute activists reacting to state policing, we should all reconsider and rethink the term and meaning with questions such as: Why is it that the only individuals classified as sex workers are those whose labor is connected to sexual pleasure? When we consider the recent declaration of the Occupy Wall Street movement with its inattention to body politics in occupying space, why is this particular form of antiwork involving sexual acts deemed illicit economy and not civil disobedience or civil resistance? If these concerns are not enough to incite thought about the existence of human work and several sex industries, then surely the HIV industrial complex, the pharmaceutical empire built on sexual dysfunction, the cosmetic surgery industry reliant on sexual desirability, the gold mine that is reproductive health and technology, the orphanages and adoption agencies, and the vice squads might compel us to pay attention to how the very industries invested in the desexualization of the body so as to make an object-subject of socially useful purposes has become a sex industry in and of itself with its own sex workers who are not antisex but antierotic sex. Black sexual cultures have demonstrated that there is not one sex industry but several industries dependent on moral panics and questionable medical and scientific ethics. However, black public spheres, politics, and knowledge productions are also marred by narratives that depoliticize work, pathologize sexual morality, and continuitize agency and subjectivity.

New Black Studies and Ambivalent Black Feminism

In part 2 of *Funk the Erotic,* I examine the visual, performative, and theatrical works of Lynn Nottage, Shine Louise Houston, and black strippers, as well as the representation of transgender sex work in the nonfiction and fiction of Toni Newman and Red Jordan Arobateau. By focusing on street parties, drama/theater, strippers and strip clubs, pornography, and self-published fiction, I am advocating for the intellectual moments in cultural performances and narratives about sex, work, and blackness when black cultural producers' imaginative knowledge challenges the way science and medicine have been the sole influence on what constitutes gender and sexuality. This new knowledge also reorients ideologies about work and art in Western civilization and modernity. However, because these figures produce sexually explicit narratives, erotica, or pornography, the critiques they offer about art, ethics, and aesthetics have not been taken as seriously in black studies as they should be. How we imagine sexuality can dictate the terms of our be(com)ing and our strategies for defeating antiblackness in the twenty-first century. Jared Sexton's "The Social Life of Social Death" offers guiding questions of why new and radical black studies must dismantle liberal humanism to provoke true revolution when he asks,

> What is the nature of a form of being that presents a problem for the thought of being itself? More precisely, what is the nature of a human being whose human being is put into question radically and by definition, a human being whose being human raises the question of being human at all? (6–7)

The dilemma of being human remains a fabrication of morality that, as Fred Moten's "The Case of Blackness" implies, can wreak havoc on black studies.[33] Yet, because the very practice and performance of sexual expression for trade/money exist before the human, it requires an ontology and phenomenology of being that exceeds the human. Therefore, reassessing the meaning and significance of sexual cultures and sex work through the African diasporic concept of funk is relevant to the project of new and radical black studies because undoing the narratives of work ethic and sexual morality also dismantles what it means to be human, to live, or to be a life form.

The racialization of sex and the sexualization of race, along with the role of biopower in white supremacy and Western imperialism, have been covered ad nauseam in black studies. On the other hand, many scientific and academic inquiries of race and sexuality begin as if moral concerns and the pathologies they create disappear in the presence of reason. According to Juan Battle and Sandra Barnes, the editors of the illuminating collection *Black Sexualities*, "Historic exploitation by segments of White society as well as hegemonic responses by some Blacks meant that . . . issues surrounding Black sexualities have either been studied based on Eurocentric or culturally biased models, tangentially included as a 'control' group in quantitative analyses, or ignored altogether" (1–2). Rationality in each context sublimates how morality/immorality function as disciplinary power. Because institutional state apparatuses seek to control and organize society through the language of rights and biopower, black citizens have provided reactionary responses to each, vacillating between respectability and hypersexuality in the cultural realm, or sexual violence, sexual policing, or sexual pacifism in the political and social realm.

Initially, however, black radical traditions have remained wary of moral agendas with regard to race and sexuality. For example, when dismissing the construct of race as scientific fact, but calling it more of a social construct, J. A. Rogers in the second volume of *Sex and Race* notes: "As for anthropological research[,] while I am strongly in favor of it I do not think that scientific pronouncements are going to help the race question much except insofar as they can be used to influence religious and ethical bodies, labor unions and other organizations, because, in its final analysis, the race question is not scientific, but highly sentimental" (278–79). Decades later, Sylvia Wynter would second Rogers's beliefs by stating, "It was in the context of this syncretized reinscription that the new criterion of Reason would come to take the place of the medieval criterion of the Redeemed Spirit as its transmuted form . . . the humanist man would therefore use the Judeo-Christian answer to what and who we are."[34] Based on Rogers and Wynter, then, the racialized Other asserting her humanity would be influenced by humanist man's morality and then rationality. When we replace race with gender, race with sexuality, or race with nation, it is obvious that any force that escapes reason (creativity, pleasure, or leisure, especially sexual) would be depicted as excess, sin, or a weapon when read as a production of Man's body. Morality becomes a way to underdevelop black America. One recent treatise of black radical thought, Greg Thomas's "The Erotics of 'Under/Development,'" examines sexual morality more specifically. He places Audre Lorde and Ifi Amadiume in conversation with Rodney, stating of their disputes with the construct of morality and immorality in Western sexuality: "[T]he supposed lack of morality projected onto the underdeveloped, the colonized, and the African may be projected foremost with regard to sexuality, which is to say, a supposed sexual morality or immorality" (152). Thomas's intervention with Rodney's work finds that "the projection of a physical lack or pathology that is manifest in an equally projected lack of morality and mental capacity (or aptitude) is part and parcel of the ruling definition of underdevelopment" (153). Therefore, new black studies must apply innovative means for ceasing this underdevelopment.

Morality remains as much an aesthetic of antiblackness knowledge as it does a disciplinary tool for black studies. Using funk as a methodology of transing can be of service to new black studies because revolutionary scholar Cathy Cohen has already asked that we rethink black politics by erecting "a field of investigation . . . that is centered around the experiences of those who stand on the outside of state-sanctioned, normalized White, middle- and upper-class, male heterosexuality" where we can talk "about a paradigmatic shift in how scholars of Black politics and more broadly African American Studies think and write about those most vulnerable in Black communities—those thought to be morally wanting by both dominant society and other indigenous group members."[35] Cohen's call reiterates Boggs's critique of rationality and revolution: "Very few logical people ever make reforms and none make revolutions. Rights are what you make and what you take" (*American Revolution,* 85). Cohen and Boggs expose how the project of morality and its emphasis on rationality undergirds black politics and various movements within it. *Funk the Erotic's* concept of funky erotixxx as sex art, with its critique of work ethic and sexual morality, also questions the symbiotic relationship between capitalism's productivity and modernity's morality, and examines specific black cultural texts' refusal to simplify this relationship. When black people develop artistic strategies and aesthetics to dismiss or deconstruct the pathology that is sexual morality, then perhaps freedom or whatever exists beyond the colonial projects of solidifying the genres of humanity—Man 1 and Man 2—will be possible. Wynter has dissected these figures as the flesh/spirit code that undergirds the Western colonial projects of overrepresenting the human with Man 1—the political subject (constructed from the physical sciences)—and Man 2—the bio-economic subject created from the biological sciences.[36] Rogers forewarned that such scientific pronouncements of race and sexuality might avoid religion and still be used to influence labor unions and other organizations, including those centered on gender.

Due to morality's vexing presence and the overrepresentation of the human, *Funk the Erotic* is an ambivalent black feminist text. Since black feminism seems to mean different things to numerous people, and sexuality seems to have multiple purposes for individuals and collectives, I am hopeful that this book's ambivalence about feminism throws sex-positivity and sex-negativity into disarray for some readers. It will certainly depend on whether the reader's feminism has a commitment to interrogating the human, as opposed to accepting a general consensus of what it means to be a human woman.[37] As such, it intends to engage M. Jacqui Alexander's statement that "[w]e would need to learn to make peace with contradiction and paradox, to see its operations in the uneven structures of our lives, to learn to sense, taste, and understand the paradox as the motor of things, which is what Marxian philosophy and the metaphysics of spiritual thought systems have in common: dialectics of struggle" (266). Alexander warns, "Still, we know that living contradiction is not easy in a culture that ideologically purveys a distaste for it, preferring instead an apparent attachment to consensus" (266). *Funk the Erotic* is certainly not the first, last, or only text vested in such struggle. Following in the footsteps of Gloria Anzaldúa, Barbara Smith, Barbara Christian, Toni Cade Bambara, Cherríe Moraga, Alice Walker, bell hooks, Kimberlé Crenshaw, Carole Boyce Davies, and Cathy Cohen, a new generation of black feminists have shown us that there are fresh contradictions and paradoxes, as well as stale ones, to be taken up. We have moved from the Combahee River Collective and *Sisters of the Yam* on to the Feminist Wire, Crunk Feminist Collective, and the House of Lorde. Mireille Miller-Young, Jennifer Nash, Marlon Moore, Treva Lindsey, Erica Edwards, Kalifa Story, Yaba Blay, Brittney Cooper, Nicole Fleetwood, Alexis Pauline Gumbs, Heidi Lewis, Joan Morgan, and many others have been dealing with the paradoxes.

Part I of this book includes chapters influenced by Richard Iton's rewriting of black popular culture in *In Search of the Black Fantastic,* in which he argues that black popular culture reinvents cosmologies. Black sexual cultures provide reinvented cosmologies for political and artistic feminist movements. By offering ambivalent feminist readings of black sexual cultures, I am reading from multiple and numerous perspectives. I am refusing the sex-determination system in biology that still underwrites segments within feminism, black feminism, and black male feminism. I am acknowledging the need to bridge and fill those spaces with new metaphysics, politics, concerns, and issues that twenty-first-century black people need to broach if they are to continue to survive and triumph over the physical, emotional, and spiritual forces that threaten to undermine black existence, and humanity as a whole. I am acknowledging the black women and men who do not live up to the mandates of black feminism, because of how knowledge about resistance, revolution, and freedom has been colonized, but whose very existence and living teaches us new strategies for resisting further colonization.

Chapter 1 explores how funk as affect directs how some black people inhabit their bodies and imagine sexuality. I examine how Paschal Beverly Randolph's occult manuscripts on sexual magic and conjoined twins Christine and Millie McKoy's autobiography as freaks provide a foundation of how black funk freakery differs from the Victorian-era freak. This, in turn, dictates whether their actions surpass the function of serving as labor to become the embodied practice of a postwork imagination and the practice of sacredly profane sexuality.

Chapter 2 opens with a brief interrogation of the sexual and racial politics of the Life Always antichoice billboard campaign to set up my argument that how black women writers' participation in what might be considered pornographic or whore industries promotes a form of guerrilla warfare whose objective is to protect and secure women's erotic sovereignty and reproductive freedom. I rely on interviews and close readings of erotica and porn composed with and by Wanda Coleman, Miriam DeCosta-Willis, and Zane. Chapter 3 examines Chester Himes's and Hal Bennett's fictional representations of BDSM and sex work to creatively theorize other articulations of masculinity in the domestic sphere seldom covered in black public spheres of politics and the church/mosque. I also explore less talked about class elements and affective ramifications for why BDSM might be practiced in black communities. Chapter 4 concludes this section by previewing the importance of sacred subjectivity to various black sexual cultures. In its proposal of nonmonogamy as an alternative practice for funk's genealogy of affection, relationality, and sexuality between human and nonhuman beings, this chapter begins to answer M. Jacqui Alexander's question about sacred subjectivity: "What is the self that is made in performing labor with disembodied energies that are themselves poised to work?" (295). Using queer legal theory, debates about the marriage crisis in black communities, and cultural depictions of nonmonogamy in the science fiction of Octavia Butler and the erotica of Fiona Zedde, I reveal how funk attends to alternative models of family and community to challenge the heteropatriarchal recolonization that happens with capitalism and the Western model of family.

Stank Matter: Black Sexual Cultures' Dismantling of the Human

Metaphorically, this book is about what stinks and the forms of social power produced to cover up that stank, but it is also about the cultures least associated with intelligence and spirituality as a result of these forms of social power—the profane, the visceral or sensation, and the party. Alexander writes that "the scent of memory (our own and that of strangers) can become faint . . . when things become unspeakable and unbearable, when the terms of belonging get reshuffled" (276). As stank matter, part II of *Funk the Erotic* provides pungency to memory. Chapters in this section insist that like the erotic, the profane must be better contextualized within the histories and trajectories of the nonhuman and the ethereal. However, doing so means meditating on memory and space in ways that would showcase how the profane can be sacred. Thus, following in the traditions of M. Jacqui Alexander's *Pedagogies of Crossing* and Katherine McKittrick's *Demonic Grounds,* these chapters examine black sexual cultures as unacknowledged profane sites of memory in which the making of sacred subjectivity and sexual decolonization might be happening. Ethnomusicologist Portia Maultsby insists that "funk is an urban form of dance music (also known as 'party' music) that emerged in the late 1960s" (293), but moving beyond her assignment of it as music alone, her acceptance of its party philosophy remains crucial to a reconsideration of funk and black sexual cultures in this section.

Chapter 5 proposes partying as an alternative model of intimacy, black aesthetics, and art inclusive of nonhuman being. I read eroticism and representations of sex work in the plays of Lynn Nottage and the films of feminist pornographer Shine Louise Houston as cultural recognitions of sex as it is mediated through what Katherine McKittrick and Sylvia Wynter assess as demonic grounds, as opposed to what Michael Warner and Lauren Berlant wrote of as sex as mediated through publics.

In chapter 6, I argue that funk produces mythologies about the body, labor, leisure, and pleasure, and that these occur in music as well as in black fiction, art, and performance centered on the potential force or energy that excites or that neutral sexual pleasures might yield. Adding to Tony Bolden's "Groove Theory: A Vamp on the Epistemology of Funk" where he argues that "the sensing techniques that black dancers employ have been central to innovations in black musicianship generally" (29–30), I discuss how funk's sensing techniques innovate sexual cultures as sites of memory. I bring three disciplines together—literature, performance, and dance—to theorize nonhuman agency in the street party Freaknik, as well as black strip clubs. I use these fields to intervene on debates about art, aesthetics, labor, play, obscenity, and excessiveness, and demonstrate why rethinking sexual cultures through human and nonhuman relationships is important to how we study, analyze, and regulate sexuality and gender and art and work. In chapter 7, I am concerned with how two writers, Toni Newman and Red Jordan Arobateau, rely on sex work, spirituality, and deconstructions of Western embodiment to theorize transgender subjectivity away from medical and classed models that do not account for race, culture, and pleasure.

In the end, *Funk the Erotic: Transaesthetics and Black Sexual Cultures* not only is in conversation with previous scholarship of funk, but it also forges an alternative trajectory of funk for future studies of black popular culture. It offers readers a needed examination of black sexual cultures, a discursive evolution of black ideas about eroticism, a critique of work society, a reexamination of love, and an articulation of the body in black movements—embodied black movements. I create valuable readings of popular written texts, visual narratives, and performance culture that will dismiss criticism that any study of erotica, pornography, or ratchet popular culture is tangential and not of practical use to future black movements.

PART I

Freaks, Sacred Subjectivity, and Public Spheres

The feminization of contemporary revolutionary epistemes then engenders, at best, an oxymoronic proposition of androgyny, bisexuality, and hom(m)osexuality/homosociality in constituting the state as national and revolutionary—an I that is collective and speaks for women.

—Ileana Rodríguez

1

Sexual Magic and Funky Black Freaks in Nineteenth-Century Black Literature

What is called the imagination (from image, magi, magic, magician, etc.) is a practical vector from the soul. It stores all data, and can be called on to solve all our "problems." The imagination is the projection of ourselves past our sense of ourselves as "things." Imagination (Image) is all possibility, because from the image, the initial circumscribed energy, any use (idea) is possible. And so begins that image's use in the world. Possibility is what moves us.

—Amiri Baraka

I believe that the healing, liberating, and rejuvenating resources we need for the planet and ourselves are restored within Black Funk.

—Herukhuti

In various iterations of funk music, we find a recurring theme and subject that many black critical traditions ignore or remain wary of—sex work and sex workers, or as I am claiming, antiwork sexual activity and funky black freaks. From James Brown and Parliament (and Funkadelic) to a great deal of hip-hop, the representation of sexual activity as trade becomes a critique of domesticity's regulation of gender and sexuality, and therefore capitalism's organizational influence on US society. Representations vacillate between depicting this activity as waged sexual labor, unwaged domestic labor, or erotic play meant for sexual leisure. From James Brown's "Get Up (I Feel Like Being a) Sex Machine," a song that addresses technology, capitalism, kinesthetics, and the automation of mankind, to Whodini's articulation of the everyday spectacular and hidden performances of freakdom in "The Freaks Come Out at Night," and ending with Lil Wayne's unforgettable refrain "what's a goon to a goblin," there remains a conscious dis-identification with the human in contemporary black cultural narratives. These narratives hail from a specific lineage that has been depoliticized by white Western histories of sex, work, and spirituality.[1] This depoliticization and misrecognition of the particular historical moment(s) relevant to funk's creation of *freak* as subject is an act of sexual pacifism, one specifically linked to colonialism and imperialism's sexual violence and sexual terrorism. The erasure of funk's *freak* impedes undoing the coloniality of being/truth/power/freedom.

This chapter utilizes funk's ideologies about labor, leisure, and imagination to counteract colonial meanings of *freak* because black funk freakery remains a significant black intervention on white America's definition of sex, work, and sex work. By highlighting the black revision of *freak* in the written narratives of three nineteenth-century black subjects, occultist/clairvoyant/sex magician Paschal Beverly Randolph and conjoined twins Christine and Millie McKoy, we can discern how black culture has redefined its humanity with a criteria of difference that has been underwritten for some time now—funk's immaterial affirmation of difference rather than a biological negation of difference. I detail how funky black freaks understand sexuality and sexual difference as originating elsewhere; that is, outside the body. On this ethereal plane, gender or sexual difference does not equate with or become sexual deviance as it does in sexology. These representations of sexual difference then provide an alternative narrative about sexuality, work, and morality that plays out in how black men and women use their bodies in slavery and freedom.

There has been a great deal of criticism about the appropriative use of *freak* or *freaks* in black American culture, with critics assuming such use accepts a hypersexualization of black bodies. Yet, long before Patricia Hill Collins engaged how "the term *freak* travels in the new racism" and argued that "the differing meanings associated with the term *freak* are situated at the crossroads of colonialism, science, and entertainment,"[2] nineteenth-century black narratives were creating a literary tradition of funk that would deploy the affects of sexual pleasure and corporeal displays to situate the freak at the crossroads of resistance, spiritual transcendence, freedom, and art and entertainment. As this chapter demonstrates, funky black freaks should not be equated with Western science and modernity's freak and its implicit biological and moral deviance created within the institution of slavery. Abdur-Rahman argues that, "despite the importance of late-nineteenth-century medical and legal discourses, which founded theories of sexual perversion and its punitive consequences, racial slavery provided the background—and the testing ground—for the emergence and articulation of those theories" (27). In agreement with her claim, I submit that although slavery may have provided the testing ground for sexual deviance and deviants, it was freedom, imagination, and imagining freedom as more than social and political and difference beyond the biological that led New World blacks to shift the definition of freak for their future living and to orchestrate sexuality as something other than ars erotica or scientia sexualis.

Fucking has always been a leisure activity with functional *and* aesthetic value, but it was civilization and then modernity's manifest destiny that tasked it with nation building and made it into a labor-intensive model of production and reproduction. Fortunately, lyrics such as James Brown's "Get up / Get on up / Stay on the scene / Like a sex machine" demonstrate how funk destabilizes the nature versus culture divide that rationalizes slavery and neoslavery if an antiwork approach and postwork imagination are maintained. It does so by sonically and lyrically recounting the organic pleasures of the body to counter capitalism's threat to consume for profit alone. Brown invokes the belief that the black body can be the site of both energy (power) and imagination. The sex machine works, but the dancing and fucking are individual labors *and* exalt uses of the body deemed excessive, leisurely, and useless in the human world. Reading the lyrics alone does not convey such meaning, for the beat and an Otherly human response to it keeps the subject from becoming a sex machine. While being like a sex machine, the individual's movement acts against future and unforeseen colonizing uses of the body: these inhuman actions form a movement against the oppressive regimes of the human's work world. These exterior and interior movements have been read as conjure and magic in black America. In addition to Amiri Baraka's reading of magic and imagination, Herukhuti's *Conjuring Black Funk* remarks upon funk as magic. Funky black freaks have always understood their identity, existence, becoming, and movement throughout many worlds as originating in magic as defined and determined by Baraka and Herukhuti. Funk's temporal displacement of a present work subject for a future unknowable subject led to the black reinvention of *freak*.

These moments of magic and play are historically shaped by, not originating in, black people's involuntary participation in what legal scholar Adrienne Davis terms the "sexual economy of slavery," as well as an implicit materialist valuation of funky black freaks in the nineteenth century rather than an acceptance of the stigmatized and criminalized white prostitute. Davis's theory of the sexual economy of slavery helps us "understand our collective sexual histories and then confront our choices, realizing that each of us makes different ones."[3] Freaks have a history in this economy that differs from slaves and prostitutes. Writings by Randolph and the McKoys are counternarratives to other black antebellum autobiographies and slave narratives about being human. What makes a black individual a freak during the sexual economy of slavery is his or her disidentification with a particular genre of the human rather than Western medical and scientific writing of corporeal difference. Because the authors of these narratives cannot depoliticize work or sex, their engagement with sexuality and leisure culture reveals black cultural knowledge about the existence of multiple sex industries that have existed since the founding of this country into our present time and the negotiation of those industries using alternative systems of knowledge. They propose a resistance to the science on race and sexuality that would write them as deviant, disordered, dysfunctional, or diseased.

The United States and its imperialist agenda have a history of simultaneously valuing human labor through a Protestant work ethic while forcing Africans and their descendants to provide free or cheap labor. The sexual economy of slavery's ethical and moral contradictions surrounding work and sex are why black people have repeatedly struggled to submit to a work ethic and a politics of representation derived from an idea of the human that could not make sense of their corporeal and cultural differences or surviving ideologies from African metaphysics. Therefore, this chapter thinks through the interior lives of those black people who might be called sex workers. From there we can ascertain how black freaks' cultural productions subvert facts of science and transgresses the so-called truths of identity politics. An examination of the freak's ontology and phenomenology in black America illustrates the creation of a subject resistant to the private/public split of sexuality and the depoliticization of work. What would the study of prostitution and sex work look like if it were not so interested in rescuing and securing the purity of white women reasoned as vitally important to projects of nationalism and imperialism?

Like a Sex Machine: The Sexual Economy of Slavery and a Phenomenology of Black Funk Freakery

The term *sex work* upholds the public/private binary that makes all kinds of repressive and white supremacist regimes possible in regard to gender and sexuality. The most amenable way to secure white womanhood, as Bernstein explains, is by framing sexuality as a private matter:

> By the end of the nineteenth century, two grand scientific enterprises were emerging side by side—sociology and sexology—destined to professionalize as two autonomous disciplines. Together, these two modernist projects would serve to institutionalize a common understanding regarding the distinction between life's social and biological realms, creating a framework which placed sexuality outside of the social sphere. (22)

Bernstein's use of *enterprise* signifies the merging of sciences with market ventures as sex is privatized. While science was used to create strategies to privatize sexuality, Kathi Weeks explains how industry was privatizing work: "But there are additional mechanisms that secure what I am calling work's privatization. One is its reification: the fact that at present one must work to 'earn a living' is taken as part of the natural order rather than as a social convention" (3). Specific bodies, however, can and will interrupt this reification. Current political actions that term the sexual bartering of men and women as *sex work* do so to access privileges that might come with being viewed as legitimate contributors to society. However, this triple privatization and the privileges derived from them can only be for humans and not their Others since the false divide between the public and private sphere has been historically vexed when the bodies or workers are not white.

Davis's work perceptively captures the history and precariousness of the split when it attempts to manage black bodies:

> The idea of a "sexual economy of slavery" may seem odd on first impression. We divide our economic relationships in the workplace from our intimate family interactions. We view these relations as taking place in two segregated spheres: the market and our intimate lives. It is in this latter space that we feel enabled to make our decisions, conduct our lives, love our families. We may experience dissonances when sex and economics are juxtaposed. . . . But the cases and rules I will examine expose a different relationship between sex and markets for enslaved black women.[4]

Davis later explains how there was seldom any separation of sex and market for enslaved black women because their bodies were used as modes of production and modes of reproduction (113), but her evaluation opens up an entirely new conversation on how all Americans should rethink the use of public and private regulation of sexual pleasure and expression. Beginning with the worker-slave, as opposed to the master-legislator, Davis reveals the dimensions of private and public spheres from a position previously deemed inconsequential—the slave's— to produce another history of sexuality.[5]

The slave, freak, and the sex worker are three subjects linked by stunted readings of difference, in addition to the historical subjugation, stigmatization, and criminalization of their bodies in the West. With an understanding of the relevance of the sexual economy of slavery, Kempadoo's exploration of transactional relationships, and Hortense Spillers's theory that all slaves become gender neutral,[6] it becomes more apparent why black culture would produce an alternative to the prostitute and prostitution: to expose the white supremacist fantasy of work as natural and to thwart human ethics and morality that justify slavery, colonization, and sexual terrorism. Staying gendered within the assignments of man and woman and accepting the boundary between public and private with work ethic and family would make it difficult for slaves and free black people to ever speak of their own intimate lives or their own right to be and become free. Funk's freakery introduced unique causality and agency that would provide rhetoric for black intimate lives.

Although this chapter does not provide a history of freak shows and race, it does briefly submit the relevancy of recognizing the freak show as an enterprise operating parallel to slave auctions and a burgeoning asexual sexual industry of Western medicine that stressed exhibition and exploitation for the sake of producing knowledge and learning. In addition, we must also remember that traveling tent shows, carnivals, and freak shows did not showcase only physical human anomalies. Each site deployed similar aesthetics and strategies, but black participants would glean maneuverable differences, whether on the slave block or the stage, and devise new aesthetics and strategies to subvert the impact of commercial economies on their families. Benjamin Reiss's *The Showman and the Slave* and Rosemarie Garland-Thomson's *Staring* do offer analyses of freaks away from the freak shows and with some attention to race, but I am interested in how black transaesthetics with the body demonstrate antiwork activity and postwork imagination. Because free blacks and black slaves were possible actors and victims in all shows, their perceptions warrant further exploration.

At the same time that freak shows were becoming a common cultural phenomenon, occultism in the United States was growing and the field of teratology (the science of studying monsters) was being founded by Isidore Geoffroy Saint-Hilaire on the basis that "monsters are also normal beings, or rather, there are no monsters, and nature is one whole."[7] At the core of this spiritualism and science was a determination of what is outside the course of nature and what is against the course of nature. Monsters were considered outside the course of nature (unnatural), while marvels were determined to be against nature (supernatural). Yet once critics ask what constitutes nature and what elements determine outside or against nature, we comprehend that subjective judgment is being made based on Western discourses of what it means to be human, to be man: "Stone Age cave drawings record the birth of the mysterious and marvelous bodies the Greeks and early scientists would later call 'monsters,' the culture of P. T. Barnum would call 'freaks,' and now we call 'the congenitally physically disabled.'"[8] These are discourses that have created divides between a human and nonhuman world that are not applicable to all societies. As Robert Farris Thompson reminds us, West African traditions of tricksters deem it useful to rethink Western medicines and popular culture representations of freaks: "As a matter of fact, both Eshu and Osanyin share the attribute of one-leggedness, and like Eshu, Osanyin was once a prince."[9] Eshu and Osanyin read as minor deities or royalty elsewhere would be read as medically and scientifically deformed and inferior. Funk's freaks challenge inclinations that would privatize their corporeal difference in the service of Western imperialism and white supremacy to remind us that "beyond voyeurism and fine art, freaks provide ready access to some essential truths about the potential within each of us."[10]

Most of the research on freak shows and sideshows[11] focuses on what Garland-Thomson articulates as cultural spectacles of extraordinary bodies. Nineteenth- and twentieth-century freaks are pathologized for their physical anomalies. Yet, Garland-Thomson's *Staring* also argues that the "term *freak* has also been un-moored in contemporary times from its original meaning. Freak meant whimsical or capricious rather than today's concept of abnormal" (164). Garland-Thomson recognizes how particular time periods determine what exemplifies a freak or what freaks mean to their communities. It remains rare to find such statements with regard to funky black freaks. Critics often harp on white inscriptions of hypersexuality introduced onto the black body in slavery and freedom alone, overlooking how funk's freak offers an alternative reading of black sexuality and black economies. Although the unstable division between public and private re-mains, the white freak's relationship to the market and consumer was different from the slave's since her labor and antiwork might at some point benefit her as much as her manager. From Eshu and Osanyin to Grandmother Eagleton and Harlan Eagleton,[12] black-Atlantic perspectives on what is marvelous or monstrous are not shaped by the schism between nature and culture, or what is normal and abnormal.

In his exploration of the house, the body, and black Americans, Robert Reid-Pharr provides an argument about antebellum black subjectivity that explains why a separate literary tradition from within would be useful and sustainable to funky freaks:

> The black of antebellum print culture was hardly a static phenomenon. It was male and female, coal black and perfectly white, bond and free, rich and poor. It could change without much fanfare from the gowns of a mistress into the rags of a concubine. . . . As a function of both social necessity and philosophical clarity, the black body had to be normalized, turned black. I contend, furthermore, that what has come to be known as Black American literature operates precisely at the site of the body's normalization.[13]

The "black of antebellum print culture" was not bound by human morality, false binaries of space, or a grammar of suffering. Reid-Pharr confirms black Ameri-can literature as a cultural site that normalizes the black body. Similarly, Jenny Sharpe's *Ghosts of Slavery* demonstrates why a cultural site less invested in nor-malizing the black body would form. Sharpe's research on West Indian slave Mary Prince reveals why the first genre in the African American literary tradi-tion, the slave narrative, would not be an adequate form for representing black women's enslavement and freedom because of its normalizing of the black body via sexual morality. Sharpe notes that "the slave narrative makes no mention of Prince attempting to gain freedom through extramarital relationships with white men" (120) and "unlike Jacobs, the conditions of her sexual relations were closer to prostitution" (123). She further explains, "The expression 'something akin to freedom' denotes the absence of a proper name for the contradictory practice of slave women achieving a degree of mobility through sexual subjugation" (xx). From Frederick Douglass to Mary Prince, many slave narratives had to suppress the contradictions of how nonhuman being and its ethics make liberation possible. But there were other narratives written by black men and women.

The narratives display the origins of black freaks as the merger between sexuality and antiwork activities by black individuals who uphold the integrity of the magical, divine, and marvelous. The stage's spectacle and the speculum/microscope's objective gaze are traded in for affective interiority and translation of difference from within, and when connected with the dismissal of a public/private divide, a new freak emerges with its own literary tradition. Despite all of the moral imperatives provided by abolitionists and fugitive slaves, when some former slaves and free black persons penned their narratives in a manner that engaged the falseness of separate public and private lives, the utility of sex for something other than reproduction, and the use of their bodies as cultural capital instead of chattel, they transitioned from sexual slaves and chattel into a different sex machine. Doing more than "writing one's self into being" human, this sex machine enacts funky erotixxx that undoes the material and capitalist ordering of its physical labor and ensures its survival as subject by producing itself.

Funk and Transracial Cultures of Sexuality

In *Dealings with the Dead,* occultist Paschal Beverly Randolph wrote, "Our principal life—for we lead several at the same time, is the life of Imagination" (254). Because his life's work was in detailing the life of sexual imagination, Randolph remains one of the many casualties of African American literary studies' dominant inclination toward excavating and examining prose about Enlightenment subjects. John Deveney's *Paschal Beverly Randolph* summarizes the absence of Randolph as a pivotal figure in early African American history and occult studies:

> Paschal Beverly Randolph was an author, well thought of in his prime in the 1860s. He was an American black man, with all the problems associated with that fact in the decades surrounding the Civil War. If this were all, he would be entitled to the obligatory footnote in works of African-American history and little more—though he has in fact been denied even this token recognition and has been totally ignored by all occult historians. (xxi)

Deveney presents the racial predicament that Randolph faced during his life, as well as that of his legacy thereafter. Despite this marginalization, Randolph created narratives that countered biopolitics of sexuality and necropolitics of sexual morality established by science and Western religion with his representations of sacred sexuality. His objective of delegitimating medical discourses on sex and sexuality, however, was secondary to his goal of pushing the United States past its overrepresentation of man. For example, in Randolph's manuscript *After Death; or, Disembodied Man,* he rejects the story of redeemed flesh, saying, "If we have ever been lost, we have been easily found again. But we have neither been lost, found, or redeemed,—not even by 'the blood of the Lamb.'. . . We have ever been in God's universe" (39). Randolph's elevation of the esoteric in his occult manuals serves as an early example of how some free black people embraced freak subjectivity. He blurs the boundary between ars erotica and scientia sexualis, and his identification as sexual magician positions him between sex worker and sexologist. His work demonstrates that another model of humanity could be made by individuals willing to articulate other means of embodiment and pleasure's significance to these alternatives.

Just as black musicians made The One essential to their invention of funk music, Randolph made the orgasm the basis of his iteration of funk, asking,

> Who of all of them has given us the rationale of the orgasm—the why and wherefore, or the cause of its being a thing of apparently no moment whatever at certain times, and under circumstances: yet at another will almost shock the human soul out of its earthly tenement the body—by its keen, incisive, cutting, awful intensity.[14]

Randolph's words return us to funk as a phenomenon descended from Africanist traditions, an immaterial reading of affective and pleasurable difference. This is funk even if it is not as recognizable as that of twentieth-century icon Michael Jackson's description, when he asked, "If you could keep on. Because the force. It's got a lot of power. It makes me feel like . . . Whew!"[15] Although Jackson was able to vocally capture the force of funk, Rickey Vincent has also astutely commented on a similar articulation of funk as spiritual and sexual, claiming that "the funk is rooted in ancient African spiritual systems in which sexuality and spirituality are united in harmony with the essential *life force*" (262). Randolph would call it *Aeth.* The lesser-known nineteenth-century sex manuals by Randolph articulate funk, Aeth, as a corporeal energy capable of generating a state of mind and being, as well as subject beyond the human.

Randolph continues, "[T]he body of man is a mere conglomerate of earths and metals, gases and fluids wholly material, but penetrated and permeated in every atom by imponderable elements essentially electric in their nature."[16] In addition to predating new materialism as a current object of inquiry, Randolph's instruction manuals on sexual magic also precede a major text in African philosophy that speaks on being, force, and general causality, Placide Tempel's *Bantu Philosophy,* which does not include a focus on sex. Something of a showman for his own time, Randolph takes a different approach to the subject of the human soul, work ethic, and the function or purpose of sex than the approaches shared by abolitionists and authors of slave narratives. Randolph began the narrative resistance to Western thoughts on sexuality by maintaining a commitment to nonconventional ideas about the spirit and sexual pleasure. He taunted both consumers and nemeses with advertising slogans such as "true-sex power is God-power."[17] However, in order to fully appreciate Randolph's understanding of the material and ethereal value of sexuality, we must locate and comprehend the discursive models influencing him.

According to his autobiography, *Paschal B. Randolph, His Curious Life, Works, and Career,* Randolph was born on October 8, 1825, in New York City. His parents were a multiracial woman, Flora Clark, and William Beverly Randolph, a white man from Virginia.[18] Abandoned by his father and orphaned when his mother died in Bellevue Hospital in the early 1830s, Randolph practically raised himself on the streets while under the unwatchful eyes of his half-sister and unrelated adults. Speaking of himself in the third person, he recalls his mother's death as the incident that initiated a change in his being:

> [He] had suffered to such a degree that his soul was driven in upon itself to a great extent; which while rendering him still more sensitive and morbid, also caused his soul to expand his knowledge inward, become wonderfully intuitive and aspiring . . . became very sensitive to influences of all sorts and characters, and a ready tool and subject for the exploitations and experiments of disembodied inhabitants of the Middle State. He became a Medium![19]

Randolph later claimed that a premonition about his father's death in 1842 was the first evidence of his psychic gift. By 1853, he was already referring to himself as something more than human: "Dr. Paschal Beverly Randolph, clairvoyant physician and psycho-phrenologist."[20] Interior anomalies prized in the occult aided Randolph's process of disidentification with modernity's version of the human, as paranormal activity became the antiwork activity and postwork imagination that allowed him to become black funk's freak.

Despite his immersion into the occult, he still had to deal with the social bondage of race and racism. For Randolph, and many other free and enslaved black people, the racialized body became a prison for a natural self. It was difficult for him to gain access to education, jobs, and basic decent living facilities. Such issues created an ambivalence about his racial heritage in which Randolph vacillated between denying his blackness with statements such as, "Not a drop of continental African, or pure negro blood runs through me,"[21] or privileging his Malagasian roots with this third-person reference, "[T]he penman of this book,—Paschal Beverly Randolph!—the sang melee! Proud of his descent from the kings and queens, not of Nigrita, but of Madagascar."[22] Madagascar, as Prashad's *Everybody Was Kung Fu Fighting* documents, is not the most fitting country to claim as evidence for being of non-Negro descent. Exploring how migrations and cultural exchanges happened before the Portuguese arrived, Prashad insists that East Asia, South Asia, and eastern Africa offer a history that contradicts myths of cultural purity demanded after modernity, thus:

> If the Bajuni's place in Africa can be dated to the early modern period, the people of Madagascar (speakers of Malagasy) can be traced to intermarriages between local inhabitants and emigrants from Indonesia who came to eastern Africa early in the first millennium C.E. Evidence suggests that these immigrants brought Asian yams, bananas, taro, the chicken, and, perhaps, the xylophone to this part of Africa. (7)

Prashad moves from the mixed heritage of the Indian Ocean before Vasco da Gama charted it on a map to what happens centuries after that cartography made the slave trade possible. Other scholars have proven that the Bantu migrants also crossed the channel to Madagascar long before French colonization.

What remains for descendants, like Randolph, is a struggle to assert a transracial subjectivity in a society that only works in binaries. Randolph later employs black nationalist thought when he argues against the African colonization, stating: "Are we to go to the lands of our African ancestors because our skins are dark? Ought we colored citizens to even tolerate the idea?"[23] The experience of being marked as black, as well as the experience of trying to move beyond the discourse of race, was a lifelong quandary for him as it may have been for his mother. Flora Clark might have experienced the predicament of many transracial women described by Rosalyn Terborg-Penn in her essay "Migration and Trans-Racial/National Identity Re-Formation":

> Identity re-formation has been occurring throughout the African Diaspora since the slavery era.... Throughout the centuries, African-descended people have struggled with the stigma of inferiority attached to having the dark skin color.... During the eighteenth, nineteenth, and twentieth centuries, African Diaspora women bearing children with lighter skin color became a strategy found throughout the Western Hemisphere.... In so doing, many women of African descent accepted the sexual advances of men outside their ethnic networks, while others found the process forced on them. In both these circumstances, exogamy, or coupling/marriage outside one's ethnic group, replaced endogamy, or coupling/marriage within one's ethnic group, as transnational identities formed. (12)

Although Randolph loses his mother during childhood, his conflicting feelings about his racial identity are an indication that his mother's transracial and transnational identity influenced his own. Randolph was invested in being an American, but his adoption of a transracial identity inevitably directed him to a discourse of transracial sexuality that he would call *sexual magic*.

Sexual Magic

Inderpal Grewal and Caren Kaplan's "Global Identities" demonstrates the importance of understanding Randolph's practice and promotion of sexual magic as a progenitor of transnational studies of sexuality that might consider race and culture when they write, "In the study of sexuality in a transnational frame, we need a mapping of different medical traditions, conceptions of the body, scientific discourses, and last but not least, political economies of the family" (667). Randolph accomplishes this feat and provides an example for others to follow. More than a century before pan-Africanist philosopher Ra Un Nefer Amen wrote about sacred sexuality in *Metu Neter,* Randolph took time to rethink concepts of Greek eros with the publication of *Eulis! The History of Love* and *Sexual Magic.* Writing of the kiss in the same occult language that he writes of the orgasm, Randolph paid close attention to an act that Greek philosophers, doctors, and scientists dismissed since it held no consequential value to procreation or politics. Randolph asserts:

> There are but few among the many who know the meaning of a kiss;—or that the soul, from its seat in the brain, is in telegraphic unity with the lips,—affectional, friendly, filial, parental, general, in the upper one; sensuous, magnetic, passional, in the lower; nor that, when loving lips meet lips that love, there is a magnetic discharge of soul-flame, and each party gives and receives large measures of magnetic life and fluid love at the instant of impact or contact.[24]

His breakdown of the kiss manages to take up almost all of the loves associated with Plato's *The Symposium* but does so in a way that does not negate the physical pleasure from the act. As he utilizes occult references such as magnetic charges of positive and negative, the lips, to which no reproductive function has ever been assigned, are discussed as physical transmitters of material energy. Kissing becomes a creative expression of being. Time and time again, Randolph highlights the intangible aspects of sexuality, pleasure, and desire that cannot be explained with biological or physical rationalizations.

Later, he would add to the complexity of his project by insisting:

> Which of them all has explained what everyone ought to, but does not know to be a fact, i.e., that, as explained in the "New Mola," and elsewhere in this book, human conjugation is or may be triple; that is, it may be of soul, spirit, or body, alone or

either, and the binary minglings of the three, in various degrees, even to an infinity, for instance one part soul, ten spirit, five hundred or more body, and so on.[25]

Despite Randolph's use of "human," his ideas about intercourse explode Cartesian dualities of spirit and soul. He was not a dualist, and he proposes that a fluid
concept of human being or becoming should not be displaced by the moral and
ethics of specific religions. He could do so because his theories on sexuality used
Afro-Asian foundations invested in holistic approaches to spirit and sexuality. The
choice of magic is deliberate for Randolph. He insisted that people were already
whole, but that transcendence could be achieved with sexual magic from within
rather than given by an external savior figure. His study of sexuality was influenced by personal experiences abroad in Egypt, Asia, and Palestine that exposed
him to alternative models of knowledge. He admits that a sexual encounter with
an Arabic woman in Jerusalem led him to his path of practicing sexual magic.[26]
Randolph's reclamation of Malaysian roots and his belief in the esoteric and occult
before this encounter seem more about recovering cultural history than oriental-
ism. Randolph's account of the sexual experience that leads to his "discovery" of
sexual magic occurs outside the trauma of racialized sexuality since it is a pleasurable experience with another person of color and in a non-Western country
or context. Regardless of whether we believe his sexual braggadocio, Randolph
wants readers to appreciate a spiritual conversion unlike those found in the slave
narratives of Olaudah Equiano, Phillis Wheatley, or Jupiter Hammon.

Randolph claims sexual pleasure produced from the body is the divine power
or energy: "Sex is a thing of soul; most people think it but a mere matter of earthly
form and physical structure. True, there are some unsexed souls; some no sex at
all, and others still claiming one gender, and manifesting its exact opposite. But
its laws, offices, utilities, and its deeper and diviner meanings are sealed books to
all but two."[27] Although the Renaissance humanist creation of man "would lead
to the de-godding/de-supernaturalizing of our modes of being human"[28] and inevitably make Western imperialism a moral imperative, Randolph's sexual magic
re-gods and re-supernaturalizes in an attempt to return to what exists before Man.
Sexuality must be imagined as supernatural for the Otherly human to see it as
something other than sexual terror, policing, and violence. Under the auspices of
energy work associated with the paranormal, Randolph then produces another
being—funk's freak. Funk finds a use for the excesses of the body—pleasure—and
writes them as part of transcendence rather than separate from it.

Randolph's participation in the occult has attended to other senses. Because
occult rituals employ their own particular modes of spectacle and sensory experience,[29] the freak subjectivity Randolph takes up diverges from the freak within
freak shows and carnivals and their connection to a privileging of medical dis-

courses and scopic visuality. As he continued to develop his art—that is, his dealings with the dead—he would instruct that the retina perceives a partial image
of man, stating, "You cannot see air, gas, or clear glass, yet all these are gross and
heavy. You cannot even see a man! We are just as intangible before, as after death"
(*After Death*, 26). The intersection of the paranormal with race, sexuality, narrative, and money gained from that intersection highlights how occult events and
spaces create more than secret societies but a mode of thought and knowledge
where what is seen with the mind becomes as important as what can be seen
with the eyes. His philosophy that some people could, through various forms of
sexual pleasure, reach an altered state where clairvoyance and other paranormal
activity can occur provides innovative approaches to agency and causality and
changes the conversations about sexual expressivity, sexual labor, and sex work.

Randolph's attention to the paranormal deserves overreading, especially since
the field ponders existence and experience of things and objects with no perceived
use value in current science or religion. Holland's *The Erotic Life of Racism* addresses how the overbearing dichotomy of black/white in racialized sexuality and
interracial sex has greatly shaped and hindered sexuality studies, and in this chapter we can see that such a dichotomy has speculatively eliminated entire histories
of sexualities and cultures before modernity made white people the center of the
universe. Histories in which African and Asian cosmologies informed thinking
of sexuality outside of sexual violence, sexual terrorism, and the pathology of
sexual morality were hidden away and closeted.

Sexual Magic's Early Challenge to the Emerging Industry of Sexology

In *The Sexual Demon of Colonial Power*, Greg Thomas intervenes in the troubling
trend in contemporary gender and sexuality studies to ignore the way the field
reproduces racist empire structuring of gender and sexuality:

> When questions of gender and sexuality are on the table for discussion, even if
> sex and eroticism or embodiment in general are not, who asks how they get there?
> What form should they take or not take? Why do they communicate explicit and/
> or implicit scenarios of race, class, empire? Which specific order of knowledge
> dictates the limited shape and purpose of such inquiries, artificially separating
> race, gender, class, and sexuality, without recognizing this is a very specific intel-
> lectual operation rooted in a very specific intellectual culture and history? (155)

Whereas Thomas's text poses pan-Africanist embodiment as a counterdiscourse
to Western sexual imperialism, Randolph's manuals emphasize the occult as an
alternative space where sexuality does not have to be "systematically designated

for white bodies and sexual savagery for non-white ones, Black bodies most of all" (*Sexual Demon*, 23).

A superficial examination of early sexuality studies makes it seem as if white scientists and doctors were the primary authors of discourses on sex, gender, and sexual practices. Richard von Krafft-Ebing, Sigmund Freud, Havelock Ellis, Alfred C. Kinsey, William H. Masters, and Virginia Johnson comprise the canonical list of readings in sexuality studies. Each used psychological and/or biological methodologies that have crafted the evolving field of sexology. While surgeons and scientists attempted to control the material or corporeal, psychoanalysts attempted to contain the intangible of sexual desire by creating master narratives of normalcy and deviance. Notably, most contemporary work on African American sexuality is deemed valid only when it is accompanied by this order of knowledge. However, uprooting the domination and detrimental influence of white Western imperialism over black bodies and ideologies means competing models of sexuality must be examined and analyzed. An understanding of sexuality enmeshed with the paranormal can escape these limited models. The occult, then, gives rise to several sexual histories—those specifically tethered to representation, sexual representation, and expression as a form of matter.

Sexual magic, as Randolph's work explains, is a form of matter and energies. Randolph's sexual magic relied on four supernatural principles: volantia, decretism, posism, and triauclairism. *Volantia* meant the exercising of "will in a calm fashion without nervous exhaustion."[30] *Descretism* was the "capacity to give unavoidable orders, inserting any necessary desires, thoughts, and sentiments to provoke verbal declarations."[31] *Posism* taught the "science of the magic of gesture" and how the body could learn to "sit in a receptive state so as to emit idea and sentiment."[32] Finally, *triauclairism* was the "power of evocation," which allowed "communication with those absent, the dead, and the invisible entities."[33] With each principle, Randolph materializes interior anomalies as methodically as Western medicine represents or materializes the biological/physical processes of sex without making them deviant. Randolph then establishes the possibility of relationality between nonhumans and the Other that supersedes human notions of work, production, and reproduction. His spiritual work had convinced him that sexuality preceded and proceeded the notion of human life: "A man carries himself wherever he goes . . . all his appetites and passion . . . the veil of so-called death. . . . I affirm that the marital form, in *union, essence, rite,* and *fact,* exists in the land of souls just as here; and in the *same* respect" (*After Death*, 135). Randolph's combining of sexuality with the paranormal avoids all of the pitfalls Georges Bataille finds so troublesome in sexology. Sexual magic's end goal is not to make more workers for the machine but to create supernatural beings with powers that can disassemble the machine and its asexual sex industry.

Given the nature of Afro-Asian spiritualism and folklore's trickster and ancestral presences, this might not seem like anything new, but Randolph's configuration of sexual magic as a science about sexual expressivity and representation insists on new materialisms that lead to innovative ideas about agency and causality in sex and work. After students mastered these principles, Randolph taught that individuals could then move on to the operation of sexual magic. Sexual magic also included general rules of a prayer before any sex act, mutual attraction, cleanliness, rest, and time way from the desired person to recharge magnetic forces. Call it nineteenth-century appropriation of the *Kama Sutra* and tantric sex, but Randolph's attraction and affinity for Afro-Asian sacred sexuality sought claim to an erotic inheritance that Western modernity interrupted with slavery and imperialism in Africa and Asia. He unsettles the coloniality of being, power, truth, and freedom. Bucking what C. P. Snow and Sylvia Wynter have described as the two-culture divide between the natural sciences and the humanities, Randolph's sexual magic is based on parapsychology, a transdisciplinary field without viable institutional support that bridges the two-culture divide and threatens any concepts of man and his overrepresentation because its purpose is to offer a scientific explanation for what cannot yet be scientifically explained. Randolph's occult publications challenged medical communities while still including a tendency toward sexual morality from institutional religions.[34] Further, Randolph's linking of the paranormal with sexual desire and sexual pleasure was atypical of nineteenth-century parapsychology or sexology.

Randolph's *Eulis! The History of Love* criticized the appalling lack of true investigation in the science of sexuality, and concluded that this void fosters a general ignorance on the subject in the general public:

> For gross and culpable non-knowledge, especially upon all the vital points that cluster round the one word "sex," you must look, not amidst the untaught hosts, the democratic underlayer of society, but right squarely among the so-called "learned," professional, much boasted, highly-cultured upper strata, especially in those centres of population whence newspapers by myriads are scattered broadcast over *all* the lands. (1)

Randolph astutely homes in on the distinctions of class, dispersion of information, and consumption habits of everyday people to highlight how sexual ignorance continues to grow in the United States.

Although Randolph's manuals are sacred texts, they also stand as a form of popular culture about sexual expressivity that deserve to be deconstructed as such for reasons that have to do with class and work ethic, as well as Iton's theory of the black fantastic. Despite the general acceptance of occultism as a "secret, hidden from understanding" or "relating to magic, alchemy, astrology . . . or other practical arts held to involve agencies of secret or mysterious nature,"[35] Randolph's manuals of sexuality are theorized as popular culture in this chapter primarily because during the time period of production, Randolph's work was not institutionally supported or legitimated by medical fields in the United States. They were also classified as obscene materials by legal statutes of the time, and Randolph was arrested and prosecuted for creating and selling them using postal services.[36] In opposition to the sex work of sexologists, Randolph's magic is categorized as invalid, unscientific, and esoteric superstition. He was stigmatized and criminally prosecuted for violating the pathology of sexual morality and capital uses of the body.

Randolph's writings are not without problems or concerns. At certain points in Randolph's writings on sexuality, his era's social scientific lines of reasoning foreclosed on the progressive possibilities of his work. Such is the case when Randolph writes about hermaphrodites: "Now accidents and inversion, aversions and perversions occur in all departments of nature, but none so glaring and positive as are encountered among human beings; and the mis-sexing of them is one of the most common forms of mal-construction."[37] Randolph reverts to popular thinking of his era and charges these intersex marvels of nature with being biological abnormalities. Further, his sexual teachings are in a strictly heterosexual and monogamous vein and inconsistently suggest gene pooling as the utmost importance for social progress.[38] Still, his theories on sexual desire, passion, and pleasure illuminate the very elements that medicine and science were ignoring in their theories. His conclusions are perceptive and voice futuristic claims of separating anatomy (the biological), gender (social), and sexuality (desire) for men and women.[39]

Randolph's writings on sexuality reveal a history of transnational sexuality studies in the Americas, and without it, African American thought on sexuality devolves into argumentative exchanges simply about trauma, pain, exploitative representation, and subjects with little to no agency. His teaching of sexual magic is but one way to understand how black funky freaks outwit imperialist writing of black erotic expressions as monstrous or hypersexual. He allows us to see how freak exists as something other than the "spectacle of deformity" that according to Durbach was produced in what "had become an international institution," the freak show (3). Remembering his concepts and uses of sex as magic, as opposed to a biological drive, we can see why freak becomes a sexual guerrilla subjectivity in black America. Understanding how this freak becomes a proponent of using sexual magic for material gain lies with two other figures.

Le Freak (Freak Out)

Continuing to look at narratives of funk and freaks outside of black music, I am compelled to look at *The History of the Carolina Twins: Told in "Their Own Peculiar Way" by "One of Them,"* a "slave narrative" about black trans subjects Christine and

Millie McKoy. In regard to the historical presence of black women in freak shows, the McKoys join the likes of Joice Heth and Sarah Baartman/Venus Hottentot.[40] Unlike those two women, however, the McKoys were able to move from spectacle to spectable by writing about their experiences. *The History of the Carolina Twins* is one of the first narratives in African American literature to differentiate between black respectability and black spectability.[41] As seen from its title, the narrative shares some similarities with most nineteenth-century slave narratives, but it also differs based on their unique experience of being conjoined twins:

> WE are, indeed, a strange people, justly regarded both by scientific and ordinary eyes as the greatest natural curiosities the world has ever had sent upon its surface. Physicians who have examined us say our formation—or rather malformation— is much more remarkable than the physical condition of the Siamese Twins. (5)

Born in 1851 to enslaved parents Jacob and Monemia, the McKoys' narrative documents their early childhood in North Carolina, their ordeal of being stolen from their *kind* master and exhibitor Mr. Smith and sold to another, better showman who placed them in an exhibition abroad. The McKoys' narrative overwrites the overrepresentation of man with the freak to become one of the most emblematic examples of a nineteenth-century narrative that unabashedly takes up something other than the human. Millie and Christine's point of protest and reflection of self is not Enlightenment's Christian white man or woman, nor Chang and Eng's freak, the Chinese Siamese twins who were their competition or rivals on the freak-show circuit.

Research on freak shows and freaks tends to justifiably focus on that space as dominated by a spectacle of difference (physical deformities and mutilations), but the McKoys were also slaves governed by the spectacle of the slave market. The focus on these women as spectacle for consumers in either space makes it difficult to ascertain their interior gravitas as subjects. Lithographs of the slave auction block and lynching photographs have clearly demonstrated the possible worlds in which free and enslaved blacks could exist with regard to bodies in pain. Slave narratives have always exposed the kind of mute, voiceless, and blank-slate representation these images conveyed. Slave narratives documenting the experience of the slave auction block mention holding pens where slaves would be examined, as well as market techniques to display bodies in the most masochistic fashion possible. Chattel slavery ended in 1863 with the Emancipation Proclamation, which meant slave auctions and freak shows existed side by side. Certainly, serving as a spectacle to entertain and awe curious onlookers would produce a different affect in a black subject than serving as chattel on the slave auction block. Garland-Thomson's anatomy of staring documents a level of shared exchanges that can happen in freak shows that would be severely reprimanded in slavery auction blocks. Implicitly, the participation of black people within both venues would offer a gradation of what it meant to be slave, human, or freak in the United States and abroad.

From the beginning, the twins' narrative does not shy away from spectacle. In recounting the oral accounts of their birth, the McKoys write: "Old Aunt Hannah, a faithful nurse, whose specialty was to be around and to discharge the first hospitalities to new comers of our complexion, couldn't for 'de life or soul of her' tell whether we was a 'young nigger' or 'something else'" (5–6). Memories in autobiographies are variations of truth depending on age, but the playing up of otherness in the narrative is only surpassed by the presentation of this birth as rather ordinary to Aunt Hannah whose words do not connote horror and fear, but rather perplexity that recognizes that these things sometimes happen. The spectacle is lessened. Here is another missing component to discussions of race, freak shows, and representation: Did Africans and antebellum black people with different worldviews share the same medical ideologies of freaks, or merely take up the word and give it new meaning? The McKoys refuse to make the singular body of man/woman and its experience the genesis of their selves, and they compel us into comprehending the rebellion that can happen if we move beyond humanity's man and begin with transpersonhood. The McKoys transpersonhood originates in their twin subjectivity rather than biological gender. Twins, and other multiples, are an intriguing representative of transness that exceeds gender. They can be transracial, transgendered, transsexual, and transcorporeal but still capable of being two very different individuals. Rather than viewing them as a natural existence, medicine conceives the McKoys' conjoined body as presenting deformities of sex and gender.

According to one sanitized source, "A series of experiments was then made under the direction of Professors Pancoast, Atlee, Maury, and others, calculated to demonstrate the construction of the nervous system, which showed that while above the junction the sense of feeling was separate and distinct in each, below the union it was in common. A touch upon the foot of one would be instantly detected by the other, while a hand placed upon either shoulder was only noticed by the one touched."[42] The inclination to do an external medical exam obscures what the women already felt, an individuation of being that could not be seen or scientifically recorded or made corporeally legible. The phrase in the title of their autobiography, "Told . . . by One of Them," serves as a formal testimony about their own sense of self that science ignores then and now. Prominent intersex scholar Alice Dreger notes a naturalness to the lived experience of conjoined twins in her research, saying "most such twins . . . grow up accepting the basic bodies they were born with as necessary to their selves. . . . After reading many biographies and autobiographies of people who are conjoined, one has to wonder whether we might not all benefit from more *twintype behavior* [italics mine] in this world—. . . a little less 'individuation.'"[43] The McKoys, however, insist that we understand who they are in and of themselves within the universe and not in comparison to a singular and individual experience of humanity, including each other. However, the body as legibly constructed by science and the state shapes the way Dreger reads utopic unification onto Millie and Christine.

Nevertheless, Mecca Jamilah Sullivan's short story "A Strange People" offers a reimagining of the McKoys' biography, one in which fictional imagination disputes the rational scientific narrative of Millie and Christine's unified body as a unified self. Sullivan's attention to the interiority of each sister provides shifting points of views that contest Dreger's notion of less individuation. Sullivan writes, "We-Chrissie wrote then . . . that there is only one heart in the body. We-Millie sits silent when she says this, and lets her go ahead with her show" (233). Sullivan creatively showcases why we must remember that the McKoys' narrative is both fiction and truth of two people, a glass closet of sorts. According to C. Riley Snorton, "[W]hile glass closets, stabilized by biopower and sutured together by institutional and social modes of regulation, may be a condition of black sexual representation, they are not spaces in which their inhabitants lack the capacity to act" (*Nobody Is Supposed to Know*, 34). Could Christine be read as pimping Millie, and could Millie have gone along with her sister's wishes just to have what Sharpe has noted as something akin to freedom? The imaginary realm allows us to understand the McKoys' narrative as both an autobiography of conjoined twins and as a type of glass closet for either sister's individual black funk freakery in which agency cannot be continuitized. Sullivan's short fiction reminds us that were we to begin with their imaginations, with their spirits, or the immaterial as their narrative does, we would end up somewhere less utopic, legible, and unified: Somewhere after man.

The literary first-person plural articulation of self signifies on a singular omniscient medical authority, but it also problematizes the very idea of "first-person" narration as the truth in black autobiography. This is the significance of rereading the McKoys' narrative from the ontology of black funk freakery because nineteenth-century surgery and medicine cannot convey the visual/picture that is their possible world(s) as individuals and conjoined twins. Since there was no narrative tradition of enslaved conjoined twins, the McKoys can make it up as they go along, even if it means using and subverting basic autobiographical strategies of singletons. William Andrews reminds us of the relevance of first-person narration in black autobiography, stating that it is a "redefining of freedom and then assigning itself to oneself in defiance of one's bonds to the past or the social, political and sometimes even moral exigencies of the present."[44] In the case of the McKoys, we can add scientific and medical exigencies. Their use of the phrase *natural curiosities* in their autobiography quoted at the beginning of this section implies that nature (not the human) entails ordinary difference all the time, and that such natural formations only become malformations when rational men of science attempt to delimit nature. There are other ways the McKoys' narrative writes the freak into being so as to disidentify with the type of humanism found in other slave narratives. Their narrative includes all of the artifice of any slave narrative, and relies on authenticating documents to support their posthuman freak subjectivity. Authenticating documents serve not only to validate the voice of the twins telling the story but also to provide testimony to the "realness" of their conjoined body. The use of the *we* subject position doubles and unifies the voice of two individuals. The sisters demonstrate why proving their humanity would serve no purpose in regard to trying to save their family and buy their freedom. A letter signed by five doctors and scientists verifies the condition (19), while a song composed and apparently sung in person by the sisters explicates their experiences as conjoined twins: "Some persons say I must be two, The doctors say this is not true; Some cry out humbug, till they see, When they say, great mystery. . . . A marvel to myself am I" (21). The slave narrative as a form already instills a sense of mistrust about the narrator's real feelings or thoughts, but newspapers, diaries, and their self-authored song reveal that at least one of the McKoy twins readily embraced a marvelous subjectivity rejected by other slave narratives.

Later, such self-fashioning is shown to have material benefits when they boast about their travels. When explaining how they once met the Queen of England, when so many others were denied the privilege, the McKoys detail the currency of spectacle and move away from humanism: "Poor little monstrosities, and black babies at that; we were sent for, and that without any influence at court to gain for us a Royal summons" (14). Well aware of the nature-versus-culture divide dictating the conditions of their lives, the McKoys dismiss the divide but are only able to do so through cultural sites since they are denied access to empirical knowledge. As a result of writing themselves as remarkable natural curiosities, which aligns with funk's connection to nature and the naturalness of difference, these women created erotic sovereignty around their illegibility. Beginning from their interior position where individual and communal/collective are not at odds with each other, the McKoys form a complex way of thinking through self and relationality to others. Quashie convincingly argues that "the earliest writings by black Americans exemplify this capacity to question not just the imposition of identity but also the very meaning of human existence."[45] The McKoys' narrative proves these insights.

The rendering of their life and the production of it as a slave narrative troubles all notions of human, gender, race, erotic autonomy, and cultural production. It is as much a slave narrative as it is not. It is a writing of one's self into being, as much as it is a writing of one's self into being an unintelligible being. Moreover, it is a narrative that at every turn begs us to reconsider these false Western divides between market and intimate lives, of choosing between being morally enslaved humans or free freaks. Although the women profess their Christian virtue when they offer proclamations such as, "Now, although we do not wish to speak Pharisaical, we think we can safely call ourselves really Christian children" (15), the Christian humanist project is undone by their emphasis on the "peculiarness" of their bodies. For example, during a court hearing in which their first master attempts to reclaim them, we learn of a woman who used the sentimentality of a mother's love to gain ownership of the girls so that she could make money from them:

> But her carefully told and well-rehearsed *lie* would not stand the close scrutiny of the Ministers of Law, who listened to the plain and well-told narrative of our mother, who evinced a mother's tenderness for *us*, her little deformities, and imparted a pathos to those utterances when she, in a natural unassuming way, begged for the custody of her children, from whom she had so long been separated, but from whom she could never feel estranged. The law vindicated itself, and gave us to our mother. (10)

The McKoys' narrative clearly relies on similar tropes about separation of family, a mother's love, and childhood destroyed to construct its narrative, but it also remains aware of other potential feelings that they might elicit from their audience. Their narrative does not simply rely on sympathy but voyeurism involving the "little deformities" of their bodies. These rhetorical devices of freak-show moments in their narrative fundamentally link to sexual subjugation as a strategy of survival and mobility during the sexual economy of slavery. For the McKoys, the method is not an act of sexual intercourse but a performance of corporeal spectacle. Moreover, because they are free from the burden of being human, Millie and Christine's words showcase how they understood that what they were projecting in the narrative and on the road was a type of antiwork philosophy that generated money. More important in controlling the narrative about their performances, they propose a new model for movements and debates about race and representation that carries over into discussions of labor and sexual capital.

Without guilt or shame, the McKoys provide more evidence of an interior sense of self within black freaks that directs them toward antiwork activities that can counter the asexual sex industries. These marvelous beings offer a way to deconstruct the pathology of sex work. According to the McKoys, they were marvels instead of malformed/disabled; efficient as opposed to inefficient; and functional rather than dysfunctional. The narrative's emphasis on family and its importance in their lives dictates the other possible worlds they existed in, home among family. However, their status is not the same as most free black women or slaves. While each may have worked outside the home or been wives, nineteenth-century representations of black women as financial heads of households are few, even if the reality might have suggested otherwise. The McKoys were their master's bread and butter, but even in emancipation the money they earned from freak shows and selling their book provided them with autonomy that other black women of their era could not have. The book cover or title page of the autobiography emphasizes these realities with the proclamation "SOLD BY THEIR AGENTS FOR THEIR (THE TWINS) SPECIAL BENEFIT, AT 25 CENTS" (4).

Throughout the narrative, readers gain a sense of the shrewd business acumen the twins have in regard to their unique body: "We might . . . tell many anecdotes of our travels, but we think a simple narrative of ourselves is all that at present those of our patrons who buy our little book will require" (13). Notably, the twins are not relying on the sympathy and moral turpitude of white audiences to acquire freedom; rather, they are strategically utilizing their bodies and audience's curious desire for their bodies to buy their freedom:

> The only alternative was for us to again go upon exhibition, and by our humble efforts contribute to the happiness and comforts of the surviving members of our late master's family. We are *interested* pecuniarily in the "show," and are daily receiving and putting away our share of the proceeds. (16)

In the sexual economy of slavery, the sexual laborer and the freak are one. Furthermore, the sisters refuse to separate corporeal, cultural, intellectual, spiritual, and erotic labor. Garland-Thomson writes that "commerce—the precursor of capitalism—and curiosity—the precursor of science—brought the prodigious body into secular life, enriching the exclusively religious interpretations,"[46] but as the sexual economy of slavery demonstrates, it also queered the desires of white men and women. Millie and Christine's ability to financially take care of their family, as well as their comprehension of the difference between living and earning a living, uses such desires.

In secondhand accounts of their lives, the issues of erotic sovereignty, antiwork activities, and postwork imagination surface when historians reveal that in addition to claiming money from their performance, the twins "insisted on one big change [for their performances]. . . . [T]here'd be no more intimate examinations by curious doctors in every town."[47] Although we may never know whether the McKoys were asexual, heterosexual, or homosexual, what we do know is that they understood how the medical community's scientific inspection of them was a form of sexual terrorism and exploitation. Being the entertainment in a sideshow generated a sense of self made more valuable by the their experiences as slaves and lab objects. As with narratives by Jacobs and Prince, the gaps between the women's narrative and accounts by others reveal the varying definitions of sexual labor being performed by black women and why they did so.

As with all slave narratives, we should ask, even if we cannot answer, whether Millie *or* Christine processed their individual and joint feelings about either sexual exploitation or pain. What details and experiences are being made absent? Even if they do not speak to it, the omission of the most exploitative and gruesome details from their personal narrative speaks to why the McKoy women reserved their disdain for the medical doctors instead of lay audiences of freak shows. During more than a dozen trips across states and abroad, numerous doctors examined the women, authenticating their conjoined conditions with statements such as: "The undersigned, physicians of St. Joseph, having been invited to see the *lusus naturae* now on exhibition in the city, fully concur in the statement that it is the greatest wonder of the age, having two heads, four legs, four arms and but one body, and one consolidated pelvis, and perfect sympathy of desire" (22). Like other women's slave narratives, the twins chose to omit graphic descriptions of the sexual exploitation happening during these medical exams. However, the publication of a medical exam by one specific doctor, Dr. Pancoast, records how the women's bodies were being sexually exploited. Pancoast's biographical sketch "The Carolina Twins" published in the *Photographic Review of Medicine and Surgery* was more explicit:

> About 1/2 inch below the middle of this common vulva is found the common anus.
> . . . Into this I could readily pass a good-sized probe. . . . On examining the vagina
> . . . I found no hymen present, but the orifice naturally small and contracted, as
> that of an ordinary young unmarried woman. . . . I found only one vagina, and
> no bifurcation of it, only one womb. (48)

Critic Linda Frost has already noted in her work how Pancoast's examinations of the McKoys between 1866 and 1871 "is blatant evidence of the sexual economy of slavery and the pornographic and sexual appropriation of black women's bodies that were foundational not just to slavery or the racist terrorism" (22). For this reason, the twins' slave narrative becomes more important than Pancoast's exploitation.

Rather than serving as a strictly abolitionist project arguing against slavery, their book is about erotic self-representation as a type of emancipation. The twins' narrative archives cultural labor as a counterstrategy to the institutional control over the exhibition of their body for the good of science and medicine. It reflects the ways women control the body and its labor based on their material and inner realities. It demonstrates that black women understood that economic transactions involving the body and radical consciousness do not necessarily exist in opposition to each other. Their narrative depicts their lives beyond their enslavement and into freedom.

> Perhaps, now, that we are "grown up girls," and like the rest of the sex, with tongues,
> and a knowledge of their use, we may go across the water once more. A gentle-
> man who called to see us when we were on exhibition in Baltimore, told us that

the "double headed girl" was often inquired after, and that he thought we would prove a "good card" there. At present our business relations are such that we feel in duty bound to stay at home. (12–13)

The McKoys' ontology influenced their decision to continue participating in the freak-show circuit after slavery. What are the options of survival for conjoined twins and their family? As opposed to shame or rage about their corporeal reality, the McKoys present a quiet acceptance about who they are and how they can make their way through the world:

> We wished to be viewed as something entirely void of humbug—a living curiosity—not a sham gotten up to impose upon and deceive the people. We are indeed a strange freak of Nature, and upon the success of our exhibition does our happiness and the well doing of others depend. We have been examined most scrutinizingly by too many medical men to be *regarded* as humbugs by any one. . . . If there be any such who have been to see us, and into whose hands this little book of ours may chance to fall, we beg most respectfully to offer them some medical testimony of a most positive and unmistakable character. (18)

Overemphasizing "strange freak of Nature," the phrase serves as a key point for how the McKoys' narrative designates their beings as part of nature, rather than separate from it. Implicitly referencing the intimate extremes of gynecological exams in proving the uniqueness of their bodies, none of their previous labor goes in vain. They deploy it as a means of increasing their wealth. The McKoys serve as further evidence that freaks perform antiwork activities to counter the asexual sex industries. Like Randolph, their reflections on the existence of more socially sanctioned sex industries dictates the ways in which they will choose to utilize their bodies.

In the end, the self-composed song in which they sing of their bodies as esoteric mystical forces ("great mystery," "marvel," "none like me") redefines the freak away from Western medicine. Freak continues to be a paranormal subject just as we saw with Randolph, but their transcendence subverts segregated America in a different way. The McKoys did buy their freedom and the plantation of their former mistress, as well as donate monies to black schools and communities. They did die with some level of wealth that most formerly enslaved blacks never had.[48] *The History of the Carolina Twins* offers us an opportunity to comprehend funk's subject position of freaks as very different from the Victorian model, as well as showcase that there are times when moving beyond human and its morality can be a praxis of liberation. As the closing of the narrative explains when they conclude with "hoping our little book will be found well worth the money, we conclude our plain unvarnished tale" (22), the twins could not afford to adhere to the fantasy that market lives and intimate lives needed to be separate on moral and legal grounds. They needed to operate as transitional beings given all of the possible worlds in which they existed. These lessons have proved viable for contemporary black moves involving erotic transactions.

The narratives of Pascal Beverly Randolph and Christine and Millie McKoy demonstrate that funky black freaks originate outside of nineteenth-century Victorian-era freak shows and twentieth-century black music. The recognition of an interior life, the ordinariness of difference in a nonconforming body, and the articulation of an altered state produce a freak that is not angry, shameful, monstrous, deficient, deformed, or maligned in black culture. It remains an expression of nature, a refusal to work, and an alternative use of sexuality and eroticism. These writers have provided African American literary and cultural traditions with an alternative trajectory from which to consider questions of economy, leisure, sex, erotic autonomy, and representation. Moreover, the postwork imagination made evident in each narrative becomes important to understanding twentieth- and twenty-first-century representations of black popular culture's disidentification with the human occurring in the repeated attention and embrace of funky black freaks now transitioning into goons, goblins, and martians. Delving into narratives written by African Americans that represent black characters or people as possessing an alternative state of consciousness about sex and work, we can better understand individuals who can get up on the scene like a sex machine, refusing to work but still live, as opposed to the US-constructed sex worker who works to earn a living.

2

In Search of Our Mama's Porn

*Genealogies of Black Women's
Sexual Guerrilla Tactics*

Writing or producing sexual representation to arouse can be a form of labor. At the same time, it can also be a means of eroticized propaganda. Funk and porn have each been prophesized and hystericized as the province of men. Yet Kodwo Eshun's *More Brilliant Than the Sun* proclaimed well over a decade ago that "[y]ou are not censors but sensors, not aesthetes but kinaesthetes . . . the newest mutants incubated in a wombspeaker. Your mother, your first sound" (oo1). With Eshun's decision to move us all beyond the "wish fulfillments" of black music history, I am allowed to insist that by recalling the vocal stylistics of women such as Betty Davis, Chaka Khan, and Erykah Badu in some of their dopest tracks, we can comprehend that their sonic interpretations signifying the anguish of being turned on and the fear of unfulfilled desire produce tone, pitch, and mood that undeniably register as funk in the throes of being on the one. Betty Davis's sonic choice to represent her theme of desire through guttural and throaty incantations on "Your Mama Wants Ya Back"; Chaka Khan's intentional move from breathy quietness about desire to outright screaming of an anguish that might make her go crazy on "Sweet Thing"; and Erykah Badu's expression of erotic longing by using bass-thumping beats to emulate a heartbeat and heavy breathing to match her crooning "I Want You" create all-new sensoriums for women and men. In their expressed anguish, we feel more strongly an interiority displaced by exterior mechanisms. We feel tuned up when these women capture anguish and touch us with it. Funk, then, is not only as Toni Morrison has stated, the opposite of black bourgeois repression of pleasure and spontaneity, but also an affective technology that can sustain reciprocal interactions that would improve the lives of women and, in the end, the men and children in their lives.

Tone, pitch, and mood also have a function in erotic attunement for women who might be classified as sluts elsewhere. Tone and mood enable a manner, mode, or way of living. Alternating among the various tones and modalities of emotion and experience at their disposal, individual women cull a new purpose for funk and women—namely sovereignty as addressed by Bataille: "The sovereignty that I speak of has little to do with the sovereignty of states as international law defines it. I speak in general of an aspect that is opposed to the servile and the subordinate" (301). Bataille comprehends that sovereignty requires a tone or pitch characteristic of resistance. The expression of anguish linked with sexual desire generated by funky black women is connected to resistant constructions of self and subjectivity. When women clarify the terms for sexual desires through tone, pitch, and mood, as well as words, they highlight why stating, asking, or demanding the conditions for sexual autonomy and freedom is not enough. How women pursue the terms of their liberation underscores the radical possibilities of what it means to desire versus to be an object of desire and to create versus produce. Hence, my discussion of aurality is important to debates about the erotic and pornography in the lives of black women. It suggests that we must look back on other genealogies of black feminism and womanism cognizant of the tone, pitch, and mood of sovereignty about sexual desire—mama's porn—if we ever want our own voices to be heard in political discussions of rights and sexuality.

Mama's porn—her amassing of juicy sexual gossip, new dances, dirty records/ audio files, magazines, books, videos, and vibrators—is accumulated from stores, catalogs, websites, friends, family, or lovers. It can be buried between mattresses, stuffed in the back of bottom drawers, hidden in closet spaces, bookmarked on the computer under an unassuming title, saved for nights out, or openly displayed and discussed at home or work. Mama's porn may follow Jane Juffer's proscription of "rewriting/reworking [porn] within everyday routines" (5), but mama's porn, with its explicit representation of sexuality, is also good at getting mother's body to live beyond the everyday regimen of a political economy and work society in which such rewriting may be neither necessary nor desired. It makes evident that there is indeed sexual rebellion. Mama's porn is not literally the pornography of our mothers, but it is the funky erotixxx briefly mentioned in the preface, a maternal profane imaginary and lineage, that informs cultural objects of propaganda in black women's sexual rebellion. When funky erotixxx goes unidentified, this anonymity can be costly for black men and women with good intentions.

US society has a penchant for representing mothering as sacred and political labor and woman as profane leisure. Discourses about the autonomy and sovereignty of women's bodies consistently occur in conversations about both pornography and reproductive rights. However, feminist strategies within those debates have consistently avoided understanding why or how the proporn feminist debates are a necessary alternative to the strategies within reproductive rights rhetoric and strategies, and that women's erotic and pornographic cultures produce a necessary attunement between the two subjects: mother and woman. Cristina Traina's *Erotic Attunement* argues that "women's eroticism includes the potential for maternal sexuality" (8). Traina's theory of maternal sexuality is important for intervening on the moral panics about wayward eros that influences both state mediation of women's bodies and appeals for reproductive rights. She observes, "The root of wayward eros is recognizing the 'other not as an equivalent center of subjectivity, but as an object that *must* enact a specific role or function in satisfying my desires.' If we are attuned . . . we keep amative space open, reciprocally allowing other's particular needs to speak to and work on our own subjectivity" (242). Although the reproductive rights movement remains important, the failure of its rhetorical strategies can be seen in our current era of regression regarding reproductive rights. The discursive focus on reproduction has not and cannot be effective since it fails to consider erotic attunement and because it maintains elements of sexual pacifism. Simply put, because women know that reproduction is valued by the state, reproduction has become the forum from which arguments about rights and privileges are made. This is a pacifist approach and it cannot bring the subject of mother in tune with that of woman.

My definition of sexual pacifism builds on Churchill's articulation of pacifism in his manifesto *Pacifism as Pathology,* in which he states, "Pacifism possesses a sublime arrogance in its implicit assumption that its adherents can somehow dictate the terms of struggle in any contest with the state. Such a supposition seems unaccountable in view of the actual record of passive/nonviolent resistance to state power" (3). Where Churchill takes up the violent or nonviolent approaches to state and institutional domination and repression of humanity, my definition of *sexual pacifism* remarks upon how black women's most heralded quests for liberation and freedom have consistently been steeped in epistemic nonviolence and asexual or desexualizing politics even when racial politics have alternated between strategies of violence and nonviolence.

Sexual pacifism should be understood as the willful denial of how a public/private binary of sex and intimacy is complicit with sexual violence as a weapon of white supremacy and patriarchy. Sexual pacifism should also be understood as the acceptance of false and forced social constructs of gender and sexuality, as well as the creation of political activism and platforms where these constructs remain intact. Finally, sexual pacifism accepts the pathology that has been Western sexual morality of fallen flesh/redeemed spirit. What would really be necessary for any woman to have reproductive rights is a decolonization of sexuality and sexual knowledge that would make it less necessary to separate sexuality from reproduction as the state has mandated.

In 2011, the Texas-based Christian organization Life Always, which is led by several prominent black ministers, initiated a black history month campaign against abortion that hinted at the immoral and unethical nature of black women, implicitly black feminists, with billboards that read, "The most dangerous place for an African American is in the womb." The problematic slogan from the three-story-high billboard campaign serves as a warning to anyone who would deny the importance of antiwork politics, leisure activity, and erotic sovereignty in black women's lives. This group's rescuing of black women and children from other black women indicates the ways in which, as Ileana Rodríguez voiced two decades ago, "[T]he mediation of state power, represented by the absolutism of the narrating subject, or by an I that is always singular and masculine, obstructs democratic representation" (16). Because black women have little to no control over the mediation of state power with regard to sexuality, black women's rebellion outside of such mediation will always be read as immoral and unethical, as nonexistent or backward and problematic, if such rebellion does not appear to share commonalities with existing black nationalist movements or white feminist movements.

The Life Always billboards also navigate around state power and insist on an absence/presence of black women. The billboards make absent black women's personhood, while insisting that their ever-present and fertile wombs, and by default their bodies, endanger all African Americans. The billboards' criminalization of black women as child murderers indicates that some people understand mothering and reproduction as both work and moral obligation as opposed to an act of free will and creation done out of love of self and life. It makes black women into objects serving the needs of other, more important subjects. When we look at the objectification of black women, we note that sexual surrogate, wife, and mother are the specific roles that they have been made to enact for satisfying the desires of various people, domestically and publicly. Despite our feminist heroics, there remain other paths toward attunement.

I join my prefatory thesis of the profane with Cristina Traina's thesis to show how a maternal genealogy for black women's porn can destroy the schism by serving as an erotic attunement of woman and mother. I demonstrate how funky erotixxx has been black women's epistemic self-defense against other pornographic cultures steeped in sexual violence and terror. The fantasies it elicits keep women conscious of the everyday invisible war being waged against their efforts at self-determination and erotic sovereignty in the political and religious arena. Examining the work of Wanda Coleman, Miriam DeCosta-Willis, and Zane, I zoom in on written sexual cultures sustained by black women, even as they may be shared, exchanged, and profited on by others. Given that much of black feminist criticism and theory depends upon literature, tracing genealogies of black women's erotic or sexually explicit cultures in print might produce an alternative path to follow for those persons interested in pornography debates that have to do with the visual. After all, the antipornography appeal in black feminist thought begins in African American women's literary tradition.[1]

While Mireille Miller-Young's *A Taste for Brown Sugar* and Jennifer Nash's *The Black Body in Ecstasy* grapple with the visual archives of black pornographic traditions with their focus on the first all-black film, *Lialeh*, I choose to underscore the narrative traditions that coincided with this visual feat and those that came after. These traditions also make the feminist recovery of the film possible since they operate in what were supposed to be opposing sites of representation: the popular and academic. This chapter submits that the previously mentioned black women writers of erotic literature and print media are sexual guerrillas who refused the sexual pacifism embedded within feminism or sexual terrorism and violence enacted by white supremacist capitalist patriarchy. Instead, they pursued instrumental antiviolence but proposed their own form of epistemic violence— more accurately, epistemic self-defense—as a countermeasure to structural and epistemic sexual violence carried out by the state on black women's bodies. Since epistemic violence has tended to be the basis for many wars, my reading of these women writers becomes important in making obvious a resistance to what black feminists have noted as the war against black women's bodies.

Early twentieth-century black leisure culture and sexual commerce look very different from later twentieth-century black leisure commerce. Cynthia Blair's book charts the construction and revisions of urban black sexual economy from the decline of brothel houses to the rise of sporting taverns, gambling saloons, movie theaters, cabarets, and nightclubs in Chicago during the 1920s. She argues of those early black women who traded sex, "[I]n moving from a terrain that had been identified explicitly with sexual commerce and other illicit pursuits to one that was increasingly associated with the everyday movements of black men and women, black sex workers redefined the relationship of prostitution to black urban leisure and to black community areas" (151). Moving forward in time from that era's leisure culture and its intersection with sexual commerce, we note that post–civil rights discourses about racial and sexual freedom are an important everyday reconsideration of being black in the United States. Understanding the way African American women's print and visual depictions of sexual leisure destabilizes concepts of sex and work lies in understanding that from the 1960s to the end of the twentieth century, black leisure culture and sexual commerce became more than menu items of specific sex acts offered at brothels and on the ho stroll.

With the legalization of written erotica, sexual commerce activities could be legally pursued through shipping and handling, in between brown-bag packages, under pseudonyms, in backrooms of black five-and-dime stores, in academic institutions, through independent and self-publishing, or via e-mail. Mail-order subscriptions, neighborhood adult bookstores, sex shops, and book clubs are particular spaces for sexual leisure culture relevant to black women and the considerations of race within this conversation. Before the Internet, adult book- and video stores were a particular leisure culture that operated in spatial boundaries similarly proscribed to sex work. These establishments were often built in transitional spaces on city streets, low-income urban areas populated by black and brown people, or highway truck stops. How many of these were black owned remains as unimportant as who worked in them for this study. More relevant, however, is the unknown number of black women who may have supplied some of the reading materials. This leisure culture reconstructs the sex economy from one in which participants and observers can easily and morally separate sex acts from sexual thoughts to one in which they make possible another unforeseen sexual culture as bookstores quickly became cruising utopias for men. Moreover, women did not necessarily have to work in proscribed public or private spaces to contribute to the industry.[2] This potential anonymity allowed these same women to not only change the adult sex industry but publishing industries and institutional discourses as well.

Wanda Coleman's Intelligent and Sexual Black Popular *Players*

Wanda Coleman's twenty-one-month tenure with *Players* magazine demonstrates exactly why attempts to separate the literary or academic from the popular in African American literary scholarship can disempower the radical model of epistemic self-defense proposed by black women. The tendency to discipline sexuality studies as critical writing only is flawed and contributes to our ignorance of black culture and sexuality. Coleman did not have to write critical essays stating her proporn opinions; she simply made porn—a very specific kind of porn that she would not want labeled as feminist porn. Coleman, an amazingly gifted poet of the late twentieth century, played a major role in the production and proliferation of black sexual culture in the 1970s when she served as the first editor of *Players* magazine. As Justin Gifford's *Pimping Fictions* exposes, *Players* "expanded the definition of the hustler and player to mean someone well versed in black arts, literature, politics, and music. The magazine constructed an ideal reader who is invested in a range of 'high' and 'low' black cultural products" (145). While Gifford discusses *Players* as a reimagining of the pimp and black masculine urban identity, I examine Coleman's editorial tenure as an example of the many ways in which black women's supposed sex work refuses the moral binaristic of sex and work embedded in antiporn black feminism.

In interviews with me, Coleman sketched out how she became a sex work scribe and editor, stating of her circumstances in the early 1970s, "In 1972 I was like many other divorced single moms, living in my hometown, then known as South Central Los Angeles, working two or three crummy jobs when I could get them, and if I could keep them." Up until recently, few people knew that Wanda Coleman the Watts poet was also Wanda Coleman *Players* magazine editor. She notes:

> No one except friends and my publisher seemed to know about me for decades. I did not hide it, but I never mentioned it unless asked. It was no longer part of my life. Then I was "outed" during a Q & A following a late eighties reading in the Midwest, probably in Cincinnati. I copped to it, said "Guilty as charged," and dismissed my questioner by stating that "it was a job!" I had two children to raise, alone, with no help from my ex. (interview with author, December 22, 2005)

Legitimate literary biographies and treatments of her work and importance as a black poet tend to leave out her editorial days at *Players,* as if her work in that particular space denigrates her literary legacy. Even as Coleman herself admits that she could not be both poet and editor at the same time, her defense of her work when outed brings me back to funk as echoed in the words of "Cosmic Slop": "Father, father, it's for the kids / Any and every thing I did." Her work, practically done to support her family but also as a continuation of a family legacy that began with her father,[3] is the result of funk's laboring for sovereignty. Wanda Coleman and *Players* magazine are the epitome of funky erotixxx.

Although *Players* was a men's magazine about men's desires, its formation and early development were shaped by a black woman's desire and uses of the erotic. So upon reflection, *Players* magazine is as much about black women's erotic life and desires as it is men's. As a result, its birth and success occur through Coleman's construction of an embodied eroticism that acknowledges a popular intelligence, while its demise into the realm of any other girlie magazine of exploitation is about the anguish caused by the repression of women's desire. We can only imagine how different conversations about gender, sexuality, and hip-hop might be were it not for the erasure of Coleman's role. This absence shapes contemporary concerns about black women, feminism, erotica, and pornography and further impedes progress on a new humanity and sensorium.

In the 1980s, white feminists insisted on a debate now known as the pornography wars. Focusing mainly on film and video, Andrea Dworkin, Catharine MacKinnon, Robin Morgan, and Diana Russell insisted that the production of porn was an everyday threat to women and children. As prosex feminists later determined, the problem with antipornography legislation was not simply that it was censorship, but that it was antisex or sex negative. With the exception of Audre Lorde and

Alice Walker, the absence of black women's voices throughout these early sex wars against pornography remains telling. Most research assumes black women were in agreement with this early stance or that matters of race and economics took precedence over sexuality. The truth, however, is far more complicated because black women's practice and theorization over sexual representation, eroticism, and porn reveal very different concerns that detail white supremacy and its construction of sexuality as a tool of power. Lisa Duggan observed that the 1980s porn wars facilitated a feminist silence or policing about sexuality, and thus led to what would be twenty-first-century cultural debates in which "three new focus points for cultural disputes about sexuality and representation emerge: the controversies over public funding for safe-sex AIDS prevention programs, the arts funding debate, and the debate over rap music lyrics" (16). Duggan's assessment has proven correct. Today queer theorists have noticeably moved the debate back and forth between rights and citizenship, while many black feminists have taken up the debate over rap music lyrics in a manner akin to the 1980s' antipornographers. The presence and work of Wanda Coleman reveal how black sex wars focused on decentralizing the power of work society and highlighting the limitations of movements and fields underwritten by Western sexual ethics that could imperialistically circumscribe a policing of black genders and sexualities.

The erasure of Wanda Coleman's work with *Players* allows for the formation of conservative threads stitched throughout womanist and black feminist thought on sexuality and sexual representation. As Layli Phillips observes, with the publication of her 1983 book *In Search of Our Mothers' Gardens*, Alice Walker "introduced the womanist idea to the general public, feminists of all colors, as well as women of color and others who question or reject feminism, have been debating the uniqueness and viability of a freestanding concept" (*Womanist Reader*, xix). Yet the introduction of "womanist [a]s a feminist, only more common" (7), as depicted in Walker's short stories "Coming Apart" and "Porn" comes with a certain amount of baggage around sexuality that is very much tied into the antipornography rhetoric of the late 1970s and early 1980s. The story about a woman's attempt to confront her husband's predilection for pornography does not offer the same thoughtful exploration of desire and sexuality as seen in Walker's later works. Walker explains that she wrote the story to address the ways in which black men use porn to gain access to the white female body and bond with white men over this new power, to address the ways in which black women see porn as progressive because it grants them "equal time or quality of exposure," and to confront a culture in which "the debasement of women is actually enjoyed" ("Coming Apart," 3).

Published four years after Coleman's work at *Players*, Walker's representation of sexuality and sexual representation falls in line with white feminists' appraisals of men's magazines of the era, rather than black people's sex wars. The story begins with a lament on the monotony of middle-class marriage:

> A middle-aged husband comes home after a long day at the office. His wife greets him at the door with the news that dinner is ready. He is grateful. First, however, he must use the bathroom. In the bathroom, sitting on the commode, he opens up the *Jiveboy* magazine he has brought home in the briefcase . . . studies the young women . . . and strokes his penis. At the same time, his bowels stir with the desire to defecate. (4)

Walker's representation of the husband seems as one-dimensional as her characterization of an insecure wife sitting around the house fearful of the power white women's goodies may hold over black men, to say nothing of her own sexual interest. From the story's lackluster beginning, Walker produces an obvious image of women's debasement as she equates sexual arousal and the desire to defecate and masturbate, as if all are one and the same. She quarantines sexual arousal, representation, and interest to the domestic space built to get rid of or hide bodily waste and replicates gender binaries around sexuality in general. In addition to girlie magazines, women singers who perform in popular forms, probably funk and disco, are criticized as part of women's culture of self-debasement. Walker's proposed solution to this sex war is to have the wife school her man with the words of Audre Lorde in "Uses of the Erotic," Luisah Teish's "A Quiet Subversion," and essays by Tracy Gardner and Ida B. Wells. As the short story closes with righteous indignation over the way popular culture exploits black bodies for white supremacy, it never once views black bodies, black men's and women's sexual desires, or black cultural representations of sex through the eyes of anyone except a white oppressor. This basic foundation in womanism connects to a value system that cannot account for what black bodies do to and for their own pleasures. Notably, Coleman's work at *Players* magazine provides an alternative to this prism.

Under the directorship of Coleman, *Players* magazine became an unacknowledged battleground for funk to foster its indeterminate black subjectivity and undermine the limitations of respectable movements around gender, sexuality, and race. By her own account, Coleman takes issue with the racism embedded in the feminist movement and remains skeptical of its usefulness for black women:

> I have always been cynical about the so-called feminist movement, and given the events on today's political stages, my cynicism was well-founded. Many feminists were racists (or conservative on other issues important to Blacks), just as many gay White males are racists. . . . Who needs to trade one oppressor for another? I mean, did feminism happen? (interview with author, December 22, 2005)

It is these concerns about feminism that reveal very different sex wars and dictate that black women try out different spaces and strategies from those being deployed by their white allies and foes. Coleman's editorship of *Players* refuses the antiporn model of immorality as well as the fight for censorship situated in legal discourse. Her reflections on pornography begin with her own experience, rather than someone else's or a presumed universal female experience.

Her words reveal several distinct elements missing from the previously mentioned feminists:

> In the seventies, eighties, and nineties, the Valley was known as the pornography (smut) capital of the world. By the age of twenty-three, I was editing as many as seven sixty-odd-page magazines at one time: for gay men, men who preferred women with large breasts, and men with assorted fetishes. It was a racist and sexist world in which I had to "write White." It was an incredibly wild experience and I received a shocking education about the nature of humankind, including Black folk, and I laughed and cried nine to five. After *Players* was over for me, I would return to this underground kind of work, temporarily, again in the San Fernando Valley, then living in Watts. (interview with author, December 22, 2005)

First, Coleman acknowledges the labor that she completed, and in doing so reveals the role of women and minorities in the pornography industry preceding the dominance of film and video. Her admission challenges the construction of domestic roles and the use value for sexuality that Walker creates in "Coming Apart." Coleman's real-life experience means that we can no longer read those materials solely as the male debasement of women that is brought in from the cold to shit all over sacred gender roles performed in the domestic sphere. From her reasons for why she participates in porn's print factories to her editorial position, Coleman disrupts images of pornography as something that destroys the life of women and children via its destabilization of marriage. She uncovers how biased Walker's agenda was in its assumptions of a certain dichotomy about sexually explicit culture as men's porn intertwined with misogyny or ideal sexual representation linked with heterosexual monogamous coupling as the only real expression of worth. It is as if mama would not own a stash of porn, or that she only procures it through some misguided definition of sexual freedom. Rather than shrinking in fear over the coming apart of her marriage as the wife in Walker's story does, Coleman uses the anguish and fear from her single-mother status to produce something funky.

When she conceptualizes the phrase "write White" to denote not only the dominance of a white male gaze but of white language and voice in constructing the history of sexuality and its abuses and exploitation of it, Coleman turns away from the very model Walker uses in "Coming Apart." She speaks to the importance of black women locating their own tone, pitch, and voice. To "write White," then, is to other and objectify through text first and then image. Inevitably, white feminists, even as they sought to protect children and women, could not escape what it meant to write white and in so doing continued disempowering a vast majority of women in the process. Coleman's work at *Players* acknowledges the primary way in which sexuality is regulated in the West—through discursive registers, literary and legal. Coleman's experience as a black woman and single mother, coupled with her experience of writing white, dictates her agenda at *Players* magazine.

After accepting an offer from Bentley Morris and Ralph Weinstock, the owners of Holloway House Publishers, to edit *Players,* Coleman developed a model of the material erotic that the black masses could embrace. Coleman's vision of *Players* as something more than just a men's magazine meant that it would be a form of culture wholly unaccounted for in the black arts movement or the womanist movement. *Players,* according to Coleman, would reflect the beauty of black bodies and black minds:

> In *Players,* I wanted to push that particular envelope and bust the stereotypes. I wanted to engage and present other, more favorable and healthier images of Black sexuality without ignoring what was obvious or could be found in the streets. . . . Above all, my vision for African Americans included my belief that we deserved to celebrate ourselves as sexual beings. I had no shame regarding my history as a people. I wanted the women who appeared in *Players* to reflect the wonderfully complex physical array Black women present in our society. I was especially interested in "big butt lovely" women. (interview with author, December 22, 2005)

Coleman sought to create a product that could decolonize the order of knowledge concerning black sexuality and desire. In layout and editorial mission, *Players* refused to promote Western aesthetics of beauty and instrumentalization of the senses that would separate intellect from body or privilege the image over the word.

Early issues of the magazine presented readers with the best in black fiction and nonfiction. Huey Newton, Ishmael Reed, Dick Gregory, Earl Ofari Hutchinson, and Stanley Crouch contributed pieces to *Players. Players* published comics and pictorials, included important interviews with leading public figures (republishing debates between James Baldwin and Nikki Giovanni), offered movie and book reviews, gave fashion and relationship advice, reported on political happenings across the nation, and included well-researched pieces on black history and culture. Despite comparisons to Hugh Hefner's *Playboy* magazine, Coleman's audience was not white. However, her sense that there was a black audience for her vision and its refusal to adhere to the tenets of writing or editing white distinguishes the magazine.

I believed our people wanted and deserved something that was not afraid of what White people thought, was not precious, was not academic, was not snooty, and above all *was not amateurish in its execution.* They deserved and wanted a slick, four- or five-color magazine, like *Esquire* or *Playboy,* that was unapologetic about Blackness. They deserved and wanted a vehicle that expressed/reflected what we were capable of accomplishing beyond the *defensive* subtext of fear, hate, and self-loathing that dominated the "Negro" pages of Johnson Publications. We needed a magazine that was free of self-imposed inferiority, that was not an exploitive tabloid or dumbed down. And our people needed it done with class on an adult level. With *Players,* I came as close to delivering as anyone has ever come in the history of American magazines. To the extent that I eventually failed, that was inevitable. (emphasis in original; interview with author, December 22, 2005)

Coleman notes the intraracial sex wars shaping post–civil rights black America, with the bourgeois sensibilities of Johnson Publications winning out before *Players* came along. Coleman's statement that it not be academic or snooty refers to the division between popular (low) and literary (high) created by an upwardly mobile bourgeoisie. She refused prescriptions of normalcy and respectability. *Players* became a magazine for modern-day freaks descended from the likes of Randolph and the McKoys. Understanding this group as her audience, Coleman challenged assumptions of deviance and stigma being placed on black sexuality from white and black sociologists of the time.

In one issue,[4] Coleman treats readers to a critical essay on *Lialeh,* the first major black adult film. The essay precedes criticism of porn in film studies. In that same issue, an article on disco-queen Sylvester showcases *Players*'s repudiation of rigidly organized sexuality, gender, and desire, as Sylvester sums up his funk, claiming, "My whole trip is very real. I can be a man if I want to or I can be a very beautiful woman."[5] Letters to the editor published in the "Conversin'" section of each issue demonstrate Coleman's success at filling a gap left by other black magazines of the time. Darnella Gipson, a woman from Sacramento, California, wrote, "I don't know if it is unusual for women to write to *Players* or not, but I just had to write you and tell you I also enjoy your 'Bad magazine.'"[6] Another woman, Nashua Nardone on the East Coast, confessed, "When my boyfriend showed me the article on Karry Onn, my spirits were boosted because for one, a magazine . . . brought out the fact that women with large breasts do exist and we are sometimes discriminated against because of our size."[7] College student J. E. Robinson wrote, "I would like to take a few minutes from my studies to commend you and your staff . . . for the efforts you have amassed to produce such an excellent product."[8] Jerry L. Finn, an incarcerated felon, wrote in that same issue, "Personally I dig the different articles and interviews that portray successful Black dudes as being 'Players.' I think that is [a] very broad-minded view, because the majority of 'Square' people cannot conceive a Player as anything else besides a Pimp, Dope-Pusher, or a hustler" (26). To date, we have yet to see anything quite like the early *Players* and its ability to reach and connect with a broad range of black people of various genders and sexualities. Coleman's concept, and black people's response to it, confounds antipornography arguments, black respectability tactics, and sex-negative cultural politics.

Although Coleman suggests that she failed because the magazine changed from her model to something more exploitative,[9] her anguish as felt in both the production of *Players* and her resignation from it as a result of publishers' undermining her creative decisions, signals the success of black women's intention to make use of the erotic as power through the popular (an intelligent black popular) rather than deploy sexuality as a weapon through the academic and social sciences. Coleman accomplishes what black feminists of her era could not do with rhetoric alone: provide an alternative product to counter white supremacy and its colonization of black people's sexuality—erotic attunement. Coleman's funky erotixxx hinges on her acceptance of the magic and marvel of black freaks and her faith in them being as intelligent as they were sexual and fashionable. Consequently, the result of her antiwork activity is a postwork imagination in which she successfully fulfills her desire to pursue writing poetry. After Wanda Coleman rounded up her *Players* around an intelligent black audience, Miriam DeCosta-Willis, a.k.a. Dolores of the Wayward Ways, would be another figure important to conversations about eroticism and the binaries of popular and academic, feminists/womanists and nonfeminists, and queer and straight by undertaking the production of *Erotique Noire: Black Erotica,* a collection of erotic short stories, critical essays, and poems.

Erotique Noire: How Black People Were Funky, before They Were Queer

Like Coleman and Lorde, Miriam DeCosta-Willis is a known figure. While all three women worked in university settings at some point during their careers, DeCosta-Willis, a.k.a. Dolores of the Wayward Ways, is the formally trained academic who without question debunks notions that the intellectual remains separate from the sexual. A self-proclaimed black feminist and author and college professor, before retiring she had been a faculty member of Memphis State University, Howard University, LeMoyne-Owen College, George Mason University, and the University of Maryland. She served as an associate editor of *SAGE: A Scholarly Journal on Black Women* for ten years and was an editorial board member of *Hispanic Review*. DeCosta-Willis has published eight books, including *Blacks in Hispanic Literature, Erotique Noire, Memphis Diary of Ida B. Wells, Daughters of the Diaspora: Afra-Hispanic Writers, Singular Like a Bird: The Art of Nancy Morejon*, and *Notable Black Memphians*. I state these academic credentials to ensure that we understand the extent of what DeCosta-Willis accomplishes in bridging the academic and popular long before our current milieu of black public intellectuals.

Although *Erotique Noire* was published in 1992, DeCosta-Willis began working on it in the late 1980s. Audre Lorde played a pivotal role in the success of the groundbreaking collection, as DeCosta-Willis confirmed in an interview with me: "And once we got Audre Lorde on board that kind of opened the door, and she was real excited about it, and that kind of opened the door to pull in other people" (interview with author, December 29, 2009). DeCosta-Willis notes that initially it was difficult to convince black writers to contribute selections because of the subject matter, and Lorde's influence symbolically and literally provided a foundation for how to imagine eroticism connected to material or a medium designated as pornographic during this era. "Uses of the Erotic" is anthologized in numerous and diverse collections, and Lorde's conscious participation in *Erotique Noire,* with the inclusion of her essay and poems, is certainly about the less discussed erotic literacies she gained from writing *The Cancer Journals*. DeCosta-Willis's textual love child with feminist scholar Roseann Bell sets the stage for erotica to become a genre in which black women writers, after the black women's literature renaissance of the 1970s, would find a great deal of success. It took four years to gather writings, edit selections, find a publisher, and be published, but as funk often does, it rose from below and permeated black cultural production for years.

The year 1992 was significant for the reimagining of funk and freaks, and it was important to contemporary debates about gender and sexualities in African American culture as well. In 1992, the annual spring-break party known as Freaknik celebrated its tenth year of existence, hip-hop ascended to new heights in American mainstream music, and *Erotique Noire* became a commercial success. Death Row Record's release of Dr. Dre's *The Chronic* ensured gangsta rap's dominance for the decade, along with its neoliberal management of black bodies within American constructs of gender and sexuality. Dr. Dre co-opted all of the heavy beats and synth sounds of P-Funk, but none of the visual aesthetics and kinetic philosophies. The signing of OutKast by LaFace Records this same year would see the rise of the kinetic philosophies in hip-hop two years later. Still, according to music historians and black feminists, misogyny, nihilism, and sexual violence against women within hip-hop dominated every aspect of black sexual and social life as a result of the genre's success. Nevertheless, in this same year Random House had to order an additional printing of Miriam DeCosta-Willis, Roseann Bell, and Reginald Martin's *Erotique Noire* beyond the initial printing. The book adheres to the kinetic philosophies of funk in every way. Funk has played a dominant role in the success and proliferation of both gangsta rap and black erotic fiction.

Yet the commercial success of black erotic fiction in the twentieth and twenty-first centuries and its connection to funk has been less remarked upon. In hindsight and placed alongside each other, erotic literature and gangsta rap offered black men and women cultural mechanisms to critique work society and promote leisure culture that could disassemble Western canons of gender and sexuality as well as blur the boundary between life and death. In both cases, the recording and publishing industries had not really predicted that these two products (hip-hop and erotic fiction) would so forcefully and profitably change the direction of the black public sphere. Additionally, the academic-industrial complex's pathologizing and privileging of the crisis of black masculinity resulted in a new field of knowledge now appropriately termed *hip-hop scholarship* that would overwhelmingly favor specific cultural forms and institutional knowledge of those forms rooted in hegemonic black masculinities and femininities. In the meantime, research on urban and erotic fiction has been dismissed as frivolous and antiliterary. The academic industry has yet to sufficiently deal with the ways these two cultural products demand new models of gender and sexualities then and now. Exploring why individuals may write and read erotica provides us with an entirely new discussion: how the intersection of black leisure with sexual commerce plays an important role in literacy, class, and sexual healing.

Coleman's decision to dabble in purple prose and blue images was about the economy of being a single mother, but DeCosta-Willis's reason was about the anguish of living a life different from that imagined by her family. DeCosta-Willis, in "Looking toward Arbutus: Remembering Frank," confirms that before she could turn inward and celebrate the role of eroticism in her living, she had to contend with the exterior expectations of her own family. She recounts the influence her father had on her life and identity as a woman, and in so doing demonstrates the ways in which class sensibilities shaped her early comprehensions of sexuality and eroticism:

> Sometimes I wonder if my father ever really knew the woman that I eventually became because I was always very careful, as I grew into adolescence and then womanhood, to preserve the image of the "good daughter," hiding from him the problems: financial, marital, personal, and family. Why? Because he and I were both raised in fairly "traditional" families, where a genteel formality and courteous

reserve were required. We were Charleston bred in a place where and at a time when we were expected to dissemble emotions—whether impassioned cries in the night or shouts of sanctified joy—like so many nappy edges concealed beneath the silken contours of a nylon wig. As I have matured, I have fought against that formality, that reserve, and all those painful silences, encouraging open discussion of even the darkest corners of my life. (206)

DeCosta-Willis revisits gendered dilemmas of parent-child dynamics that may prohibit erotic sovereignty for each individual throughout life. Still, anguish can artfully disassemble emotions held together by middle-class formalities. There are several ways in which funk as affect and sex enables DeCosta-Willis to transform into Dolores of the Wayward Ways.

In "Letting Go with Love," an essay that warrants inclusion in narrative medicine courses, readers learn about how DeCosta-Willis was compelled to break from sexual respectability politics. When her husband is diagnosed with cancer, DeCosta-Willis turns to the uses of the erotic to help navigate around the diagnosis and disease. Throughout her husband's battle with cancer, she and her husband progress past courteous reserve and genteel formality to sustain the affective intimacy of the living. DeCosta-Willis recalls the value placed on erotic leisure and sexual activity, stating,

> When a battery of doctors visited A the day of his release from the hospital, we handed them a list of detailed question that I had prepared. The first question read: "How soon can we have sex?" When the doctors responded with an embarrassed silence, we concluded that they could prevent dying but didn't understand much about "living." A month later, I turned to the oncologist after A's first bout with chemotherapy and asked, "What about sex?" The doctor mumbled, "Uh, maybe after six months." (63)

DeCosta-Willis comments on a medical operative who appears more concerned with the diagnosis and treatment of disease and less interested in the care of his patient. Doctors' reports assess the cellular mechanics of the disease as the most significant factor, and unless prompted they never ascribe any medical use to how the patient feels. DeCosta-Willis's elaboration on the sexual feelings of patient and family as relevant to patient treatment and health precedes narrative medicine's current emphasis on patient feeling and care. She considers them as an important designator of the difference between life and death.

Still, in between the cancer cartel's discourse and the awaiting of death, funk lies, as she later notes: "Although there were often passionless days and impotent nights, physical intimacy between us was very important because it affirmed who we were as individuals and how we connected as lovers. It reminded us that we were alive."[10] DeCosta-Willis speaks of erotic attunement as important beyond parent-child relationships and grapples with its implications for the living and the dying. She chronicles the way illness can force us to change the ways that we have been taught to contain or express desire, sensuality, or pleasure. She recognizes the way in which it can affect our connection to those closest to us: "The hardest part," she continues, "was dealing with powerful contradictory impulses: attraction to a man I deeply loved, but aversion to his wasted, scarred, sickly body; desire to spend time with him, but feeling trapped."[11] Funk bares truths that would otherwise be ignored or made simple by Western medicine or bioethics. Just as funk can grapple with morbidity, loss, and death, it also concurrently reinforces the spontaneity of life. DeCosta-Willis transitions through the melancholy caused by her husband's death, and she resists a return to the numbing bourgeois sensibilities she had been raised with as a result of an unexpected eruption of funk in her life.

When she meets her coeditor and coconspirator Roseann Bell, DeCosta-Willis recounts:

> Roseann and I just hit it off beautifully. I brought her to LeMoyne College where I was teaching. I'd started an honors program there. And got a grant to bring someone. And she came and she was just a delightful person. Real down-to-earth and *FUNKY* [emphasis hers]. She started telling me about some of her stories and in order for her to. . . . You know she was at Cornell and she had money problems, and so she signed on as Tantra or something like that. I forgot what her name was. But you know where you make erotic phone calls. And so she got into that. She told me about some of her experiences when she was living in the Caribbean. And I mean the girl was way out, you know. . . . So we just got to swapping tales. I realized my own experience was extremely narrow. (interview with author, December 29, 2009)

DeCosta-Willis's and Bell's friendship leads to a further redefining of eroticism and erotica based on girlfriend subjectivity.

In *Black Women, Identity, and Cultural Theory,* Kevin Quashie uses *the girlfriend* as a metaphor for how black women writers create subjectivity in their narratives:

> The girlfriend is that other someone who makes it possible for a black female subject to bring more of herself into consideration, to imagine herself in a wild safety. A woman is encouraged by her girlfriend to be herself radically, even as the heft of doing so might be too much for their connection to bear. (18)

Rather than the Morrisonian tragedy of black womanhood that is Nel and Sula in the bottom, DeCosta-Willis and Bell anchor each other in an experience of the bottom where there is wild safety. Although both DeCosta-Willis and Bell made contributions to the collection as authors, the girlfriend subjectivity extends to their joint editing of *Erotique Noire*. This is not the sad representation of pornography decimating a marriage as presented in Walker's short story. DeCosta-Willis and Bell openly discuss intimacy and pleasure with each other, and they feel no shame about it. Rather than view erotic material and form as excrement, these women demonstrate what can occur when the gaze on the body is one's own or same sex. The book, and all erotic writing read and written by black women thereafter, becomes quite potentially a girlfriend relationship in which funk can find a space to grow, prosper, and create radical black female subjectivity in wild safety. DeCosta-Willis and Bell's friendship demonstrates the ways in which girlfriend subjectivity shapes black women's permission to represent the erotic as sexual and spiritual. Girlfriend subjectivity also makes it possible for them to invite and include Reginald Martin, a third editor who happens to be a man. As a praxis of liberatory black erotics, they offer an example of women and men practicing reciprocating ideas about sexuality and valuing women's erotic sovereignty across the diaspora.

More than a translation from English to French, *Erotique Noire* urged readers to imagine the representation and study of black sexuality as relevant, to understand the importance of eroticism in black life, and to value sexual leisure and cultures but not necessarily be resigned to its rules as sexual commerce. As black women academics writing and editing sexually explicit literature, Miriam DeCosta-Willis and Roseann Bell contribute to a further transing of research on sex and work and black literature since they offer a less pathological and more nuanced understanding of sex and work. In the introduction to *Erotique Noire,* DeCosta-Willis clarifies capital as necessary for revolution and eating.

> Roseann is, perhaps, the most experienced (in terms of her, uh, writing) of us erotophiles because she got her first piece . . . published, that is . . . back in the sixties when she and another colleague, both strapped for money, wrote an x-rated book and sold the rights—for just three hundred damn dollars (shades of Anaïs)—to a publisher who supplied porn shops. Ever the innovator and entrepreneur, she later teamed up with another friend and started a sexy phone service called Tantra. (xxiii)

Not unlike Coleman, DeCosta-Willis goes on to note that she also made a few bucks. She amassed a little over one hundred thousand dollars from *Erotique Noire*'s royalty checks (interview with author, December 29, 2009). Many of the writers in this study share similar biographies in this regard, and their work might be readily classified under the moniker of sex work. Unlike the rest of the writers in the tradition of funky erotixxx, DeCosta-Willis was not a creative writer but a scholar who traded in sexual ideas.

DeCosta-Willis's alter ego then offers writings and work that serve as a reconsideration of the erotic from a black feminist, prosex perspective, and one wholly and consciously connected to the academy. There remains considerable anguish for black women about what it means to be sexual and intellectual in the academic-industrial complex. The 1990s was a decade filled with writing by black women academics who also happened to be queer or queer advocates: Cathy Cohen, Evelynn Hammonds, and Laura Alexander Harris were the most vocal voices. Still, the erasure of *Erotique Noire*'s sex-positive black feminism also matters for black queer studies. Because 1980s' black feminist literary scholarship gravitated toward the politics of reconstructing the cult of true womanhood, Evelynn Hammonds vigilantly declared in the late 1990s that something else needed to be offered, when she wrote:

> In the past the restrictive, repressive, and dangerous aspects of female sexuality have been emphasized by black feminist writers, while pleasure, exploration, and agency have gone underexamined. . . . Reclaiming the body as well as subjectivity is a process that black feminist theorists in the academy must go through themselves while they are doing the work of producing theory. Black feminist theorists are themselves engaged in a process of fighting to reclaim the body—the maimed, immoral, black female body—which can be and is still being used by others to discredit them as producers of knowledge. (99)

What Hammonds called for is exactly what DeCosta-Willis and Bell offered in their efforts in the early 1990s. *Erotique Noire* includes the works of black lesbians Audre Lorde, S. Diane Bogus, Ann Allen Shockley, Jewelle Gomez, and Alice Walker, as well as Opal Palmer Adisa, Beryl Gilroy, P. J. Gibson, Kristin Hunter, Toi Derricotte, and Barbara Chase-Riboud. *Erotique Noire* documents the way intellectual corporate regimes might attempt to repress black women's knowledge on sexualities by privileging an order of knowledge from the social sciences. Though not a theoretical or historical analysis of black women's sexuality that Hammonds argued for, *Erotique Noire* exceeded the capabilities of history or literary history.

Likewise, this praxis of black feminism meant that readers would peruse the writing of Essex Hemphill and Bruce Nugent alongside Kalamu Ya Salam, Trey Ellis, and Chester Himes. *Erotique Noire* becomes the practice of a theory on erotic culture meant to subvert the stigmas of racialized bodies. Specific sites of knowledge cannot be privileged in any study or representation of sexuality if the process of sexual decolonization is to succeed. In many ways, the edited collection's various eruptions of funk work better than an extended narrative would in reordering knowledge about bodies forced into performing normative behavior. The collection blurs the boundary between the academic and the popular. Be it the introduction that states that "[b]lack erotica is fertile terrain for scholars of Afro-American literature" (xxxvi) or the inclusion of essays such as Audre Lorde's "Uses of the Erotic," Sandra Govan's "Forbidden Fruits and Unholy Lusts: Illicit Sex in Black American Literature," Charles L. Blockson's "African American Erotica and Other Curiosities," and Françoise Pfaff's "Eroticism in Sub-Saharan African Films," the editors of *Erotique Noire* refused to section off the analytic discursive models of sexuality from the creative forms of poetry and fiction to avoid legitimated institutional protocols that value history over culture, social science over humanities, and the ethnographic accounts over the fictional prose.

When *Erotique Noire* became a reality, Reginald Martin decided to publish a story under his real name, but DeCosta-Willis and Bell decided their short stories in the collection would use the pseudonyms of R. Pope and Dolores DeCosta to subvert the protocol of which bodies can respectably produce sexual representations and knowledge. DeCosta-Willis explained at the time that "Reggie can be brave if he wants to—he's a man—but we're gonna be chicken and go undercover" (*Erotique Noire*, xxiii). Aware of the notions of womanhood impressed by external forces onto the lives of black women in the academy and beyond, they overcome such impediments by outing themselves in the introduction. DeCosta-Willis exposes how institutions of higher learning and the black public sphere attempted to stamp out funk. Martin has also warned that we not "fall into the binary-opposite game that white publishing and white media have set up."[12] Where then do we place the DeCosta-Willis, Bell, and Martin collection other than in the tradition of funky erotixxx? Since they were as humorous and playful as they were serious and introspective about the significance of what they were doing, the collection remains one of the few places unbound by moral pathologies. Such was the case with the inclusion of Jewelle Gomez's "Piece of Time," a steamy foray into black women's same-sex corporeal leisure:

> "Carolyn," she said softly, then covered my mouth with hers again. We kissed for moments that wrapped around us. . . . Then she rose. . . ."I have my work, girl. Not tonight, I see my boyfriend on Wednesdays. I better go. I'll see you later." Ella arrived each morning. We made love. . . . We talked of her boyfriend, who was married. (389)

In an era when pathologies of down-low and queer times were in their infancy, the collection remained one of the few spaces where representations of black sexuality and sexual desire were not segregated with regard to gender and sexual identity, where a politics of respectability was addressed, maintained, or dismissed, and where a broad range of discourses and interpretations on black sexuality and eros existed alongside each other. Initiated by two black women invested in polymorphous erotics and completed by three African American literary scholars constructing discourses and representations of race and sexuality that engaged the popular and the academic, *Erotique Noire* stands in stark contrast to the queer studies and theory that would initially make the white male body, gay or straight, the center of sexuality studies. This woman's work has implications for other work that she does as the machines take over.

Zane: The Anguish of Respectability and the Hedonism of Artificial Intelligence

Because Wanda Coleman and Miriam DeCosta-Willis provide a phenomenal foundation from which to rethink the possibilities of black sexual cultures, black feminism, and public spheres, others are able to follow a different path going into the twenty-first century. Enter Zane, a Howard University graduate of chemical engineering, daughter of a theology professor and retired schoolteacher, paper saleswoman, mother of two, and bored, unhappy housewife. As Coleman and DeCosta-Willis situated their cultural products in a non-Western and liberating exploration of funk, Zane's efforts exhibit a rough struggle to work within the painful rigidity of high literary aesthetics and Western assignments of sexuality and eros for women, not unlike many of the characters that she writes about.

> He spread my legs open and went to work on my pussy. Tyson's technique was different from Quinton's. He bit on my clit, and while it was painful, it made me come almost immediately. I was discovering yet another part of my sexual desires I never knew existed. I discovered I liked it rough. (*Addicted*, 177)

Rough sex and rough writing can be pleasurable. Zane's erotica, based on writing aesthetics and style rather than theme, is for those who like their fiction less polished than that found in *Erotique Noire*.

In Zane's first novel, *Addicted* (1998), readers take a journey with protagonist Zoe Reynard, a married mother and successful businesswoman whose "disease" of "sexual addiction" leads her to have multiple extramarital affairs that could cost her the joys of family and domestic bliss. Unfortunately, unlike Zoe Reynard and Zane's fan base, some reviewers of the novels do not like their erotica rough or formulaic. Book reviewers and literary critics have not been kind in their assessments of Zane's work. Sam Fullwood submits in his "Before Zane Was a Star" that he advised Zane with these words: "I don't think any publisher in New York would touch your work with a ten-foot pole. It's too graphic and explicit" (19). Salon.com writer Charles Taylor has argued of Zane's novels, "Great writing? Not by a long shot. Psychologically nuanced? No." ("Libertine or Prude?"). AfroerotiK owner and blogger Scottie Lowe was more loquacious and less flattering in her "The State of Black Erotica," when she lamented:

> She's single handedly reshaped the face of Black erotica and opened the door for anyone, ANYONE who writes about sex to get a publishing deal, regardless of talent, or in most instances, the lack thereof. Sentence structure, spelling, grammar, and editing be damned. Publishers have taken the Zane story and capitalized off of it.

None of the reviewers explicitly say what factors serve as criteria of good writing. Reviewers who may prioritize Strunk and White's parameters of mechanics and style tend to deny the magic of storytelling for readers, be it oral traditions or free-verse poetry. The presence of good grammar or artistic metaphors and symbolism for sex does not ensure capturing the minds and imagination of "the people."

Zane's funky erotixxx might be more consistently valued and understood as a guerrilla tactic and expression of anguish if we examined it through Sylvia Wynter's thesis in "Towards the Sociogenic Principle," which asserts that in order for (wo)man to be set free, "the study of rhetoricity of our human identity" must occur. This new science is needed because

> [s]chemas, whether in their religious or in their now secular forms, can be recognized as the "artificial" behavior motivating "narratives" whose "vernacular languages of belief and desire" . . . structure our culture-specific orders of consciousness, modes of mind, and thereby of being. It is these schemas and the coercive nature of their systems of meaning that make it possible for each mode of sociogeny and its artificially imprinted *sense of self* to be created as one able to override, where necessary, the genetic-instinctual sense of self, at the same time as it itself comes to be subjectively *experienced as if it were instinctual.* (48)

The pseudo-pop-psychological tropes in Zane's works, the narrative economy of language within it, and its origins in cyberspace demand a Wynterian reading. If we begin here, then the last part of Wynter's essay changes from "black" to what it is like to be a repressed black woman. From the beginning of *Addicted*, Zane highlights the artificial behavior that will motivate her narration of Zoe's fictional life, which begins in first-person narration: "As much as I wanted to forget about the whole therapy session, the alternative was not acceptable. I desperately needed help, and it was time for me to face my fears. When I was a little girl, my mother always told me that courage is simply fear that has said its prayers" (1). Zane's depiction of Zoe's faith in prayers and therapy to help resolve her issues about sexuality would be admirable except that there is nothing redeemable about the religious and secular schemes excerpted from the pathology of Western morality and the overrepresentation of man. As the plot progresses, the author's elevation of this artificial intelligence does not overwrite the struggle of an erotic self with the discourses of religion and psychology outside of the fictional world. The study of Zane's words reveals as much. Zane's mode of writing and themes reflect an ongoing struggle against artificial intelligence that would wipe out nonhuman being or abort the other models of human being. Like Parliament's use of the synthesizer in funk, Zane uses technology to arrange the frequencies of her anguish into something funky.

Zane's biography alone provides the perfect example of why the erotic and funky erotixxx will be important to ensuring the survival of arts and humanities in this era's overinvestment in a society and humanity ordered, educated, and organized around a STEMocracy.[13] The genderless and asexual formulas and codes that led to new technologies created by Bill Gates, Steve Jobs, Mark Zuckerberg, and other white men have led to leisure activities organized around virtual networks and realities in which sexual violence and sexual pathology of white male supremacy can be imprinted onto human and artificial intelligence alike.[14] Digital media humanities and new media studies are already debating the racist and sexist implications of virtual leisure in gaming technologies.[15] Most recently, techies have linked the success of *Fifty Shades of Grey* with white middle-class women's desires and the innovation of Kindle and Nook because the e-readers ensure privacy for respectable women willing to cerebrally roll around in the muck.[16] Few, however, have really paid attention to the way the paper saleswoman who, without creating a single code or program, utilized low-tech communication to challenge the gendered and sexual configurations of communication and technology being dominated by white men so that maybe one day the shit Siri says will not only be dictated by white male supremacist fantasies. One woman's bad writing is another's hope for revolution as the machines infiltrate every aspect of our lives.

Prince Rogers Nelson's search for his love life in the song "Computer Blue (Till I Find a Righteous One)" leads him to recognize the symbolic usefulness of formulas and codes in the interim of finding a long-term level of intimacy and human contact. The same might be said of Zane's career and writing, which reflect a narrative economy of frugality ensconced in the interim space of everyday life and set free by the promise of the Internet. According to Zane, her forays into erotica begin during the midnight hour, after she had put her kids to bed:

> "I wrote an erotic story called 'First Night,' e-mailed it to three friends, and they forwarded it to other people. Then, I started getting e-mails from random people asking if I had more stories." She posted her next two stories on free websites set up through AOL and Yahoo[!] and says within three weeks she had over 800 hits. But because of the sexual content of her stories, she says, the Webmasters kept shutting down the sites.[17]

From that point on, Zane's eroticanoir.com was born, a site that still exists today. Astrid Ensslin's *Canonizing Hypertext* explores the relevance of new media to literary studies, asserting, "[T]he new Media revolution has radically changed public discourse, verbal and nonverbal communication as well as the concept of text in much the same way as it will, to an increasing extent, change our notions of the forms and topics of literature" (162). Although e-mails of the late 1990s may not have been as hypertext-capable as their current iterations, Zane's use of pre-W3 text—Ebonically enhanced narration—on the computer digitizes her narratives of sexuality. Ensslin states that hypertext is said to "have a nonlinear compositional structure and thus categorically deviate[s] from other digitized forms of writing, often called 'paper under glass' . . . in other words, there are multiple possible reading paths through a hypertext" (5). Sociolinguistic research on Ebonics in literature and culture, especially signifying, already underscores the proliferation of metatexts layered within black culture. In addition, media studies that focus on language, rhetoric, and media technology offer us further methods of reading. Although Ensslin admits that hypertext is a "colonialist media genre," she does little to separate how racialized communities' traditional and improvisational relationship to colonialist media has unforeseen results.[18] Black literacy adaptability allows Zane to improvise her use of technology to thwart an artificial self that might limit the pursuit of erotic sovereignty.

Criticism about whether sex acts should be written about, and thus how they should be written about as either formulaic or nonformulaic, has made it difficult for literary critics to engage the writing of Zane or others who fit within the tradition of urban erotica or urban fiction. "First Night," a nine-page short story, gives readers an economy of words steeped more in corporeal angst or discomfort than titillation. The first-person narrative traffics in what sociolinguist Arthur Spears notes as directness:[19]

> I can feel the head of your dick inside my stomach. It is a confusing mixture of pain and pleasure, but I want it all. I want you to tear my pussy up, fuck me like I have never imagined, so I take it and I come over and over again. Orgasm on top of orgasm.[20]

Metaphors and poetic prose could indirectly reveal information, but such tactics would mask the layers of code, formula, and directness that continue to work in accord with artificial intelligence (AI) of Western humanity. Zane's use of directness, however, confronts the coercive nature of language to shape modes of being. Thus, instead of asking if the writing is bad, we might ask if the writing resists in form as well as thesis;[21] or what the writer's relationship to her words and to her body or other bodies may be. Is that relationship best conveyed on the page in directness or poetic prose? That would depend on the writer's relationship to her body. What are readers' relationships to words and their bodies, and does what takes place on the page exemplify that relationship? These questions and their answers should be used in determining the value of Zane's work. The process and struggle over words determines one's awareness of the artificial intelligence Fanon and Wynter regarded as precarious.

Zane and her readers locate themselves in an economy of words based on repressed bodies and literacies, as opposed to grammar and mechanics established to discipline bodies into social categories of race, nation, class, and culture. Again, considerations of labor, leisure, eros, and funk can determine the methods of literary critics whose very work is to figure out how certain texts do what they do to and for what reading audiences. Critical work that distinguishes between bad writing and narrative economy or the rhetoricity of words could prove useful in recognizing alternative literacies—sexual literacies. Zora Neale Hurston has shown, more times than not, that one can be literate and intelligent while Ebonically speaking on any subject. Zane writes about the repressed in the language of the repressed. Likewise, her audience is composed of those who speak and read in a similar manner. The task of writing to help revise the self, voice, and consciousness happens in the everyday of what others have read as bad writing.

Zane demonstrates a preference for first-person narrative economy in her early works. When discussing first-person agency in essays and autobiographies, Quashie insists that "it is use of first-person that generally gives an essay its rhetorical power" and "the first-person narrative not only speaks for its narrator but speaks of his or her condition representationally, iconically" (*Sovereignty of Quiet*, 37). Though not an autobiography or essay, Zane's use of the first person in the short-story form and the erotic genre becomes an important marker of what her work does and why it appeals to certain women readers. Zane's first-person narration resembles a crisis around sexuality, voice, and agency. There remains great value in overstating the significance that she was a mothering woman bored with her career and periodically unhappy in her marriage who found pleasure in laboring over words that would validate fantasies of black bodies in motion: fantasies that threaten the everyday domestic labor practices she upheld. If Zane writes in the first person because it is rhetorically powerful or confirms its narrator's condition, we might understand that it also confirms the author's condition in fiction and reality.

By writing, Zane can pause her domestic labor, but long after work society's labor hours when sleep should happen. A culturally shaped first-person narration that acts as a writing style that can present such sentiment in aesthetics, pace, and mode cannot only be bad writing. Certainly, a large readership that supports this style of writing challenges all of us to reconsider what constitutes good writing. *The Sex Chronicles: Shattering the Myth*, a collection of stories made up of Zane's late-night computer blues, reflects all three of the elements in "First Night." Committed readers have seen the mechanics of Zane's writing improve, despite her use of the same narrative economy in her short stories, novels, and edited collections. One literary writer who made it her life's work to fictionalize the rich experience of black women provides further evidence to support such claims.

Toni Cade Bambara once explained that "short stories are a piece of time" and that her affinity for the short-story genre came from its ability to allow her to economically convey human living in the break between work society's wage and domestic labor. She said, "Writing had never been a central activity in my life," and then continued, "It was one of the things that I did when I got around to it or when the compulsion seized me and sat me down" ("What It Is I Think I'm Doing Anyhow," 154). The compulsion that seized Zane was no different, as she began writing erotica when she could get around to it. I am not suggesting that Zane's work shares a quality akin to Bambara's, but I am insisting that they share similar writing circumstances that produced different texts with their own valid aesthetics therein as opposed to what others have said.[22] Zane's work exists in a distinctly different narrative economy from Bambara's fiction and nonfiction. Bambara's attention to time and women's writing showcases what we rarely consider in all these conversations about black literature, fiction, and quality, and that is the economy of time and space and who has access to more of that than others. I mean this not simply in regard to material time and space, but with regard to subject matter that we may have been trained, taught, or conditioned to disregard or give less attention to in our everyday home and professional lives.

According to Taylor, "[Zane's erotica] is the damnedest mix of libertine and prude. Explicit, raucous and profane sexual descriptions stud her prose, along with bromides on infidelity and homosexuality that would do any far right-winger proud."[23] Such a review implicitly calls out the facile ending of *Addicted*, reminiscent of the film *Fatal Attraction*, in which Zoe is literally scared straight by a crazy bisexual woman. Zane continues this representation of madness, women, eros, and sexuality in another novel, *Nervous*, in which the female protagonist, Jonquinette Pierce, has multiple personality disorder/dissociative identity disorder that results in a sexually transgressive alternate. With improved grammar and mechanics than those found in *Sex Chronicles*, these novels, which are steeped in the formulaic fairy-tale romance of first young loves marrying each other, traumatic childhood sexual abuse, and promotion of psychotherapy that can heal the wounds of trauma, deserve the ire of critics because these characters' actions on the wild side can, in the end, be forgiven once they are diagnosed as part of a mental illness. The fairy-tale and moral endings of the novels acknowledge Zane as a writer aware of an audience that may very well be struggling with situating eros in the in-between of their wage and domestic labor, but who are still on the fence about validating antiwork activity.

As a form of sex-based work that does not have to take place in the street, black text-based erotica on the white space of paper and the cyberspace of the Web during the 1990s creates transitory spaces and sites for the black bodies, literal and symbolic, displaced by many city ordinances and zoning of sexual commerce and leisure. From her days as a self-published author to her current partnership with corporate publishers Simon and Schuster,[24] Zane's endeavors have created new models of erotic and sexual literacy. Simon and Schuster's publication of reading guides for the novels identifies a specific consumer—a middle-class readership invested in guidance via book clubs. The guide affirms the legitimacy and validity of that consumer's point of origin with regard to sexuality and speaks to a possible evolution that can happen as a result of reading and discussing the text. Question 5 from *Addicted*'s reading guide demonstrates the potential to change the way we think about literacy, literature, and representations of sexuality:

> One of the reasons *Addicted* is such an entertaining book for reading clubs and discussions among friends is there are so many different ways to come at this novel. It's an action-packed, sexy novel, but it also takes on some serious issues with which we all contend in our personal lives. What kind of a novel is *Addicted*? Suspense thriller? Love story? Modern-day morality tale? Erotica? How would you describe this book to a friend?[25]

Far different from the conduct and sexual health manuals of the nineteenth century or the late 1960s' Greenleaf Classics pornographic-pulp paperbacks masquerading as sociological and medical instruction manuals, the reading guide for *Addicted*, a novel most easily attached to the damaging rhetoric of psychoanalysis and the discursive violence it inflicts on women's personal sexual evolution, resists the educational inclination toward behavior modification.

The reading guide leaves space for the reader to decide what to do with the embedded schemas. It promotes a discussion that might make readers in the group aware of institutional state apparatuses, in addition to placing a value on any differences exhibited in the various responses to the novel. Although Zane's women characters have been regarded as merely reinscribing heterosexist paradigms, the short stories and novels inevitably make it clear that without the destabilization of heteropatriarchy, there could be no new woman, no better marriage, no great love story, and no moral redemption at the end of the orgasmic rainbow. Zane's preoccupation with creating characters who need another self or life outside of their proscribed lives should be overread, especially since this method disappears as she continues to publish her own work and the work of others.

Zane's novels and edited collections begin in the popular public sphere, but they soon exceed print media to forge new enterprises dependent upon a wider reach made possible by technology and an audience of women like Zane. Taylor and Lowe argue that Zane's technique reveals a certain prudishness, but critics such as Shayne Lee classify the heteronormative dominance within most of her books as revolutionary. However, the truth remains a lot more complicated. The lauded puritanical values within Zane's novels would be an effective and valid critique save that Zane's sex-based work does not end with her fiction. As a result of her publishing successes, Zane comprehends an already existing market based on the freak, as opposed to the spectators who come to see the freak. Typically, these other industries only recognize and market to a majority of white men. Understanding that there exists a consumer in search of leisure entertainment and spaces, as her funky erotixxx does, Zane reaches out and appeals to freaks whose anomalous interiority invests in the body at play or in pleasure. Her fiction validates existing freaks who may still be searching for a space that will not be vulnerable to state actions. Because Zane's work has transitioned from this to less problematic representations of female sexual exploration, the reading community that she has built possibly transitions with her. For someone who does not have the Kensington Ladies' Erotica Society on her side, Zane continues to defy odds of what a readership and following would look like.

The publication of collections such as *Purple Panties* and *Honey Flava* confirms that the chances of any real erotic revolution remaining straight and racially segregated are slim to none. While *Erotique Noire* decimated the wall between the academic and popular, Zane's fiction bridges the gaps between public and private spaces by erecting a new leisure industry built around digitization, technology, media, intimacy, and erotic literacy. The book is only the beginning. She creates a transcultural narrative that is able to travel across forms such as print media, Internet, film, social networking, and tourism. Perhaps a psychoanalytical reading would reveal how Zane's affirmation in erotica created from her own imagination allowed her to change the real and material conditions of her own life. Yet, such a reading does not seem necessary for this chapter, since Strebor—Zane's empire, like a T. D. Jakes megachurch—has corralled a contingency of freaks. In *Essence* magazine, Lynya Floyd showcases the commercial enterprise that is Zane, Inc.

> Welcome to Zane's first Freak Dating party, the new singles frontier, a heady mix of speed dating (where you're paired with someone new every eight minutes), erotic adventure (the mask, the names, the rules: You're only allowed to talk about your sexual desires), and a lot of nerve. As the Heat Seekers—one of the evening's signature cocktails—begin to flow, and the sounds of Prince and Rick James thump from the speakers, things get rolling. (196)[26]

The only other notable authors that have been able to create a book with philosophies to live by and then amass disciples and other followers, according to the myth, is whoever wrote the bible and L. Ron Hubbard. Zane's potential to promote erotic autonomy far exceeds the limited configurations of the information superhighway, which has changed the way we read and why we read, but it is up to her readers to create movement from it.

Throughout this chapter, I have advocated for black feminism to acknowledge how black women's production and use of erotica and porn among each other matters to its sexual politics. Distinct from their nineteenth- and twentieth-century foremothers, black women writers producing erotica and porn seek to construct a new offensive model of womanhood based on resisting the threat of sexual violence and the repression of desire that manifest destiny and manifest domesticity inflict upon women. Black women's erotica and pornography opens up an amative space vested in reciprocity for another and self for numerous genders. These black women writers, wives and mothers too, figured out how to use what others classify as profane, obscene, or taboo to bridge the intellectual, spiritual, and sexual to counter state and religious institutions' separation of the maternal or mother figure from woman.

To this end, black women writers' pursuit of erotic sovereignty through creative expression of sexuality and the fictional representation of that pursuit for women readers reveals how the rhetoric of choice/right as well as the rhetoric of life/moral fails to adequately address the dilemmas of black women dealing with state and communal sexual terrorism. For the difference between living (life) and dying (death) has never simply been about biology. One's perception of the erotic inevitably informs one's definition of what constitutes life and living, as well as who has the freedom that makes choice a reality. What is the definition of life in prolife rhetoric? If it remains the biological alone, then this also confirms why eros, eroticism, and maternal sexuality have been made obsolete. Such an absence is why women who have multiple abortions or women who have multiple children out of wedlock are made less visible in prochoice and reproductive rights strategies as well as appear inhuman in prolife rhetoric. Without a third eye that truly sees erotic autonomy as essential to life, the rhetoric of choice and rights is utterly inefficient when compared with the rhetoric of morality and ethics.

In a network of women, safe and discreet, funky erotixxx provides epistemic self-defense against sexual violence and terrorism purposely different from that of antipornography rhetoric and creates a space for the construction of a sexual guerrilla. The women writers and producers of erotica took an encroaching fixed identity and essentialized body that was becoming the foundation of black feminism and womanism and gave it permission to cruise in and out of different public spheres until a new subjectivity with many lives emerged. Their creative endeavors have reimagined and continue to reimagine desire for women from the gaze of a nonwhite and male entity, captured the gender-neutral anguish of being turned on, and played with the masculine fear of unfulfilled desire. Black women making erotica created a form about sexual anguish originating in the repression of women's desire and the threat of such force to the formation of an autonomous self that could live instead of die. Wanda Coleman, Miriam DeCosta-Willis, and Zane remake sexual commerce in the asexual and sexual sex industries. In doing so, they force us to consider the very definition and meaning of life and living.

3

"Make Ya Holler You've Had Enough"

Neutralizing Masculine Privilege with BDSM and Sex Work

In *Sounding Like a No-No,* Francesca Royster beautifully writes about black masculinity, the performance of imaginative freedom, and an aesthetic of silliness in P-Funk music. Her black quaring of the group and her question, "What do we make of the fact that this dance of masculine dreaming, of freedom and future and found community, is all to a song of lost women, mothers whose smiles mask the fact that 'life is really tough'?" (90), have significant ramifications for black political projects and black public spheres invested in dismantling gender hierarchies. Likewise, Sharon Holland asks, "But what if our erotic selves have been compelled not just by state intervention but also by such terms as 'community,' 'home,' and 'race'? (47). Having answered their own questions about family and gender, Royster's and Holland's questions allow me to bypass their focus on familial dynamics and eroticism and community responsibility so that I may focus on how play with power in nonfamilial erotic relationships, as well as a deployment of transaesthetics, in the fiction of Chester Himes and Hal Bennett intends to undermine gender and sexual-based epistemological violence maintained within and by black public spheres. As Erica Edwards educates us about charismatic leadership in black communities, she notes in *Charisma and the Fictions of Black Leadership* that it entails three forms of violence:

> [C]harisma is founded in three forms of violence: the historical or historiographical violence of reducing a heterogeneous black freedom struggle to a top-down narrative of Great Man leadership; the social violence of performing social change in the form of a fundamentally anti-democratic form of authority; and the epistemological violence of structuring knowledge of black political subjectivity and movement within a gendered hierarchy of political value that grants uninterrogated power to normative masculinity. (16)

Thus, in order to interrupt these three forms of violence and the erotic life of racism, funk proposes a blend of parody, irony, communal intimacy, and temporal violence that is satire and BDSM (bondage, domination, sadism, and masochism) to critique masculine privilege and eroticize male submission that would embrace nonnuclear and unpatriarchal traditions of family.

John Clark's "Formal Straining: Recent Criticism of Satire" tells us that "rigorous formalists have felt that satire lies outside the pale of aesthetic criticism" (499), while Charles Knight's *Literature of Satire* discloses why satire epitomizes what transaesthetics can do in the literary domain: "Satire also imitates . . . speech genres, the characteristic or conventional utterances developed in various spheres of communication. . . . Satire is thus pre-generic. It is not a genre in itself but an exploiter of other genres" (3–4). Remembering that transaesthetics demand a reorganization of the senses, then, we must also be mindful of what pregeneric satirical forms could exploit in their effort to observe, represent, and attack their critical objects. The body as text and sex as art are pregeneric forms. Knight continues, "Satire . . . is a parasitic form, imitating other forms by way of parody or using such imitation as a way of fixing points of reference and judgment" (5). As a result, I am arguing that funk makes BDSM a postgeneric form of satire in Himes's and Bennett's novels.

Unclassifiable as Horatian, Juvenalian, or Menippean because it does not meet the literary requirements of prose, poems, novel, or plays, BDSM can be classified as a contemporary embodied subgenre of satire, but only when it possesses a performative mode that does more than imitate numerous historical and social narratives. It must also attack and critique these narratives so as to expand and reinvent pleasure in accord with its denunciation of specific societal ills. Black public spheres too reliant on nostalgia and respectability can be reinvented using cultural legacies of transaesthetics to create new political strategies. Eliminating gender hierarchies and sexual colonialism in black communities hinges on black men and women accepting systems of knowledge that would teach them that forgoing masculine privilege and rethinking the feminine is not only morally and ethically right, but also that there is pleasure in it if everyone involved is willing to submit to funk's emphasis on The One.

In "Maid to Order," Anne McClintock asks, "Do men indulge in submission only when dressed as women and slaves, dogs and babies?" (96). This chapter's reading of funk's freaks in fiction serves an emphatic no. For men and women to neutralize masculine privilege, men must first indulge in the fantasy of submission, but for some black men that fantasy will not necessarily see them dressed as slaves, dogs, babies, or women. They might, however, indulge in the fantasy of submission within black men's culture where physical, performative, and economic androgyny are eroticized—black funk freakery. Such was the case with

Rick James. James was someone blacker than Prince Rogers Nelson, a little more heterosexual than Sylvester James, and the personification of an ecstatic androgyny that could coalesce black men and women into perversely playing with antibourgeois performances of gender and sexuality.

From the moment Motown released Rick James and the Stone City Band's *Come Get It!* (1978), black cultural representations of BDSM would be shaped by fantasies of drugs, glitter, leather, and funk. Braids of bondage rope would give way to braids of kinky black hair, and the ethos of a black underclass would insist on the submission of the black middle class and its work ethic. The front image of the album cover for Rick James's *Street Songs* (1981), a conceptual album about sex workers and antiwork activities, hardly personifies the James Ambrose Johnson who was raised as a devout Catholic by a single black mother in Buffalo, New York. It does, however, feature Rick James with luxurious flowing cornrow locks of hair and lip-glossed poppin' lips dressed in tight leather pants and bright red thigh-high boots as he holds a guitar and offers a cold-blooded stare. The back of the album depicts the singer being arrested along with several women of the night. This back cover displays James's funky fashion sense working in accord with powerful sultry glances from ebony eyes. His demeanor projects an ambiguity that makes it difficult to discern whether James is a hustler or a john. He appears especially feminine and vulnerable as the white cop pats down his tooted-up ass. That was Rick James: 1980s' icon of funk and superfreak extraordinaire.

James was a freak in the Baldwinian sense of the word, and his brand of funk was far from silly.

> Freaks are called freaks and are treated as they are treated . . . because they are human beings who cause to echo, deep within us, our most profound terrors and desires. . . . Most of us, however, do not appear to be freaks. . . . We are for the most part, visibly male or female, our social roles defined by our sexual equipment. But we are all androgynous. (Baldwin, "Here Be Dragons" 258)

I invoke the superfreak Rick James as a way to complicate the tensions around black male eroticism to the feminine and power and to reassert the androgynous nature of freak that Baldwin engaged. The freak proposes an alternative trajectory, especially since it allows us to eroticize black male submissiveness through funk. Baldwin uses a less material concept of androgyny to revise the meaning of *freak,* which also entails a critique of masculine privilege and racialized concepts of hypersexuality. While the demise of hypersexualized black bodies seems less likely, the neutralization of black male privilege, according to James and Baldwin, would occur when black men and women incorporate androgyny into their definition of *freak.*

For all of the ways in which James performed a mode of masculinity that ex- emplified Baldwin's understanding of how a freak's embrace of feminine qualities could reorganize the hypermasculine black male body as androgynous matter, and whose performance of sexual freakiness via BDSM could inspire others to pursue sexual autonomy that might wreak havoc on domesticity and the identity politics that accompanies it, he was not that thing Toni Cade Bambara theorized about when she mentioned the "task of creating a new identity . . . an androgynous self."[1] Such an androgynous self could "fashion . . . revolutionary lives, revolutionary relationships."[2] James's real-life practices of BDSM demonstrated how easily male privilege could negate the radical potentialities of such transgression and turn them into a form of sexual terrorism.[3] He was far from exemplifying the gender progressiveness of such feminist politics. What he symbolized, however, could have been because his performances of gender and sexual transgression did not fit neatly into black political projects situated in heteronormative masculinity and a cult of domesticity.

Years earlier, however, James's brand of commercial fetishism had already been imagined outside of black music, and it was very much attuned to the task of fashioning revolutionary lives and relationships. Chester Himes and Hal Bennett are highly regarded satirists, but what makes them emblematic of funk is that they utilized commercial BDSM and male hustling as both symbolic and mate- rial means to critique the inherent gender and sexual hierarchies dominating and delimiting black political platforms reliant on charismatic leadership and a cult of domesticity in the late twentieth century. They did so by replacing the conjugal union exacerbated in African American literature with the commercial fetishism and gender power contained in sexual subcultures.

In *Conjugal Union,* Reid-Pharr submits that in black antebellum novels, and literary criticism of those novels, "proper black bodies can only be produced in proper black households" (11). To this end in African American literature and literary studies, the cult of domesticity has been predominantly associated with the cult of true womanhood and its message of uplift.[4] However, Wallace's ap- praisal of the autobiographies of Frederick Douglass and Booker T. Washington in *Constructing the Black Masculine* establishes a link between antebellum black masculinity and the cult of domesticity. Because these representations can in no way sustain alternative models of black manhood, nor eroticize male submis- sion, to offset conventional ones set up by the overrepresentation of man and his ideologies of eros and eroticism, we must heed the words of Reid-Pharr at the end of his examination of the conjugal union and its value when he asks,

[A]s we approach the millennium, how much longer can this particular set of ideological and discursive strategies serve our interests, especially in the face of the constant reports of black bodies and households under siege? What is to be gained in the often precious manner in which we cherish the common sense of black ontology? What worlds will collide if black bodies continue their promiscuous, self-interested longing? What catastrophes await the erection of improper households? What more is to be achieved through this union? (131–32)

Nothing more can be gained from this union in a new millennium.

Chester Himes's *Pinktoes* (1961) and Hal Bennett's *Lord of Dark Places* (1970) had already deduced that equality lay in the erection of improper households. Attending to the antiwork politics within superfreaks' sexualities, Himes and Bennett propose that black men would need to refashion themselves as an androgynous self and refuse an interrogation of the erotic that deduces its uses through a binary of phallus and anus complex—who is penetrated and who is penetrating. Such men would also need to avoid writing black women as "revolutionary pussy" or as a romanticized domesticated half of a revolutionary couple.[5]

Rather than adhering to the divide between the public and private sphere for traditional representations of sexual barters so as to safeguard masculine privilege, Himes and Bennett highlight the divide as false by writing novels featuring black women characters who make black male submission pleasurable and profitable. Himes provides his black woman leader, Mamie Mason, with a unique political sphere in which race men submit to her desires and political aspirations. Bennett takes on the black church and sacrifices the race man, as well as the black buck and queen, while extolling black androgynous libidinal economy. Anne McClintock offers one perspective as to why Himes and Bennett chose this particular form of representation.

> By cross dressing as women or maids, by paying to do "women's work," or by ritually worshipping dominas as socially powerful, the male "slave" relishes the forbidden feminine aspects of his own identity, furtively recalling the childhood image of female power and the memory of maternity, banished by social shame to the museum of masturbation.[6]

As this chapter shows, Himes and Bennett write women characters, gangstresses,[7] who deal in illicit trans(actions) or commercial fetishisms. By operating outside the confines of the traumatic site of slavery in a black/white binary, they reveal the other elements shaping power struggles and abuses within and outside of black communities. In each case, new black masculinities are carved out and away from white hegemonic masculinities from which the old black masculinities were made. These men would transition into freaks. Although the freak and superfreak originate in gender-neutrality, black feminist thought has engaged the gendering of the figure as feminine much more, albeit in negative ways.[8] Regardless, funk's freak provides an important figure and history for black masculinity studies These figures demonstrate black masculinity submitting to androgynous living, which is a cultivation of sexuality and gender across a wide range of bodies and practices where new economies are imagined.

Pinktoes: Satire That Hurts So Good

In their attempts to explain why women writers seldom write satire, some (male) critics have asserted, "Satire is not, on the whole, private and domestic. It tends to be concerned with public issues and with public examples of those issues (Knight, *Literature of Satire*, 7). Although he is not a woman writer, Himes's conscientious intent to critique social fictions of race, gender, sexuality, and class refute the general parameter of Greco-Roman traditions. In recent years, critics have done a fabulous job of exploring the importance of Himes's well-known and lesser-known domestic fiction. For Himes, domesticity was not simply about representing black households with a mother, father, children, and a house. He often referred to his street-centric novels as domestic fiction.[9] Readers of the Coffin Ed Johnson and Gravedigger Jones novels can glimpse Himes's preoccupation with representing a variety of black sex workers.[10] Himes's only novel to be classified as an erotic text—*Pinktoes*—creates a type of domestic fiction out of improper households where sex and work are inseparable. Foreseeing the role integration would play in building a black middle class and creating class-segregated suburbs, Himes takes his domestic series away from the gritty realism of the streets into the cozy comforts of domestic bliss. Writer John Williams documented upon *Pinktoes*'s publication, "[T]he use of satire today (although used sparingly by black writers in the past) could signal a new approach in writing technique" (74). Critics Edward Margolies and Michel Fabre document the ways in which Himes saw *Pinktoes* as a way to change the very fabric of black writing during his time: "'Mamie Mason' would be a different kind of Negro novel. Readers, he said, were tired of protest fiction arousing pity for poor downtrodden Negroes" (91). Himes himself stated, "I had the creative urge[,] but the old tired forms for the American black writer did not fit . . . I wanted to break through the barriers that kept them labelled as protestors" (92).

In telling the story of Mamie Mason, a married Harlem social matron and dominatrix, Himes imagines a world in which black women direct conversations and circumstances around sexuality and the Negro problem. Mamie approaches the Negro problem in a way not many socialites would use—through interracial orgies and select practices of BDSM. Himes doubly interrupts the leadership scenario of black politics and its representative form, the African American narrative, with orgy scenes and sex work in the novel. Negro race leaders and preachers, white patrons and benefactors, black matrons and black club women make up the list of characters in Mamie's Harlem. If something or someone is going down, Mamie is usually the fellatious force dictating such happenings.

Mamie aspires to be the perfect host at her orgies, and other characters view her as capable of more self-control and restraint in light of their sexual gluttony. Himes establishes Mamie as the epitome of restraint and control by detailing Mamie's rigid dieting process. Throughout the novel, the narrator notes the actual physical effort it takes for Mamie to get her size 12 frame into a size 6 dress. Corsets, tied knots, sucking in of stomach, stockings, too-tight shoes, and various diets represent the painful and difficult attempt to keep Mamie's voluptuous frame disciplined and in place. When Mamie's best friend Zoe decides to lure Mamie away from her diet out of fear that Mamie's dieting efforts are about seducing her husband Zeke, she prepares a dinner for all of them. The narrator explains, "Zoe set the table for three and called Mamie to dinner, saying she . . . roasted a big milk-fed turkey cock especially for her, knowing how much she liked er, ah, turkey" (*Pinktoes*, 31). *Pinktoes* contains numerous moments of signifyin(g) that shape and direct the satire about race, sexuality, and power. Zoe takes sadistic pleasure in enticing Mamie to break her diet. Though the dinner is tempting, Mamie refuses it while in the company of Zoe and Zeke. These skills of restraint enable her to convince wealthy whites and middle-class blacks to contribute to her worthy social causes for Negro uplift.

However, one of the ways in which Himes foreshadows Mamie's fluidity and mobility comes through an exposition on the fragility of such control, which is delivered through wordplay and double entendres about sex and food. Once Zoe and Zeke depart for the night, Mamie's alone time with the food showcases Himes's critique of sexual restraint, decadence, and overindulgence. In the case of Mamie and the turkey cock, she could not resist the temptation to taste a little of the turkey before she "made it back to her room" (34). The narrator continues, "She was still ravenous for some turkey cock, but she had herself well under control and the weakness had left. The only thing now was that her empty stomach, suddenly confronted by a small token of cock, had pounced on it with all its juices, and had become woefully inflated, such as happens to the female stomach when it samples too much cock. . . . And Mamie wasn't mad at anyone. It was just a case of a month of privation confronted with a tremendous cock" (34). Himes successfully makes indigestion a double entendre for masochistic sexual excitement and anticipation created from specific bodily discipline and concerns about race and representation.

Research on the Marquis de Sade and BDSM has generated a general consensus that BDSM remains a practice of the elite and upper-class segments of society;[11] it becomes clear that Himes revises these theories to take into consideration black historic experiences with physical torture and sadism of slavery transitions into a vacillation between physical and mental sadism and masochism in Jim Crow emancipation. Greg Thomas's elucidation of the connection between colonialism, torture, and sadism in the work of Fanon has broader anticolonial implications for Himes's novels *Plan B* and *Real Cool Killers*: "The writings of Fanon and Himes amount to a twin testimony to this violence and the necessity of violence as an anti-racist, anti-colonial remedy to violence" ("On Psycho-Sexual Racism," 229). Reading BDSM in the context of colonialism reinforces the idea of BDSM as some white European practice, but Thomas's reading also proposes why it might be relevant to black people during and after segregation. Just as neolynching of police brutality exists alongside black sexual cultures of bondage and domination, the same might be said about lynching existing alongside eroticized BDSM and interracial relationships in segregation. Rather than expel or avoid these practices, black people, Himes tells us, reinvent them.

Pinktoes underscores the importance of comprehending BDSM as a practice meant to challenge bourgeois conformist ideologies of domestication and civilization[12] that are not solely in the de Sade province of colonialists or elite aristocrats. Although bourgeois mores and manners remain the object of the challenge, the manner and means in which different classes oppose these norms varies. Here again is why my earlier reference to Rick James remains important. The practice of BDSM play, and any depiction of it, has symbolic and material consequences for the underclasses and working classes, women, and black people for the way it proposes violence as a solution to violence.

Himes proposes that the affect generated by interracial orgies and BDSM are contemporary sexual magic, more secular than sacred, that can be used to dismantle black public spheres underwritten by the charisma scenario and manifest domesticity. Mamie's orgies symbolize a public space that offers a democratic experience unlike any public sphere available during the time period of the novel's setting or in the era in which the novel is published. At one of Mamie's parties, the narrator tells of a distinguished white woman who becomes enraptured with a nameless black man who reminds her of her black chauffeur Jackson, a would-be Negro poet. The doppelgänger's shared physical attribute is his black skin. Nevertheless, the two end up leaving the party together to have sex. The narrator comments on the call-and-response nature of their sex: "This poetry is not only being made but it is being said, between pants and grunts and groans, that is. He: Birmingham / She: oh, you poor lamb / He: klu klux klan / She: oh you poor black man / He: lynch mob / She: oh, you make me sob" (*Pinktoes*, 109). This poetry, a form of sexual culture and epistemic violence, counters the colonial history of sexuality that erases racialized sexual terrorism. The themes of suffering and release expressed with this one couple are representative of the interactions occurring at Mamie's orgies. The sadism and masochism play and fantasy is organized around racial trauma specific to segregation, but Himes does not foreclose on how class matters either since the exchange happens as a result of the erotics of class fantasies.

Mamie's orgies are situated around white fantasies, but the political economy gained from them goes toward black people. These gains are the result of Mamie's (Himes's) commercializing BDSM from a particular race and class perspective that cannot rely upon public sex cultures of dungeons and community groups organized around BDSM proper. She turns instead to groups organized around racial uplift and its race leaders, and even these interactions would not be possible were Mamie poor. Most recently, Margot Weiss's *Techniques of Pleasure* offers that "SM play with social power, especially cultural—and national—trauma like slavery and the Holocaust, is contested and politically complex. Such play echoes and plays off traumatic histories; indeed it is this dramatization of historical structures of exploitation in the guise of fantasized or performed display that makes SM play erotic" (188). Adding to the conversations of S/M as a public and political problem about private desires, Weiss's work attends to class and capitalism in her performative materialist methodological approach to studying BDSM.

Himes, however, understands that within US colonialism, violence can be both physical and epistemic and come from above or below. He uses *Pinktoes* to remind readers that class is a form of social power with its own traumas sometimes legibly played out via gender, race, or nation, and other times illegible and unimaginable in current circuits of sexuality. He pays particular attention to one aspect of BDSM prevailing in the United States: "Psychological aspects (negotiations, relationships, polyamory, aftercare, violence, trust, land mines, personal fears)" (Weiss, *Techniques of Pleasure*, 9). Himes focuses on the psychological aspects to center his appraisal of the epistemic and physical violence of BDSM in a manner that deals with the interior affect of class for African Americans. Race and gender have been the dominant ways in which critics have focused on theories and performances within BDSM practices and communities, but too little attention has been spent on power relations among class groups within the same gender and racial communities—that is to say, black on black BDSM where the circuits are not public. There seems to be an unknowability as to what rules of class categories can be transgressed if hyperbolic performances of power play are deracinated. Because, according to Weiss, "changing forms of community, identity, and commodity exchange produce BDSM and its pleasures" (229), then we should consider what exists in the absence of dungeons, clubs, organizations, and sex shops. The social relations of power that produce class hierarchies also create erotic power and tensions originating in individual fantasy but regulated by institutional forces.

Himes's *Pinktoes* asks us to think about what the historical and personal traumas of class may be for black society as a whole and for black individuals: slavery is certainly one, but racial and class segregation are the others. The history of lynching has demonstrated that transgressing the boundaries of legal segregation in the South and self-imposed segregation in the North involves risk and consent, which is why Mamie's orgies are very much a subculture community of uplift and risk made possible by income. Dominant ideologies of safety in BDSM community philosophies, from safe, sane, and consensual to risk-aware consensual kink, are deemed safe and protected from outside forces due to class privilege. Cultural and institutional responses to play and practices within edgeplay highlight the prominence of class privilege in the communities.[13] Do the poor have techniques of pleasure that they enact against the rich that would not land them in jail or an asylum, or have the fantasies of the poor as nihilistic, ignorant, lazy, and childishly hedonistic made the question of little consequence? What does it feel like for a poor black woman to make a submissive of a middle-class black lady? What is it like to imagine BDSM play as the homeless man pissing or shitting on any willing WASP couple? For a scene to consist of the foster-care kid beating and flogging his parents? For a black professional businessman to stop, frisk, handcuff, and beat the working-class white cop? Although white communities can ignore questions about what happens if the colonized want to practice and play at BDSM in a manner different than that established by capitalism, neocolonialism, and domesticity, black communities cannot. Himes's characterization of Mamie as a black woman from a questionable class background pursuing power through BDSM orgies rejects safe, nonviolent, asexual, and moral platforms of the black public sphere because he recognizes such elements as a form of colonial violence.

A simple parody of slave-master relations will not sufficiently represent how and why black men and women might participate in BDSM in the everyday or in subculture communities. Satirically representing the eroticization and fetishization that happens in the historic parameters of white patronage does. McClintock has shown that "an important theoretical distinction therefore needs to be made between reciprocal S/M for mutual pleasure, and consensual S/M organized as a commercial exchange. Whatever else it is, commercial S/M is a labor issue."[14] Mamie organizes consensual S/M for political capital. Himes's depiction offers that such affective collaborations can potentially interrupt the political work of a singular authority figure. As the previously mentioned couple continues interracial intercoursing, the chauffer continues to moan and groan an oppression caused by the Negro problem answered by an appropriate white liberal response until the final climax in which he groans "Oooooooo!" and she moans "Negro" (*Pinktoes*, 110). Mamie's house parties are a way for black and white men and women to invoke incidents that will lead to revolutions. Lest we forget, interracial sex was once an antiwork practice that could produce sexual citizenry and freaks.

Brown v. Board of Education typically stands as the landmark moment for retrospectives on integration and equal citizenship, but that case is for considerations that make absent the role of manifest domesticity. It was *Loving v. Virginia* that would sustain a square world of domestication, despite its queer interraciality. When federal circuit court judge Leon M. Bazile initially delivered a ruling on the 1965 *Loving v. Virginia* case, he claimed:

> Almighty God created the races white, black, yellow, malay and red, and he placed them on separate continents. And but for the interference with his [arrangement] there would be no cause for such marriages. The fact that he separated the races shows that he did not intend for the races to mix.[15]

Bazile's argument meant that any defense of interracial contact must have at its center a moral contract and an ethic of productivity. The *Loving* story has been written as a romanticized citizenship narrative in which love conquers all, even the racist aftermath of slavery and segregation. The plaintiff Mildred Jeter pursued a legal challenge to Bazile's ruling because she wanted to raise her children near her family in her hometown in Virginia. Still, *Loving* never toppled the pathology of sexual morality or work ethic in Bazile's idea of citizenship.

Family and home are powerful social narratives that are complicated by interracial sex as opposed to interracial marriage, and the power of these narratives has silenced the questions about who Mildred Jeter was before she became wife, mother, and defendant. She was a woman bold enough to date, on and off, a white man who frequented drag races and was six years her senior.[16] The leisure activities of interracial contact convey a story of play before the work of citizenship. In another time and place, could Mildred Jeter have been as like-minded about interracial contact as Mamie Mason? Certainly, Himes's depiction of Mamie's affinity of interracial intercourse critiques sexual identities and political institutions in ways that Jeter could not through a court of law. He intuits the simultaneous privileging of white male sexual citizenship and continued denials of black women's sexual agency and erotic autonomy in *Loving v. Virginia*.

Written in Paris, France, during the early 1950s, but published three years after *Loving v. Virginia* began making its way through the courts, *Pinktoes* does what the very adult case of *Loving v. Virginia* failed to do: rewrite considerations of race, sexuality, labor, and citizenship. Immediately preceding and after *Loving v. Virginia* and the publication of *Pinktoes,* the climate surrounding black sexuality and mores was still clearly aligned with righteous propagation of a bygone era. According to Mitchell's *Righteous Propagation,* this was an era in which "women and men would nevertheless explore ways in which sex could bolster the literal reproduction of the race, secure a healthy presence in the national black politic, and strengthen the collective integrity of Americans with African heritage" (79). Interracial intercourse, for a number of reasons, could not be classified as righteous propagation for white lawmakers like Bazile or black political leaders invested in segregation or integration.

Himes's representation of Mamie's promotion of more interracial intercourse, therefore, is not only about his personal preferences for interracial sex but a rejection of Christian moral agendas undergirding Reconstruction-era platforms and the black civil rights movement. Satire, as Knight observes, "sees morality as hypocritical, or as a presumptuous effort to assert a social control to which the moralist has no right. . . . Satire, then, is independent of moral purpose" (5). Just as Randolph, the McKoys, and Lorde were skeptical of Western medicine and science, Himes conveys the same level of skepticism toward the US legal system's supposed objectivity in regulating bodies and in enforcing the public/private divide in US society.

The title of Himes's novel, the vernacular term *pinktoes,* provides black people in Himes's fictional world with what *Loving v. Virginia* could not for black people in reality: an admonition of the white hypocrisy and sexual morality. Himes understands that the emerging superfreaks deserve a viable discourse that can overwrite Western medicine and science's biologic of sexual identity, a variant in the overrepresentation of man, when he states the definition: "Pinktoes is a term of indulgent affection applied to white women by Negro men, and sometimes conversely by Negro women to white men, but never adversely by either" (*Pinktoes,* 7). In stating the power dynamics of sign/signifier and meaning, and who gets to say who is and is not a pinktoe, Himes situates that this novel and its depictions of sexual mores will determine its meaning and pleasures from African American culture and discursive mechanisms, rather than those established by white Americans of the time. For these black people, sexuality will no longer be what the colonizers do to themselves or the colonized, but what the colonized do to themselves for their own pleasure.[17]

Finally, the term *pinktoes* remarks upon the beginning of new and ignored sexualities that comprehend race, not gender, as the definer of a particular sexuality. Himes makes obvious how Freudian binaries and Kinsey scales are schemas preserving institutionalized white supremacy and sexual imperialism in the lives of people of color. Were interracial sexuality ever theorized as sexual identity and orientation, what would theories of BDSM look like? Would BDSM become akin to the differential markers of so-called homosexual sex acts: buggery or tribadism? Or would its disregard for gender as an object of sexuality do that? *Pinktoes* illustrates how ridiculous the disavowal of interracial sexuality as a sexual identity is in several laugh-out-loud scenes.

Himes does not focus on the heterosexual aspects of this interracial sexuality alone. He also engages white male obsession with the black phallus to underwrite the elements of S/M that might be eroticized in interracial sexuality. When the black Reverend Riddick and the white Professor Samuels end up wrestling buck naked after leaving one of Mamie's parties, Professor Samuels's wife, Kit, becomes so excited by watching two differing racially marked bodies in a sort of dance that she begins calling out epithets such as, "Oh, big black Riddick, I'm a bitch. I'm a bitch in heat" (113). Her cries incite her husband and the reverend to wrestle even more vigorously until finally, as the narrator tells us, Professor Samuels "gripped Rev. Riddick's most vulnerable limb. The only thing was he was too weak to take a good hold and his hand kept slipping up and down" (113). Throughout the narration, as Kit Samuels grows more excited, and her husband becomes more physical with Riddick, Himes displaces psychoanalytical analysis of interracial cuckoldry as a practice in which white men take pleasure in watching their wives or girlfriends with big black bucks, with a reading that acknowledges the agency and autonomy of all three people in the equation.

Himes's omniscient narrator shifts the gaze of the spectacle from black man to white man, from white man to black man, and from white man to white woman. Kit Samuels is not the passive virginal white woman servicing men. She is the voyeur getting off on her white husband vigorously "wrestling" with Reverend Riddick. The interracial tryst moves from the private boudoir of the Samuels to outside on the city streets, and it ends with Professor Samuels and Reverend Riddick in a jail cell. Black men as the object of desire for white men and white women is confirmed when our narrator proclaims, "Which just goes to show that the Phallus complex is the aphrodisiac of the Negro problem" (115). Himes's phallus complex is meant to differentiate itself from the white Oedipal complex that writes the father's law. The race question is about sexual desire. He constitutes a BDSM scene where white women's desires are placed alongside white men's desires. Words reinforce violence. Private desires give ways to public abandon.

Mamie's efforts at using interracial intercourse to racially uplift the black race are not in vain. Later, in a chapter appropriately titled "Hold That Devil," Himes gives the finger to both racial propagation and the sexual demon of colonial power when Reverend Riddick and another white woman, Peggy, end up marrying each other. He hilariously criticizes the sexual morals that accompanies colonialism and enslavement spiritual conversions, when in faux marriage vows to Peggy, Reverend Riddick proclaims, "By holy heavens, I'll dedicate the remaining years of my life to the exorcism of your devil" (223). Power, Himes writes, can be obtained not only in sexual violence and terrorism, but through sexual conversion or sexual salvation less pathologized as immoral or deviant. Himes then undermines black nationalist agendas of same-race relationships by positioning Reverend Riddick's engagement as *Pinktoes*'s righteous screwing. Reverend Riddick becomes another example of how political uplift becomes a form of sex work in Himes's fictional world. Ironically, these acts disturb the boundaries of black leadership, the project of manifest domesticity, and pathologization of sexual morality.[18] Propagating, righteously for the nation or otherwise, will not be a sufficient means of sexual decolonization.

Himes depicts Mamie as creating a black public sphere in which freak subjectivity informs her platform for attaining equal citizenship. She understands that she and other Negroes will always be outsiders. So she works from a position as outlined by Blair's assessment of black sex workers in the early 1900s:

> Black sex workers also resisted the exhortations by leaders within the emerging African American community to conform to expectations of public propriety and sexual purity. As they publicly labored to earn money in the sex industry, black sex workers challenged the discourse of respectability, implicitly questioning its relevance to their experiences in [an] industrial economy. (3)

More interracial intercourse promotes sexual leisure among the races instead of sexual utility and labor that will reproduce more bodies. To further insist that he is not simply advocating racial propagation but funk's rebellion, Himes's narrator provides a lesson on faith, screwing, and the history of black people in the United States. In the case of the Harlem inhabitants in *Pinktoes,* he offers that they have faith in "the wonderful exhilaration derived from screwing" (23). He continues,

> One desires to employ a term less idiomatic than screwing in this historical treatise, such as fornicating, cohabitating, or even plain propagating, but there is nothing plain about this propagating; one is limited by a language that was not designed to describe the acrobatics and athletics involved in this contest . . . and the beautiful part about screwing is that it does not require the assistance of either the Lord or the Jew. (23)

Himes attacks both morality and capitalism's underdevelopment of black America. He uses sex to displace organized religion as a spiritual site and to overwrite political economy of rights with the possibilities of sex as material resource. The distinction the narrator makes between screwing and propagating clearly rests on the lack of depth, tone, and touch to translate the feeling and funk the act of sex creates. Propagation is a utilitarian act, a work assignment, or it has a biological and then political imperative to reproduce. Both, then, would involve outside interference. Screwing does not. Himes's novel considers a purpose of black sexuality that cannot be controlled or policed by those within and outside the black community.

BDSM, Interracial Sex, and the Classless Society?

Pinktoes, in form, structure, and theme, is funky. It continues what critic Kevin Bell sees as a pattern in Himes's other widely read works, specifically the ability to "create worlds of movement, sound, texture, lines, and breakage that interact directly with bodies, institutions, laws, and cultures, amplifying the singularity of each, by addressing not its power of instrumental language, but of affective furor, of each field's individual idiom of pure expressivity, its abilities to convey meanings that operate in excess of language" (858). BDSM interracial sex serves as the affective furor and becomes symbolic of how a classless society might come to be through human relationality and affect as opposed to political organizing in the United States. James Boggs recaps the difficulty of creating a classless society in his reading of Marxist theory:

> Yet ever since the Russian Revolution, all kinds of socialists have differentiated themselves from the communists in terms of political policy and political organization but have never tackled this question of Marxist theory that socialism is just a transitional society on the way to communism and that only under communism can there be a classless society. (107)

Based on Bell and Boggs, movement in a class society—class mobility—would not necessarily be movement in a classless society. Likewise, interracial sex that does not depoliticize work and that does not remind its agents that the taboos and boundaries of interracial sex are themselves a form of automation that maintains a class society is the reality signified by *Loving v. Virginia*. Himes's glorification of interracial BDSM extends the socialist moments that otherwise would transition into communism. His pornographic satire suggests BDSM techniques provide approaches from which to form a classless society, specifically when initiated by black women class outsiders who have contact with the elite. With Himes ridiculing the historical necessity of white patronage to all black racial uplift efforts, his representation of Mamie refuses simple readings of her absolute submission to male power, as black freedom has covertly manipulated white patronage support of spectacles of black sexuality.

White patronage stands as a class performance of BDSM very different than that enacted by slave-master narratives. Chattel slavery's whip is replaced with wallet or pocketbook, and the services being purchased satisfy both interior and exterior desires. As readers learn, Mamie faces some difficulties in convincing prominent members of the white community to attend the wedding and reception of Reverend Riddick and Peggy. Each of them has offered an excuse for not attending, as their presence might be read as public approval of this social taboo. Mamie strategically makes the reception a masked ball to entice and protect the identities of "three distinguished doctors of philosophies and humanities, Dr. Oliver Wendell Garrett, president of the board of the Rosenberg Foundation, Dr. Carl Vincent Stone, president emeritus and chairman of the board of the famous Negro College . . . and Dr. John Stetson Kissock, chairman of the Southern

Committee for the Preservation of Justice " (227), who she needs to attend the wedding reception. Throughout the novel, these three men have been engaged in the social uplift work of fixing the Negro problem. Himes showcases how these men's approval, delivered by their appearance at the wedding reception, symbolizes the ways in which white masculinity is privileged in social and legal matters of society.

Bell's assessment of Himes's novels as possessing affective furor is multiplied several times over in the closing scenes of the novel in which Mamie acts as the primary instigator of a BDSM scene meant to gain political benefits. The climatic scenes are crafted to reject sexual civility and explore animal urges. On the day of Reverend Riddick's wedding and Mamie's masked ball, readers learn that the three doctors, Garrett, Stone, and Kissock, are more than Mamie's lovers. They are her bottoms. Having fasted once again to look her best, Mamie slips into an "absolutely fabulous rhinestone-ornamented gold lamé costume, size twelve" (243), and not a minute after she slips into it, Dr. Stetson Kissock arrives demanding that she take off the dress lest he tear it off her. Soon they both undress with our narrator observing of Mamie's body after her fast that "she bore a striking resemblance to a skeleton clad in a skin four sizes too large," and noting of Dr. Kissock without his clothes, "The other was not Dr. Kissock at all. It was a round happy porker fresh from the scalding pot" (244). Here, Himes cleverly mocks the removal of all airs of respectability with the removal of clothing. Neither individual is who he or she represents him or herself to be, and once these fabrications of race and gender are removed, nature or common human-animal remains.

Having already exposed the role of biopolitical theory in his critique of miscegenation laws, Himes addresses and neutralizes the deployment of biopolitical theory used in social contracts to ensure black women's posthuman future. Cary Wolfe's *What Is Posthumanism?* details the role of biopolitical theory in creating laws and agendas for medicine, science, and technology, offering: "For biopolitical theory, the animality of the human becomes a central problem—perhaps the central problem—to be produced, controlled, or regulated for politics in its distinctly modern form" (100). Himes refuses to separate the human from the animal as Western civilization has done. Himes suggests that for complete racial liberation and sexual freedom to happen, black women must do more than throw off respectable dress (that is, get rid of respectability) or work away from racial scripts. Black and white men have to bottom themselves out as well. Everyone has to get on the one. Furthermore, his disidentification with the human means that immorality, not morality, will be the distinguishing basis of black satire.

Mamie's performance as dominatrix allows her to manipulate this central problem outside of the ways that modernity deals with it. Going against the grain of rights rhetoric, Himes opts to move readers from liberal humanism using BDSM.

Himes's depiction of BDSM exceeds theories of it as performance and scene centered on the ocular. He presents BDSM attuned to other senses, through funk's sonic emphasis of being on the one and its kinesthetic emphasis on movement and smell.

The final scene of the novel details how the success of Mamie's political efforts depend not on her strict masochistic control over everything, but in her ability to move between masochist, sadist, and dominatrix, specifically in her ability to do a funky dance that generates power from below. Kissock does not come to Mamie's house so that they can engage in interracial intercourse centered on phallic penetration, but instead so that Mamie can whip him into ecstasy with "a miniature bullwhip, black and a foot long" as he sympathetically laments "Oh! Oh! the poor Negro!" (244). Mamie obliges him until they are interrupted and he has to hide from Mamie's next client, Dr. Stone. Dr. Stone's sexual pleasure comes from sniffing, snarling, biting, and groveling at the musk-bathed bosom of Mamie as he professes, "Can't bear to hear black women singing spirituals . . . Oh, how I hate the Negro" (245). A few minutes later Stone has to hide from Dr. Garrett who has come to spank Mamie with his own bullwhip while he chants, "Oh, how I love the Negro." Love, hate, and pity are what Mamie experiences from them. As each lover unclothes, Himes employs the same strategy of suggesting that the clothes were hiding a mad dog and a billy goat. Stripped of their basic Westernized humanity, the façade of white heteronormative masculinity is dropped when each discovers the other. Upon recognition of each other, no one wants to leave. All four of them, with Mamie setting and establishing a rhythm with her bullwhip, excite and incense each other into "a sighing climax" (249). This is the absurdity of racism, but it is also the inescapable pressure of capitalism.

With his representation of Mamie as domina, Himes continues to exemplify how writing S/M as a scene reflective of race and class dynamics matters. McClintock reminds us that "[i]n commercial S/M, the domina acts as an official, if forbidden, witness to private anguish, baffled desires, and the obscure deliriums of the flesh" (109). Himes's representation of the syncopated S/M exchanges between Mamie and her lovers are simultaneously oral (confession and moaning), olfactory (sniffing fetish), and haptic (bullwhip beatings and biting) rather than privileging the visual, which would highlight racial difference and its hierarchies organized around those differences. Despite the verbalization of racial absurdness, Himes focuses on sensations that would move beyond race and racial discourse of the human. How these people come to locate and understand themselves entails a new order of the senses in which interior and social differences of race, sex, and class would also be smelled, felt, and tasted. They are white and black, but more than that as well. Their getting off depends upon the latter.

Satirizing racial uplift through parodic accounts of interracial sexuality and BDSM provides a humorous but powerful examination of the absurdity of racism and the horror of class mobility as it operates in the lives of black men and women in the United States. In discussing the issue of racism in his autobiography, Himes assessed that "racism introduces absurdity into the human condition. Not only does racism express the absurdity of the racists, but it generates further absurdity in the victims. And the absurdity of the victims intensifies the absurdity of the racists, ad infinitum" (*My Life of Absurdity*, 1). To match this absurdity, Himes manufactures this group BDSM scene as an affective critical procedure, Wolfe's meaning of posthumanism, that distinguishes itself from the critical subject of humanism because it does not need the biopolitical. He relies on BDSM to critique white desire for black bodies but also to emphasize how the restraints middle-class black Americans place upon themselves as a solution to solving the Negro problem are a form of BDSM.

According to many African American cultural critics, the tendency to eroticize BDSM arises from sociohistorical positions of power and privilege typically shared by white males. Audre Lorde, in her anti-S/M essay with Susan Leigh argued, "Sadomasochism is an institutionalized celebration of dominant/subordinate relationships. And, it prepares us either to accept subordination or to enforce domination. . . . Sadomasochism feeds the belief that domination is inevitable and legitimately enjoyable" (*Burst of Light*, 14). Years later, intersectionality has shown us that there may be little to no exchanges that are completely equal to funk's emphasis of being on the one. Elizabeth Freeman's *Time Binds* would assess sadomasochism, temporality, and history to argue against Lorde's reading: "[I]t is inescapably true that the body in sadomasochistic ritual becomes a means of invoking history—personal pasts, collective suffering, and quotidian forms of justice—in an idiom of pleasure" (136). Written decades before Lorde's or Freeman's theories of S/M, however, Himes's final scene in *Pinktoes* goes beyond invoking history and the social discourses of race. Himes invokes the history of white patronage, over white master, to complicate black action and movement as it pertains to capitalism. Identification of the up-and-down exchange of power between black people becomes all the more relevant for black futures. Since he begins with the black female body and then engages BDSM through the body and experiences of a black woman expressly and intently interested in wielding power, Himes invokes futurity, coincidence, and fantasy beyond black domesticity and citizenship.

Having moved back and forth between black respectability and white hate, white pity/guilt and respectability, and white exoticization and desire, without ever losing sight of what she desires, Mamie advances her cause for "more . . . interracial . . . intercourse" during this last ball. Her efforts compel the real proper

Negro woman of color, Maiti Brown, to exclaim, "Move over, Pinktoes, we're a hundred years behind" (256). Brown, still stuck in a nationalist mind-set, cannot see that Mamie has created a necessary incident that will propel all forward rather than backward. Despite its focus on uplift, bourgeois posing stagnates and is without movement. Brown sits, observes, and comments, while Mamie has been acting all along. Mamie's dedication to upholding respectability, metaphorically represented by her fasting and dieting throughout the novel, is done not so much because she believes it will yield political power and social mobility, for as Himes reveals, it is her willingness to not adhere to respectability that does that. Mamie is less interested in individual social mobility and more vested in socialism's classless society. For Mamie, respectability and social mores are a form of strategic dress, something to be taken on and off when it is convenient for the wearer. Her movement in and out of that dress generates and conducts power, economic and political. Understanding that, in middle-class black America, racial constructs and identity politics take precedence over rebellions, Himes allows Mamie's faith in the fluidity allotted from sexual acts to make a movement.

Mamie's faith symbolizes interior movement and exemplifies funk's attention to what is not seen, what is psychic, and what is magic. Himes's narrator explains of Mamie, "What made Mamie Mason great was that she capitalized on coincidences. And she could capitalize on them in such a singular manner because she believed in them. She believed that all life from the womb to the grave was a coincidence" (68). Western modernity's rational human does not bet on coincidence because it does not have to. So much of history's linearity is based on a grouping of important series of events whose outcomes we would have never deemed as significant as they were lived out. History, or science for that matter, cannot account for coincidence or who will capitalize on coincidence. Mamie's faith in coincidence, not order, raises questions about concepts of organized time and political organizations arranged by things and beings seen as inanimate and without movement. Such an organization of time is based on what is externally seen and not what is internally felt. Himes's representation of BDSM as a dance based in black funk arranges time around internal and external rhythms. Mamie's faith in coincidence serves as Himes's recognition of funk as black affect, and her faith in what is felt as a submissive or dominatrix is an acknowledgment of racial uplift as a practice of commercial S/M among black people playing with and working to gain power.

Himes offers black respectability as a trauma far different from the transatlantic slave trade, and its historical costumes and props are not "Holocaust, slave or Inquisitor paraphernalia" (Freeman, 143), but the paraphernalia of marriage, family, debutante balls, and uplift clubs. Further, the last scene between Mamie and her three lovers best articulates this text's argument of funk as fundamentally necessary to a reordering of the senses for posthumanity. Satire allows Himes to locate the less discussed eruptions of funk in black middle-class life, as well as its tendency to take on the role of sadist within its own community policing of black bodies and bedrooms as a way to enjoy the pleasurable dangers or taboos of funk. Notably, Himes's representation of the black bourgeoisie also confirms the charisma scenario's intersection with black race leaders' predilection for BDSM. Mamie's sex work interrupts these fictions about black leadership. Because Mamie chooses these antiwork activities and dismisses concerns of sexual morality, she can become a mechanism that demonstrates the manner in which black female bodies and black women can interrupt white heteronormative masculinity and the domestic space that would continually cultivate patriarchal dominance.

As Himes's depictions show, black women's sexual agency and autonomy would force all of us to create innovative models of sexuality and masculinity, models very different from those of modernity that still uphold masculine privilege and access to women's bodies bestowed by white men's laws and regulations. When woman cannot be read as sister, mother, or wife, narratives of masculine identities that tend to reinforce unequal power dynamics have to be rewritten. Himes's representation of Mamie as a gangstress transes the domestic sphere and black men. Typically we have seen how such Queen B (?) figures matter to black women's empowerment,[19] but Himes suggests how entire black communities might benefit from this woman's hustle (postwork imagination). He takes the publicly stigmatized spectacle of the sex worker, removes it from the public sphere, and situates it within a domestic space, thereby changing the conversation and direction of discourses that could be used to examine race, sexuality, and class for those descended from the sexual economy of slavery. *Pinktoes* stands as a successful reorganization of the domestic sphere that includes a critique of masculine privilege and male self-interest. Chester Himes would not be the last black male writer to do so in a manner befitting the aesthetic acumen of funk.

Born-Again Sexualities: Funk's Spiritual Conversion and Currency

Hal Bennett fictionally examined black men's hustling as a reordering of domestic space and a sacrifice of male privilege in *Lord of Dark Places*. Bennett's novel was critically acclaimed but went out of print soon after its first edition. As Ronald Walcott noted in his review of Bennett's tour de force: "It is surprising that his performance in *Lord of Dark Places* has not earned him recognition for what he is: one of the most original and gifted Black satirists to come along since Wallace Thurman."[20] Satire was one method, but Bennett also practiced authorial reinvention as another method for destroying the era's established possibilities and tropes for black men, black masculinities, and black writers. That Bennett took up the pseudonym Harriet Janeway when writing a romance novel that breaks with form and tradition, as well as assuming another pseudonym, John D. Revere, for his *Assassin* series, signals his consistent sense of what being a writer means: "So I think that what the black writer should attempt to do is to examine himself profoundly and see if he cannot strike out into diverse directions" (Newman, "Evening with Hal Bennett," 367). As satirist, Harriet Janeway, and John D. Revere, Bennett broke away from the black masculine protest tradition.

In an interview with Katharine Newman, Bennett acquiesces regarding his writing about black America: "I do think that we feel unclean, and I'd like to carry it to all its very finest ramifications "(359). He continues, "What I'm trying to do is be a counterpoise to James Baldwin. He is trying to be a conscience. I'm trying to undo the sense of being a conscience" (365). Without explicitly saying so, Bennett establishes a precedent for funk as a particular model of writing that can undo the sense of being a conscience—a disidentification with the human. Funk gives us movement, or a movement—social transformation that comprehends how strategically undoing the sense of being a conscience ensures continuous social transformation. For if we are always trying to be conscience, how do we recognize, once we have fixed one thing, what the next change in our liberatory process will be and how to do it? Bennett plays with the tropes of spiritual conversion and nuclear family conversion and their importance to enslaved and colonized black peoples' humanity, and then he juxtaposes them with a spiritual tradition and domestic space built from funk.

Royster's reminder that the black family has been the authorized space in which heterosexual black men can be productive citizens suggests why Bennett needs to address "spaces in which [black men] can be nonproductive."[21] She explains that funk provides a space where "black men who are heterosexual can talk about their . . . nonreproductive sexual desires . . . and claim public space in which to talk to each other about those desires."[22] Underneath the organized privileging of the nuclear family in black nationalism are not only concerns about citizenship but also the remnants of two dominant forms of organized religion in black culture— Christianity and Islam. Religious faith becomes a marker of productivity that influences eroticism and sexuality or questions of work and sex. US citizenship, as post-9/11 politics have shown, depends upon Christian morals. That political movements during and after the civil rights era would inadequately examine sex and work in their strategies has a great deal to do with deeply ingrained class conflicts and ideologies about morality and consciousness. Depictions of black masculine nonnormative sex acts around work society and domesticity overturn the spiritual colonization still influencing black political life. Though they seem distinct causes, *Lord of Dark Places* shows that each are linked to one another.

Bennett's novel about how huckster Titus Market creates a new religion involving sexual rites that include paid-for sexual activities with his son Joe Market, a.k.a. the Naked Disciple, was out of step with the political and artistic movements of the time. The development of Joe as a religious witness to Titus's race man savior complex allows Bennett to take readers on a cosmic voyage that demands something other than the black Christian church's overrepresentation of man. Bennett once scoffed at its erroneous and insipid foundations in the colonized mind saying, "Something happens to the mind [of a person] who is using the Bible which has been put together by white people, which insists upon the basic Divine-mandated inferiority of the black man, and this same document is then used to show me how to achieve salvation" (Newman, "Evening with Hal Bennett," 366). Moving away from this model of black humanity, Bennett offered up one radical solution—a new world order based on androgyny and its ideologies about work and family.

Bennett begins his creation of new black masculinities through pansexuality, rather than hyperheterosexuality, culled from southern geographies outside of the urban. When readers first encounter Joe Market, he is a physically strapping, carefree twelve-year-old catching catfish naked in Lee's Creek in the spring of 1951. In Joe's hometown of Cousinsville, biblical morality exists side by side with cosmic oneness, and this in turn produces a form of black power that exceeds phallocentric ideologies. According to Rickey Vincent, the African ontology of funk emphasizes "a cosmology of 'oneness' in which everything and everyone in the universe is interconnected" (258). While in music that philosophy might be practiced or enacted by musicians "locking in" "on the one-count of the beat" (Vincent, 258) and "getting the band to key in on the dynamic parts of the one instead of playing all around it" (Danielsen, 121), in other cultural sites that means demonstrating an interconnectedness between body, spirit, and nature and getting humanity to focus on the interconnectedness/unity of all three rather than the forced division Judeo-Christian tradition and psychoanalysis enact.

Early in the novel, Joe's innocent but sensual relationship with nature establishes funk's cosmic oneness as distinct from Baldwin's conscience. After seeing a water moccasin move toward him, Joe decides to exit the creek. Before he can get out of the water, his father approaches him with news that his mother has died during and from their lovemaking. Rather than be comforted by his father, Joe

> stood stock still in the water. From the corner of his eye, he saw the snake glide into the mud blossoming around his leg. . . . All of a sudden, he felt its long, cool body sliding like slow music across his leg. He was filled with self-loathing, and he thought, *Joe Market, you ain't nothing but a dirty good for nothing black nigger.* A snake touching him like that. He expected to fall down dead in the water. Instead a hot, happy chill shot through all of him, the snake had felt that good and cool. (2)

Here, Joe prefers the comfort and intimacy of Mother Nature, signified by elements of the mud, the serpent, and water, to the sometimes false emotional bonds created out of Western constructs of family established by bloodline narratives. The narrator's metaphor of the snake as slow music across the leg takes us outside of what it means to be human or animal since the ear is ordinarily the organ associated with musical sounds. But emphasizing how music feels on another part of the body captures Joe's enjoyment of this moment and shows that readers should understand that Bennett is interested in an alternative order of being made anew without human morality.

The spiritual symbolism of water and the water moccasin enables Bennett to destroy any preconceived notions of Cousinsville as a biblical Garden of Eden. Western traditions would deem the water moccasin as a phallic symbol, but in other spiritual traditions, serpents and water symbolize creative and feminine tools for innovation and fertility. Bennett implores that we understand how nature (land) and Joe's connection to it represent a humanity that would not rank the binaries of masculine and feminine, rational and irrational, or civilized and primitive. The water moccasin inhabits land that is both beautiful and ugly, dangerous and serene, and is quite often associated with spiritual traditions that are the antithesis to Christianity. Bennett provides descriptive imagery of Cousinsville as an isolated and tight-knit community separated from the city by the lushness of nature. Historically, black communities such as these were like islands capable of sustaining their own spiritual beliefs, cultural traditions, and economy. Thus, this metaphorical connection offers Bennett's readers an opportunity to rethink the meaning of sex and work and sexual morality and work ethic in the exilic and counterexilic lives of persons residing in rural spaces. Bennett's setting also deliberately removes us from the Southern gentility of a black middle class and refuses an Ellisonian-Trueblood marginalization that cannot self-actualize its exile as resistance.

The water moccasin symbolizes feminine power, and well before Joe migrates north, he instinctively embraces it and refuses the father's law and mandate in his decision to stay in the water and be comforted by nature. Despite what appears to be Joe's cosmic oneness with nature, a social mistrust of nature created by a patriarchal arrangement of the human family makes Joe hesitate to accept what feels good to him at that time. As readers learn, Joe's mother had consistently warned Joe to be wary of sexual advances from his own father, a lesson his mother had taught him but never learned herself. Bennett explores a decisive separation between man and nature that leads to a speciesism that would make Joe feel unclean, but he then undoes the sense of being and the consciousness that comes with it by casting aspersions on the institutional model of family that contributes to such consciousness. Funk, as Bennett notes, compels us to undo the sense of being a conscience. It allows Joe to delve into the filth represented by the mud opening up around his body and not fear the moccasin approaching him. Later, Joe's self-loathing turns to sexual excitement, where he feels that the "snake's touching him had baptized and purified him in some way" (9). The celebration of nature, its spirit and force, as it interacts with Joe's black body and thought delivers Joe from the auspices of shame, humiliation, and abjection. Here, the snake so vilified and maligned in the Garden of Eden will lead not to the fall of man or sin, but to rebirth and an alternative sense of self.

Titus instructs his son early on in the new doctrine, "Always give in when you're tempted. . . . That way, you'll never have problems with your conscience" (20). Over the years this philosophy plays a role in both their lives, and the transient nature of their living in marginal spaces allows it to remain central. The scene provides a groundwork for readers to resist seeing the novel in black protest tradition or to criticize Bennett's novel as being representative of a moral black masculine conscience,[23] rather than undoing that sense of being the conscience that Bennett advocates above all else. Bennett's own words about writing dispel theories that incorporate the pathology of sexual morality that undervalues the erotic and deems Joe's story as one about a failed journey of recuperating black manhood through the powerful black phallus. Bennett has expressed a more nuanced way of thinking of the phallus and linking it to funk: "Consider language is a tool. A pen is a tool, a gun is a tool. A penis is a tool, usually. It is a tool. . . . I'm not talking about weapons. But I will suggest that sometimes it is used as one." Later Bennett claims, "So many women I've come across do their utmost to inspire a man to use his penis as a weapon against him and against her" (Newman, "Evening with Hal Bennett," 368). In *Lord of Dark Places*, Joe's mother literally exemplifies Bennett's theory about women because Titus uses his penis as a weapon, killing his wife with it. As Bennett's novel later surmises with another female character, there are women who recognize the penis as a tool. He outlines the potential practice of something other than sexual pacifism and sexual terrorism by suggesting the penis as possessing creative energy, as well as destructive potential, and his novel and representation of Titus and Joe Market function in this way.

Titus creates his unique religion, and he uses the tent-church tradition to remain mobile but also because it allows him and Joe to take advantage of nature and avoid the institutional edifices of a church building that usually require performances of shame and inhibition carried out via dress and ceremony. As Joe ages, his oneness with nature contributes to his status change from Naked Child to Naked Disciple since his relationality with nature teaches him "the human body was sacred" (*Lord of Dark Places*, 235). Although Titus pimps out his son, Bennett's ironic use of sacred sex work to counter the schism of body and soul that the Christian church promotes is nothing short of genius. The success of Titus's church depends upon his recognition that there is an overrepresentation of man, which then leads to a type of faithful masochism and subservience from his congregation.

His awareness derives from a family tradition of hypocritical religious missionaries. His mother Madame Eudora married her nephew Roosevelt, and they started their own church—the Church of Stephen Martyr. The novel narrator describes it as a church that taught that "niggers ought to stay in their place, and die like dogs" (12). Bennett's satire works with an understanding of Christian morality as a form of masochism since the Markets' black wealth hinges on the husband's and wife's subverting of work society and their calculated investment in the morality and the overrepresentation of man. Yet, Eudora and Roosevelt's own faith in their self-devised religion is questionable since Roosevelt, as a man, is not the preacher. Eudora leads and preaches. Eudora, like Mamie Mason, symbolizes the commercial S/M domina. Upon Eudora's death, Roosevelt fails to revive her religion and thus he and Titus must move. In an unfamiliar location Roosevelt loses his life when one night a white mob comes to lynch him for supposedly winking at a white woman.

The trauma of witnessing his father's lynching, as opposed to the successful union of improper bodies, leads Titus to deploy the phallus as a weapon for the remainder of his life as well as in the religion he creates. When Titus flees from North Carolina to Virginia, he vows, "No son of his would die like his father had died. He'd do anything to keep that from happening to a son of his" (4). Titus then creates a religion that exalts the black male body rather than fears it, but because this religion still seeks to maintain faith in masculinity and masculine privilege organized by white heteronormative designs, Titus shares the same fate as his father. The last time readers see Titus he is being arrested, but not before he is able to deliver a sermon that calls for charismatic leadership through organized religion instead of politics:

> What I am saying, then, is that salvation *might* be possible if slavery itself does not drive the black man into the hell of madness. And if he can distort the Christian values until they are clearly seen to be just another way of holding him satisfied in bondage. And if he can manage *not* to become the sum total of his surroundings, which is the ghetto rung. . . . And—finally—if he can raise a man from among his own ranks who has sufficient courage and strength to be the black man's king and deliverer. (55)

Bennett's attention to charisma and madness as filtered through Titus's sermon shapes his exploration of various ways to submit and share power. Bennett highlights the benefits of spirituality and the misuse of it through organized religion.

Given that Titus creates Joe as a black embodied text and the weapon as a savior, he and Joe must be murdered and reborn for others to live. Though Titus's congregation views him as a madman, he becomes Bennett's voice of harsh criticism against the church as a formal institute of confinement similar to Foucault's iteration of the asylum and its recursive making of man.

Foucault, in treating the history of the asylum and its connection to the prison industrial complex in *Madness and Civilization*, writes of the nineteenth century's introduction to madmen occurring more formally with the 1656 decree founding of the Hôpital général de Paris: "From the middle of the seventeenth century, madness was linked with this country of confinement, and with the act which designated confinement as its natural abode" (124). However, Western rhetoric about savagery, immorality, and underdevelopment insists that we understand that asylums were for white people who were deemed unfit humans, but slavery, the chain gang, and prisons have been built for black Others. An actual building for those who would be erroneously diagnosed as black madmen (enslaved persons who wanted to be free) was not cost-efficient in antebellum slavery and neoslavery institutions. Nevertheless, the plantation erected an asylum that could be situated on the plantation and in the field. The church and the slave's formal indoctrination about the fallen man and redeemed flesh became a structural and mental asylum within slavery.

After emancipation and during racial segregation, the prison industrial complex and the church become the structures and institutional asylums where black bodies in the United States would be housed. Like the asylum, once the chains and physical restraints are removed, we find in these institutes the ideas espoused by Foucault: "There, the religious and moral milieu was imposed from without, in such a way that madness was controlled, not cured" (*Madness and Civilization*, 143). The asylum always attempts "to place the insane individual within a moral element where he will be in debate with himself and his surroundings: to constitute for him a milieu where, far from being protected, he will be kept in perpetual anxiety, ceaselessly threatened by Law and Transgression" (*Madness and Civilization*, 144). From Bennett's representation of Madame Eudora, Roosevelt, Titus, and Joe, churches, mosques, and religions are asylums where black madness and madmen go to be controlled but never cured, and its ministers, preachers, and prophets become charismatic leaders and teachers of knowledge that enhances the real madness of being human.

Even as Titus argues against the tenets of white Christianity, he reinstalls them with his call for a black savior and leader. *Lord of Dark Places* emphasizes that the madman, the race man, and sacred martyr might be one and the same. Titus's church may appear different from Madame Eudora's, but they are bound by the same cultural lineage and their lack of faith in religion to save anyone. Sacred martyrdom can only produce necropolitics. In a hilarious turn, readers learn that Titus delivered the radical sermon only because he envisioned that Joe would bear the repercussions of it. Titus, therefore, is no Nat Turner, and because he never understands that the body and manhood that needs to be sacrificed must be his own and not Joe's, he meets the same fate as his father. Once Joe sees the cops hauling Titus off, there are no impediments for his transition from the Naked Disciple into superfreak. As Joe migrates from the South to the North, his story does not entail innocence and moral righteousness lost and destroyed by northern, inner-city blues. Funk's superfreak confronts the three means (silence, recognition by mirror, and perpetual judgment)[24] by which orders of knowledge, the state, Western medicine, and judicial systems attempt to categorize and cure "madness and insanity." Cosmic oneness displaces recognition in the psychoanalytical mirror; Titus's advice to give into desires dismisses perpetual judgment; and with migration, silence is replaced by movement and the motion of sex acts rather than voice.

Joe Market stows away on a train headed north and literally cozies up to another stowaway, an asexual and androgynous homeless man named Pee Wee. By the time Joe and Pee reach the North, Joe has turned from sacred whore to urban hustler and Pee Wee from transient to pimp. Each is now shaped all the more by the transitional space offered by "the street" instead of the edifying structures of a house, and they create an alternative society where other genders and sexualities grow and multiply: "Then Pee rented a room on West Market Street and started bringing clients home for Joe, men or women, it was all the same to Joe, he wasn't prejudiced a bit" (67). Pee Wee's management of Joe differs from Titus's abuse, molestation, and manipulation of Joe. As Titus's son, Joe had less agency and autonomy. Because Pee Wee and Joe share a collaborative relationship in which neither fits traditional hegemonic masculinities, Bennett's male characters in the novel can transfigure masculinity. As a hustler, Joe has agency and autonomy that does not have to be regulated through heteronormative masculinity.

In order for black male femininity to have some value in projects about new black masculinities, the antiwork politics of black men and women during the sexual economy of slavery and beyond has to be remembered and valued. Bennett chooses to interrupt ideologies of the male breadwinner who, unlike his woman/wife, does not have to use his body to make ends meet. Bennett's antiwork politics and postwork imagination occur due in large part to the way he uses androgyny and hustling to address Weeks's concerns about entanglements of work and family:

> The wage system, work processes, work ethics, and modes of worker subjectivity are intimately bound up with kinship forms, household practices, family ethics, and modes of gendered subjectivity. Attempts to challenge or reform any one of these—like the schedules of and dominant values attached to waged work—must take into account the complexity of the entanglements here. (163)

Joe's occupation as a male hustler who sleeps with both men and women inter-rupts the belief that black women have been the sole disturbers of the modern boundaries of public and domestic spaces organizing actions of sex and work. Even after meeting and marrying a classmate, the respectable Odessa, Joe con-tinues his sexual bartering to support his home and family. This antiwork activ-ity lets him disavow traditional black masculinity and productivity. Later, when Joe has been arrested for solicitation, he has to sit in the police station where he wonders, *"Do they know I'm a queer hustler? Or do they think I'm queer?"* (italics in original; 234). Bennett writes Joe Market as pansexual, and his depictions of Joe trading sex transes black masculinity.

At the time that Bennett wrote this novel, there was only a simplistic articula-tion of black male heterosexuality and black male homosexuality. That he has Joe distinguish sex acts for pay from sexual identity is key here, but we see its distinc-tion played out in the way performances of gender and sexuality are organized in antiwork societies versus work societies. Besides Pee Wee, Joe's interactions with the secondary characters of the African American prostitute-gangstress Mavis "China Doll" Lee, the Italian policeman Tony Brenzo, and the African American effeminate friend Lamont Cranston are juxtaposed with his actions of pursuing Odessa as his wife and later setting up a household with her.

As Joe chooses antiwork activities over wage labor in the North, his residency in a boardinghouse introduces him to Mavis Lee/China Doll and Tony. Joe meets Tony during a sting operation in which Tony arrests a naked Joe for solicitation of sex in his own apartment. Their bedroom meeting offers alternative possibili-ties for black and white masculinity that do not occur in the public sphere since they are constructed around superfreaks' pansexuality and androgyny. During the bust, Joe gets an erection and loses it, then becomes erect again. The nar-rator offers, "The cop was looking at his dick, that's why it was doing that. He wasn't queer, but he was interested in something that had to do with Joe's dick" (72). When Tony moves in closer to Joe to look him squarely in the eye, Joe, in all his naked glory, confesses, "I can see completely inside you" (73). Joe's detec-tion bespeaks a shared pansexuality and androgyny that is revealed later when Joe uncovers not simply Tony's interracial desire for black women, but Tony's mourning and love for his deceased black wife. Because Tony's Italian heritage racializes him throughout the text, Joe takes this racial ambiguity and reads it as androgyny. Their friendship confirms the close proximities of the asexual sex industries (vice squads) and the sexual sex industries (prostitution).

Joe shares similar moments of recognition with Mavis. During one of his at-tempts at asserting his heterosexuality, Joe goes to Mavis's apartment showered, groomed, and completely naked. Upon seeing Joe at her door, she tells him, "All that powder on you, you smell like a woman," and he later refutes her claim with a "cruel, grinding fuck" (82). The narrator shows that before Joe can ever sleep with Mavis, she must recognize and accept his feminine attributes. Joe and Mavis's interactions have them both exhibiting gender fluidity. Joe desires women as evidenced by his pursuit of Mavis and Odessa, but he goes on hustling men, claiming to do it only to make a living. His protestations about not being queer do not indicate a denial of his queer identity since he is funk's superfreak like Mavis.

Joe's only enduring and egalitarian relationship with a woman is with Mavis because they share similar ethics regarding work and family. Mavis, then, not only serves as the object of Joe's sexual desire, but she unravels the manufacturing of a moral consciousness that domesticity and marriage was producing for him. Readers learn that Mavis works as a prostitute when Joe brings his boss, Mr. Yen, back to the boardinghouse to meet her. When Mr. Yen decides he wants to stay, Mavis tells Joe: "He's the first Chinese customer I ever had. I want to see if it's true what they say about Chinese men" (90). Mavis's trading in sex leads to her then marrying Mr. Yen. Like Joe, she continues her antiwork activity while married. From that point on, Mavis Lee becomes China Doll. The change in name symbolizes what will later be revealed as her gangstress persona who traffics in illicit economies. These illicit economies enable her to continuously refuse participating in domesticity as other men and women do throughout the text. Notably, Mavis's new name comes from an outdoor plant that horticulturalists attempt to grow indoors—that is, domesticate.

With Mavis and Joe, Bennett moves his critique of sexual morality from the Southern church to the bonds of matrimony. By writing Joe and Mavis as continuing with their antiwork activity while participating in the institution of marriage, Bennett refuses to adhere to conclusions that the public and private spheres never meet, while also informing readers that marriage cannot be divorced from capitalism. Joe attempts to revise his familial legacy through secular means rather than the spiritual terrain of his grandparents and father. He locates a community and family of androgynous beings, Pee Wee, Mavis, and Tony, that can sustain the birth of his new being. His unabashed physical and emotional nakedness in the presence of all of them at various moments in the novel represents his willingness to make himself vulnerable to others like himself. However, his lack of language or discourse for what he is affects others who may still be invested in masculine privilege. The Market genealogy of black male femininity runs counter to the shamed queerness of Joe's friend Lamont Cranston, a male character wholly invested in black nationalism and white patriarchal supremacy's domesticity.

Bennett's recovery of an androgynous superfreak, through the hustler, emphasizes how devoted he is to reconfiguring the domestic space and killing off the overrepresentation of Man. If we begin with a lineage that does not position the black male femme as abject of the black masculine line of patriarchy (effeminate, which in itself implies a kind of distaste or hatred of femininity or women), then fear of emasculation rhetoric becomes moot. Bennett's black femme male bodies are specifically tied to a matrilineal lineage that counters the abject sissy of white and black patriarchy. This black male femininity and its body locate their salvation in an embrace of fluid black womanhood, as opposed to a singular recuperation of phallic manhood or cult of womanhood. It would be simple enough to view Joe Market and Lamont Cranston as polar opposites with regard to masculinity, but they are both emblematic of a thread of black male femininity typically unseen in African American literature in the late twentieth century. Nevertheless, Lamont's attempt to place himself in the domestic sphere and nationalistic recouping of black masculinity ultimately undoes his radical potential.

Lamont, also a friend and employee of Mavis, forms a contentious friendship with Joe that culminates in Lamont committing suicide. The tension in the relationship stems from the different ways in which both men deal with and articulate the feminine, with Joe positioned as black male feminine and Lamont as black effeminacy. Joe qualifies the difference when he submits, "But he didn't especially like Lamont. For one thing, there was something very sissified about him that went against Joe's grain. He certainly didn't have anything against sissies, although they were very different from out-and-out queers. Joe defined a sissy as an undeclared queer" (105). For Joe, Lamont's femme attributes alone are not what makes him unappealing; rather, it is his failed performance of aggressive masculinity—"to come on like a real he-man" (106)—as well as failed femininity. Joe reads this as Lamont's denial of his true sense of self, but we should not necessarily assume that his reading is based in misogyny and hatred of the feminine. Here again, the notion that Joe prefers or embodies hypermasculinity is destroyed by how he privileges interior ordering of self over social scripts. Bennett's representation of Lamont encompasses the gendered roles established by domesticity.

In the novel, Lamont's performance of masculinity is motivated by his mother's disapproval of what she perceives as her son's queerness. Lamont tells Joe, "I didn't turn out to be the kind of man my mother wanted me to be . . . And that's why she's trying to kill me. . . . I think she thinks I'm *queer*. I can see it in her eyes" (108). Bennett notes that female lovers of black men are not the only ones who promote the phallus as weapon; black mothers can do so as well. The queer in this context, undeclared or not, is one who would use the phallus as a weapon in a queer nation, just as it would be used in black nation building. Ultimately, Lamont participates in events and actions that he believes will bestow a masculinity of which his mother can be proud: he kills Mr. Yen's turkey, he enlists in the army with Joe, he does illegal jobs for China Doll, and he eventually sleeps with her. Throughout the entire novel, he never admits to being queer and tells Joe after he sleeps with China Doll, "So you see, Joe, I can't be queer. . . . I made it with a woman, I enjoyed it, I've never made it with a man" (222). The more Lamont protests his queerness, the more contempt Joe feels for him. Lamont's actions and protests, however, demonstrate that he, like Joe, struggles to escape necropolitics. Although Bennett presents them in divergent ways, Lamont's struggle against domestic black masculinity in proper households coincides with Joe's struggles. Their enlisting in the army and their dedication to nation and some version of proper family leads to violence enacted against others and by them. Joe kills a soldier and later his infant son in attempts to escape the prison of domestication-heteronormative masculinity and its execution of his androgynous being.

Joe's third murder comes through the act of sexually bullying Lamont into performing fellatio on him and then asking for payment for the act. Joe then verbally abuses and shames Lamont for his weakness. Confronted with the effect of his actions and Joe's words, Lamont commits suicide. Joe deploys his phallus as a weapon, as opposed to a tool. That it is aimed at a man and not a woman continues Bennett's point that men must disengage from masculine privileges that make male femininity untenable. Later, in acknowledging his influence on Lamont's suicide, Joe compares it to the murder of his son, thinking to himself, "*I did good when I killed my son, Lamont, this ain't no world for him to grow in, this ain't no world for you*" (227). And later "*you betrayed your queerness and that's why you died. You fucked China Doll, and that gave you the balls to make it with me, and that's why you died*" (250). Even in death, Lamont's sexual identity is unclear, but his gender presentation is clear. Because Lamont has accepted the gender ideologies of manifest domesticity, he had no way of knowing that neither gender nor sexuality ever has to align with the other. Joe's lessons about domesticity remain very different from Lamont's. His mother never held Titus up as the paragon of model masculinity, but instead warned Joe of the violent risks of the father's law when she asked that he tell her if Titus ever tried to touch him (13). Joe's revelation to Lamont that fathers kill their sons, not mothers, accepts this wisdom (107). Patriarchy and participation in it can only lead to death and violence, and escaping this narrative means moving away from Western canons of gender and sexuality.

Because the rebirth of fallen man contains damaging ideologies about the body and pleasures of it, Bennett insists on having his protagonist challenge the ways in which birth and rebirth occur in Western society in an important plot development at the end of the novel. He creates his own form of sexual magic through secular invocations of cosmic oneness. Joe, dislocated from the rural country, educated, a veteran, and properly married to Odessa, finds cosmic oneness in a threesome with Tony and Mavis. By having an experience in which he transcends his social self, Joe opts out of the usual dynamics of what Joe references as their Triple S scene in which he had always "insisted on being top man" and asks this last time to "let me get on the bottom" (252). Joe, at the bottom of the heap of stacked, three-way intercourse on Mavis's kitchen floor, gets to partake in an experience where he can reorder knowledge he has amassed from Titus, from white America, and from black America. In *A View from the Bottom,* Tan Hoang Nguyen observes that "[a]ffirming bottomhood, femininity, and race together rewrites abject masculinity without writing off femininity and the feminine, thus enabling a new mode of social recognition" (19). In writing the Triple S scene, Bennett makes the human body sacred again in a manner mindful of funk's kinetic energy of getting down on the One.

In many novels depicting the domestic and sex, the bedroom situates bodies in the narrative of romantic love, and sex acts can typically be relegated to this private space for decent couples and their conjugal unions. The kitchen has often been gendered as woman's domain but reserved as a communal place for family (husband, wife, child) to eat. Bennett's domestic scene, however, shares few commonalities with that idyllic family kitchen but instead attends to Gwendolyn Brooks's kitchenette. Bennett describes Mavis's kitchenette as a place where collard greens simmer in a pot as three people fulfill dreams of temporarily fashioning revolutionary selves out of pansexuality and androgyny on the floor as a red-bearded poet squats in a corner with his guitar watching and "strumming a sad accompaniment to their undulations" (253). The sardonic description of the scene makes for a surreal representation of uncoupled desire that is radical and revolutionary. Surrealism, after all, requires a lack of reason, spontaneity, and surprise, and an elevation of transaesthetics, to be a revolutionary movement. Bennett remains mindful of sexuality as an expression of creativity and art when he invokes smell, color, and sound. The threesome is "psychic automatism in its pure state,"[25] but so is the guitarist's song, which is inspired by their Triple S scene. This is funk's emphasis on getting down.

With everyone in rhythm, the narrator describes that "Joe was glued to China and Tony, they were suffocating him with their bodies, he was his mother and son rolled into one, powerfully male and female at the same time, dominating in sex and being dominated by it" (252). Bodies oscillate between being male and female, where funky acts and funky families can feed and sustain each other. The Triple S scene also serves as the most emblematic secular representation of funk's idea of being on the one: "Joe moved in a kind of slow fury; China squirmed to meet him. Tony said over and over through his teeth *O goddamn goddamn goddamn*" (253). As Himes had done with his gangstress Mamie Mason, Bennett makes it clear that Mavis controls the rhythm of these sexual acts. Men are made and unmade by her desires, her autonomy, and her sexual agency. On this night, she had initiated it, asking them both until they gave in. Mavis asks, but not as a sacred martyr sacrificing her body for the good of men. She asks as a secular witness to the creation of new masculinities that she makes possible.

Bennett's description of the three-way emulates Danielsen's analysis of the one, where "the One starts to swell . . . heavier and more unifying than the other heavy beats, to such an extent that it is about to become *the* heavy beat—that is, the only one that really matters" (118). Tony, Joe, and China Doll's recognition of each other as androgynous superfreaks is based on fair exchange and an understanding that they will not categorize, classify, and claim ownership to the fixed binaries of gender, race, and sexuality. The Triple S scene allows them to practice ways of being that have no language, where there is no fence, and no intellectual or moral barriers in between these bodies. The trauma of molestation, incest, war, marriage, infanticide, and suicide induced by racial oppression are released for Joe when he bottoms out in a manner his paternal forefathers, Roosevelt or Titus, never would:

> For perhaps a full minute, he could not breathe—China's mouth plugged his own, Tony's forearm dragged him closer around the neck, cutting off his windpipe—nor could he see . . . The double sensation of choking and blindness filled him with an almost powerful elation. I cannot love, I do not deserve to live. (254)

For Bennett then, Joe Market's turn away from the Judeo-Christian cleansing or washing away of sin for the cosmic oneness of a Triple S scene is not meant to change sentiments with external judgment but to maintain the connection to an interior divine force. The corporeal baptism of the Triple S scene in no way segregates mind, body, and soul. It acts as a spiritual experience of death and rebirth returning us to the words of Reverend Cobb. Mavis, Tony, and Joe bathe in each other's funk and write themselves away from the orders of knowledge that would make false the admissions stated in a simultaneous tri-climax where China Doll's postcoital "O God I love you, both of you" rings as true as the tender actions of two men: "Tony reached underneath Joe and dragged them closer together. Joe ran his hands up and down Tony's back, the ivory feel of it" (255). There is no male self-interest in this Triple S scene, only male self-inquiry. The Triple S scene gives Joe the strength to confess a murder and propels him to commit another. In being on the bottom, Joe lets go of seeing himself as a savior figure and martyrs himself, rather than asking for martyrs. He creates an incident that might just lead to a revolution.

The characters in the novel who are very concerned and attuned to the project of domesticity that seeks to make normal black bodies through proper households are the figures for whom the protagonist and narrator show little sympathy: Mary, Odessa, Titus, and Lamont. Their exclusion and deaths by the hands, words, and actions of Joe, China, and Tony are purposeful. Bennett continues to move us beyond the overrepresentation of man, with which black nationalism and post-blackness remain stuck. Joe's coming into a conscience and then undoing that conscience serve as the impetus for other characters to continue to work toward social transformation. At the end of the novel, Joe sits in the electric chair for killing the elderly white woman, Mary, who had watched him kill his son and later blackmailed him with that knowledge. Mary serves as a metaphor for sexual morality based on disembodiment because her name references the mythological figure who endured the Immaculate Conception that gave Christ to the world, and thus anyone who believes in this myth cannot live. Joe kills Mary because, as Mary tells him before he commits the act, "*You want to kill a white woman and I am a white woman who wants to be killed*" (282). The deaths of both Mary and Joe, or symbolically Mary and Joseph as the human parents of the Messiah—Jesus—are crucial to Bennett's masterful critique of how Christianity contributes to the dehumanization of black people. Bennett successfully uses funk to challenge Christian doctrine in the lives of black people and creates his own unique version of cosmic slop. Movements of social transformation may invoke rhetoric about being conscience, but as funk explains, strategically undoing the sense of being a conscience is just as necessary for new forms of being to be born.

In the end, Himes's Mamie Mason and Bennett's Mavis/China are culled from an admiration of the feminine and a reading of male submission as pleasurable and valuable. The authors' representation of sexual antiwork by men and women actively seeking to deinstitutionalize family and nation reconstructs black genders and sexuality away from a work society and domestic institutions. By depicting the illicit economy activities within legitimate social institutions of marriage and family, they situate male submission and black women's mobility as new archetypes for black liberation. Moreover, the fantasy of male submission and its erotic affect in each novel reflects on how pleasure must figure into the sacrifice of those masculinities in favor of androgyny. The representation of BDSM in the literature of Himes and Bennett serves as a critique of charisma and its three forms of violence as well as recognition of the erotic as that deeply feminine space or plane remarked upon by Lorde. Such ideas remain a key factor missing in debates about gender equality, racial progress, and sexual freedom. If the goal is merely to covet power, it would be insane for black men to give up a privileging of masculinity for androgyny, to do away with sexual violence for sexual utility, to sacrifice themselves for a greater good not of their making. If the goal is freedom for all, then it really is time for black men to bottom out, toot up, and serve as witnesses to something other than their own interests.

4

Marvelous Stank Matter

The End of Monogamy, the Marriage Crisis, and Ethical Slutting

What is love? What does funk do to love? And when it does whatever it does to love, what happens to the concepts of family, friends, relationships, husband, wife, monogamy, or marriage? The omission of funk in philosophies about love and eros, with its imperative proposal of sexuality as imaginative experience, becomes all the more relevant to restructuring intimacy and affection. Because Western relationships and marriages are often mandated as coupled, chapter 1's queries about Christine and Millie McKoy's unified or individual subjectivity and their prioritizing of the marvelous influences this chapter's reading of intimacy and relationships. The marvelous, as René Ménil explains in "Introduction to the Marvelous," "is the image of total freedom" (82). This chapter dissects the ways in which black cultural producers have used funk to destroy Western humanist concepts of love and their social contracts and products.

When the US Department of Labor published the infamous "The Negro Family: The Case for National Action" by Daniel Moynihan in 1965, it not only motivated decades-long black scholarship that would seek to redeem black women, black men, and black families in the eyes of US white society, it basically ensured a premature end to the funking of love and eros that black people had been developing and working through for centuries in response to racism and capitalism. *Funky love* can be defined as publically radical configurations of family, love, and relationships where monogamy and marriage are not situated as the ideal praxis. Reactionary responses to the report ensured what has now become known as the marriage crisis for black women, a crisis that law professor Ralph Richard Banks writes as a national concern in his book to preserve the institution of marriage *Is Marriage for White People?* Rather than attending to marriage as an underdevelopment of black America, Banks sees preservation of it as a form of social progressiveness: "Marriage survives because its symbolic significance persists. Marriage confers a sort of social prestige. . . . Marriage has become a marker of status and achievement" (21). Despite his later statement that "marriage is more a relationship and less an institution these days" (25), the remainder of Banks's study geared toward saving black marriage disproves this statement since much of the book includes uncritical acceptance of monogamy as central to functional families and stable marriages.[1] Marriage comes to be an economy of love, a sexual industry whose product continues to be monogamy and its advancement of ownership and possession. Yet a century earlier, sexual magician Paschal Beverly Randolph was opposed to this economy of love, saying that "the idea of ownership is what has made marriage as it is today,—a jangle, wrangle, tangle" (*Eulis!,* 80). Nevertheless, in 2008, Barack Obama provided the presidential stamp of approval on gay marriage accompanied by an addendum of monogamy, and a few years later the archandroid mediator Janelle Monáe explained that she dates androids because they don't cheat.[2] In either case, it becomes clear that aspirations for a progressive society and imagined futuristic models of being posthuman remain linked to a form of humanism that cannot make legible nonmonogamous sex and love.

In opposition to such a perspective, jazz vocalist Abbey Lincoln basically tells us that marriage is an institution that promotes necropolitics, and in doing so, her wisdom and boldness reveal why a marriage crisis must be manufactured specifically centered on black women:

> People don't understand. Max [Roach] was not a womanizer. He wasn't running around. But I don't want to have to answer where I was last night! I don't want him to divorce his first wife if he can't have me. I don't want my sister to be without. I would never do that again. . . . But the whole thing—I never had any rights [to Max]. What rights have you? Unless you can kill him. The African women could do that! . . . What was wrong with Roach and me was the approach to marriage.[3]

The marriage industrial complex remains a sex industry regulated by sexual morals and work ethics that center monogamy, coupling, and heterosexuality as less illicit than other trade activities. The task of "saving" marriage in black communities continues to be a priority that continues to overlook the antiwork activities and postwork imagination of black beings still resisting past and present sexual terror of US imperialism and capitalism. Nevertheless, the representation, theory, and practices of a funky love remain with us though not approved, legislated, or legally recognized in ways other than criminalization and stigma.

In this chapter, I discuss my own use of what I am calling *stank matter*—that is, a form of creative energy generated by the self and the self's relationship to sacred forces. Stank matter writes and orders my relationships as imaginative freedom for a sacred subjectivity that exists before the narratives of gender hierarchy and sexual pathology can coerce it into a social and political subject that is not of my own making. Though its praxis into nonmonogamy or polyamory can also be examples of what Carolyn Cooper calls *erotic maroonage,* or undomesticated female sexuality,[4] which confronts the privatization of black women's bodies, my concept addresses love and intimacy as an esthetic experience. Of esthetic experience, Dewey explains, it "is not possible to divide in a vital experience the practical, emotional, and the intellectual from one another and to set the properties of one against the characteristics of the others" (56). Because the narratives of affection between human and nonhuman being require transaesthetics, whereas narratives of love between some human beings apply monogamy as a formal aesthetic, I use black women's consideration of funk, affection, and intimacy in popular fiction to theorize nonmonogamy outside of human being. Specifically, the science fiction of Octavia Butler and the erotica of Fiona Zedde are examples of funky erotixxx's counterlineage to narratives of Western eros's romantic and coupled love or black polygamy's marriage, which locates its roots within Afrocentric thought, capitalist privileging of masculinity, or Islam and other religious institutions. These novels serve as a rejection of social categories and practices that promote ownership and possession of bodies and emotion that inevitably are invested in maintaining the status quo of white male patriarchy, heteronormativity, and capitalism.

In the 1990s, reading Dossie Easton and Catherine Liszt's *The Ethical Slut* (1997) was one of the failed ways I sought to validate my stank matter. *The Ethical Slut* debunks five myths of monogamy: long-term monogamous relationships are the only real relationships; sexual desire is a destructive force; love equals control of the loved one; jealousy is inevitable; multiple involvements lessens intimacy in a primary relationship (21–25). While I agreed with the debunking of these myths, the writers' promotion of ethical polyamory and polysexuality was a problem for me since the inclusion of ethical in discussions of polysexuality assumes a deviant practice that also falsely reiterates its counterpractice of monogamy as an ethical practice. Although *The Ethical Slut* and other texts such as Celeste West's *Lesbian Polyfidelity* (1997) and Deborah Anapol's *Polyamory: The New Love without Limits* (1997) were popular and accessible self-help books with a welcomed critique of monogamy, their focus on ethical, responsible, and fideled polyamory was from the liberal settler colonial perspective and seldom had to consider a Moynihan Report, state interference, welfare-queen stereotypes, black political uplift rhetoric, and the preservation of sacred subjectivity in their practice of ethical polyamory. How could these ethics ever allow the twenties me—poor, black, woman, nonmonogamist, and bisexual—to arrive somewhere after man?

Ironically, my familial legacy has become the motivation of why I theorize my practice of funky love and erotic maroonage. I am from a family in which members have either endured name-callings, beatings, or divorce for publically incorporating stank matter into their lives, discreetly participated in open-secret extramarital affairs, or unsuccessfully attempted to fit into traditional models of relationships and marriage. But even for family members not schooled in feminism or black queer studies, praxis has led to theorization. A few years ago, one of my more outspoken cousins declared the descendants of this inherited generational practice of nonmonogamy as part of "a long-long, long-long, long-time line." Her naming of the practice has become an important recognition for our generation and the next to accept without shame the familial practice that has never aligned with the notions of simple and serial monogamy so deeply linked with matrilineal and patrilineal models of family and marriage that will property and reproduce ideologies of possession that dispossess. Nor has it ever looked like ethical polyamory and polysexuality or the aspirations of black respectability and black heteronormativity within political projects of black nationalisms.

Understanding that they may never get back what has been displaced and lost, stolen and redistributed as a result of slavery, forced spiritual conversion, and racial and economic segregation, my long-long long-long long-time line demands that I take the time to reflect and be creative and critical in articulating their affective modalities for countering the dispossession and displacement that happens through privatization and politicization of love and intimacy via monogamy and marriage. This chapter reads black women's representation of funk's conceptualization of nonmonogamy as a method of self-defense against sexual pacifists' proposal of monogamy and marriage as solutions to black feminist concerns about family and community in America. The assumed naturalness of one and morality of the other have gone unchecked in black political projects and therefore remain depoliticized. Together they are a form of dispossession and displacement of poor people through the US empire's management of intimacy and relationality revealed most succinctly when we begin with black women's stank matter, rather than black men's and white women's practices of nonmonogamy. I do so by way of funk.

It was funk, said Rinaldo Walcott at the 2011 Collegium of African American Research (CAAR) conference about circulation dispossession, and transformation that allowed Sylvester James to bring love into the hypersexual arena of disco. Walcott may have been referencing James's hits "Do Ya Wanna Funk" and "You Make Me Feel (Mighty Real)," or other songs from *Step II*. It was a timely affirmation and appropriate example, and a useful one since Sylvester also took wedding vows when gay marriage was not an agenda and then practiced polysexuality during that marriage. Sylvester's race, his understanding of gender and sexuality, as well as his music arises from a different way of being human and begins a conversation about nonmonogamy as an act of creativity and creative expression, as well as an everyday ordinary practice of resistance that funks with

Greco-Roman and Enlightenment humanist ideals of love. It is a conversation typically impeded by race politics, defense of marriage acts, and perceived crises about the black family and black men and marriage for black women that takes us away from how concepts of love and any interrogations of them could change our society. Marriage needs to be rethought, not love, and when love is revised, as noun or verb, it still incorporates its primary subject—the human who privatizes love with monogamy and marriage, while also publicizing love as a political act for moral nations. This is why I bring critical race feminist and legal scholar Adrienne Davis into a conversation with Ralph Richard Banks's limited ideologies of a marital model of heterosexual coupledom.[5]

Although Davis does not engage Banks's work, her arguments in "Regulating Polygamy" offer some reasons that other marital models are avoided in discussions about the future of marriage.

> [T]he gay marriage analogy invoked, on the "left" and the "right," is a red herring, a distraction from the real challenge polygamy raises for the law—how plural marriage transforms the conventional marital dyad and whether law is up to regulating marital multiplicity. . . . [P]olygamy's distinctiveness lies not in the spouses' gender (as is the case for same-sex marriage) but rather in its departure from the two-person marital model.[6]

In their examinations of polyintimacies, two women from different professions, Davis and Lincoln, are bound together by a different history of sexuality, what Davis has termed *black sexual economies*. Together, they provide an alternative to Banks's perspective on marriage. Black sexual economies provide a different history of both the US empire's modern morality and its human subject, and the discourses that create both.[7] Further, Davis's solution to cease decriminalization of polygamy and to regulate marital multiplicity using commercial partnership law, as opposed to family law, highlights the benefits of acknowledging the overrepresentation of man in theories of love, marriage, and sexuality. As Davis has noted elsewhere,[8] her legal arguments are consistently influenced by her study and appreciation of black women's literature and culture. These foundations, or lack thereof, matter to other legal arguments about polyamory and polysexuality.

Legal scholarship by Ann Tweedy and Elizabeth Emens builds a case for polyamory and polysexuality by correctly arguing monogamy as a social fiction rather than a biological fact. Emens explains, "Polyamory is a lifestyle embraced by a minority of individuals, with an ethical vision that . . . encompasses five main principles: self-knowledge, radical honesty, consent, self-possession, and privileging of love and sex over jealousy" (282). Emens does insist that polysexuality's deconstruction of monogamy inevitably underlines how most people, serial and compulsive monogamers, are not monogamous. Still, the practice of nonmonogamy over time, and not the rhetoric, illuminates the conflict and precarious-ness of these ethics. Undoubtedly, the emphasis on consent within sex-positive cultures and communities versus those built on sexual violence should not be contested. However, the alignment of consent with honesty and being honorable with self and others miscalculates the infinite possibilities of multiple and poly entanglements, as well as the interior fluidity of individuals whose very being can shift and change based on contact and intimacies with others in this world and other worlds. While we can always insist on consent, total or complete honesty and being honorable requires an essential and unchanging self. It would require prefabricated knowledge of a coherent stable self that is overwhelmingly rooted in a type of humanism that enables dispossession. Sexual orientation has become such a fabrication in sexual politics.

Ann Tweedy's "Polyamory as a Sexual Orientation" debates whether "sexual orientation" in antidiscrimination law should be revised to include polyamory as a sexual orientation so as to provide better legal strategies for polyamorists involved in custody cases and employment lawsuits. She avoids using biology to confer an essential polyamory identity when she suggests that "we should con-sider including a person's self-identification, along with perceived orientation, as part of any legal definition of 'sexual orientation'" (1477). However, this approach does not take into consideration the way religion, race, class, and gender would dictate what gets to be legally defined as a poly relationship and how polysexuality would be ranked or valued against monogamy. It ignores that some communities resist orientations. It also continues to lay a foundation in which sexuality has to be categorized, as opposed to ceasing categorization that creates hierarchies.

Emens's and Tweedy's legal arguments about sexuality or ethics of love are limited because they cannot escape a specific notion of the human and its over-representation. As Emens herself admits, "[I]f we try to imagine desire itself separate from the normative conception of desire, we can think more distinctly about how law might be shaping those desires" (354). In the end, both Tweedy and Emens could do more to question, as Elizabeth Povinelli has asked, "how a set of ethical and normative claims about the governance of love, sociality, and the body circulate in *liberal settler colonies* in such a way that life and death, rights and recognition, goods and resources are unevenly distributed there" (3). Therefore, I want to propose that judicial and everyday advocates of polysexual-ity pay attention to texts seldom used and communities rarely seen as part of the discussion: black fiction, nonfiction, music, and black women.

Beginning with these marginalized texts and individuals as valid knowledge production delimits future defense of marriage acts and orientation categories, and offers a basic understanding of why monogamy and Western marriage itself can still become a form of oppression and inequality in the twenty-first century, even if one does not choose to participate in the institution. Comprehending the value of funk's practices of affection and intimacy, as represented and theorized in different sites, relies upon recognition of nonhuman genealogies of affect and intimacy, which also produces radical genealogies that thwart capitalist arrangements of family and intimacy that continue to place black women and black women's freedom in limbo, or what I refer to as the *myth of black love* and uncritical monogamists refer to as the *marriage crisis*. Thus Lincoln's earlier statement about her relationship with Max Roach offers a moment where we understand how modernity and Enlightenment humanist tradition have placed limitations on how we live and invent affection for self, others, or communities. Her statement contains an angst and impatience with that mode of being human and its dominant genealogy of love, sex, and art—eros. Lincoln's and Davis's theories about love and marriage rely on funk as an additional genealogy of affection, sex, and art that disidentifies with the human: more explicitly Western concepts of eros (love and creativity) bound by human ethics.

From its origins in West Africa to its cultural formation in the Americas, funk has offered a critique of labor, sex, work, intimacy, and family with a philosophy about aesthetics rooted in sensory experience of the Other that does not see man as separate from nature or superior to animals, as opposed to eros's human ethics foundationally situated in rationality and the polis. Here I would like to add nonmonogamous sexuality and love as another form of secular humanism[9]— sustained by funk's transaesthetics of self and its order/definition of knowledge. These elements problematize agency in discourses of monogamy and marriage by revoking the tendency to privilege the human over the nonhuman and otherly human. Karan Barad's "Queer Causation and the Ethics of Mattering" explains why such efforts are noteworthy:

> [B]ecause it is symptomatic of a widespread predilection, shared by post-structuralist, feminist and queer theorists, as well as more traditional theorists, for presuming that causality and agency need to be thought and rethought once again in terms of the human. The constitutive outside—the nonhuman, in its entanglement with the inhuman, the differentially human, and the otherwise than human—haunts these accounts that think and rethink causality in terms of the field of human sociality and processes of subjection. (313)

Although Barad's theory demands a queering of causality and agency, it sticks with what is measurable in science. Discussing desire and love as creative forces aligns with the transaesthetics of what is more than human and sacred subjectivity. Funk, then, is about a different genealogy of affection and sexuality, rather than operational capabilities or normative social functions. It can be further defined as the nonhuman practice of preserving the infinity within by improvising on Enlightenment human knowledge about affect and social structures.

As Rickey Vincent explains of funk's philosophy on the "infinity within," the infinity within is about an individual's quest to "obtain self-knowledge, rather than follow a certain lead, and the more graphic the knowledge, the more self-aware the individual."[10] The infinity within confronts how "god as love" organizes relationships. It provides a transaesthetics of self that reveals how funk has been offering a different genealogy for our present and future intimacies and relations. Monogamy is a narrative scripted around, on the one hand, rationality, objectivity, and biology and, on the other hand, irrationality stemming from very specific religious traditions. It is sustained by human concepts of love. Nonmonogamy, however, can be human, animal, or nonhuman, but when sustained by funk's emphasis on affect, creativity, aesthetics, and improvisation, and the fact that it does not require Cartesian dualities to hold it in place, new sociality and intimacy happens. When black people have thought through affective relations with nonhumans and their distinctions against their human counterparts, the field of human sociality and being vibrates into something else.

In an interview with Amiri Baraka, Abbey Lincoln explained herself as part of the modern tradition of funk affection when she explained, "I'm an African woman. Really. I'm not a monogamist." In another interview, Lincoln returns to indigenous humanism and exposes the infinity within (a transaesthetics of self) when she boldly explained of her eight-year marriage to Max Roach:

> It's a hard thing to do to live with a man in this approach to life. I mean where a man and a woman live in a house together. She lives in his name and things like that. I don't wanna do that anymore. . . . I embraced the arts before I embraced anybody. I met my music before I met any man, and I will never put away my music for anybody.[11]

Monogamy, polygamy, polyamory, and polysexuality defined within the boundaries of science and law for human colonizers, classified as an orientation or not, bound affection and desire of objects/subjects to a particular model of the human. Lincoln informs us that there may be other human and nonhuman concepts of intimacy and relationality less concerned with material ownership and possession created by a capitalist society. When Lincoln equates her art with a man or anybody, she argues against compulsive monogamy and ranking Western human love and erotic attachments above her creative relationships or nonhuman affection. Creativity, imagination, and improvisation are not words typically associated with polyamory and polysexuality because human ethics and biology are usually the basis for a defense for them, but stank matter intends that we understand why this other genealogy is relevant. To dismiss what the creative expressivity and aesthetics of stank matter intend to teach and make us feel means impeding new knowledge systems, relationality, and a decolonizing of the empires of love in black women's lives.

Octavia Butler and the End of Monogamy

In his "Coming Out and Stepping Up," Francisco Valdes argues that critical race theory, feminist legal theory, and queer legal theory need to better collaborate in combating heteropatriarchy. Consequently, if polyintimacy has any use beyond introducing new marital models, then we must push critical race theory, feminist theory, and queer legal theory to advocate for rethinking love and sexualities away from human ethics. All three must deconstruct the human and its ethics. In addition to this deconstruction of the human, integrating philosophies about the posthuman and nonhuman could lessen the chasm. In another article, "Afterword and Prologue: Queer Legal Theory," Valdes underscores why narratives other than those in legal and biological terrain should become points of reference for policies about polysexuality. Two of his proposed suggestions have particular relevance to my argument for the use of black popular culture and literature to rethink polysexuality so as to account for multiplicity and intersectionalities: the use of narrative scholarship and a better conceptualizing of sexual orientation. Of the first method, Valdes explains,

> The third tactic or method entails recognition of scholarship's limits: even though social science data is critical to advancement of sex/gender equality, by itself it simply cannot be, and is not enough. To enlist legal culture earnestly in the battle against heterosexism, Queer legal theory must supplement the use of social science scholarship with narrative scholarship. ("Afterword and Prologue," 366)

Valdes's warning about the limitations of social science data confirms my previous use of personal reflection and my future analysis of black popular culture and film. His comments are why Emens and Tweedy utilized narratives such as Deborah Anapol's *Polyamory: The New Love Without Limits,* Ryan Nearing's *Loving More: The Polyfidelity Primer,* and Easton and Liszt's *The Ethical Slut: A Guide to Infinite Sexual Possibilities* in their legal articles. However, these narratives fail to explicitly consider the implications of race and class.

Emens's, Davis's, and Tweedy's inclusion of narrative and narrative scholarship draws from what Valdes writes of as inherent in narrative: "the capacity of stories to elicit a sense of empathy with sexual minority claims and in its corollary ability to root both action and theory in reality" ("Afterword and Prologue," 366). Yet, such empathy cannot be sustained without a deconstruction of the human in general. For these reasons, fiction and popular culture become as necessary as social science data in extolling the radical potentialities of nonmonogamy. As many literary scholars and theorists can attest, fiction and nonfiction stand as narrative scholarship about future subjects. With regards to sexuality, something as lengthy as a novel or as brief as a personal ad queers the organization and classification of genres that might define or constitute narrative scholarship. Fiction's use of imagination and fantasy in developing alternative social arrangements and social justice creates posthuman "ethics" not easily recognized as that.

The assumption that there is anything ethical about monogamy and its inherent ideologies about possession, love, and intimacy must continue to be rigorously disputed, and the ways in which it is contested become just as important as the dispute. Octavia Butler's speculative novel *Fledgling* provides the perfect foil to legal theory's elevation of human ethics that sound good but remain empty of sustainable meaning in regard to polysexuality. Ethics containing rhetoric such as "we are ethical people, ethical sluts. It is very important to us to treat people well and not hurt anyone. . . . Most of our criteria for ethics are quite pragmatic. Is anyone being harmed? Is there a way to avoid causing harm?" (*Ethical Slut*, 16). Undoubtedly, the emphasis on consent within sex-positive cultures and communities versus those built on sexual violence should not be contested. Yet, a close reading of stank matter in Octavia Butler's *Fledgling* unveils how fiction serves as theory for the posthuman black female subject's life after love. Moving beyond the legacies of segregation and slavery that served her so well in *Kindred*, the *Lilith* trilogy, and the *Parable* series, Butler confronts ideologies of a postracial America in a manner especially cognizant of genders and sexualities. She provides readers with an allegorical tale that demonstrates the necessity of African American women to reimagine the genealogical society of the West and its human concept of love, if not in policy and public sphere, at least in consciousness. Steeped in the poeticizing tradition of secular humanism, Butler's protagonist offers a genealogy of affection and intimacy written by funk.

The opening of the novel begins in disorientation. Protagonist Shori awakens alone in a dark cave with amnesia. Absent visible signs, Butler emphasizes her character's other senses such as smell, sound, and touch. Butler provides Shori's interior monologue to accompany the narrative's emphasis on affect versus signs: "Somehow, I had been hurt very badly, and yet I couldn't remember how. I needed to remember and I needed to cover myself. Being naked had seemed completely normal until I became aware of it" (4). Because no one else is in the cave, Shori's pain and how she feels inside becomes her guiding force. In addition, without memories, Shori is neither animal nor human. Shori's memory loss symbolizes the transitory nature of human ethics. In addition, her memory loss makes it possible to create a narrative where the grammar of suffering usually associated with black characters can be overwritten by nonhuman grammars. What feels right when there is no memory and no one to tell us what to think? What is "love" when there is no Greek philosophy, no rational moralizing or sentimental romance narrative, or translations of other concepts of affection? Shori's memory loss becomes a metaphor for the experience of New World black subjects whose physical and cultural memory of affection and relationships have been erased or colonized. After the initial disorientation from memory loss, Butler continues to disorient readers and Shori.

Later readers learn that Shori is a fifty-three-year-old vampire and that no matter how she feels, in terms of health, age, and species, she looks like a child. This state of being produces disorientation for readers, Shori, and her lovers. Shori's lovers are Wright Hamlin, a twenty-three-year-old white man, and a lonely middle-aged white woman, Theodora Harden. Before tackling the taboo of nonmonogamy, Butler has to disidentify with the temporal logic of human development and its organization of love, sexuality, and affection. She does so by centering her novel on the least empowered subject in US society, a representative that connotes the othering of little black girls. Butler describes Wright as being genuinely concerned for Shori, who he perceives to be a lost child until she bites him on the hand. Terrified, appalled, and enticed by Shori's biting and licking of blood from his wounded hand, and the pleasure he receives from it, Wright becomes Shori's first lover/partner. Acknowledging his sexual excitement and repulsion at Shori's appearance as a human child, he says to her, "And you're way too young ... Jailbait. Super jailbait" (12). Other adults, like the lonely Theodora Harden, become the other would-be child molesters compelled by Shori's bite to ignore her visible presentation as a human child. Because Theodora and Wright have little knowledge of who and what Shori is, they struggle with the moral and legal implications of their physical and emotional interactions with Shori in ways that human symbionts knowledgeable about the vampiric Ina do not have to.

As long as Wright and Theodora remain obligated to the human, Shori will be that, but once they understand her as something nonhuman, their relationship and interactions with her will move them onto alternative ways of being human. Butler's heroine forces readers to comprehend that time and family are not natural arrangements, and that the social construct of time fabricates orientation as much as sex or gender. Indeed, the ordering of time and space orients. Sara Ahmed's work on disorientation offers a reason for why Butler's novel continues with this disorientation: "What happens if orientation of the body is not restored? What happens when disorientation cannot simply be overcome by the 'force' of the vertical? What do we do, if disorientation itself becomes worldly or becomes what is given?"[12] If disorientation becomes worldly, then old ethics dissipate and new ethics are not as rigid. Aside from disorientation centered on taboo sex across age boundaries, Butler continues to use disorientation in her depiction of nonmonogamy. From there, her novel can avoid the anthropocentrism and androsexism upheld in many polyamory/polysexuality debates.

Butler's decision to withhold Shori's memory strategically prohibits readers from becoming oriented into the ethics of the Enlightenment human, so that we can understand the limits of that way of being human. When Shori does find her Ina "family," we understand that even as she learns her family genealogy, she never recovers her memory. Memory is both affect and information. Butler's construction of Shori as a blank slate without memory, land, or orientation does not keep her from having a family, intimacy, and relationships; it simply insists that she can have them without any prior knowledge of how to make them. When a secondary character and another lover, Celia, explains Ina and human relationships to Shori, she explains as best she can that "the relationship among an Ina and several symbionts is about the closest thing to a workable group marriage. . . . With us sometimes people would get jealous and started to pull the family apart" (127). Yet Butler refuses to let human paradigms shape her nonhuman exploration of intimacy and affection when Celia shares a key difference between the Ina and human.

Celia recalls a memory of her previous Ina lover Stefan and his inability to circumvent human jealousy because of his own disorientation and confused feelings. She tells Shori, "He didn't say 'jealous.' He said 'confused'" (127). Butler's characters differentiate confusion from jealousy to showcase jealousy as a human emotion, and confusion as a nonhuman affect. Confusion is situated in disorientation, while jealousy manifests in orientation of possession and ownership. Ahmed explains, "Disorientation can move around; it involves not only bodies becoming objects, but also the disorientation in how objects are gathered to create a ground, or to clear a space on the ground (the field)."[13] Jealousy is the result of human ethics, while confusion is an affect of living beings disoriented as they relate in accord and against each other. Human beings in Butler's novels have to consistently see themselves in relation to the Ina and vice versa so they too can make their way through confusion. Such an approach is the opposite of ethical polyamory and polysexuality, which consistently seek to orient.

Disorientation permits Butler to align her heroine's quest of self-discovery with the scent of memory and the sense of smell symbolizing the infinity within— stank matter. Soon after Shori meets Wright, she explains, "Now that I'd had a few moments to absorb his scent I realized he smelled . . . really interesting" (9), and regarding Theodora, "The woman didn't smell as enticing as Wright had. . . . She didn't smell of other people" (24). Butler's focus on funk's privileging of olfacation provides an out from the Western romance narrative that suggests one love to complete or fulfill the self as modern and civilized. As Alain Corbin explains in his consideration of smell, "Unlike the sense of hearing and sight, valued on the basis of a perpetually repeated Platonic prejudice, olfaction is also relatively useless in a civilized society."[14] Olfaction, in stark contrast, is not a platonic sense. To walk with it and to make it a part of one's culture evokes a new understanding of life and humanity. Despite an entire civilizing industry built on getting rid of smell or masking it, funk determines how these other scents work. Butler rewrites olfacation and uses funk to produce other genealogies of love as a defense against modernity's monogamy or ethical polyamorous, polysexual, or polygamous loves. Shori chooses her partners based on how much pleasure they give her in regards to smell. Sex, gender, and race never matter, and thus they are not the orientation. Yet, Butler does not allow smell to become just another biological or chemical explanation for polysexuality because she emphasizes the sensual differences and evocative pleasures of odor as an aesthetic for love and sexuality art forms.

Butler's focus on smell as an affect of erotic attraction versus biological factor for reproduction gives her vampire and human characters an out from human ethics consistently legislated to preserve and protect white male supremacy and patriarchy. After Shori has taken another male lover, Wright asks, "Do you love me, Shori, or do I just taste good?" (139), but in another instance, Shori observes of her relationship with Theodora, "She was like Wright. She had some hold on me beyond the blood" (137). Wright calls what he feels love because he identifies as human, going as far as proclaiming Shori's feelings as basic biological instinct. Yet Shori's feelings, as she notes, are more than that. Untethered from human ethics, they do not have to be called *love* and therefore cannot invalidate her simultaneous feelings for both Wright and Theodora. In having to consider the nonhuman and human, human beings like Wright are not placed at the center of relationships and family for characters and readers, which means new ethics are constantly being created for human beings throughout the novel. These ethics erupt from the aesthetics of how they feel in relation to humans, Others, and nonhumans. Butler's heroine forces readers to see that the social construct of time fabricates orientation as much as sex or gender.

Butler's novel fosters a greater comprehension as to why polysexuality should not simply be written as another sexual orientation because it stands as one of the few remaining challenges to, or proposes an alternative to, how enfranchised and violently powerful interests abuse space and time. She does this through affect, emotion, and disorientation rather than policing, classification, and orientation via biology, science, and the law. Nonmonogamous love and sexuality must be understood as necessary disorientation for posthuman formation since it confronts the very speciesism embedded in "ethics" to disallow the anthropocentrism and anthronormativity that underwrites sexuality, marriage, and monogamy in the United States. These strategic moments of disidentification with the Enlightenment way of being human in black culture and communities decolonize approaches and debates about polysexuality and the alternative families and communities they propose. It allows us to understand alternative and affective responses to dispossession that occur as a result of the privatization of sexuality and love elsewhere.

Fiona Zedde and Jamaican Funk:
Who and How Long We Love

Another reminder that the publicness of women's sexuality can be a radical confrontation with the status quo can be seen in the ways in which women who are not heterosexual or monogamous can be stigmatized, criminalized, beaten, jailed, or killed for making public sexual desires in the United States and abroad. Heather Russell's "Man-Stealing, Man-Swapping, and Man-Sharing," a heterosexually inclined essay about the open-secret practice of nonmonogamy in some Caribbean communities, has argued that "the ideology of proper women's behavior, coupled with the materiality of unequally distributed resources, helps to explain such dialectics of 'man-stealing' and its corollary, 'man-swapping,'" (283) in the Caribbean. Analysis of Carolyn Cooper's concept of erotic maroonage within Fiona Zedde's lesbian erotica, on the other hand, considers nonmonogamy from black women's third-eye perspective centered on women's relationships with each other.

Zedde's first novel, *Bliss* (2005), plays up maternal sexuality as informing black women's eroticism and methods of self-defense of nonmonogamy, fluid sexual desire, and erotic maroonage even as she captures the destructive violence embedded in sexual terrorism enacted by men's polygamy and femicide. Zedde also uses antiwork activities to reconfigure typical conversations about women's erotica rooted in the square and straight, by thematically embracing maternal sexuality as a component of erotic sovereignty. Zedde's characters are often lesbian and bisexual Caribbean immigrants moving back and forth between national borders.

Before Zedde, black lesbian erotica was included in several notable lesbian erotica anthologies, including the stories of Blake Aarens and Pat Williams, as well as the authors within Naiad Press collections. Zedde's novels, however, become important because they are stand-alone novels that intend to dismantle imperialist readings of Caribbean sexualities as homophobic. Capturing the ways in which the erotic should be conceptualized as a journey to evolve modes of being human, Fiona Zedde's Lambda-finalist novel *Bliss* draws our attention away from the obvious intersection of desire and sexual identity to focus on what happens when feelings and affect are arranged by black-Atlantic's funk instead of Greco-Roman eros.

Bliss is about protagonist Bliss Sinclair's search for her own symbolic namesake, bliss. Referred to as Sinclair throughout the text, the protagonist takes readers on a journey from Atlanta to Jamaica, where she is confronted with same-sex desire, homophobia and hate crimes, alternative communities and families, and a deeper understanding of how to make a claim to her own bliss—a state of ecstasy. As the novel demonstrates with characters other than Sinclair, bliss may or may not be romantic love, monogamy, or marriage. By "making female subjectivity central to a queer diasporic project," Zedde's fiction demonstrates the ways in which funky erotixxx can, as Gayatri Gopinath notes, "conceptualize the diaspora in ways that do not invariably replicate heteronormative and patriarchal structures of kinship and community."[15] Moreover, Zedde's queer diasporic project also refuses to pathologize funky bodies that resist Eurocentric definitions of queerness or sexual identity.

Bliss, as well as Zedde's other novels,[16] adds to black theorizations of the erotic with its transatlantic reconsideration of the very concept of leisure and love. Zedde's first novel attacks the ordering of feelings, the politicization of monogamous love and sexual desire (hetero and homo), and the privileges of each in configurations of national identity for men and women by using funk to substitute ecstasy in the place of love. The current work of sexual identity politics to domesticate bodies and strengthen unified imperialist nations exists in opposition to the black quests for bliss that can thwart sexual imperialism. Given what we know funk can do with sound and the visual in the black Atlantic, we can begin to speculate about what funk can do with love and Western sexual identities and politics. Black funk's organization of love continues to be represented via olfaction and noninstrumentalization of the senses.

Bliss begins with a day in the life of protagonist Bliss Sinclair, an editor at Volk Publishing, who meets Regina Valasquez, a woman who will change her life in many ways. Representation of same-sex desire for black women is initiated outside of the Western ordering of sense and the psychoanalytic beginnings of subjectivity, sight, and the visual.

> Just as the doors began to close, a woman slid quickly between them. She brought with her the light, mossy scent of Chanel No. 19 and nodded briefly at Sinclair before staring ahead at the mirrored wall of the elevator. Despite her coolness, the woman immediately drew Sinclair's attention. (1)

Corbin notes that the perception has been that "the thick vapors of impregnated flesh, heavy scents, and musky powders were for the courtesan's boudoir or even the brothel salon,"[17] but just as Lorde did in *Zami,*[18] Zedde begins with funk's privileging of the sense of smell and expresses a correlation between an appreciation of feminine musk with regard to same-sex desire. It matters not that the scent is fragrant rather than foul for funk, or that it is Western perfume rather than some fragrant oil.

Moreover, after the narrator provides descriptions of how Regina smells, readers find out how she looks, how she talks (with a southern drawl), and what she does. The narrator provides more details about this subject than the protagonist of the novel. Soon after Sinclair's encounter with Regina in the elevator, readers learn that, despite an attraction initiated by the baser instinct of smell, Sinclair is not a lesbian. Corbin established that traditionally, smell "was elevated to being the privileged instrument of recollection, that which reveals the coexistence of the self and the universe, and finally, the pre-condition of intimacy."[19] The narrator's descriptions about Regina's mossy scent, then, provides that smell, as a precondition of intimacy, could care less about the gender of such intimacy.

Writing against the binary established in a system of sexual terror and violence, Zedde's novel insists that the visceral and intellectual can coexist. Sinclair and Regina value both. Sinclair works as an accountant for Volk Publishing, but she wanted to be a poet. The object of her desire—Regina—writes nonfiction books and essays with titles like *Making Sex and Having Love* that begins with "The first time someone else touched me with the intent to pleasure, I fell in love" (12). Zedde begins with the primitive sense of smell and moves on to touch, although it is not tactile touch but affective imagined touch produced from nonfiction discourse. Reading continues to be an act of leisure for many people, and for Zedde to write women characters with careers that depend on the promotion of reading, this use of intellect seems especially relevant to revising eroticism and black women's hypersexual representations. The author's attention to intelligence and imagination confirms what Corbin understood as innocuous to the Western culture's opinion of smell where "the development of the sense of smell seems to be inversely related to the development of intelligence,"[20] and Zedde's depiction of Sinclair and Regina's first encounter with each other understands that "in contrast to the claims made in association with the first paradox, the extraordinary subtlety of the sense of smell appears to grow with the development of intelligence."[21] Senses, memory, imagination, and intelligence are linked in the early character development of Sinclair as she moves through heterosexual designs to same-sex desire: "All these things that [Regina] wrote about aroused Sinclair's curiosity. . . . Regina's words made her long for them" (12).

Sinclair's visceral response to the scent of Regina during this incident will be relevant because the strong physical attraction that she experiences for Regina initiates her transition from being a heterosexually square women to a queer one. Regina undoes the way Sinclair has organized her senses and therefore her way of being and living. Before meeting Regina, Sinclair had never been with a woman, participated in public acts of sex, or imagined herself as needing to open attunement and amative space. Theories on African cultural survivalism focus on language and aurality, but Zedde's depiction of Sinclair and Regina confirms that we need to add West Africa's notion of funk as smell and intuition. In *Bliss*, sexual identity and domesticity's romantic love will consistently be undermined by the depth of feeling and sensations introduced into Sinclair's life after her first interaction with Regina. Although the southern girl Regina sets Sinclair on her new path, it is Hunter, a Jamaican self-exiled to England but returned home, who provides the final queer diasporic underpinnings of Zedde's erotica.

In *Bliss*, purposely or not, it is not until Regina has turned Sinclair on to same-sex desire, and turned her out using the transgression of homonormative and heteronormative sexual activities of orgies and S/M that readers learn that Sinclair is Jamaican American. Feeling out of sync with what her immigrant experience of growing up in the southern United States has taught her, Sinclair attempts to normalize the intensity of her desire and the freakiness of her sexual experiences by ordering each around a disastrous concept of human love and work society's ordering of time far removed from alternative genres of the human less inclined toward monogamous and homonormative labor. Unwilling to convince Regina to do work and organize her leisure around the domestic, a heartbroken Sinclair must go home to Jamaica to mend her heart. This trip reveals that she has a closeted lesbian half-sister, Lydia, a result of her father's extramarital affair. She later learns that her mother Beverly had several female lovers over the course of her life while married to Sinclair's father.

Despite these unexpected surprises that provide alternative models of love and sexuality to heteronormative and monogamous love, Sinclair views her return home to Jamaica as good medicine since she meets Hunter, her next lover. However, rather than depict this monogamous love for the sake of ensuring monogamy's longevity, Zedde contrasts the representation of Sinclair's parents' nonmonogamous marriage with Hunter and Sinclair's monogamous homosexual love to make obvious how both women's Western experiences have shaped their views about sexual identity and women's public sexual lives. The sexual and emotional interactions between Sinclair, Regina, and Hunter provide a triangulation of black-Atlantic funk as affect that values the feminine and thus challenges Greco-Roman eros. Zedde's novel proposes that these poor cousins of modernity have developed and created affect that deconstructs the West's ordering of feelings through their own construction of time and space.

Rinaldo Walcott offers evidence for why beginning in the black Atlantic, rather than the Americas, is crucial to comprehending the reconsideration of black love in Zedde's *Bliss*. Speaking about the poor cousins of modernity, black people in the Americas and Europe, he asserts:

> But we do belong in the Americas now. We came in the belly of the slave ships and so how do we negotiate this very complex place and make a claim to it? Trying to figure out a new place in this world that is willing to grapple with at least the . . . three inheritances of what it means to be black in the Americas. Europe, First Nations, Aboriginal, and African. . . . We can think of ourselves as being Western and modern with a tremendous inheritance from the continent of Africa and at the same time we can recognize that our own Westernness, our own modernness, is often not synchronous, it's in disjointed time to Euro-American modernity and Westernness.[22]

To contextualize Walcott's statement with this text's preoccupation with writing away from Western considerations of eros, which includes its definition of love, we might do away with the very heteronormative notion of black love and think instead of black funk. Walcott's statement compels us to ask what it means to love and be loved, to fuck and be fucked, for the descendants of those who made it through the middle passage, for those funky bodies out of sync with modernity and Westernness, and thereby modernity's constructs of time and space and its ordering of feelings. The answer to the question might also enable us to see how we can make a claim to the Americas now, outside of marriage debates and sexual identities. Out of concern that national politics and culture may in some sense advocate or incite homophobia, heterosexism, and violence (gay bashing), much of contemporary debates about the Caribbean islands and sexual identities revolve around how to connote or define same-sex desire and love outside or within Western binaries of homosexuality/heterosexuality, in the closet or out. Within these oppositional paradigms, sexual identities produce politics but also taboos that would make the getting off or the coming more intense for those who subscribe and submit to them, as well as those who resist and transgress them.

Omise'eke Natasha Tinsley's *Thiefing Sugar: Eroticism between Women in Caribbean Literature* does an amazing job of answering a question once asked by Caribbean writer Michelle Cliff, specifically: "What would it mean for a woman to love another woman in the Caribbean?" (Raiskin, "Art of History," 69). Examining the works that depict same-sex love and desire of both cisgender women and transgender women, Tinsley adds to Cliff's question by asking, "What would it mean for a woman to love another woman in the Caribbean, and to plot her bodily and imaginative work of womanness, eroticism, and decolonization nowhere stable, nowhere fixed, nowhere conventional . . . but in the malleable, explosive, volcanic force of the so-often buried words she puts together to speak her body, her desires, her work, her island" (28). Zedde's novels contribute to this work initiated by Cliff and continued with Tinsley by asking what does it mean for women (and men?) in the Caribbean to do whatever comes before, during, and after love to each other? When same-sex love is not all unicorns or rainbows, or, more culturally relevant, all Afreketes, Osuns, Mami Watas, and Ofo Oshes? What happens when writers attempt to trans love, move beyond, across, and through it, and when they attempt to translate that undertheorized entity known as black love via same-sex representation?

In Jamaica, Sinclair and Hunter's relationship develops slowly, and the leisurely pace is due to Hunter's complicated past with Lydia and the threat of homophobic violence on the island. Shortly after recognizing their attraction for each other, Sinclair and Hunter publicly flirt with each other but are then confronted by a group of men who yell, "Pussy don't belong with pussy," before physically accosting the women and drawing them into a brawl that Lydia thwarts (113). Zedde's characters resist dwelling on the trauma, but they are also distressed by the everyday hate unaccounted for in hate-crime rhetoric. The incidents force Hunter to verbally lash out at Lydia and suggest that Lydia's closetedness was part of the problem. Lydia refutes Hunter, arguing, "This is not America, Hunter. This isn't even your precious England. I can't walk around here holding my girlfriend's hand like it's nothing. Women get raped and beaten for that kind of stuff around here" (113). Hunter's reply to Lydia, "I'm talking about your family, your friends," is met with even more skepticism by Lydia, who exclaims, "You are so damn naive" (114). Although her more traveled characters are critical of Jamaica's homophobic violence, Zedde allows Lydia's reading of both family and nation as being one and the same to call attention to something more insidious shaping public and private ideals about sexuality. Lydia's status as a bastard child also shapes her comments about family, friends, and nonnormative sexualities and relations.

Yet Sinclair's relationship with Hunter continues to be shaped by a transing of love incomprehensible in the United States. Sensing that she may be out of place and out of time when her father casually insists on her getting to know Lydia without speaking of the affair he had, she thinks, "*Maybe that was the way men and women dealt with each other here. What's a lover or two in a marriage?*" (italics in original; 94). As same-sex marriage activists continue to advocate for marriage, critics continue to engage closets and down-low debates, and non-Western nations continue to be presented as the monstrous spectacle of out-of-control and rampant homophobia and sexual violence, there is a conversation about sexual identity being avoided. Yet fundamentally what is at the heart of these conversations and being taken for granted is love and its intersection with sexual identity, specifically contrasting and contested notions of the concept of love that if not understood produces a monstrous other incapable of loving and only hating. In promoting black women's leisurely search for bliss with each other and remaining conscious of keeping that search as an antiwork activity, Fiona Zedde reminds her readers of the importance of erotic attunement necessary for all black women by introducing readers to maternal sexuality in the Caribbean.

In the novel, this maternal, nonmonogamous sexuality has been carried on in house parties. It is a house party for the lesbian community in Jamaica where Lydia notifies Bliss that one of the attendees, Della, is a family friend. Lydia informs Sinclair, "She and your mother were lovers for a while, too" (139). Learning about this affair becomes one of the reasons that Sinclair can move away from the judgments she made about her father as immoral and uncaring. As she continues to socialize with Della, Sinclair learns more about Beverly as a woman, which complicates the comforting memories of maternal love. Later in the novel, Della tells Sinclair, "You never knew your mother, little girl. I knew her inside and out. . . . Better than anyone she'd been with before or after me" (149). Della destroys any notion that Beverly only stepped outside her marriage once. She continues, "She was my next door neighbor growing up. I was her first lover and her last. Despite the others, she always came back to me. And I to her" (149). Sinclair's knowledge about her mother's same-sex relationships with women while married produces a funky translation of black love, where we see the eroticization of sexual identity and the transatlanticness of love give way to erotic maroonage instead of marriage.

Erotic maroonage not only avoids the black marriage crisis, but it recognizes the bonds of matrimony and its privileging of monogamy as neobondage. While Greg Thomas has traced erotic maroonage within the diaspora in his *Hip-Hop Revolution in the Flesh,* Richard Price's *Maroon Societies* reminds readers of the basic etymology of what constitutes maroon societies: "[D]omestic cattle that had taken to the hills in Hispaniola; Indian slaves that had escaped from the Spaniards; Afro-American runaways: strong connotations of 'fierceness,' of being 'wild' and 'unbroken.'"[23] Understanding marriage as a form of bondage that might impede the infinity within, some black women's practice and representations of nonmonogamy rely upon erotic maroonage. That means not only undomesticated sexuality as described by Cooper but also differentiating between models of maroonage as Thomas does:

> On the one hand, *"grand" maroonage* signifies maroonage "on a grand scale with fugitives banding together to create independent communities of their own," which physically and symbolically strike "at the heart of the plantation system." On the other hand, *"petit" maroonage* signifies "temporary" flight or "repetitive or periodic truancy with temporary goals."[24]

Thus, rather than all-out rebellion against domestication—that is, marriage rooted in monogamy—we get temporary flight from the institution or a group of fugitives banding together to create independent nonmonogamous communities even within the institution of marriage. That means wife-swapping, mate-sharing, and party subcultures of married and single women having sex with each other.

Cooper's *Noises in the Blood* explains that typically in conservative fundamentalist Christian ideology, "erotic maroonage" must be repudiated since "it has the smell of prostitution" (161). Yet, its funkiness continues to be important because, as she details, it has been a "tradition of resistance science that establishes an alternative psychic space both within and beyond the boundaries of the enslaving plantation" (4). Maroonage conceptually highlights why ethical nonmonogamy may not be applicable to some communities because ethics assumes a free state or level playing field with the state, as well as assumes a human subject for those ethics. Erotic maroonage understands monogamous marriage as conceptually linked to an institution of bondage that oppresses women. If the goal remains freedom of self rather than marriage, funk's privileging of erotic maroonage also becomes another way in which maroonage's connotation of flight and resistance dictates some black women's practices of nonmonogamy. These moments of what Thomas and Cooper note as collective flight and resistance point to a crisis less about the saving grace of marriage and more about a process of decolonizing love and sexuality in black communities. Zedde's depiction of erotic maroonage demonstrates why erotica is a genre that transes narratives about sex work.

Erotica is a sort of traveling genre not necessarily tied to the idea of a national literature or culture. From Anaïs Nin to Chester Himes, the transatlantic nature of the genre refuses traditional modes of literary analysis. It is a genre immersed in what Wai Chee Dimock has termed *deep time.* Deep time, Dimock observes, "produces a map that, thanks to its receding horizons, its backward extension into far-flung temporal and spatial coordinates, must depart significantly from a map predicated on the short life of the U.S. . . . a world that predates the adjective *American.* . . . Deep time is denationalized space" (160). Zedde's erotica reflects Dimock's definition of deep time because the characters, or more succinctly the characters' sex acts, sexual desires, and sexual longings, reflect a recognition of deep time as a counter to work clock, queer time, or reproductive time. Deep time, as suggested by Zedde's writing of Sinclair's same-sex desire as intertwined with a longing for home and maternal sexuality, writes around these borders. Zedde intrinsically returns to deep time again with Bliss and Hunter.

The novel needs this transatlantic framing of deep time to deal with conventions of diaspora and the impossible desires of these two women who have returned home. Shortly after Sinclair and Hunter become lovers, Hunter provides Sinclair with a touristy perspective on the island by taking her on a tour of Fairfax Castle, a faux English castle described in the guidebooks as "a national landmark" that is "exotic and mysterious" (206). According to Hunter, "Some Englishman apparently built the place in the image of his ancestral home, complete with stone walls, servants' quarters, and a little upstairs prison for his certifiable wife" (206). Though the tour is clearly set up for an imagined white tourist, the Caribbean tourism industry is built upon a conventional diasporic discourse that only ever renders itself in past colonial relationships. However, Zedde's novel intends to undo diasporic discourse of nationalism and colonial desires mapped onto black bodies through heterosexuality. As Gopinath reminds us:

> If conventional diasporic discourse is marked by this backward glance, this "overwhelming nostalgia for lost origins, for past times," a queer diaspora mobilizes questions of the past, memory, and nostalgia for radically different purposes.

Rather than evoking an imaginary homeland frozen in an idyllic moment out-side history, what is remembered through queer diasporic desire and the queer diasporic body is a past time and place riven with contradictions and the violences of multiple up-rootings, displacements, and exiles. . . . Queer diasporic cultural forms and practices point to submerged histories of racist and colonialist violence that continue to resonate in the present and that make themselves felt through bodily desire.[25]

The tour of the castle becomes a reconfiguration of BDSM as presented to readers early in the novel when Regina forced Sinclair into participating in bondage play at a warehouse orgy. Together, the Jamaican-born women who grew up abroad in the United States and England use the tour of the castle to step out of the time and space assigned to them by modernity and colonialism and claim self and land by acknowledging the racist and violent past through sexual movements. The women's presence in the castle signifies the structure as a symbol of modernity and the women, as Walcott explained earlier, as the poor cousins of modernity. They will continue to be so as long as the narration of this tour experience writes away from the island's past history of slavery and colonization and its present colonization at the hands of global imperialism via the tourism industry.

However, Zedde insists that these women make a claim to the island that sent them abroad as teenagers and welcomed them back with homophobia and vio-lence. Though the characters make no critical comment on the ways in which Fairfax Castle is part and parcel of the plantation system of Spain and later the English and British colonial rule, Zedde's novel articulates the funky triangulation of desire via their bodies. Zedde has her characters listen intently to Mavis the tour guide as they take in the castle known as "one of the most beautiful lookout spots on the island" (208) until Mavis tells her tourists, "Our next destination is the former slave quarters, a place that the mistress, as well as the master of this house, visited at regular intervals" (209). Rather than follow behind Mavis, or even voice some concern about seeing the slave quarters, Zedde presents us with Hunter and Sinclair straying from the group to stake their claim to the castle and island: "Hunter kissed her again then pulled her away from the stairs, toward the small back room with its barred windows and glimpse of paradise. Sinclair's body was wet with anticipation" (209). The history and memory of slavery is im-printed onto the reader and the characters before they decide to step away from the reproduction of Western modernity that the tour enacts.

These two women are not tourists to this place, and as they kiss, grope, and reach for each other, it becomes all the more plain how natural their presence is on the island as opposed to the castle constructed to overlook the landscape of the island. As Hunter instructs Sinclair to "hang on to the bars" of the window and slips a strapped phallus into Sinclair, readers immediately grapple with the affective ways in which possession of bodies and land create various narratives of modernity and identity. Their fucking, out of place and out of time with the castle's regulation of their bodies as women and blacks, insists that we consider a presence before the Spaniards, the British, and the Americans, but that we also consider moments before they were Jamaican, Spanish, or British subjects.

It also demands that we consider the present imprisonment of such imagined moments between women as erotically restricted and constrained by nation and sexual identity. When Sinclair thinks that she hears footsteps from the tour group, the narrator explains that "her body tensed and, despite her earlier bravado, fear of being caught ricocheted through her body. She tried to push Hunter away, but the other woman held her, trapped between the wall and her body" (210). The pleasure of their lovemaking in that space intensifies with the possibility of being caught. Lest any readers forget, the policing and surveillance of black and native bodies by imperialists inform the disjointed nature of violent responses to same-sex desire and love, but it is the continued impetus to transgress and eroticize such transgression that makes change possible. *Bliss* successfully accomplishes what Gopinath provides that culture assigned as queer diaspora should do; it "enables a simultaneous critique of heterosexuality and the nation form while exploding the binary oppositions between nation and diaspora, heterosexuality and homosexuality, original and copy."[26] It avoids a neocolonial policing mandated by faraway queer nations situated within a lens of morality and underdevelopment that continues to write the exotic contours of the Caribbean as the sexual retreat for economically advantaged white and black consumers.

Zedde's *Bliss* refuses a sexual morality that would invalidate alternative heterosexual love and fucking as well as queer's identity politics and its liberal subject,[27] which refuses to engage colonization and imperialism as forces that also impede same-sex love. Zedde demonstrates that same-sex love, same-sex fucking, and nonmonogamy are not synchronous but disjointed because they remain nonhuman, antiwork activities. Her novel is crucial to seeing how the black Atlantic offers a different articulation of love from that conceptualized in black America as black love. Because Zedde's work is funky erotixxx, it stands as a part of popular culture outside the typical considerations of Caribbean popular culture and eroticism, such as the dance-hall space. Similarly, because it is funky erotixxx, it stands outside the traditional and current canon of Caribbean women writers represented by Jamaica Kincaid, Michelle Cliff, Merle Hodge, Jean Rhys, or Lorna Goodison. *Bliss* becomes the textual "Funkin' for Jamaica" and the fictional transing of black love.

Black popular culture and fiction provides legal scholarship with narratives that call into question the dominance of "human" ethics and the empires of love in laws regarding monogamy, polysexuality, and heterosexuality. These expressions become all the more relevant for black people forcibly relocated from native lands, and who for centuries were unable to own land to pass on. They also exemplify a questioning of human ethics as it relates to black being and living that begins in the slave narrative and continues today. Stank matter as I have theorized cannot be located on the dominant genealogical grid of imperialism, since it differentiates Western forms of genealogy from local practices of corporeality. How we read polyamory/polysexuality in African American women's culture depends on whether we accept the idea that all African Americans are a part of the same genealogical society as other Americans, or if we accept, based on our own freedom dreams and sacred subjectivity, that there are those who have relied upon erotic maroonage to intervene on genealogical societies and its bondage. In addition to using fiction and music to explore ethics of ethereal matter, the key to locating models of affection and intimacy less invested in Western imperialism or global patriarchy would mean not only entering into innovative negotiations around human genealogies like Davis's attention to partner contracts, but also letting go of linear genealogies of bloodlines and a privileging of human romance that continues to infringe on the *infinity within* of black women.

PART II

Superfreaks and Sites of Memory

Reforms and revolutions are created by the
illogical actions of people.

—James Boggs

5

Sexuality as a Site of Memory and the Metaphysical Dilemma of Being a Colored Girl

> Where there is a woman there is magic. If there is a moon falling from her mouth, she is a woman who knows her magic, who can share or not share her magic . . . this woman is a consort of spirits.
>
> —Ntozake Shange

> Still, like water, I remember where I was before I was "straightened out." . . . All water has a perfect memory and is forever trying to get back where it was.
>
> —Toni Morrison

My ancestors were superfreaks, and I have clearly become a conduit for their continued activities in the afterlife. We have an understanding. They help me conquer the metaphysical dilemma of being a colored girl, and I help them get their life in this world. They usually visit me a couple of nights before the unexpected bacchanalian events ensue to prepare me so that I do not ruin their plans. In return, I am rewarded with renewed energy, new purpose, or some windfall of an opportunity. I like to believe that they come to me because my body serves as a site of memory for them and because we have a shared understanding about how to approach this world's manufacturing of the publics of sex—that it should not be the primary mediator of our sexuality. In accord with M. Jacqui Alexander's reminder that we must know who we walk with and create sacred subjectivity in order to fulfill our calling,[1] these last chapters examine how sexuality is a site of memory for the nonhuman presence just as it can be a site of memory for human beings. Like water, it is forever trying to get back where it was. As this chapter declares, Lynn Nottage and Shine Louise Houston devise fictional plots and women characters that confirm how and why sexuality exists as a site of memory for some black women.

Women's bodies and sexualities are their canvases and creative tools. Although the end result may become representations for national ideology or products to be consumed, the process of creating out of the body and sexuality is in and of itself evidence of power that exceeds the human. Terms such as *sex work* and *sexual labor* perpetuate the imperatives for sexuality set by colonial or imperialist projects, but men and women's decisions to use sexuality outside the moral mandates of these projects should also be read as a challenge to the subordination of sexuality in most modern religions, as well as a means of improving the material realities of everyday living. Political activism has yielded improvements and impediments for black people's lives, but to write of black women's sexual expressivity as productive labor, a right of citizenship, free speech, and political activism alone would simply maintain the Western use of sexuality as terror and violence. The function of sexual culture can exceed its uses in this world. Such is the case with how black women use unfettered sexual expression between the human and nonhuman in a public sphere that has only been written as a political concern about men's and women's human relations.

More than a decade ago, Michael Warner and Lauren Berlant's "Sex in Public" added to Pat Califia's work on public sex, or "sex as it is mediated by publics" (547). Looking beyond pornography, print erotic, strip clubs, and queer zones, they interrogated national cultures' emphasis on privacy and theorized the possibilities of radical sex when the heterosexual couple is not at the center of policies about public and private intimacies. They argued that "making a queer world has required the kind of intimacy that bears no necessary relation to domestic space, to kinship, to the couple form, to property, or to the nation" (558). That is, a queer world requires the logic of creating a queer counterpublic that "support[s] forms of affective, erotic, and personal living that are public in the sense of accessible, available to memory, and sustained through collective activity" (562). Ironically, this queer counterpublic remains most useful to queer men since Rodríguez reminds us that the public (counter or not) continues to be mediated through a masculine *I*. Alternately, if the black public sphere remains the only way that black women can theorize identity, culture, and movement, then all is lost. However, as Shange's and Morrison's words demonstrate, the public sphere does not have to be the primary mediator of black women's sex. When memory, or a site of memory, is afforded the same value as history, then we might gain a better sense of what has been wagered.

I highlight Pierre Nora's distinction between memory and history in "Between Memory and History," as well as Toni Morrison's "Site of Memory" as a significant feature of black communities' politics and culture. Nora reminds us that "history . . . is the reconstruction, always problematic and incomplete. . . . [H]istory is a representation of the past. Memory, insofar as it is affective and magical, . . . installs remembrance within the sacred; history . . . releases it again" (8–9). He later claims that "memory attaches itself to sites, whereas history attaches itself to events" (22). Reducing the power of history even more, Morrison would later claim that fiction could be a site of memory for attempting to reconstruct the lives of black people: "Because, no matter how 'fictional' the account of these writers, or how much of it was a product of invention, the act of imagination is bound up with memory" (199). Imagination as bound to memory holds information vital to the shifting research and study of sex work and sexual cultures. Having already asserted the importance of seeing sexuality as an object of imagination, I subsequently propose that imagination as bound up with memory further advances sexuality beyond objective knowledge as power. The nonreproductive uses of sexuality, sexual expression, that would be seen as immoral or hypersexual are instances of sexuality trying to get back to where it was—a space where human coupling is not at the center of sex and intimacy and a time when women had moons falling from their mouths. The publics of sex as it interferes with sexuality as a site of memory is Shange's metaphysical dilemma for the colored girl, and that dilemma is why the chapters in part 2 of this book demand alternative definitions of intimacy, black aesthetics, and art inclusive of nonhuman and human relations.

Each chapter highlights black women's and men's cultural recognitions of sex as it is mediated through demonic ground as opposed to sex as mediated through publics. The demonic, Katherine McKittrick tells us, "invites a slightly different conceptual pathway—while retaining its supernatural etymology—and acts to identify a system (social, geographic, technological) that can only unfold and produce an outcome of uncertainty, or (dis)organization, or something supernaturally demonic" (*Demonic Grounds*, xxiv). Thus, Lynn Nottage's creative statement that theater is "a place where we can experience catharsis and exorcise demons"[2] leads her to a different conceptual pathway—atypical representations of sex and work in African diasporic communities—for challenging sexual violence and the mediation of sex through public spheres in her plays *Intimate Apparel* and *Ruined*. Similarly, Shine Louise Houston once explained of her filmmaking process: "What we do is nonexploitative . . . primarily because we don't take a technological view of our talent and their sexuality. All the talent have a wide range of autonomy when they shoot for us."[3] Houston's statement emphasizes that the film of feminist pornographers is integral to new movements around sexuality, gender, art, and work.

Black female cultural producers insist on a commitment to both real-world sexual politics and the intuitive knowledge that comes from the ever-present, ever-evolving memory of sexuality as sacred energy. Talk of public sex—that is, pornography, sex clubs, strip clubs, and sex work—seldom begins with a consideration of the spiritual in black feminist thought, let alone black studies. However, because of the immediate memory of relatives who have transitioned in my lifetime, as well as ancestral presences that I only have blood memory of, I am motivated to be mindful of what they ask of me, when they might ask it, and how they ask, especially when it might conflict with what is known as black feminist thought and its sexual politics. Jennifer Nash warns us that "in focusing on pornography as solely a gendered site, and not as a complex field of signification where gender and race function as intersecting visual tropes, feminist legal theory has remained haunted by its continued failure to theorize 'intersectionality'" ("From Lavender to Purple," 309). The same can be said for other sex work and sexual cultures.

The pornographic and erotic are key cultural components for validating human and nonhuman relationalities that exceed biopolitics and necropolitics. They help theorize intersectionality from its original concern with embodiment as opposed to policy discourses alone. What do those of us who promote a feminist praxis, but who also walk and talk with ancestors who predate feminism, sex wars, and pornography, do with not only our sexual pleasure and corporeal aesthetics but also whatever their ideologies of pleasure may be? These are pleasures embedded with foresight and futurity about who we could become. If we value our spiritual world as much as our public world, how do we maintain this sham of favoring human-to-human relationality regulated by the public/private divide over human-to-nonhuman relationality? Ishmael Reed fictionally explored what could happen should we not feed the loas,[4] but Toni Morrison's appraisal of the novel as a form rooted to an ancestral presence resonates for this chapter:

> I could blend the acceptance of the supernatural and a profound rootedness in the real world at the same time with neither taking precedence over the other. It is indicative of a cosmology, the way in which Black people looked at the world. We are very practical people, very down-to-earth. . . . But within that practicality we also accepted what I suppose could be called superstition and magic, which is another way of knowing things. But to blend those two worlds together at the same time was enhancing, not limiting. ("Rootedness," 2288)

Morrison confronted the imposed divide between nature and culture in the West, but she also dismantled the binary between life and death based on notions of Western embodiment and Cartesian dualities. Morrison's statement becomes a building block for black feminist cultural studies,[5] and now black sexual cultures. Morrison's words remain powerfully useful: a blend of the supernatural and a profound rootedness in the real world can be enhancing. If we accept the African diasporic concept of ancestral presences and that these ancestors walk with us, guide us, and visit us, then the current geographies of sex and work that were established based on where human/human or human/otherly human interactions take place can no longer dominate.

The etymology of the demonic in ecclesiastical terms (spirit) and scientific terms (nondeterministic schema), as McKittrick previously noted, documents why transaesthetics become important not solely to artistic production but to scholarly production as well. With funk as a research aesthetic and methodology, part 2 of this book invokes the lost meanings of art as an orgy of the senses and an orgy as an important spiritual ritual. Historically, art as public culture and orgy as counterculture are affiliated with the aristocrats or elite members of a society. While art provides an aesthetic experience that intervenes on bourgeois sensibilities, orgies promote ritualized sharing of creative human expression that could be classified as sex and art.

Overviews of orgies within religious studies detail how the orgy's function has been shaped by its locations in Western or non-Western cultures. Scholars have charted the practice of orgies in many societies across the world, with the most ancient origins traced to festivals and rituals in Egypt (Bubastis), Greece (Dionysus), and medieval Wicca. Women and the feminine heavily influence these traditions. Orgies have also served as external physical crossroads for men and women where catharsis and ludism are possible in Christian and Greek societies:

> The rites whose religious—or more precisely, orgiastic—basis is understood consist of fantasy incarnate. The word *incarnate* here carries its full semantic force: it indeed refers to aggressive, caressing, colliding, loving bodies. And before they were sanitized in the familiar political and religious rituals, these rites were truly and intimately a violent or tender confrontation, involving fantasy, exertion, loss—in a word—the unproductive.[6]

Despite the emphasis on physical or bodily contact, this definition's explicit attention to fantasy and the imagination demonstrates why the orgy should be classified as an art form as well as a spiritual tradition. It also configures art as a type of orgy and connotes its function as a crossroads for human and spirit exchanges in pre-Christian and non-Western societies. Other contemporary considerations reveal the orgy as a cultural site where ritualized and physical interactions involving sex, art, or both can occur.

Setting aside the emphatic dominance of libertine literature as a major factor in theorizing about the pornographic and the erotic, Karl Toepfer's *Theatre, Aristocracy, and Pornocracy* engages theater and its connection with the orgy to document six primary components of orgy as practice and metaphor:

1. An orgy is a manifestation of excesses which . . . must be hidden to be experienced.

2. The motives for excess and secrecy have a metaphysical foundation in the desire to get closer to god, to feel a divine energy within the body.
3. [An orgy] entails an erotic, carnal pleasure in *worshipping* someone.
4. An orgy involves *groups* of bodies, group eroticism, communal ecstasy.
5. [It is] a type of aesthetic performance (such as "singing" and "dancing") which develops *theatrical* qualities to achieve ecstatic effects.
6. [It] signifies a current of exclusivity within a society, a magnitude of pleasure reserved only for an initiated class of persons. (10–11)

Toepfer goes on to classify the orgy as a category of ecstatic experience and ecstasy as a category of aesthetic experience (11). He insists that the demise of the orgy cult occurred because of the promotion and rise of Greek theater. Because Greek theater, "as a public cultural event, function[ed] to institutionalize, objectify, and control the phenomenon of impersonation, the human capacity to change identity at will" (20), Greek public identity came to be based in catharsis and representation instead of ecstasy and ritual.

Conversely, black culture's transaesthetics and sexual economies certainly reflect the religious and cultural connotations of orgy, and for some time the conditions of segregation manufactured a type of racial exclusivity relevant to the reception and consumption of black art and black sexual cultures. In black political and cultural spheres, manifestos on the revolutionary nature of black literature, art, music, and theater detail the aesthetic elements and functions for each form as containing rituals.[7] Beyond these considerations, however, the orgiastic properties of black art proper include a more radical thesis as a result of its own transaesthetics: that sex is art.

Politicians, lawyers, writers, artists, intellectuals, and laborers within modern society have developed discourses, philosophies, and institutional systems that give credence to sex work, sex wars, sex surrogates, sex laws, and sex economies. Sex is so weighed down by human ethics that there is little to no simultaneous valuing of sex as art, performance, collaborative interaction between humans and nonhumans, and as a nonhuman force acting and being aesthetics beyond sight. Were it not for modernity's creation of interior and exterior selves, the order of knowledge's separation of logic and rationality from eros and creativity where the exterior social self becomes ranked over the interior, or the human construction of time where conscious, living, and organic matter takes precedence over dead and inorganic matter, then what has been named fantasy and imagination might be legibly written as one possible reality in which eros and creativity could be transferred into powerful individuals.

However, demonic ground revises these affiliations. Plays and films by Nottage and Houston write sexuality as an art form that can then become a crossroad for human and nonhuman intimacy in which ancestors provide a specific vision of sexual cultures as antagonistic material that confronts the influence of organized and institutionalized religion on the public sphere and questions its dominance as the singular moral authority on sexuality. They do so through transaesthetics that disorganize cultural and religious institutions in order to clear out space for ritualized exchanges of communal intimacy. The first three items in Toepfer's list of orgy elements direct my study of how Nottage's and Houston's investments in the ecstatic and ecstasy result in sexuality as a site of memory as opposed to the publics of sex or private intimacy. The ecstatic experience enables resistance to the necropolitics, biopower, and sexual pacifism within various black public spheres that endorse domestic narratives of intimacy. Theorizing black sexual cultures and leisure as decidedly interested in ecstasy and an ecstatic experience rather than domestic intimacy signals a radical shift for how to understand sexuality, sexual expression, sexual ludism, and sex work in black political and artistic movements. It also has implications for sexual decolonization, the study of sexuality, and institutional monopolies profiteering on creative expression (museums, theaters, halls, and so on).

Lynn Nottage's Black Orgy on Demonic Grounds

Lynn Nottage relies upon black transaesthetics to transition Western theater from its Grecian roots as just another public sphere to that of demonic ground of orgy, where characters' stories remind audiences that sexuality is a site of memory for the living and afterliving. With *Intimate Apparel* and *Ruined,* Nottage turns away from blues legacies, black feminisms, and womanist literary traditions and refuses to allow either the politics of respectability or stereotypes/scripts of Jezebel, Sapphire, or Mammy to dictate the construction of her female characters and their performances onstage. In Nottage's two plays, there are no organized religions, no God-fearing/bible-toting matriarchs, no black churches, no mosques, no temples, and no missionaries. Without these, moralizing narratives become obsolete, which may explain why the endings of both plays are inconclusive and open. The plays serve as a space where characters and theater audiences can seek out ecstasy and ecstatic experiences that metaphorically recall the orgy's communal rituals as a site of pleasure-knowledge for women.

In *Intimate Apparel,* lingerie becomes a creative vehicle for ancestral presences to exorcise the demons from the sexual economy of slavery. Nottage offers complex female characters to her audience in the form of two friends who live in the boardinghouse of another strong black female character. Esther, an illiterate but intelligent seamstress who specializes in lingerie, and Mayme, a prostitute/call girl, live in the boardinghouse of Mrs. Dickson at the beginning of the twentieth century. At the other end of the spectrum, in *Ruined,* the brothel serves as a sub-stitute for churches and museums where sexual terrorism goes unacknowledged. Nottage's plays are not sociological treatises, but they do consider the historical facts about black women's experiences as well as current and future considerations of their subjectivity and agency from those experiences. In several interviews, Nottage explains that *Intimate Apparel* is loosely based on her own family his-tory, and that *Ruined* was motivated by her experience of listening to so-called ruined women from the Congo talk about their experiences of sexual violence and war.[8] Nottage's plays transform African diaspora memory about sexual coercion, sexual policing, and sexual terrorism in the lives of black women into lieux de mémoire. Esther, Mayme, Mama Nadi, and Sophie act as the unwritten interior life of black women's eroticism and sexuality, including economic aspirations and sexual violence. As sites of memory encased by imagination for the human and nonhuman, both plays exemplify radical philosophies about the work, sexuality, leisure, artifice, and intimacy that go into understanding their art as sex.

With *Intimate Apparel,* Nottage intervenes on philosophies about art and sexuality, as well as violates the rules of domesticity and the way the true cult of womanhood writes the conditions of intimacy. First, Nottage does not accept a separation between art and sex but understands them as emanating from the same source. Second, she does not divorce this sacred or spiritual element from the profane or material realities of the human world. She accomplishes both of these tasks by exploring her women characters as things that feel. As Mario Perniola's *Sex Appeal of the Inorganic* theorizes, "[A] thing that feels seems somewhat dif-ferent from a thing that thinks" (7). Nottage rearranges modernity's instrumen-talization of senses and focuses on feeling that arises from touch and the haptic. In a forum in which the sense of sight could dominate, Nottage intends that her theater audience be cognizant of another sensory experience when she centers her play around Esther. Esther's artistic and creative expressions fixed on haptical-ity expose sexuality as a site of memory, as opposed to discourse. When Esther convinces her employer, Mrs. Van Buren, to write a letter to her long-distance suitor, she asks, "Do you think we could describe this silk. . . . Will you tell him what it feel like against your skin? How it is soft and supple to the touch. I ain't got no words" (23). Esther may not have words, but her imagination's approach to fabric, style, and senses proves that making someone feel is an art whose form does not necessarily rely on using words.

We see the same emphasis on the haptic in the sentiments expressed by Es-ther's best friend Mayme. When Esther brags about the diversity of men she has bedded, she tells Esther, "I been with a Jew, with a Turk even. And let me tell ya, a gentle touch is gold in any country" (23). Mayme's comments about her trade corroborate sex as part of an illicit global economy market, but in a way that acknowledges that lack of feeling and touch in the world is as important to the development of an industry as is greed. Other comments highlight that Mayme has not reduced herself to her economic function while sexually bartering: "[A]ll that pawing and pulling. For a dollar they think they own you" (21). She insists that she is more than property or an object of desire. Nottage's characterization of Mayme as literate and more culturally savvy than Esther ignores narratives that pathologize women who trade sex as uneducated, without culture, and tragic. Nottage's depiction of Mayme as a sex artist, as opposed to sex worker, had been foreshadowed in the play's stage directions: "*Mayme's boudoir. A canopy bed dominates. Mayme . . . sits at an upright piano*" (20). A bed and a piano are tools and canvases that can produce different art and affect, and for poor black women in the early twentieth century, the bedroom becomes the demonic ground for both since there was no separation of public and private spheres.

Nottage's depictions of Mayme and Esther's private interactions become metaphorically representative of the orgy cult where feminine power is exalted over male public spheres. During one scene, Mayme performs a blues piece on the piano for Esther. Mayme makes art and sex in the same space, but that space implies that the two are inseparable expressions of the imagination. Nottage reveals Mayme's skill and craft as a blues musician not on the public stage but in her private boardinghouse bedroom. The stigma around women's nonreproductive sexual bartering and creative expression is reiterated when Mayme explains of her long-abandoned proper family home with an abusive father, "My daddy gave me twelve lashes with a switch for playing this piece in our parlor. One for each year I studied the piano . . . a syncopated beat was about the worst crime you could commit in his household" (21). Nottage's emphasis on the blues genre's sonic aesthetic rather than lyrical content confirms that what is beautiful, proper, or civilized is conveyed outside of language. For Nottage, the repression of sexual autonomy and women's creativity are linked, and therefore the productive and nonproductive regulation or policing of each through laws or aesthetics must be challenged. Otherwise, every act of eros, of sexual pleasure, of creativity without productivity becomes a crime or sin within what Wynter notes as the "secularizing behavior-regulatory narrative schema" of Western imperialism ("Beyond Miranda's Meaning," 361). Nottage's choice of the bedroom setting importantly indicates how we should understand both characters' artistic expressions: Sex and blues for Mayme, but lingerie for Esther as a seamstress.

Rather than premise her exploration of sex work as based in organic conceptions of the body designed by a mind-body split, Nottage implements a philosophy that offers an answer to Mario Perniola's question: "What does it mean to feel one's body or that of others as clothing" (46). According to Nottage, it means that concepts of truth, beauty, sex, art, man, woman, dead, and living have to be redefined. Nottage's play is set not too long after emancipation, and her work expresses the newness of hapticality for the shipped, the formerly enslaved, or the undercommon. Harney and Moten remind us that hapticality is "the capacity to feel through others, for others to feel through you, for you to feel them feeling you, [and] this feel of the shipped is not regulated" (98). The play's representation of sex work begins and ends with hapticality and the undercommon's deregulation, consciously and unconsciously, of this feeling. Though Esther is a seamstress by trade, she chooses the expression of the trade. She does not have to design lingerie, but she does so because she exists as a thing that feels. Nottage's representation of Esther and her work as a seamstress symbolically touches on why contemporary debates about what does and does not constitute sex work and sexual economy matter less and less to the undercommon. Though not porn or erotica, Esther's creation of intimate apparel speaks volumes about art as sex and the importance of both to creating and becoming a thing that feels in black women's sexual cultures.

Nottage provides extravagant attention to the details of early twentieth-century women's lingerie in stage directions and setting. Scenes have subheadings such as "Wedding Corset: White Satin with Pink Roses," "Hand-Dyed Silk," or "Gentleman's Suit." Italicized stage descriptions explain: "Esther laughs and returns to examining the fabric, reveling in the tactile pleasure of its texture. There is a sensual quality to how Esther regards the fabric" (19). In the same way that Shange utilized dance and poetry to convey sensory experiences that were different from the visual in theater, Nottage relies upon clothing, apparel, and fabric to do the same. An emphasis on touch and tactile movement or expressions invokes orgiastic expressions where "the body experienced by neutral sexuality is not a machine, but clothing, a thing. It is made of many types of fabrics juxtaposed and interwoven among themselves" (Perniola, 10). Through Esther, audiences glimpse black women's sexual culture as an ability to produce things that feel and promote neutral sexuality.

In one scene, Esther fits Mrs. Van Buren with a corset she designed, to which Mrs. Van Buren replies upon seeing herself, "Ha! I feel like a tart from the Tenderloin. Granted I've never been, but I'm told. Are you sure this is what you made for that . . . singer?" (13). Just as Esther's corset design for Mayme made her feel "like a Fifth Avenue bird" (22), her creative efforts have an affective impact on Mrs. Van Buren. The corset was introduced to heighten feminine artifice for upper-class women who did not work, but its uses extended into being apparel meant to transgress sexual chastity (for example, for prostitutes and fetish BDSM). Esther's lingerie does not simply accessorize what is generally seen as the main object, women's bodies; rather, it provides a way to become a thing that feels.

Mrs. Van Buren is not coming to Esther simply for clothing, but for a specific type of clothing that she herself connotes as hardly seeming "decent" and "a bit naughty" (12–13). Although Esther is not engaged in sexual intercourse, her work functions as a bartering in neutral sexuality, which Perniola claims "emancipates sexuality from nature and entrusts it to artifice, which opens up a world where the difference between the sexes, form, appearance, beauty, age and race no longer matter" (3). Through her design, Esther has facilitated a fantasy of intimacy and sexual desirability for Mrs. Van Buren that frees her from the burden of white womanhood and its duty to produce children, which we later learn she cannot perform. Esther's dramatization of bodies as clothing, not the lingerie, creates the taboo feelings Van Buren covets. Yet, Esther's trade constructs an interzone not imagined by the vice squads and political officials regulating public red-light districts of New York, Chicago, or New Orleans. She creates lingerie for whores and ladies, white women and black women, and purchases fabrics from men outside of her specific black community or women's boardinghouse. The crossing of racial, cultural, and geographical boundaries, however, does not happen in the street, but in the bedrooms of other characters in the play: Mrs. Van Buren, a white wealthy socialite, and Mr. Marks, a Jewish tailor. Mrs. Van Buren's homoerotic desire for Esther as well as Esther and Mr. Marks's interracial longing for each other are indicative of Esther's trafficking in neutral sexuality, an art form suited to the undercommon.

Though Esther never offers physical sexual services like Mayme, the lingerie and lingerie fittings provide a neutral sexuality that has emancipated Mrs. Van Buren and herself from what Perniola sees as a vitalist premise of sex, or orgasmomania, "an instrumental conception of sexual excitement that naturally considers it directed toward the attainment of an orgasm" (2). Esther makes Mrs. Van Buren a thing that feels during the fittings. Foreshadowing Van Buren's attraction to Esther,[9] Nottage uses parenthetical directions to build upon Van Buren's brief mention of sexual thrills and escapism later when "*Esther runs her fingers gracefully along the seam, down the curve of Mrs. Van Buren's waist,*" and "*Mrs. Van Buren tenses slightly at the sensation of being touched*" (13). When Mrs. Van Buren attempts to kiss Esther after another fitting and intimate contact, Esther comes to understand that she was providing something that "feels" like what Mrs. Van Buren likened in fantasy to sexual thrills to be found in the Tenderloin district—orgasmomania. As a result of the time that they have spent together as customer and worker, Mrs. Van Buren attempts to kiss Esther and explains it as a gesture of friendship in which she exclaims, "I just wanted to show you what it's like to be treated lovingly" (59). Esther responds, "How we friends? When I ain't even been through your front door. You love me? What of me do you love?" (59). For white women, transgressing the established boundaries of class and race in a private sphere like a bedroom means "love," but it is less so for black women. Esther's performance, her art as sex, was a form of shared ecstasy aesthetically created: even if the feelings it invoked in Mrs. Van Buren were not intimacy, they were feelings elicited by an ecstatic experience between Esther, her sewing machine, and the bedroom. Nottage, unlike Perniola, refuses to rank neutral sexuality over profitable sexuality where orgasm seems to matter most. She recognizes the use value of both in the lives of black women.

Nottage's depiction of Esther's artistry and work offers a nuanced understanding of sex work and race sorely missing from numerous critical studies of how relationships between white women and black women figure into what and how we discuss sex work and prostitution. The sexual economy of slavery, "something akin to freedom" (to quote Sharpe), unequal class and race relationships between servants and employers (Mammy romances), and even early twentieth-century representations of sex work stressed that Elizabeth Bernstein's bounded authenticity[10] predates a postindustrialist society. This is why when Katherine McKittrick intervenes on what geography means for black women, we should apply her arguments beyond slavery and understand them as important to the "real"ity and imaginary of sex as work or art:

> So, what philosophical work can geography actually do for us, as readers and occupiers of space and place, if it is recognizably alterable? . . . And what do black women's geographies make possible if they are not conceptualized as simply subordinate, or buried, or lost, but rather are indicative of an unresolved story?[11]

Public and private divides contribute to what we deem to be art or work, or what is criminal and morally heroic. Ironically, the beautiful configuration of desire constructed within the close quarters of the bedroom and through the fantasy constructed by the lingerie and lingerie fittings for Mrs. Van Buren and Esther is remade into ugly intimacy in another Nottage play—*Ruined.*

Although there has been an increase of moral panics about human trafficking and prostitution, Nottage once again interjects a perspective that can only be classified as one wholly aware of demonic grounds. In *Ruined,* a public brothel becomes a historical site of memory meant to encompass the themes of intimacy, art, and commerce of sex in the face of atrocious violence. With characters such as Salima (an exiled wife), Sophie (a disfigured songstress), and Mama Nadi (a madam), Nottage has no room for overextended debates about the Hottentot Venus and exploitative representations of black women taken out of historical context. As Mama Nadi, the tough and compassionate brothel owner in *Ruined,* defensively suggests of her decision to run a brothel in war-torn Congo, functionality of one's creative expressions matter: "They're safer with me than in their own homes, because this country is picked clean, while men, poets like you, drink beer, eat nuts, and look for someplace to disappear" (48). Mama Nadi accepts that her brothel is a business, but she also contends that it serves as an important site of memory unlike books of poetry and fiction and art museums. Her sentiment exposes that the same public cultures that mediate family, nation, sex, and women's lives are often the same ones that deradicalize and privatize the art and creativity of women.

For the women in the play, intimacy remains a fictitious narrative entangled with the romance narrative of patriarchy and nationalism in colonialism. For example, when Mama Nadi catches Sophie reading pages from a romance novel to Salima and Josephine, she tells them why she does not care for such novels: "The problem is I already know how it's going to end. There'll be kissing, fucking, a betrayal, and then the woman will foolishly surrender her heart to an undeserving man" (35). Later, when Salima mentions leaving Mama Nadi's for home, Sophie does not share in the romantic fantasy of home as safety but asks, "Where will you go? Huh? Your husband? Your village? How much goodness did they show you. . . . There is a war going on, and it isn't safe for a woman alone" (22). Nottage details that Mama Nadi's and Sophie's sentiments are undergirded by life experiences in the Congo long before either became a madam or a singer in a brothel.

When Mama Nadi and Mr. Harari, a diamond trader and customer, haggle over a diamond she has been keeping hidden, she explains to him and the audience that her current hustle is not of her own making:

> When I was eleven, this white man turned up with a piece of paper. It say he have rights to my family land . . . Just like that. Taken! And you want to hear a joke? Poor old Papa bought magic from a friend, he thought a hand full of powder would give him back his land. . . . I don't want someone to turn up at my door and take my life from me. Not ever again. But how does a woman get a piece of land, without having to pick up a fucking gun? (19)

Like *Intimate Apparel*'s Mayme, Mama Nadi understands the material value of sex, but she also conceptualizes it beyond its patriarchal uses when she articulates an antiviolence appeal of sex work that is rooted in the knowledge of her ancestors and in the material realities of the human world. Women fuck so that they do not have to kill. Magic, violence, language, and land have always existed, but black women have become adept at building their lives on demonic grounds. Nottage's play consistently asks audiences to rethink domestic intimacy and recognize how other affective relations organized by elements of orgy provide alternative modes of being that may not end in murder or death.

Nottage's play is filled with women singing, dancing, and drinking with men and each other. She invokes the orgy cult to debunk myths of prostitution and war as solely segregated gendered spaces. Mama Nadi's bar-brothel is depicted as a sanctuary from the violence and terrorism of war for both men and women who, despite temporary pleasures and reprieves from violence, can never seem to escape capitalism's reach. War, and the material acquisition at the center of most wars, impedes human connection and intimacy. Sites of memory such as museums, memorials, or ruins are supposed to restore such connection. However, the significance of cultural institutions can be lessened when these institutions become national projects of imperialist design. The living and afterliving cannot wait for wars to come to an end to be remembered, or to remember their connection to each other. Sexuality is a site of memory.

In *Ruined,* there are no museums, theaters, or dance and concert halls in the war zone, and war has destroyed the preciousness of domestic bliss personified by wife, husband, and child. There are no churches, mosques, or altars. There is only Mama Nadi's bar-brothel, where Sophie sings to Congo soldiers, "You come here to forget. / You say drive away all regret. / And dance like it's the ending. / The ending of the war." (14). War and colonialism anesthetize feelings and produce machines through the art of killing, but in the absence of cultural institutions to elicit alternative feelings and methods of expression, black orgy serves as a viable substitute for culture and ritual. In one scene, Salima translates what she intuits as the difference between leisure culture and ritual exorcism in her differentiating between time spent with miners and time spent with soldiers: "Them miners, they easy, they want drink, company, and it's over but the soldiers, they want more of you" (22). While intimacy and leisure might be enough for the miners whose labor does not entail the taking of life, it is not for the soldiers or the women who sell their bodies. They seek out an ecstatic experience, one that will forgive instead of love.

Salima later explains to Sophie, "Sometimes their hands are so full of rage that it hurts to be touched" (22). Here and elsewhere in the play, there is no way to avoid making parallels between the women in the brothel and the soldiers. Salima and the other women are all filled with rage and touch does not come easily. Soldiers weep after fucking and still want to be held. Sophie sings, "praying the pain will be gone," and Salima hides from her husband Fortune because she cannot forgive or forget that he let her be exiled because soldiers raped her (45–47). Intimacy, sexual or otherwise, cannot combat sexual violence alone. Sensation and a rearranging of the senses matter for the colonized. This is the missing component of nonimaginative studies on sex work where we assume the tragedy is sex work itself and not anything that comes before. Nottage refuses to let her audience engage in pathologizing of sexual morality that has too often uncritically accompanied debates about global sexual trafficking while ignoring the unethical policies of colonialism and global capitalism. Spaces must be cleared out in order for individuals to have ecstatic experiences that can contend with the interior lives of black people as well as the exterior lives.

Because Nottage's plays thematically focus on sex work, she deftly centralizes the orgy cult and the feminine power associated with orgiastic performance as methodical means of disrupting institutional forces of work societies that stigmatize and oppress women. *Intimate Apparel* and *Ruined* also subvert the original designs of Western theater to displace the orgy. In an appended section specifically on orgy cult and slave culture that further explains the link between the rise of theater and the demise of the orgy, Toepfer posits that "the use of theatre by the Greek patriarchy to marginalize the Dionysian orgy cult and the violent 'feminine' power associated with orgiastic performance was possible only because the theatre functioned in conjunction with ideological structures controlling other institutions within Greek society, such as family and slavery" (176). Relationship and commitment to nation-state had to take precedence over relationship and commitment to self and a higher power, especially when the subjects in question were women. Theater became a tool to ensure this philosophy. Toepfer reveals the historical politics behind the Western tradition of theater and how it evolves over time in response to a perceived lack of political mandate in orgy rituals.

This marginalization of orgy performances and its significance to black women's sex work, sexual leisure, and sex as art is made all the more obvious by theories in Sylvia Wynter's "Beyond Miranda's Meanings." Wynter deconstructs Shakespeare's *The Tempest* and questions the most significant absence within criticism of the Shakespearean drama: "For nowhere in Shakespeare's play, and in its system of image-making, one which would be foundational . . . to our present western world system, does Caliban's mate appear as an alternative sexual-erotic model of desire; as an alternative system of meanings" (360). Wynter continues, "The absence of Caliban's woman is therefore an ontological absence, that is, one central to the new secularizing behavior-regulatory narrative schema" (361). The erasure of the orgy, its aesthetics and performance, and the absence of Miranda prove that alternative approaches can modify ideologies about black women's participation in sexual economies. Such efforts are not about performance theory alone since the foundations of Western psychoanalysis are rooted in Greek theater traditions and plays. Thus, when Shange combines dance and poetry to invent the choreopoem in her play or the theater, she resists the political agenda of Greek theater and patriarchy. The same might be said of Nottage's depiction of sex, work, leisure, and creative expression in her two plays. They are the epitome of black orgy's revenge on a Greek theater tradition and Shakespeare's image making so readily adopted and minimally revised by white American theater tradition.

Nottage boldly reintroduces Miranda and her meaning so that an alternative sexual erotic model of desire can establish a different system of meaning for sex, love, intimacy, and work.

Nottage's settings of bedrooms and brothels in every scene demarcate a typical architectural domestic space made into a broader geographical public space upon black women's entry into it. While such deliberate settings solidify one play's title and theme about intimacy, they also make a strong statement about another play's title and theme that emphasize how black women's sexuality, both ruined and as ruins, revel in ecstasy and the ecstatic as much as they politicize the intimate and domestic. They become demonic grounds that allow for a possession less influenced by capitalism.

Shine Louise Houston, Penetration, and the Art of Possession in Queer Black Pornographies

Ecstasy, as Jennifer Nash instructs in *The Black Body in Ecstasy,* refers "both to the possibilities of female pleasures within a phallic economy and to the possibilities of black female pleasures within a white-dominated representational economy" (2). It is easy to "read for ecstasy rather than injury" (Nash, 4) when the subject is filmmaker Shine Louise Houston. Houston released her first feature movie, The *Crash Pad,* in 2005 and utilized the LGBTQI film festival circuit in the way numerous marginalized filmmakers before her had done. The difference was that she adamantly understood and marketed her work as a specific type of pornography meant to challenge the definition of pornography as well as the parameters of black and queer cinemas and black queer cinema. In her own words, she claims, "I know what the holes are in the market. I know there's a need for that. Fuck it, I wanna make it. I wanna make a porn" (Lo, "Shine Louise Houston Will Turn You On"). She quickly followed up her first film with *Superfreak* (2006), *In Search of the Wild Kingdom* (2007), and *Champion* (2008), as well as started an ongoing web series based on *The Crash Pad* and a digital media forum entitled *Heavenly Spire* focused on masculine beauty, sexuality, and masculine appreciation. To date, most of the productions have received notable LGBTQI press, awards, and profit.

Houston provides an ideal model upon which we can build a critical foundation that would mean moving beyond tainted readings of representation in video pornography. As porn scholar Mireille Miller-Young explains in *A Taste for Brown Sugar,* "Pornography created by black women attempts to expand black women's sexual representations, performances, and labor beyond the current limits of the mainstream porn industry and the confines of pervading stereotypes" (264). Miller-Young's brilliant project on porn attends to the actresses, but her theory of "illicit eroticism,"—that is, "how black women use, manipulate, and deploy their sexualities" within porn (182)—becomes relevant to nonactors as well.

Houston occupies an interstice of multiple and simultaneous cultural trajectories. *Interstice* is defined as an interval of time or space, as well as a small or narrow space between parts of things uniformly organized. On the importance of interstices to black women's sexual cultures, Hortense Spillers's "Interstices" noted their presence as important to intergenerational communication and discourses. She theorizes that we must develop an interest in "what we might call discursive and iconic fortunes and misfortunes, facilities, abuses, or plain absences that tend to travel from one generation of kinswomen to another, not unlike love and luck, or money and real estate" (73). Houston's *The Crash Pad* and *Superfreak* acknowledge those passed-on things by uncovering what has traveled from one generation to another—the superfreak.

Houston's films graphically document the false dichotomies between black feminist thought, antipornography, and antisexual rhetoric and cogently explore symbols, myths, and representations that early black lesbian filmmaking left alone—less conflicted *representations* of interracial desire and black butch and trans expressions—while also capturing the spirit of 1980s' and 1990s' black independent filmmaking. Houston's journey into filmmaking is decidedly different from a number of black women filmmakers often geographically situated on the East Coast (Philadelphia, DC, and New York) and the West Coast (LA). As Claudia Springer's assessment of black women's filmmaking in the mid-1980s alludes, the University of California at Los Angeles and the University of Southern California are responsible for educating a number of known and unknown black women filmmakers whose main artistic mission was to challenge the misrepresentations of black men and women in Hollywood:

> The emergence of university-trained black filmmakers on the West Coast since the late 1960s has included a significant number of women. During the summer of 1982, I met with fifteen black women filmmakers who work in Los Angeles, and I viewed thirteen of their films. All but two of the women were working toward or had received an MFA in motion picture and/or television production at UCLA; one had a BA in art from UCLA; one had received an MFA in cinema production from USC. . . . They said they chose filmmaking as a way to express their ideas, to influence or enlighten audiences, and to counteract the damage caused by Hollywood's inadequate treatment of black people. (34)

To this end, many black women filmmakers have a vision of what films they would like to make and why. The same can be said for Houston, who was similarly motivated by race, gender, and sexuality. She has recounted in several interviews how her directorial path to pornography happened as a result of going to film school and because she worked at the sex-positive store Good Vibrations, where she noticed a dearth of lesbian pornography available to customers.

Additionally, Houston's biography provides insights into how we might contextualize her concerns about race because most of the attention has been from white media that seldom mentions it. Black media outlets rarely acknowledge her work. Houston, a 1998 graduate of the San Francisco Art Institute film program, describes her familial and social roots as "Southern California, mostly in San Pedro/Long Beach area, by the beach, beach culture. Surf punk—so punk music, surf culture" (Lune, "Interview"). Houston's background both as a filmmaker and black lesbian occurs in cultural milieus and geographical locations often associated with white masculinities rather than black female experiences on the West Coast. Moreover, her interests in punk music and surf culture forge a vision of black culture less defined by normative assimilation and accommodation with regard to gender and sexuality. She does not fall into the standard paradigm of black and queer filmmaking.[12] Additionally, the pornography industry's most successful productions are not black, lesbian, or female ventures. In Hollywood, despite critical and sometimes commercial successes of any black women filmmakers, the industry is slow to support and promote future films on a consistent basis. Thanks to visionaries such as Michelle Parkerson, Cheryl Dunye, Yvonne Welbon, Shari Frilot, Debra Wilson, Tina Mabry, and Dee Rees, black lesbian filmmaking has been steadily increasing its presence on the Hollywood and independent filmmaking landscape.

Houston emerges in the interval of each industry ready to deliver black women's queer sexuality, and explicit representations thereof, back to the future without having to strategically contain it in cinematic biopics and historical documentaries geared toward making visible invisible lives. She has expressed specific personal aspirations for herself and her work. As a filmmaker Houston commits not only to being inclusive of sexual identity on-screen, but also to the various ways to express such identity on-screen. While the tagline for Houston's media empire claims to be "porn for pussies," the stated mission of the company reflects more complexity and the key ingredients for Houston's vision as a filmmaker:

> Pink & White Productions create adult entertainment that exposes the complexities of queer sexual desire. Taking inspiration from many different sources, Pink & White is dedicated to producing sexy and exciting images that reflect today's blurred gender lines and fluid sexualities.[13]

Houston's film production company skips right over any configurations of itself as lesbian porn, and it is designated as queer instead. To date, she has won several Feminist Porn awards for her work, and such acclaim suggests that she is changing the way that women desire. Houston's work does not intend to simply show what it looks like for black women to love and sex other women; it means to show what it *feels* like for black women to love and sex each other and other women. She does so by framing lesbian penetrative sex as affect of interior possession instead of spectacularized effect that ends in orgasm.

In her queer pornographies, Houston emphasizes fucking as an act of spiritual possession as well as an act of human penetration. Houston's films demand to be read through the act of possession instead of the Western male gaze of objectification, whose limited temporality omits all of the possible selves that one can be. Bliss Cua Lim explains in *Translating Time*, "The time of spectatorship . . . may not always coincide with the temporal rhythm of the object of our gaze. Human perception contracts an image that possesses a much different duration into the terms of our own temporality" (66). Lim's structural and technical critique of temporality and spectatorship spotlights why Houston's pornography serves as an evolution of sexual magic. Houston's own recognition of temporality based on something other than human perception structures how she uses the camera to show both forms of possession and thus devise her narrative approach to sexuality on film.

Houston's first film *The Crash Pad* is an orgiastic meditation on the domestic sphere and the superfreak. Houston designs her scenes out of orgy's other context—its parodic scene. Lucienne Frappier-Mazur's perspective on this element of orgy insists that "*parody,* which may reflect admiration as much as censure, . . . can be defined in two essential ways: it can either reinscribe some classic discourse, and thus have limited relevance, or else convey a subversive, innovative, and plural discourse" (2). *The Crash Pad* encompasses the latter. Refusing models of lesbian U-Hauling and bed death, romance narratives of homosexual monogamy, fixed sexual identities, and the taboo of interracial sex, she constitutes a new scene for lesbian domesticity. According to Samuel Delany, G. Winston James, and José Muñoz,[14] cruising has been a utopic space for gay and bisexual men for decades. Unfettered mobility as a privilege of masculinity allows the public spaces of bathhouses, parks, gyms, and nightclubs to serve as an oasis for single, partnered, and married men who wish to escape social constraints geared toward sexual domestication. Because historically women have not been allowed such physical mobility without the threat of violence or criminalization, cruising has not figured heavily into the sexual imagination of women until quite recently. Yet the physical dangers and risks linger.

Mindful of these realities, Houston includes riffs on cruising and domesticity in the plot of *The Crash Pad*. The opening shot of the film simulates a gaze peeking into a room where a black woman and white woman engage in penetrative intercourse made possible by a leather-strapped harness that secures a black, silicone cock. Having established the strapped-up black woman as a top and the white woman as bottom, the scene shifts from color to black and white and back to color. Houston offers almost five minutes of these women fucking and kissing, and kissing and fucking, in various positions so that viewers understand that oral and phallic penetration, as she has visually represented them, are equally relevant forms of penetration depending upon where the audience enters sensation in the scene, from the exterior or the interior. Houston's opening montage of the diverse and broad range of sexual penetration distinguishes itself as explicitly different from other films that recreate women's sexual penetration on-screen.

Dennis Dortch's *A Good Day to Be Black and Sexy* (2008) delivered six vignettes on black sexuality, and one specific short—"Reprise"—wasted an opportunity to take up the interiority of women's fucking. "Reprise" depicts the comical experiences of a woman who has repeatedly attempted to enter her male partner's anus with her finger. Dortch emphasizes the issue of male vulnerability and the heteronormative fears that understand anal penetration as a threat to masculinity. At no point does the director attempt to explain the significance or affect of the act for the woman. The power symbolism of what it means to be physically penetrated or to penetrate, specifically when *penetration* is defined as "to pierce or pass into" (*Oxford English Dictionary Online*), has been regurgitated by both feminists and misogynists alike. Straight and gay pornography adeptly convey back-breaking and ass-splitting penetration as a piercing, powerful, and brutal force. There has been much less effort expended on understanding the affect of penetration more closely aligned with its other less violent meanings of "to arrive at the truth or meaning"; "to enter and diffuse"; and "to obtain a share of" (*Oxford English Dictionary Online*). Coincidentally, this definition echoes elements in Toepfer's orgy theory: "[W]hen ecstasy is possible only through an excessive mode of appropriation in which the 'other' to whom one has abandoned oneself to has 'too many' bodies" (11). Houston's camera alternates between kissing and fucking to visibly illustrate and capture the interiority of penetration as arriving at truth, sharing, or diffusing—as possession, specifically as a ritual meant to elicit ecstasy that is only possible from excessive spirit and human appropriation of each other.

As the two nameless lovers in *The Crash Pad* continue being physically and metaphysically engrossed in each other, another interracial couple awkwardly stumbles into the room feigning surprise at the sexual escapades unfolding before their eyes. When the boyish Asian woman attempts to leave, her white femme partner insists that they stay and watch. In a satirical nod to formulaic straight porn, the newly arrived couple enjoys a voyeuristic show until they are invited to participate with a come-here motion conveyed by finger and eyes rather than cheesy one-liners. The Asian stud undresses to reveal that she too is strapped up with an artificial black phallus. She eases into a threesome as her partner watches the multiracial trio engage in fellatio, cunnilingus, double-penetration fucking, and masturbation. Viewers can see that, based on the director's choice of shot angles and coordination of bodies and movement within the scene, her gaze touches and penetrates the threesome enough to excite them into further sexual frenzy. The camera, the performers, and the direction of the scene make it clear that there are various ways for women to give, receive, and take sexual pleasure. Although the spectacle of the strap-on phallus remains, due in large part to Houston's signifying on black phallic supremacy, the emphasis is not on penetration tied to male pleasure and the privileging of it. Houston's method of capturing the interiority of what it means for women to strap on a phallus moves beyond misconceptions of women who strap up as only interested in imitating male power.

The women's simultaneous touching of their breasts as phallic penetration occurs for both top and bottom, the expression on their faces as the dildo is orally consumed by the lover, and the gaze of everyone in the room confirms penetration as a felt act of sharing, diffusion, and interior recognition of self outside the confines of gender, race, sexuality, and ability. Real or performed, the penetration from the inside and outside, as Houston directs it, is distinct. The women's feelings arise from the inside as well as any exterior sensations that may occur from straps against skin, rhythmic dildo thrusts, and engorged wetness instigated from collaborative fantasies and movements of self and another. Notably, despite the intercourse with black phalluses, the scene ends with the threesome engaged in masturbation, oral stimulation of breasts, and kissing, but most important with the fully clothed participant who chose to watch offering viewers a female gaze that conveys breathless awe and complete sexual satisfaction though she never touched or was touched by anyone. In this house setting, Houston dictates that same-gender loving can exist alongside same-gender fucking that is not confined to one partner.

From this early scene in *The Crash Pad,* the film's setting transitions to an outside scene where two lesbians stand and converse about the operations of the house. One woman (Houston in character) explains to another that she has the key to the crash pad, a place where she enjoyed a phenomenal sexual experience, and so she wants to pay it forward and pass the key on. As if she were conveying ancient secrets of how to care for a Mogwai so that it doesn't turn into a gremlin, the lesbian benefactor explains to the new recipient of the key to the crash pad: "You have to call first. If nobody answers then it's vacant, and it's first come first serve. Two, if you're in the crash pad leave the phone off the hook or else pick it up and let people know that you are in there, or invite them in. Last, you can only use the key seven times. . . . After seven uses you gotta pass it on" (*The Crash Pad*). These rules convey that normative ways of approaching sexual relations are not what the crash pad is for despite domestic implications laid out by the early representation of homosexual coupling. In hippie and punk culture, crash pads are a squat location for communal living. However, Houston remakes it to provide lesbians with something akin to a safe cruising space for women.

Users of the crash pad are not simply going to have sex but to have specific sexual experiences that might exist outside the lives of domesticity for single, partnered, and married women. Viewers have no clue what the relationships of these women might be in the opening scene. They could be longtime partners or one-time stands since the women do not intend to play house but rather use the house to play. The remainder of the film works to disrupt any domestic projects, and the film also insists that anonymous sex can be a transcendent experience. Houston's film asserts that women need more than a room of their own to write: they need a space that can handle the crashing messiness of their desires.

The Crash Pad presents viewers with differently sized and shaped bodies, differently racialized bodies, and differently gendered bodies fucking each other. From stud-on-stud wrestling that leads to two bois sexing each other without a dildo or harness in sight, to femmes fucking butches, and butches fucking butches, Houston chooses to ignore gender roles that would make the crash pad like any other house. As a result of her queer interpretations of sexuality, Houston's films have also been construed as operating outside of what might typically be considered black filmmaking aesthetics because of her casting choices and her representation of explicit or hard-core sexuality. In writing about black women pornographers, *Clutch Magazine Online* blogger Arielle Loren described *Afrodite Superstar* (2006) by Abiola Abrams, a.k.a. Venus Hottentot, as "the first adult film directed by and for women of color" (Loren, "Black Feminist Pornography"). However, a year earlier, Houston had released and toured *The Crash Pad*, which brings up the question of what Loren might myopically mean when she says "by and for women of color." Loren's assessment of *Afrodite Superstar* as black feminist pornography by and for women of color presumes to identify aesthetics and themes for all women of color, as if there exists a universal and essential way for black women to have sex and represent sexual activities.

Afrodite Superstar and *The Crash Pad* are films directed and written by women who identify as black. Both films utilize women of color in the story line, and both address representations of black women's sexuality in pornography. But the main difference seems to be that Abram's film explores race in a traditional and obvious black nationalist and womanist vein, recouping the Hottentot Venus to engage black female hypersexuality, while Houston's work offers an uncharted path of exploring butch women of color and trans women of color locked out of black nationalist and feminist cultural frameworks. Thus, the femininities that submit Abrams as a black feminist pornographer who directs for women of color dislocate the female masculinities that Houston as a black queer feminist pornographer engages. Such a dislocation also seemingly disqualifies Houston from being a filmmaker whose work could be for women of color.

If there is going to be such a thing as black feminist pornography, we need to remain mindful of what Kara Keeling has observed:

> [The] current thinking about and studies of race and representation customarily acknowledge that theories and assertions premised on any assumption that racial categories neatly and predictably organize living beings are problematic. Yet those studies fail to interrogate the mechanisms that authorize their own embrace of racial categories to describe that which they presume is represented via the visual media. (27)

Keeling determines that such moves simply reproduce the hegemony of (neo) colonial discourses that their subjects and their actions initially subverted or challenged. Houston's *The Crash Pad* and *Superfreak* present viewers with the mythic being of superfreak and the interiority of women's fucking so that black women have greater options of when and where to enter on-screen and off. As if she were invoking the visual work of Adrian Piper, Houston uses pornography to present a different conversation on entry and black women. She reflects a vision of transfiguration C. Riley Snorton views as necessary to black culture, and in this case produces black sexual cultures that represent "black transfeminism, black butch feminism and the varied experiences of masculinities that exist within blackness—to reflect an understanding of gender multiplicity with and without a penis."[15] Houston's second film, *Superfreak,* offers viewers a more nuanced glimpse into the interior lives of superfreaks that are not bound by time or space.

Superfreak provides an amalgamation of black funk references that can be traced to masculinities expressed by Rick James as well as Prince. At the beginning of the film, a blond-haired white woman in a symbolic S(uperman) T-shirt masturbates while reading a magazine in her room. The woman's self-gratification is interrupted by a spectral presence that begins to form while the woman grows more excited. White mist solidifies into a figure with beaded and braided hair, Rick James (Houston in drag), who watches and exclaims, "I like that" before jumping into the white woman and possessing her as she masturbates herself to climax. The director's intent to transmit the sound of the possessed woman as she speaks, "That's freaky," occurs with a vibrational echo meant to convey the spectral presence from within hitting up against the possessed woman's own pleasure. Time and space are altered. *Superfreaks'* activities suggest that kink is about geography and temporality. In the film, the woman continues pleasuring herself, as she and the viewers maintain an awareness that something also comes from within. Houston's use of the ghost and possession as a trope distinguishes itself from the psychoanalytic construction of id and ego in Zane's work and opposes the early argument of ghosts and haunting presented in Avery Gordon's *Ghostly Matters.*

Gordon explains that "haunting raises specters, and it alters the experience of being in time, the way we separate the past, the present, and the future. These specters or ghosts appear when the trouble they represent and symptomize is no longer being contained or repressed or blocked from view" (19). Houston's use of James correlates with the first part of Gordon's statement, but because Houston divests her specter from sociological narratives ruled by trauma, her cinematic haunting extrinsically links to an African humanist tradition where ancestral presences can be as dedicated to trouble and pain as they are to parody and pleasure. *Ghost Images*, a book charting the development of ghosts and spectral presences on film, views the trope of possession outside the horror of demonic possession needing exorcism and finds that in some films "the idea of possession blurs into mediumship, where a medium invites communication, but it is not clear how far control is exercised over the spirits" (Ruffles, 98). Rather than reproducing haunting as a narrative of pain and trauma, Houston's film relies on this blurring of possession into mediumship and places the audience into Randolph's realm of sexual magic in which sexual excitement and energy form a spiritual bridge where otherworldly contact happens. Moreover, Houston's trope reflects a postwork imagination where there are no clocks or calendars that would establish leisure or work time. As Lim states, "Ghosts call our calendars into question. The temporality of haunting—the return of the dead, the recurrence of events—refuses the linear progression of modern time consciousness, flouting the limits of mortality and historical time" (149). The film's theme and the film itself, as a genre in the fantastic, make us aware of the plurality of time that historically bound political and artistic movements fail to capture because they are linear.

Following the opening masturbation scene, the film depicts the same woman getting ready for a party with the ghost of Rick James still inside her. This socio-spiritual collaboration means not only that the white woman has become Rick James, but that Rick James has become a femme white woman. Again, Houston has found a way to express the affect of penetration as sharing. When the possessed woman arrives at the party, Houston provides visual and sonic cues that the energy of the ghost, rather than the white woman's beauty, makes the women all pause when s/he walks into the room. Throughout the party, the ghost of Rick James continues to possess various women's bodies along the racial and gender spectrum. Houston explores possession as a form of orgy, but does so through the ghostly presence. Given James's real-life proclivities with women of all races, Houston's decision to invoke James here particularizes her superfreak in a manner cognizant of interracial sexual desires as well as sexual and gender fluidity. Some thirty years after the height of James's funk ascension, Houston perfectly captures why he was such an intriguing figure for men and women who wanted to embrace kink beyond their racialized bodies. In doing so, she confirms sexuality as a site of memory.

Houston's manifestation of Rick James as ghost coincides with Gordon's other understanding of ghosts and haunting: "Haunting and the appearance of specters or ghosts is one way . . . we are notified that what's been concealed is very much alive and present, interfering precisely with those always incomplete forms of containment and repression ceaselessly directed toward us" (19). With *Superfreak,* Houston changes how viewers desire by showing them the superfreak gazing inside self and staring back at others. The gaze is the subject of much film analysis, but with regard to African American women, it seems all the more necessary to subvert dominant gazes of men when dealing with black women's sexual representations. In *Superfreak,* the gaze is not gendered, but always in process and changing since it is foundationally based on the superfreak. Houston asks us to reconsider how women watch other women and to consider what that might feel like from the inside. This is an important task when we consider how critical such gazes could be to conversations about the divide between antisex feminist agendas and sex-worker agendas.

Houston remains invested in using her film to present women in the vein of what Gordon has explained as *complex personhood.*[16] Houston's gaze as a black lesbian director and her minor acting performance as the ghost of Rick James perform a double duty of haunting. Her use of possession gets at the contradictions, recognitions, and misrecognitions of being instead of representing "black," "woman," and "lesbian." Houston makes the ghost of Rick James a tool to possess and have sex with women, but she also possesses and penetrates Rick James with her camera. Considering the plurality of time, rather than time's linearity, this black female masculine gaze with its double penetration of representing the exterior and interior disturbs fundamental arguments of a singular male gaze. In all of her films, Houston critiques theories about the gaze that prove why it is so vital to have black women in control and directing films, both mainstream and porn. Her films envisage this claim by representing diverse women, and I mean diverse regarding body shapes, hair aesthetics, and gendered roles and identifications, as opposed to monolithic racial diversity.

Superfreak also has implications for black men and masculinities less sustained by the biological. *Superfreak* makes explicit what *The Crash Pad* and other films have made implicit: the drag of black masculinity as articulated by Rinaldo Walcott when he explains that masculinity "as a performance [becomes] conditioned by myriad other performances, encounters, and interpellations" ("Reconstructing Manhood," 80). Houston's films remind viewers to pay attention to the fluidity of women's bodies, pleasures, and freak's belief in magic. As the ghost of Rick James, Houston artfully uses strap-ons and dildos as a modern-day nkisi charm to grant magic and healing to its wearers. Robert Farris Thompson explains that "an nkisi (plural: minkisi) is a strategic object in black-Atlantic art, said to effect healing and other phenomenon" (*Flash of the Spirit,* 117). Minkisi containers can be "leaves, shells, packets, sachets, bags, ceramic vessels, wooden images, statuettes . . . among other objects" that would be "spirit-embodying materials"

(*Flash of the Spirit*, 117). Used in divination practices, these items are said to be portable graves or objects that can be infused with the power of the dead. Strap-ons and dildos can be infused with the power of the "dead." Houston's use of the black phallic object serves as a nice accompaniment for the ghosting of black masculinity, and it further transes all bodies so that we might better understand the pleasure in consuming self. Houston reconfigures the phallus as an altogether different object to showcase that black funk's superfreak occupies a self-made interstice.

Given the wide variety and artistry of harnesses and dildos, as well as the artful performances that may occur when a person wears them together, Houston visually elevates the black dildo on film by assigning it a supernatural function that exceeds the mythic black cock of white imagination. She creates rituals and sacred objects. Her phallic ghosting becomes a haunting aesthetic of rituals despiritualized over colonized time.[17] In her representation of these haunting sexual encounters, Houston's films insist that what happens inside a woman who uses a strap-on might be as affectively powerful as being penetrated or penetrating with flesh if one's point of origin is not the biological human. From plotlines to symbolic recognition of phallic penetration as something other than piercing force and power, Houston tackles the necessity of sensation to the interior and exterior spaces of women's lives and culture, where she as a black woman filmmaker can rebel against work society and sexual morality.

Crash Pad and *Superfreak* showcase Houston as a beacon for the ideology that porn can be just as constructive and creative in the right hands as it is destructive and damaging in the wrong hands. She has proven critic Angela Carter's thesis that "there is no question of an aesthetics of pornography. It can never be art for art's sake. Honorably enough, it is always art with work to do" (534). Because sexuality, desire, the erotic, and sexual acts are more than three-dimensional, the toil involved includes moving representations of sexuality beyond two-dimensional visual perception. Like any superfreak, Houston conjures black funk to do so.

By design, and as it has been theorized, the black public sphere traffics mostly in nostalgia, discourse, and moral narratives. It remains ill-equipped to deal with fantasy and the hold of the undercommon. Be it democracies or monarchies, Harney and Moten are right when they say, "Governance is a strategy for the privatization of social reproductive labor" (53), which is why insurrection, guerilla warfare, and revolutions signal that politics alone will not create a postwork world. We take for granted and assume it is normal that the places where we can pray, dance, or have sex have been architecturally separated from each other by ordinances and policies that regulate space, or that where we can find books, view art, see plays, hear music, or think and learn have all been cordoned off without our consent by the human concept of work. The imposition of designated spaces and its disciplining of our minds and bodies, however, is often undone by funk's philosophy of sexuality as imagination, of sex as art. Freaks provide critical memory that reminds us of the existence of something before the black public sphere: physical or mediated spaces where people gather to share information, debates, and opinions.

The juxtaposition of the high-art theater of Lynn Nottage with the low culture of Shine Louise Houston's queer pornography demonstrates why the functions and aesthetics of art and sexuality have to shift from public/private domain to demonic grounds. Each woman uses her creative art as demonic grounds where ritual and feminine power can disempower the mediation of sex through publics. In the next chapter, I propose that the orgy and carnival enable unique theories promoting communal intimacy in black communities. As opposed to being nostalgic or critically nostalgic for the orgy, freaks insist that elements of the orgy can be used to create demonic grounds where people can meet to have nonverbal exchanges, performative relationality, and networking and movement, and to initiate the future of thought. These elements help overcome the numbness of organization and its lack of focus on feeling.

6

From the Freaks of Freaknik to the Freaks of Magic City

Black Women, Androgyny, Dance, and Profane Sites of Memory

To begin with, there must be a will to remember. . . . Without the intention to remember, lieux de mémoire would be indistinguishable from lieux d'histoire.

—Pierre Nora

Have we developed a new metaphysics of political struggle?

—M. Jacqui Alexander

Who needs confession when there is music, dance, a party, and sexual magic? The will to remember is very different than Foucault's will to knowledge. Many black men and women continue to be especially vigilant about a history of sexuality and sexual terror and violence, while they ignore memories of sexuality that precede and follow such terror and violence. Recently, in response to Slut-Walk, the organized march against sexual violence, one civil rights organization wrote and circulated "An Open Letter from Black Women to the SlutWalk." The collective authors of the letter detail the reasoning behind the letter as follows:

> We are deeply concerned. As Black women and girls we find no space in SlutWalk, no space for participation and to unequivocally denounce rape and sexual assault as we have experienced it. We are perplexed by the use of the term "slut" and by any implication that this word, much like the word "Ho" or the "N" word should be re-appropriated. The way in which we are perceived and what happens to us before, during and after sexual assault crosses the boundaries of our mode of dress. Much of this is tied to our particular history.[1]

This letter refers to a "particular history" of sexual exploitation that rarely includes the issues of sex and work taken up in *Funk the Erotic*. How black women respond to sexual violence often reflects strategies that might either nullify resistance or encourage it. This well-intentioned letter invokes amnesia because it refuses the ways in which some black women have affectively and politically responded to sexual violence and terror. "An Open Letter" nullifies and limits how black women might resist sexual violence because it assumes a singular path of resistance. The letter's critique of the white feminist movement and its lack of concern with intersectionality does not negate the authors' particular class privilege or the unintended disavowal of antiwork efforts and postwork imagination carried out by black women seldom associated with political work.

Additionally, it remains unconcerned with Western privilege since it ignores more radical and non-Western and African diasporic protests involving nudity, as well as cultural traditions and modes of becoming that have denounced sexual violence explicitly though the body or sexual expressivity. The letter about Slut-Walk favors history and the public sphere and ignores any sites of memory that would reveal how and why black women, even without having to protest SlutWalk, have found ways to not let the fear of sexual terror and violence deter the use of sexuality as magic or divine power. The letter also denies a particular history of colonization that privatized sexual desires and clothed bodies even before it physically enslaved them, and it ignores a mental enslavement that would do the same. This mental enslavement would also erase a memory of black female beings who had moons falling out of their mouths and substitute a subject more interested in being a female citizen. Fortunately, for some black women, the will to remember sexuality as a site of memory for human, nonhuman, and inhuman relations has been taken up in movement and action as opposed to words alone.

This chapter theorizes that some black women may utilize sexual cultures as demonic grounds to erect profane sites of memory for individuals who would dare to accept sex as art (sexual magic); value aesthetics as much as ethics; lessen the influence of a singular black public sphere; have a different relationship to time, space, and geography; and sustain fluid androgyny so as to undo fixed binaries of gender that uphold work society's divisions of sexual labor. The cultural sites are deemed profane because of how capitalism's ideology of possession (accumulation of material things) structures the will to remember and threatens or conflicts with the orgy's ideology of possession if the subject stops moving.

Beginning with an ecstatic analysis of the street party Freaknik, I detail Freaknik as an exemplary model of the "queer art of failure."[2] Freaknik's failure to adhere to heteronormative common sense and black respectability results in a liminal space of undomesticated black communal eroticism that overcomes the class divisions set up by work society, as well as the public mediation of black women's mobility and sexual expression. Building upon my alternative reading of Freaknik, I then offer a theoretical claim, as opposed to a materialist claim, as to how Freaknik's failure generates a psychic space for black women to further develop sexual magic in the twenty-first century. This psychic space clarifies black women's presence as consumers and dancers in black strip clubs in the twenty-first century, as well as consumers and practitioners who transform public sexual cultures into profane sites of memory. These examples exemplify how forms of bodily movement retain public memories of sexual expression meant for material and spiritual gains in black communities. I collapse three disciplines onto each other—literature, performance, and dance—to reexamine methodologies and ideologies commonly used to research strip clubs and to understand black dance in strip clubs as a means for making sacred subjectivity in the absence of historical African cosmologies and Randolph's theories of sexual magic.

My perspectives on Freaknik and dance in black strip clubs in this chapter are derivative of the previous chapters' theorizations of sexual magic, transaesthetics, and demonic grounds, which provide entrée into matters of perception and observation that undermine dominant theories of a Western gaze derived from film studies. Modernity's visual economies cannot erase what the sensitivity to light and the funk of onions tell us—that the eyes feel as well as see. I demonstrate what happens when black women enact memory of black orgy's communal erotic gaze over a visual economy sustained by a singular male authoritarian gaze. The communal erotic gaze exemplified in voodoo initiations, carnival, chitlinality, the soul-train line, or orgies enact an interior ocularity that reorganizes the senses to detect sacred energies of others in relation to the self so as to produce a new metaphysics of political struggle, rather than a movement that will simply mediate sex through a public sphere created and maintained by the authors of sex as knowledge, terror, or violence.

Although museums and other cultural institutions supplement the political sphere and serve as sites of history, there continue to be sacred and profane sites of memory. Studies on African deities, Zora Neale Hurston's *Tell My Horse*, Paule Marshall's *Praisesong for the Widow*, Ishmael Reed's *Mumbo Jumbo*, or Maya Deren's *Divine Horsemen: The Living Gods of Haiti* provide keen insights about extinguished and surviving rituals and sacred sites that once contained alternative knowledge about sexuality and eros. Yet, as much as the representative texts about such sites change and evolve, the sites themselves seem to be static in form and representation. Subsequently, given the spiritual assimilation of black people, it is easy to wonder about where the tricky tricksters, the living gods, and ancestors go when they come back; when they come looking for someone to get down with. Might they need to trek to what would be called profane sites of memory in this world because patriarchy, colonialism, and enslavement forced indigenous rites, rituals, and shrines to go underground and replaced them with churches, mosques, and sacraments.

Equally, if black women have the will to remember sexuality as a site of memory, but the histories of sexualities, empires of knowledge, Western capitalism, and missionaries have made it difficult to access that memory, then black women must also consider the other spaces in which such recognition can happen. Dependence on institutional spaces—feminists and nonfeminists—to enact, regulate, organize, or synthesize black sexual expressivity and imagination is to also risk ingesting neoslavery and neocolonial aesthetics and ethics. Accessing sexuality as a site of memory in the reverse means the will to remember in Western culture might require erecting or dwelling in profane sites of memory. Nora and Morrison remind us that sites of memory do not really have to be institutions architecturally built for the purpose of remembrance:

> Lieux de mémoire are simple and ambiguous, natural and artificial, at once immediately available in concrete sensual experience and susceptible to the most abstract elaboration. Indeed, they are lieux in three senses of the word—material, symbolic, and functional. . . . [T]he three aspects always coexist. (Nora, 18–19)

Brothels, sex clubs, BDSM clubs, or strip clubs might be classified as profane sites of memory. To comprehend the magnitude of what profane sites of memory attempt to make known is to turn away from the political world's emphasis on movement (or a movement) as buttressed by walks and marches and turn to the party's articulation of movement.

Party and Bullshit: Transaesthetics in Profane Sites of Memory

The orgy in the West has been represented as a very particular scene in which all subjects are humans and the entire purpose is to escape the conditions and limitations of civilization and its ever-evolving work society. In *A History of Orgies*, Burgo Partridge's classic explanation of orgies, the author argues that "an orgy is an organized blowing off of steam; the expulsion of hysteria accumulated by abstinence and restraint, and as such tends to be of an hysterical or cathartic nature" (7). Whenever the practices of orgies have been discussed and researched, *man* has been privileged as the subject, and thus his quests for freedom and sexual liberation placed at the center. What does freedom feel like and look like for him? Deracinated, depoliticized, and despiritualized intercourse. Such points of origin are why, literally and metaphorically, Jean Baudrillard can assume that in the eras after the 1960s, everyone needs to figure out what to do now that the orgy is over:

> If I were to characterize the present state of affairs, I would describe it as "after the orgy." . . . Now everything has been liberated, the chips are down, and we find ourselves faced collectively with the big question: WHAT DO WE DO NOW THAT THE ORGY IS OVER? Now all we can do is simulate the orgy, simulate liberation . . . because all the goals of liberation are already behind us. (3)

To believe that society currently exists in a state after the orgy, we must accept that Baudrillard's metaphor of the orgy as political or artistic revolution is apt for black communities, when it is not. We would have to accept a universal subject and participant, accept it as man's psychological connection to another, primitive self, and comprehend the orgy as a less sacred space divorced from the realities of life and afterlife as Baudrillard does. The connection between the orgy and revolution as worked out by Baudrillard hinges on an investment in the polis as well as a national consciousness that Frantz Fanon determines to be an empty shell for the wretched when he writes:

> The birth of nationalist parties in the colonized countries is contemporary with the formation of an intellectual elite engaged in trade. The elite will attach a fundamental importance to organization, so much so that the fetish of organization will often take precedence over a reasoned study of colonial society. The notion of *the party* is imported from the mother country. This instrument of modern political warfare is thrown down just as it is, without the slightest modification, upon real life with all its infinite variations and lack of balance. (italics mine; 108)

Fanon's sweeping commentary closely examines "the party" in black communities as succumbing to the pitfalls of national consciousness,[3] but as the introduction to this work has shown, funk as "party music" demonstrates more than a slight modification of party as an organization into party as a ritual occasion for freaks interacting with nonhuman sacred forces. Party has become a reasoned, imaginative, and pleasurable study of colonial society. From the rent party to the block party, funk reiterates early twentieth-century revisions of the orgy. As opposed to merely serving as a metaphor for revolution in the way that Baudrillard theorizes, the orgy in black communities provides a mechanism in which the pitfalls of national consciousness can be avoided because the orgy avoids the fetish of organization. The black orgy, or rather its scene, does not look like a white Western orgy of purging the ethics of its own modernity or its histories of sexuality. Black communities' acceptance of transaesthetics have led to cultural practices that merge the rituals embedded in orgy with those of carnival so that party fulfills the exterior needs of social advancement and the interior needs of individual transcendence. As Toepfer notes,

> Carnival is a public event, democratic in appearance if not in function, whereas the orgy is for the elite and performed behind closed doors. Most of the actors who take part in the orgy are aristocrats, and the action is played out amidst luxury and abundance. (2)

Black communities' revision of party and dismissal of the element of exclusivity in orgy for the publics of carnival become the basis of its sexual leisure culture for very strategic reasons. When a person is part of a group, both in slavery and segregation, that has very little to say about mandates of public and private space, adaptive measures become necessary. Maintaining these elements ensures the link between an interior life suited to the ecstatic and aesthetic experience in orgy while doing away with concerns about exclusivity. Integration and economic advancement would necessitate new models of privacy and secrecy for some while retaining the process of creating a community beyond the human world of man and work.

Black communities also facilitate a neutral sexuality in their praxis of orgy—exhibitionism and dance. Again, neutral sexuality refers to a sexuality not centered on orgasm and penetrative intercourse, or any intercourse so visibly rendered in Eurocentric paintings of orgies. Popular artist Ernie Barnes left us with the most visceral and lasting example of the black orgy, *Sugar Shack*. From its association with Marvin Gaye's *I Want You* album cover or the opening sequence for the television show *Good Times*, *Sugar Shack* really ushered in the transaesthetics necessary for translating the eroticism of antiwork activity in black art. As Barnes critically explained of his own work, especially his *Beauty of the Ghetto* series: "Being an athlete helped me to formulate an analysis of movement and movement is what I wanted to capture on canvas more than anything else. I can't stand a static canvas."[4] In its privileging of dance as a force and ritual and black subjects as worthy of representation, Barnes's *Sugar Shack* reenvisions the orgy from a stance centered on neutral sexuality and transaesthetics. Barnes evokes perception and sensation at once so that he does not rely only on visual codes but body memory of how the limbs and body extend in movement or retract in close quarters. The symmetry of faces with closed eyes and dancing bodies in motion replicates what others might statically offer of those same bodies partaking in an orgy. The subjects in the painting worship and find their ecstasy not solely with each other (their dance partners) but with the greater force not seen but felt by everyone all at once. While the expression of the body—sex as art—is key here, it is the shared communal expression of humans with a higher power rather than each other that leads to the ecstatic moment.

The privileging of neutral sexuality, communal eroticism, dance, and music in black orgy is a modification that ensures the strength of spontaneity Fanon sees as so necessary for revolution and allows us to overcome the pitfalls of national consciousness and the fetishizing of organization. Without a doubt, the gendered assumptions entailed with leading a party or partying have been made into a masculine dilemma where work and productivity separate the legitimate race men from the minor posers, and this gendering results from the male privilege of unencumbered mobility in this society. Because black men have consistently dominated the public sphere, the devaluation of orgy's transaesthetics have yielded infinitely more negative consequences for the uses of women's bodies and creative energies in the popular arena versus the uses of women's bodies and developing ethics in political machines.

Freaknik and the Queer Art of Failing to Be Good Black Men and Women

In the past five years or so, some black feminists have been vehemently opposed to the SlutWalk movement, providing statements such as, "I understand and even support the goals of the SlutWalk, but for me trying to reclaim and reframe 'slut' is just as fruitless as efforts to take back and tame the 'n-word'" (Marjorie Valbrum, Slate.com), or "But sisters did not line up to go on symbolic, collective ho strolls. And for good, and I think, obvious reasons."[5] However, from the 1980s to the 1990s, sisters, real and fictionally televised, did not have to create SlutWalks since they were busy recovering and reclaiming freak by lining up to go to Freaknik. As the 1990s saw the rise of white queers and queer theory in the academy, outside the walls of the ivory tower, the freak was being elevated, policed, and admonished in black communities all at once as a result of Atlanta's annual spring-break event Freaknik.

The ultimate example of youthful black leisure, Freaknik was where G-funk aspirations and erotic noire fantasies intersected with each other. There was drinking, drugs, cruising, dancing, music, parties, and violence. Most media accounts and historical writings about Freaknik consider it a failure. Marian Meyers, in "African American Women and Violence," offers close readings of the *Atlanta Journal-Constitution*'s coverage of Freaknik to explore the rise of violence at the event. The spring-break extravaganza of street parties and cruising that originated in 1982 as a "'modest picnic in the park for a couple of hundred students' from historically Black Morehouse and Spellman colleges. The event attracted, at its peak in 1994, up to 200,000 student and non-student participants" and ended in 2000 after severe policing (95–96). By the time it waned, any narratives about it as an event that allowed decolonized expressions of race, eroticism, and sexuality were displaced by Atlanta's dedication to a civil rights narrative of chaste and asexual black social and economic progress, or lost to the sexually exploitative video enterprises like the *Girls Gone Wild* franchise.

From their black vernacular inception of contracting "freak" with "picnic," the middle-class and aspiring-middle-class organizers of the event would solidify their efforts to have "good clean fun" as a queer failure. Judith Halberstam has noted that "the queer art of failure turns on the impossible, the improbable, the unlikely, and the unremarkable" (88). So although socializing over flag football, cooking out, and music might be good, clean, and unremarkable fun for some people, for freaks whose point of reference is funk, it would have been impossible. The organizers contractually wrote into existence a black orgy even if that was not the intention. When *Atlanta Journal-Constitution* reporter Ernie Suggs interviewed one of the founders of Freaknik, Sharon Toomer, she responded with sensibilities reflective of sexual morality as pathology. Toomer insisted to Suggs of Freaknik: "It was very innocent. . . . Even the name. Throughout the year, we had this thing about the Freak. There was a dance called "The Freak," Rick James had a song out called "Super Freak," and Chic had "Le Freak." So we named it Freaknik. That was it. It was a sign of the music at the time."[6] Toomer's explanation signals a failed translation of funk as an improvisational force capable of deconstructing the overrepresentation of man and its models of sexuality and class. She displaces funk's powerful sonic force of being with a sexual innocence ascribed to youth under middle-class sensibilities. The songs referred to by Toomer certainly serve as a sign of the musical times, but her disconnection of freak's sexual transaesthetics from funk are invalid. Funk bombs any public sphere that would segregate dance from partying and partying from fucking.[7] Toomer's comments emphasize how black people have repeatedly tried to ignore the erotic and sexual implications within funk music because open and frank sexuality did not align with the soul and post-soul civil rights policing of black bodies.

Like Toomer, the city of Atlanta demanded disconnecting funk from freak for reasons that were about violence but also sexual morality. Halberstam reminds us that "heteronormative common sense leads to the equation of success with advancement, capital accumulation, family, ethical conduct, and hope" (89). Despite these efforts, Freaknik had awakened the will to remember sexuality as a site of memory, especially for black women. In episodic representations of Freaknik, black network television shows committed to middle-class values, such as *A Different World* (1989) and *Sister, Sister* (1999), capture the titillation and danger of Freaknik as it intersects with the tensions of black common heteronormative sense for black women, while eliding the potential of its gender and sexual decolonization. Given Atlanta's fascist response to black youth, black bourgeois insecurities, and the fact that black women's mobility was no longer work-related, the freak was misperceived as embodied in a black female gender without magic or marvel. Nevertheless, black men and women descended upon the street to try and capture the marvel and magic of black funk freakery since Freaknik was shaped by both the carnivalesque and orgy theory.

> Carnival is a pageant . . . without a division into performers and spectators. In carnival everyone is an active participant, everyone communes. . . . [W]hat is suspended first of all is hierarchical structure and all forms of terror, reverence, piety, and etiquette connected with it. . . . [A]ll distance between people is suspended. (Bakhtin, 251)

Both carnival and the orgy can hypothetically exalt and balance feminine and masculine energies and bodies without the colonial politics of gender hierarchies and segregation. The funk origins of Freaknik are essential to redirecting black feminist debates about pleasure, autonomy, and black women's participation and creation of black sexual cultures. For as much as Bambara's androgyny matters to new black masculinities and their politics, Baldwin's androgyny matters as much to black women's political projects and futures.

Some years after James Baldwin showcased androgyny in reference to freak, Adina Howard would capture how party transaesthetics promoted androgynous communal eroticism for a post–civil rights era generation when speaking about Freaknik:

> Freaks—male and female alike, just a bunch of freaks. Probably the best way to look at Freaknik was the Woodstock of the Nineties. Being out there just doing whatever, not really thinking about consequences to the actions that are being executed. Let's just go and have fun, and do what we want to do—how we want to do it, when and where and why we want to do it. The atmosphere was just crazy. Freaknik was one of those things we had the privilege of being able to enjoy. Men and women were just out there uninhibited, like, "It's on, let's party!"[8]

Erica Edwards has shown how the fictions of black leadership make gender revolution nearly impossible. The subject of party politics has and always will be man or woman, with man being the point of orientation. However, party's transaesthetics orient subjects in androgyny. Howard conceptualizes freak as representing both genders. She underscores androgyny as spatial mobility and ludism as opposed to fixed anatomy and work. Sexual excess and hypersexuality always assume a norm or universally correct amount of sexual expression and activity for black women and men. Androgyny does not assume a norm for sexuality, and black communities' articulation of freak and sexual magic ensures the reproduction of beings capable of sustaining communal eroticism and ecstasy where there are no men and women.

Moreover, although Howard references Woodstock, the activities and behaviors of Freaknik were akin to activities taking place in another city and street party—New Orleans's Mardi Gras.[9] New Orleans possesses a much different history of race and sexual cultures, but Mardi Gras's continued existence in spite of sexual violence, sexual exploitation, and natural disasters such as Hurricane Katrina indicates how narratives about Freaknik are too often conveyed via moral panics of black middle-class sensibility or controlling master narratives of white patriarchy and paternalism. In documenting the well-intentioned goals of Black Men for the Eradication of Sexism (BMES), Omar Freilla explains, "My class decided to organize a speak out on Freaknic [sic], Atlanta's Black College Spring

Break weekend festival where nudity and the lewdest, 'freakiest' behaviors are encouraged. It is also a weekend where women are raped, harassed, and generally disrespected by male participants" (79). I juxtapose Howard's and Freilla's different perspectives about Freaknik, and the divergent ways of reading Freaknik and Mardi Gras, to highlight how the event could mean something different for multiple people at any given time during its tenure. Meanings hardly captured in the histories of Freaknik as antithetical to black politics but that remain in profane sites of memory built by funk.

Freaknik has not been written as a site of black women's sexual leisure or their demonic grounds, nor has it been written as a site of androgynous sport and play. Yet black women who were not classified as cultural producers emulated what Morrison, Nottage, and Houston had done with fantasy on the page, stage, or screen, and they made the streets of Atlanta a profane site of memory, rather than a sight or scene. The key to such comprehension comes in acknowledging that Freaknik was an economically feasible form of communal erotic expression. Black women rarely, to this date, own leisure spaces where public sex and neutral sexuality could happen. In her study of black women's sex work in Chicago, historian Cynthia Blair illuminates one facet of leisure and sex work when she explains, "The transplanting of black women's sex work from the red-light district to black community networks was both geographical and institutional. . . . Significantly, as black women's work in brothels waned, the role that black male leisure entrepreneurs played in the sex economy expanded" (151). The same has been said about Storyville in New Orleans, in which the world of sexual economy and leisure was both predominantly heterosexual and thought of as men's leisure.

Alecia Long's *The Great Southern Babylon* describes the red-light district of late nineteenth- and early twentieth-century New Orleans as a "year-round erotic space, inside the boundaries of which men of all descriptions and convictions could indulge in a variety of sensual, even sinful, pleasures for days and nights on end, free from the moral restraints that their home communities imposed on them" (170). Whereas Blair contextualizes her history in terms of male leisure and sexual economy, Long documents Storyville as a site of sexual tourism or a "sexual amusement park" (169). In either case, as we move forward into the twenty-first century and beyond, women's leisure culture is imagined as not intersecting with illicit economies and men are configured as the only persons of leisure, the only consumers. Thus, my configuration of Freaknik as sexual leisure and sexual cultures is intended to rewrite heteronormative and masculine paradigms of sexual leisure where homosocial bonding, heterosexism, misogyny, and capitalism dictate the meaning of every interaction.

Writing Freaknik as a profane site of memory also recognizes that black women's sexual leisure aspires toward androgyny, as opposed to womanhood, and understanding why such aspirations might produce artistic and political values not seen in black male sexual leisure. One of the many privileges of hegemonic masculinity occurs in its geographic mobility to feel less pressure to cordon off sexuality to the private sphere. Barring the use of *ho, slut, nympho,* and *freak,* there are no celebratory terms and stories of women coming out as sexually free, and being LGBTQI has not solved this dilemma. The fantasy of lady in the street but a freak in the bed continues to be a modern-day philosophy of good black women and communities. Yet, if we consider the words of James Baldwin and Adina Howard, freaks until the day and dawn, we might understand why so many black women, despite all claims of being misguided, created their own demonic grounds at Freaknik. More than an annual purging of respectability, Freaknik provided black women with an opportunity to mirror each other's uninhibited-ness across classes, sexual identities, and public spaces.

Black middle-class women and men mingled with street aficionados to form a combustible combination of clashes around morality and antiwork activities. Racial anxieties and sexual violence eventually led to the demise of the young black middle class's attempt to freak out. Krista Thompson, in her essay "Perform-ing Visibility," does a great job of documenting the city of Atlanta's militaristic response to Freaknik, explaining that "the event agitated and transgressed the racial, gender, and class boundaries upon which the city of Atlanta is built" (25). Freaknik, she contends, was "about the city . . . and the right of African Americans to claim and possess space in the city environment," and that fight was "mapped specifically onto the black female body and mediated through the camera" (26). Freaknik, then, reflects a contemporary quandary of context and domesticity. Here is where we must return to testimonies of participants in Freaknik and suggest that for the participants in that moment, Freaknik was never specifically about the black female body mediated through the camera alone.

When *Complex* magazine's "The Oral History of Freaknik" was published, the article provided oral commentaries from well-known music performers and pic-torials without context. Some of the people interviewed corroborated the most vocal critiques of Freaknik. But what if we had asked in the moment, and what if the media coverage had included perspectives of the young people in that moment as opposed to white Atlanta's fear of blackness and black Atlanta's anxiety about black sexuality? As Jermaine Dupri suggested, "The problem was that, and I say this all the time, the city never paid attention to the entertainment part of Atlanta the way they should have. There should have been a committee in the city that took over and kept it going. They said it became something that was bad, but it wasn't."[10] Still, Nika Watkins claimed, "At first it was chill. Guys would ask where you're from, what school you went to, etc. It meant a fun weekend partying in Atlanta. It eventually changed to a sex fest. It was the weekend guys knew they could get laid."[11] However, Watkins's comments seem to mean that only guys were attending Freaknik to get laid.

Were there few to no women attending Freaknik for the sake of getting laid? Were there no lesbian or queer women at Freaknik who took pictures of each other as an invocation to their own desire? Can those who never attended actually know the context of half the images left from biased media coverage? And what of multiple perspectives of the many participants? One person's experience at an orgy is never the same as the next. Moreover, given the current mass communication of dick pics in our present technological era, are we to believe that there are no such predecessors before the twenty-first century? Are we to believe that there are no dick pics from Freaknik, no Kodak moments of body-building poses, muscle shots of chests and abs, and crotch grabbing? More likely, the media's lack of circulation of such pictures is a result of prioritizing male privacy. I hold out hope that these images could be hidden in a former freak's basement or trunk, awaiting their future discovery by a young archivist searching for freaky-deeky life forms of a bygone era. Racial anxieties continue to make it difficult for the freaks to come out in broad daylight rather than the night. I wonder what the deliberate silencing of black women through omission of their desires or shaming then and now means for how we understand what Freaknik was (an outward expression of some black women's interior sexual lives) and what it has led to for black women: black sexual leisure and sex as art.

Chester Himes viewed the leisure activity of fucking, specifically the orgy, as a new strategy in the public sphere to combat the restrictions and ills of black respectability. Consequently, it is not surprising that even as Freaknik became more dangerous, black women continued to attend it each year. McKittrick offers some ideas about how knowledge about the impossibility of black self-government may have informed black women's participation in the street party:

> Black women's unique geographic concerns are concealed by racial, sexual, and economic processes. That is, the dispossessed black female body is often equated with the ungeographic, and black women's spatial knowledges are rendered either inadequate or impossible. . . . [T]he real and imaginary geographic processes important to black women are not just about limitations, captivities, and erasures; they are also about everyday contestations, philosophical demands, and the possibilities the production of space can engender for subaltern subjects. (121)

Black women lacked a viable interzone, a red-light district, a club, or a city ordinance to call their own, so their sexual leisure in the street became a temporal space of black female self-government given that they perfectly understood that the city is not the black man's land. Sexual leisure becomes a part of black women's culture because it provides interclass and androgynous contact very different from uplift work of past generations, and in black communities that began with less tidy categories of gender and sexuality that were assimilating into more strict models of gender and sexuality, such interclass contact lessened the affect of assimilation.

Though Samuel Delany's *Times Square Red, Times Square Blue* was a very geographically specific and, some would say, gendered eulogy of an important district in New York City that changed as a result of gentrification, much of Delany's argument resonates with this chapter's exploration of sexual leisure. Specifically, what Delany notes as the two modes of social practice, contact and networking, are especially relevant to why sexual leisure matters for black communities. Delany explains, "Contact tends to be more broadly social and appears random" (129). He suggests that public-space exchanges like grocery-line small talk, bar conversations, front-porch/stoop dialogue, and, most important, "intercourse—physical and conversational" (123) are when interclass encounters happen. On the other hand, networking "is what people have to do when those with like interests live too far apart to be thrown together in public spaces through chance and propinquity" and "is heavily dependent on institutions to promote the necessary propinquity (twelve-step programs, conferences, reading groups ... social gatherings, workshops)" (128–29). Delany's arguments demonstrate how work society impinges upon every facet of life, even leisure. Thus, in addition to blue collar versus white collar, or domestic family labor versus public corporate labor, the organization and ordering of leisure via networking ensures barriers to a postwork society.

Given the effect integration has had on class stratification in black communities in which the black bourgeoisie, black working class, and black underclass remain geographically segregated in the suburbs, city interzones, or rural farms in ways that they had not during segregation, there are fewer opportunities for interclass contact to happen. Interclass contact remains an important mechanism not simply for black nationalist agendas organized around race alone but also for moving away from the gender and sexual categories of Western imperialism and colonization. Freaknik was a failed attempt at sexual decolonization through the sacredly profane site of communal erotic intimacy that could initiate interclass contact. Black women, however, would have to take what they had learned from Freaknik and set up demonic grounds elsewhere: in black strip clubs in the late twentieth century.

Magic Cities and Remembering Miranda's Meaning

Freaknik's queer art of failure invoked a shared memory of sexuality for some black women. The will to remember and the desire to transgress race, class, and sexual boundaries were not quelled by one city's control of the street. It was reborn in the elevation of Magic City from a basic strip-club joint in Atlanta, Georgia, to a black cultural institution with a fantastical philosophy about sexual leisure shaped by new configurations of geography and black women. Too often, conversations about strip clubs and women revolve around men as patrons and consumers; however, the remainder of this chapter discusses the ways in which black women shift how scholars should think about any strip clubs that showcase the particular practices of black dance. Such clubs become cities, magic cities.

Magic City is not a city in the traditional sense of a permanent landmass or settlement where citizens reside, but it is a city as outlined by Elizabeth Grosz in "Bodies-Cities":

> The city provides the order and organization that automatically links otherwise unrelated bodies. For example, it links the affluent lifestyle of the banker or professional to the squalor of the vagrant, the homeless, or the impoverished without necessarily positing a conscious or intentional will-to-exploit. It is the condition and milieu in which corporeality is socially, sexually, and discursively produced. But if the city is a significant context and frame for the body, the relations between bodies and cities are more complex than may have been realized. (243)

Many strip clubs could be examples of being cities unto themselves based on this definition. With regards to Magic City, however, seeing it as more than a building structure or strip club means acknowledging that it remains indelibly shaped by a black sense of place[12] where we truly understand the complexities between bodies and cities—that is, black women's bodies and their cities, rather than owners and male patrons. Their operation of sexual magic with no intent toward human reproduction or production, we learn, gives birth to cities in which the method of charting or mapping is based on what is felt inside the body as opposed to codes and regulations organizing the body or landmasses.

Artemus Jenkins's *Power of Pussy,* a web documentary series about the dancers featured at Magic City, adequately captures the way a focus on demonic grounds and aesthetics shapes black women's sex as art and black women's sexual leisure. In the first episode of *Power of Pussy,* "Beginnings and Endings," Jenkins begins his documentary with a sound bite from a Bernie Mac monologue about how strip clubs came into existence. Mac begins, "Stripping business started in Africa . . . a long, long, long time ago." Considering the African Dionysus tradition of the orgy mentioned earlier, as well as the absence of a moral pathology that would deem dancing nude or minimally clothed a horrific sin, Mac's humor unintentionally aligns with black orgy tradition. This sound bite is accompanied by footage of a number of abandoned buildings like Club Nikki's and Jazzy T's, establishments that used to be strip clubs. The last club viewers see during this opening has a shiny sign and in the backdrop is a faux skyline of Atlanta. Under the sign Magic

City, the filmmaker includes the heading "Open Over 25 Years." What makes Magic City different from Club Nikki's and Jazzy T's cannot be conveyed via a typical history of the city of Atlanta or the strip club industry. Instead, we would need to consider the affective moments and the materiality of certain forces to understand why a quarter of a century later, Magic City not only endures but also receives platitudes in black music and film, as well as corporate imitation by other strip clubs.

Jenkins is not alone in documenting black strippers and strip clubs. Since 2011, Leilah Weinraub's Kickstarter-funded documentary about a lesbian strip club party in Los Angeles, *Shakedown,* has had limited viewings.[13] In the film, Weinraub focuses on the performances and lives of Ronnie Ron (butch/stud emcee), Egypt (femme star dancer), Mahogany (lesbian trans woman stripper), and Jazmyne (another headliner) before the club was shut down. Both Jenkins's and Weinraub's films contribute to analysis about the role of aesthetic elements in stripping, but Weinraub differentiates her film from Jenkins's by using a visual focus on dollar bills linking work society (the club) with domestic (family). Such emphasis indicates how money gets recirculated and how sexual and asexual industries support each other. However, rather than view what happens in Shakedown as especially different from what happens in Magic City, I propose that these films, forever conscious of the male and Western gaze, can never adequately capture why black women watching black women dance completely or partially nude creates a different vibe and magic, whether the space is specifically catering to heterosexual or homosexual desire.

Black strip clubs, like all other black culture, are distinguished by their inclusion and reproduction of transaesthetics. This is what makes them different from white strip clubs. It is why clubs such as Magic City, Strokers, Stadium, King of Diamonds, Onyx, Erotic City, Starvin Marvins, Silver Fox, Sunset Strip, and the Player's Club have a steady consumer base of black women, rather than a minimal mandate to admit women without a male companion. It is also why lesbian clubs and entertainment production companies such as the Shakedown, Girlicious, Neshe Entertainment, and others remind us all, in the words of Cheryl Clarke, that living as a lesbian entails more fluid and transitional ways of becoming based on something other than domestication. Although the initial clientele of the clubs and production companies might be assumed to be different based on biological writings of sex and gender, their commonality remains communal erotic intimacy shaped by the practice and aesthetics of black dance and its resistance to being colonized into "appropriate" social spaces, venues, functions, and moral purposes. Black dance becomes the alternative cartography, the demonic grounds, that make any strip club an erotic city come alive.[14]

There is no doubt that strip clubs are inventions of capitalism and patriarchy, but like everything else that arises from the institutions of white supremacy,

African Americans can shift such institutions to their own purposes. Demonic grounds redirect us away from histories of theater and burlesque as the most relevant cultural institutions to provide other narrative contextualizations for black strip clubs.[15] Moreover, they compel scholars to rely on methods that can grapple with the unseen elements of particular significance to black survival outside of politics.

To formulate how black women's will to remember can transform architectural spaces meant for white and black men, such as the black strip club, I briefly attend to my own experience as a consumer in traditional strip clubs and with Neshe Entertainment, a black lesbian production company in Jacksonville, Florida, to suggest other possibilities left unexplored (for practical reasons) in inquiries of black strip clubs and black women. From 2005 through 2008, I attended Neshe Entertainment's First Friday events at Mills Cove Golf Club. Although Neshe's First Fridays were certainly a gathering place for black lesbians, they were also events for any black woman to display a talent, whether it was black women showcasing athletic and dance skills by stripping or others reading poetry or singing. The audience and performers were comprised of local businesswomen, professors, navy personnel, radio DJs, and television newscasters.

During those three years, I watched black women consider stripping as artistically equivalent to poetry and singing; I watched women generously tip poets, singers, and strippers alike. They did so for the same reason they could create a lesbian space to gather: because First Fridays enabled a different arrangement of time and because Mills Cove Golf Club, a haven for male bonding over golf during the day, was not on First Fridays a golf club, nor was it the theater. It served as demonic grounds:

> Like other human geographies, black expressive cultures do not communicate whole geographies. Instead, the mixture of presentation, music, noise, bodies, performance, and musical arrangements are used to exploit existing geographic arrangements and push narratives of normalcy out of the comfort zone. (McKittrick, *Demonic Grounds,* 140)

Black women took over this very specific leisure space centered on what some still see as a sport of white elite and upper classes and made it into a venue for sexual leisure and a plane capable of making sacred subjectivity, but a history of burlesque and theater omits or minimalizes such moments. Just as a golf club can become a makeshift lesbian strip club, strip clubs can also become sites of memory when transaesthetics are deployed. Although Randolph's sexual magic resided in occult rituals, several of its principles of volantia, descretism and posism are practiced in black cultural practice of dance. Uncovering the ramifications of sex as art, we must turn to theories of performance that undermine the finality of sex as work and that require us to remember Miranda's meanings that Wynter has explained as offering an alternative set of erotic schemas. The collaboration between female audience and dancers as well as certain aesthetics of dance provoke the will to remember, and it is why some black women find themselves as patrons in strip clubs marketed toward male consumers.

Dance Apocalyptic Methods and Profane Sites of Memory

Time and space are human constructs. Dance is an inhuman force. Dance does more than defy time with its dismantling of the virtual and actual binary of space and matter created by human work society—it generates new matter and methods. In current black queer communities, we have come to understand dragging as gender performances that can be political and artistic, but we have yet to understand and appreciate how gender and sexual performance and expression in strip clubs can have artistic, as well as economic, implications. Most recently, Siobhan Brooks's *Unequal Desires* and Katherine Franks's *G-Strings and Sympathy* have moved beyond the kind of analysis that assumes a pathology and stigma attached to those working in the industry and its consumers. Both scholars include their own actual experience as strippers into their sociological treatises, but they seldom move away from the narrative of work that generates particular citation practices around gender and sexual performativity in strip clubs as Judith Butler's theory on performativity tells us about words and their affect when she insists that "performativity must be understood not as a singular or deliberate 'act,' but, rather, as the reiterative and citational practice by which discourse produces the effects that it names" (13). When stripping is labeled as sex work, it becomes work no matter the space. The female ethnographer, researcher, stripper, and patron are each locked into a narrative not of her own making. No matter what attempt is made to better understand, each person in this forum can only regulate the other and others through discourse that dismisses affect and aesthetics. Alternative methodologies are necessary to counter the citational practices that create automatons. Devising methods from cultural traditions in which seminudity, nudity, and eroticism are not antithetical to the concept of "dance" can be a useful starting point for more radical analysis.

Black dance refuses written narratives about stripping that have become a type of performativity of sexual pathology that travels across generations. In doing so, it provides radical methodologies about how movements arrive long before thoughts do in black women's production of space and being. Dancer and critic Brenda Dixon Gottschild reiterates the point, stating, "I've never understood why 'black' dance has been characterized as narrative. Africanist dance is symbolic movement. It may tell stories, but these stories are about the movement itself and about concepts—the body dancing its symbols" (261). Black dance has typically been studied as black national culture that incorporates Africanisms essential for the sustenance and survival of black communities confronting cultural assimilation, but it also remains a site of memory that far exceeds the politics of racial difference. Sometimes it is about stepping out of time and place.

Women of color and transnational feminism have consistently been concerned with elevating other epistemologies of knowledge so as to avoid the epistemic violence carried out on women of color by Western "discourses" of knowledge.[16] With her work on Haitian dance, Katherine Dunham forever changed dance and dance scholarship. As Dunham offers in her "Notes on Dance: With Special Reference to the Island of Haiti":

> Dance is a rhythmic motion for one or more of a number of reasons: social cohesion, psychological or physiological catharsis, exhibitionism, auto-hypnosis, pleasure, ecstasy, sexual selection, play, recreation, development of artistic values, stimulates to action, aggressive or non-aggressive, extension and affirmation of social patterns and others.[17]

Dunham's statement on dance codifies why research on black strippers and strip clubs requires research methods that would understand the relevance of research aesthetics. In "Terra Incognita," Jane Desmond begins her important intervention with: "I suggest that we use the potential of fieldwork—that is, the sustained participation in and observation of communities, institutions, and practices—and apply this widely to a variety of sectors in the United States, including modern dance and ballet companies, dance institutions such as archives, training schools, community dance centers, and even our own scholarly organizations" (43). What she does not include in that list is strip clubs. Sustained participation in and observation of communities, institutions, and practices with regard to strippers and stripping would inevitably mean that researchers would have to consider the technical limitations of their methodologies as well as the aesthetic and ethical limitations.[18]

When Desmond explains what ethnographic research entails, she initially privileges an ethnographic approach over textual analysis, overlooking the existence of competing narratives that will require textual analysis in order for an ethnographic approach to avoid epistemic violence of its subject.

> What an ethnographic approach requires that textual analysis does not is actually speaking to people, participating with them in their activities ("participant observation"), and trying to understand their own interpretations of what is going on. This requires sustained engagement with communities, not just going to a performance

several times, or spending a couple of months in an archive. Researchers must arrange their lives and resources to spend (at the very least) months at a time working "on site." (46)

Participant observation offers a wealth of information, but it is always information shaped by textual analysis of somebody's narrative, somewhere. A methodology mediates an experience as much as narrative encapsulates experience. What questions an ethnographer asks and how she speaks to people or participates in their activities are shaped by competing narratives of the West and its Others. How research subjects answer a question or engage a researcher is influenced by narrative traditions associated with their race, their gender, their sexual orientation, their occupation, and their "work ethic." Most helpful is Desmond's suggestion that "we combine ethnographic approaches with historical research and with 'cultural studies' tools for the analyses of 'texts'"(45). Like Desmond, Omi Osun's/Joni Jones's theory of performative ethnography[19] proves why traditional ethnographic method and its attention to the real and the material should not be the sole authoritarian research method. Juana María Rodríguez's *Sexual Futures,* with its focus on gesture and affect, theorizes why innovative methods might be useful for understanding sexual expressive labor where fantasy and leisure play such a significant role in why people consume other individuals' sexual expression. Rodríguez suggests that "[b]oth dance and sex create opportunities for new interpretations that are performed and received in each instance of their production, making each articulation simultaneously wholly iterative and wholly new" (100). In addition to video documentaries like *Power of Pussy* and *Shakedown,* black women's music videos have become mediations and a type of methodology for studying black women's dance out of time and out of place as far as aesthetics and politics are concerned.

On her second album, *Electric Lady,* Janelle Monáe takes up the importance of all types of dance for black women. On "Dance Apocalyptic," she riffs and revises Juicy J's strip club anthem "Bandz a Make Her Dance," while her collaboration with Erykah Badu has Badu proclaim on "Q.U.E.E.N." that "the booty don't lie." Monáe exhibits a Dunhamesque ability to understand the link between the strip club anthem and her own revolution that recognizes and refuses the moral split between dance as sacred movement, dance as sexual expression, and dance as art. Alan Ferguson's amazing music video for Monáe's single "Q.U.E.E.N." cleverly visualizes this alternate reality by depicting things that feel like rebels of a future revolutionary movement. Ferguson's video opens with a voice saying, "It's hard to stop rebels who time travel." From there the monologue tells of a living museum that has displayed the rebels frozen in suspended animation for its patron's cultural enjoyment. As Fanon warned in his discussion of party politics and nationalist organizations, movement police—singular authoritarian leadership—are real. He expands this warning with a statement about violence: "This consideration of violence has led us to take account of the frequent existence of a time lag, or a difference of rhythm, between the leaders of a nationalist party and the mass of the people" (107). Violence, however, is not the only way in which such gaps can be seen. Dance is another.

The "Q.U.E.E.N." video makes correlations between the political, artistic, symbolic, and a time lag between leaders and the people when Monáe, Badu, and band members are presented as such rebel artifacts. The members of the video's "time council" inevitably become movement police who attempt to determine what constitutes "crucial activist energies," as well as artistic representations. Yet, the dominant narrative of a council who could freeze rebels is interrupted when a patron places a vinyl record onto a turntable, and the frozen objects/subjects are brought to life by a banging beat. Monáe's lyrics suggest that time travelers are funk's freak and dance is the crucial activist energy of their future movements: "Am I a freak for dancing 'round / Am I a freak for getting down / . . . / Yeah I wanna be, wanna be Queen" ("Q.U.E.E.N."). Monáe is vying to become queen of something other than a Western empire. The video depicts one way in which black women and men have been making themselves into things that feel and taking in things that feel to experientially create an experience that can "free sexuality from its dependency on the organic"—that is, the genitals (Perniola, 46). What the song undeniably explains is that we do ourselves a disservice and miss the movements happening before our eyes when we consciously separate "Make it rain trick," "The booty don't lie," and revolutionary thought. "Q.U.E.E.N."—the song and video—demonstrates that the gap created between aesthetics and ethics is one created by work society's construct of time and hu(Man) values, but its oppressive hold lessens when we become things that feel. We also become black art with multiple functions beyond consumption.

As Maulana Karenga explains of any black art, "If we must paint oranges and trees, let our guerillas be eating those oranges for strength and using those trees for cover. We need new images. . . . All material is mute until the artist gives it a message, and that message should be the message of revolution" (2087). Understanding sex as art, or mute matter, we also understand that it can have an individual artist or collaborating artists who give it a message or force. Black women make each other's material art, their work, with messages of a revolution that only they seek out. They keep giving mute matter force through their exchanges with self and others. The dance of strippers is no different.

"Her ass has a life of its own. We got her ass running a classroom," exclaims Rihanna of dancer Candace Cane on the MTV show *Making the Video* for "Pour It Up." Written by Rihanna and Michael Williams, the song is a strip-club anthem, but the video is also performance ethnography as *Making the Video* demonstrates. Long before Rihanna was criticized by feminists for exhibiting her pole skills in the video, she was a student of strip-club choreography. In the "Pour It Up" video, she reworks and restates danced events to create new mythologies that unbreak the hold of the Western gaze and reject the polis and church as sites of miracles. Jesus walked on water, but as Rihanna says to the camera, "I bet you never seen bitches twerk on water. My bitches twerk on water" (*Making the Video,* "Pour It Up"). Rihanna's video for her single "Pour It Up" and *Making the Video* take seriously the "really artistic things happening"[20] in black strippers' choreography. They act as evidence of noninstitutional knowledge production that demonstrates the link between choreography, performance, and ethnography.

For example, in discussing Katherine Dunham's choreography and ethnography, VèVè Clark reveals:

> Dunham's research became the basis for character dances and ballets, all of which demonstrated her extensive knowledge of dance forms re-created from African diaspora memory. When the dance steps, music, and other cultural forms were transformed for stage representations, they become lieux de mémoire. . . . Dunham's lieux de mémoire became at once a celebration of Caribbean memory and history preserved in dance form and a reminder of cultural artifacts one should not forget. . . . Her writing on the dances of Haiti applied a form/function, structuralist analysis to the dances she observed, while her choreography belongs to the narrative, modernist tradition. . . . The challenge, then, is to develop a critical literacy for dance analysis so that we may decipher and interpret choreography just as we read literary texts closely or "read" the language of cinema.[21]

Recognition of narrative's influence on methodologies centers Clark's study of Dunham and Dunham's own work. Dunham chose radically different methodologies of investigation while in Haiti.[22] Had Dunham visited Haiti and viewed the dancing that happens within voodoo ceremonies as primitive and beneath her, there would be an enormous void in dance.[23] Instead of allowing her perception of art or her own art to be determined by a schema not of her own making, she reclaimed Miranda's meaning. Such is the case when Jenkins's documentary spotlights former Magic City dancer Gigi Maguire. Viewers see a woman who has moved on from Magic City to open her own business, PoleFanAddicts, a fitness studio where aerobic activity and workout routines are created around stripping culture and dance moves. Viewers get to see Gigi direct a class on the "stripper bop" before hearing her testimony about being a former headliner and bartender at Magic City for about five years. PoleFanAddicts, however, allows her to establish a venue where she teaches "pole fitness, booty bounce, sweat dance, and pole parties for any occasion" (*Power of Pussy*). She creates a critical literacy around her techniques and utilizes performance-to-pedagogy method. Gigi's students at PoleFanAddicts, however, are not considered clients or johns even though they are customers. Just as Dunham challenged both anthropology and dance with her research-to-performance method, Gigi's pole-fitness studio and Monáe's and Rihanna's music videos also express this same understanding. They provide a method for studying black women's dance that differs from burlesque or theater. Black women audience and patrons in strip clubs critically challenge modes of analysis of black women's sexual expression for money as work alone, and theorize the aesthetics and space with movement as opposed to words. Such a threat does not go unnoticed by those seeking to profit from women's art.

At Sunset Strip, one of the few black-owned and oldest strip clubs in Indianapolis, Indiana, a handwritten sign reads "All Female Customers: No Dancing" and "If you have on less than appropriate attire or are 'scantily' dressed you will be refused entry." Women patrons have been escorted out of the club for dancing while scantily or fully dressed. Ironically, Sunset Strip, unlike some other clubs, allows women in without male accompaniment and has a visible lesbian and bisexual clientele and workforce. The sign with its rules about dancing and dress, however, serves as a deployment of power and consideration of violence in the sex wars and demonstrates the time lag and difference of rhythm between men and women. The need for these rules also indicates that women on stage and in the audience accept the dances in the club as valuable beyond men's consumption of them, and although the women at Sunset Strip are not professional dancers who have theorized in words, they do move in accordance with Dunham's stated elements of dance. They continue to dance to their own rhythm, not keeping time with a work society that deems them as either customer or performer, and the establishment that would market itself as on time and in time with today's black (wo)man has to mark and make legible performances in order to contain and order them. Patrons and dancers alike participate in dismantling systems of knowledge that segregate work and play, art as spiritual enlightenment, and art as objects of consumption. However, the regulation of space and aesthetics has happened outside of Sunset Strip, specifically with regard to race and culture.

Despite the designations of street art and performance, the valuation of its images are never quite ethically and morally attuned to Western civilization to make it simply art, and never as aesthetically pleasing to make it an object or performance worth collecting, buying, stealing, or heralding as artistic expression in concert halls, theaters, museums, and galleries.[24] Fanon's always-useful consideration of spontaneity conceptualizes why stripping has not been classified as a form of dance that is artistic, although capitalism has designated it as worthy of study. This is not because there are no skills involved, but because no formalized school of thought has been accredited.

Toward a Black Stripper Aesthetic

From ballet to break dancing, why do upper-class white men and women get to dictate what is art, work, or culture? Why must sex-negative approaches be the only viable and valid research methodologies for sexual cultures? The pole is to the stripper what the tap shoe is to a tap dancer. Currently, black strippers are students of various forms of dance, including hip-hop dance as Thomas DeFrantz has defined it when he explains, "[W]e can understand how dance is performative, mirroring the way in which speech may be equated with action. Dance movements convey speech-like qualities which contain meaning beyond the formal aesthetics, shapes and sequences of movement detailed by the body in motion" (66). DeFrantz's work on hip-hop dance allows others to think beyond just break dancing, which has been so extremely imagined as masculine. Black women dancers in strip clubs have been relegated to an unauthorized and illegitimate division of the hip-hop dance tradition, but they consistently make the black beat visible.

During *Power of Pussy,* Jenkins moves us from Gigi Maguire's small business to the locker room of Magic City where we are introduced to another dancer, twenty-two-year-old Callie (Cali), who moved from California to Atlanta and has been dancing at Magic City for a little under a year. She begins her explanation of why she works at Magic City by discussing issues from the minimum wage to the lack of family in the area should she need help. Callie then explains, "The club hires you. They give you the rules and they put you on the floor. . . . There's no training session. Nobody tells you how to dance, how to interact with the clientele, what to say, what to do . . . you learn by watching. You learn how to dance by watching the girls on stage" (*Power of Pussy*). While novices may assume that exhibiting nude and naked bodies is the extent of what these women should do and can make money from, the women actually have another narrative, one not recognized by critics who only study stripping as a form of sex work.

In another scene from *Power of Pussy,* viewers watch Snack Pak, a trio comprised of Gigi, Virgo, and Simone, practice and formulate routines. Jenkins interweaves footage of Gigi proclaiming, "Being a stripper isn't just getting on stage and shaking your ass. There's more money than stage money, but when you have a background in gymnastics, technical dance, it helps your stage presence a little more" (*Power of Pussy,* part 2). As they try out a particularly difficult routine, Virgo climbs the pole until she reaches the top, then Simone climbs and maneuvers her body below Virgo's, then stretches and planks her body on the pole before Virgo lowers herself down in a sitting position on Simone's thighs still wrapped around the pole. She swings her legs as they slide down the pole together. At the end of the successful routine, Virgo proclaims, "We gone call that the swing set." What follows are other pole moves that they also name: "the Bicycle, Sideways, the Bench Press, United We Stand, the Pack Back, the P-90." We learn that they name their moves based on "whatever it looks like, or however they [we] felt when . . . doing it." Dancer Virgo, who earlier informed viewers of her background training in ballet, theorizes about the booty clap/pop: "Didn't nobody teach us how to do it. We had to observe. See what's going on and you gotta practice it. You just know that your thighs are going in . . . and it's an ankle movement" (*Power of Pussy*). Thighs going in and ankle movement denote the simultaneous isolation and movement of specific body parts. More instruction is provided on technique in part 2, and by the end of part 3, there remains little doubt to the artistry, in addition to work, of these dancers. But these moves are also memories. Gigi's and Virgo's comments are relevant to the new dancers hired, but I am suggesting that they also apply to women who might come to watch other women dance. The memories and lessons, however, are more than self-objectification.

More Than Pussy-Popping on a Handstand: Dancing in and out of Gender

Black women's dance in the strip club reminds us that sexuality is a site of memory, as opposed to a history of violence and terror. As Dunham tells us, "Alone or in concert man dances in his various selves and his emotions and his dance becomes a communication" (262). Dunham's use of "dances in" signals a different grammar or order of knowledge about dance—dance as possession (of self and others). If one attends to kinesthetic energy, movement, and communal ecstasy, then dance as neutral sexuality becomes a mechanism for escaping the colonial binaries of gender and inventing sacred subjectivity from unmarked performances. As Peggy Phelan explains:

> By locating a subject in what cannot be reproduced within the ideology of the visible, I am attempting to revalue a belief in subjectivity and identity which is not visibly representable. . . . *Unmarked* examines the implicit assumptions about the connections about representational visibility and political power which have been a dominant force in cultural theory. (1)

There are marked and unmarked performances happening between women and men in the strip club, but Phelan returns us to highlighting interactions between female dancers and patrons as unmarked performances between a higher immaterial self and a material subject matter. When we foreclose on any imaginative practice, sexual or otherwise, what dated worldview and systems of oppression are we enabling? The unmarked performances occurring in strip clubs are exactly why women can be thrown out of strip clubs for dancing or denied admittance without a male escort. Unmarked performances are acts of possessing multiple genders that critique patriarchal systems of gender using movement and the haptic instead of discourse.

Dance in black sexual cultures is not a one-way linear exchange. It involves collaboration between several participants taking on different roles who agree to participate in communal fantasy making that has become obsolete in the era of organized religion's displacement of the orgy cult. Understanding dance as ancestral rootedness and dance performance as a site of memory, Robert Farris Thompson explains, "There is further evidence, on this point, centered on the notion that the ancestors, in ways varying with every culture, continue their existence within the dancer's body. They created the steps, the dancer moves, in part to bring alive their name" (*African Art in Motion*, 28). Party aesthetics reminds us to pay attention not only to the marked performances by those on "stage" but also the unmarked performances by those not onstage. Certain forms of black dance evoke gender and sexual difference at the metaphysical rather than biopolitical level, and when some of these forms have occurred in what might be considered profane or obscene spaces, the metaphysical promise has been ignored.

Irrespective, dance is a superpower rooted in the androgynous nature of spirits according to Gottschild, who insists that

> any dance can capture the spirit. It is not a matter of what a dance is about—the what—but the dancing body's performance, the living dance in the present moment—the how—that is the essential ingredient. Nevertheless, there are certain movement techniques and motifs that help to harbor spirit. (260)

Gottschild provides a means of looking at a stripper's dance outside of moral narratives about sexuality and work because she relies upon Africanisms where the sacred and profane can exist in accord with each other. Such ideals reverberate elsewhere. Dance within certain black spiritual initiations provides maneuverability around the usual discourses of erotic performance in sexual leisure because dance is, as Dunham and Gottschild have shown it to be—psychic materiality and communication. We need not read strippers as voodoo priestesses, mambos, or horsemen being ridden by particular loas to translate the benefits derived from their dance, but we can access how black women dancers conceptualize their dancing as in and out of gender to overcome elements of sexual colonization and carry on black funk freakery's sexual magic and neutral sexuality. At these profane sites of memory, neutral sexuality persists, and Perniola reminds us that neutral sexuality "emancipates sexuality from nature and entrusts it to artifice, which opens up a world where the difference between the sexes, form, appearance, beauty, age, and race no longer matter" (3).

In *Shakedown, Power of Pussy,* and numerous performances of dom stud strippers, the unmarked performances of dancing in and out of gender are only made visible because of audience participation as it intersects with movement of the dancer. Clothes and removal of clothes are marked performances, while movement of the body captures interior and unmarked hapticality. For example, in one series of YouTube videos centering on EZodiac the Entertainer, a traveling stud stripper from Texas, these unmarked performances highlight androgyny in varied and unexpected ways. In one taped performance, EZodiac flips, bounce-grinds across the floor, strips off her pants, and works the audience into a tipping frenzy before removing her sports bra. It is clear that even if a ceremony has not been announced, the spirits have come out to play. I have witnessed EZodiac's dancing of marked and unmarked performances, with its specific acrobatic bounce, staring, and rhythmic isolation of gluteal muscles, elsewhere without the stylistic intricacies of masculine performance. Just as high-femme Snack Pak defies gravity with their bounce and pole dances for Magic City, EZodiac demonstrates the mutability of the body to perform many genders. The black arts have taught us that spirits are androgynous, and when presented with a funky beat they can possess and ride anybody.

EZodiac's performance captures the affect of freak's androgynous gender, and the dancer is being ridden as well as riding its human and spirit audience. The performance of masculinity remains even after the emcee's sonic iteration, "The titties is out bitch." The spectacle of exposed breasts speaks to the performer's creativity and art of illusion, as well as the stud's skills and strength as a dancer. As Leilah Weinrub admits of her filming of stud strippers at the Shakedown, "The interesting evolution of Shakedown has been that studs strip and that phenomenon is gaining more popularity. There is still some tension about being completely nude and a stud/masculine of center/trans [or androgynous]. But I'd love to encourage it, 'cuz the girls definitely want to see it."[25] Yet, the spectacle of a stud's nudity cannot erase the way the dance moves blur what a male or female body should or can do. Therefore, these aesthetics in the strip club have to be contextualized outside of the Western gaze and examined through another lens in which we understand black dance as linked with an elevation of androgyny. In several clips, EZodiac performs for a mixed audience of queer men and women. These are the political economies of black space where gender segregation may not be efficient, but the transaesthetics of black dance as something that defies gender and sexual categories of the public ordering of sex and gender remain in the movement, the bodies, and the eroticized interactions between dancer and audience. However stud or butch a performer might be standing still, dance as neutral sexuality refuses binaries of butch and femme. The same can be said for high femme women in male and lesbian strip clubs.

During Neshe Entertainment's First Fridays in Jacksonville, one of the high-femme strippers, Eden, would seductively grind against butches and studs, but she would then move toward an unsuspecting femme and lift her up or flip her over, and then simulate cunnilingus or anal rimming before maneuvering down to simulate missionary and/or scissor copulation. As opposed to pussy-popping on a handstand, this was Eden's go-to move, a crowd-pleaser rooted in the spontaneous nature of the music's beat. Eden's performance, like that of other black femme strippers, incorporates an unmarked performance of the tomboy. She was soft, sexy, and feminine but capable of dexterity, strength, and athleticism. Tomboy is a gender category, rather than a script, that has allowed women to escape the categorizations of hot women, fast girls, and hypersexual women for eons. Black women's performance of tomboy in popular culture, like hip-hop's b-girl, is not a script or type that gets much attention because its roots are in performances of androgyny that are more felt than seen.

The *tomboy* has been defined as having characteristics or behaviors attributed to the gender role of boy or males, from wearing masculine clothing to taking up activities that are physical and athletic in nature. Of course, the pervasive debates about tomboys or androgyny attend to the visual manifestations of appearance or dress, but black women in strip clubs as dancers and patrons return us to an interior expression of self articulated in black funk freakery where notions of androgyny have to do with race, work, play, and art, as well as gender. Historically, it has been more affectively stylistic than other cultural traditions. Rihanna, Aaliyah, Ciara, and the women of Magic City use the term *tomboy* in reference to themselves, despite their performance of hyperfemininity. They do so because *butch, stud,* and the like cannot convey what *tomboy* does in black cultural traditions.

Tomboy is a particular term of youth often conflated with other adult gender roles that are taken up by women, but tomboy's link with androgyny stems from its roots in play rather than a woman's investment in domesticity and work society. The behavior of separating work from play, or from understanding men as privileged enough to do both and maintain separation, continues heteropatriarchy and male supremacy. Androgyny demands something else. Some black women use the term to read themselves as antiwork beings in everyday play centered on human and inhuman forces, people, and objects. An androgyny informed by the dismantling of the boundary between work and play looks different in specific cultures, and to read women in the strip clubs as mere performers of hyperfemininity misses all of the ways in which gender and sexuality can be undone by the imagination.

In *Power of Pussy,* dancer Simone enlightens viewers about her skills of guise and artifice, and confesses, "I used to wear my hair a certain type of way. I used to not know nothing about lashes. I was like a real tomboy just like her [Callie]. So when I saw her I just kind of took to her and told her about her eyebrows, makeup." Still, this tomboyishness does not only refer to makeup and hair but to physical abilities and presence as well. Simone continues, "Like I said, I'm a tomboy . . . so I know how to perform I guess, but I don't know how to seduce," and then she shimmies as if to equate the motion with the affect of seduction. The shimmying motion of seduction that she does, as she notes, is not what she does on the pole. When different members of Snack Pak explain their artistry, the women tend to describe themselves as tomboys.

Later, Virgo the ballerina explains, "I'm just crazy and wild. Honestly, I know how to climb poles 'cause I use to climb trees and jump fences . . . so I just go. I just go" (*Power of Pussy*). Virgo's "I just go" might as well be "I just play," as opposed to "I just go do this domestic work for the neoliberal nation or the black nation." The tomboy serves as an unmarked performance in the strip club that is erased by the marked performance of hyperfemininity and the prioritizing of a male gaze. Eventually, every tomboy confronts the false fixed realities that are gender roles and sexual identities, and that confrontation showcases why these strippers should be recognized as referencing an alternative gender that can also illuminate and intervene on other performances of masculinity and femininity that have arisen from biological theories of gender. Indeed, Virgo's words and the names given to Snack Pak's dance moves expose the documentary's contradictions about professionalism and work as separate from the play or antiwork activity that each woman does with dance movement. Black women patrons recognize and embrace these unmarked performances, memories of play.

Although ample scholarship has detailed black women's participation in sexual economies and labor as the failure of both feminism and black liberation rhetoric, and therefore the success of capitalism and continued oppression of black women, I have argued that some black communities have generationally insisted upon and accepted an unacknowledged black women's uncredited intertwinement of philosophy and sexuality—the orgy theory, party aesthetics, neutral sexuality, and demonic grounds as a will to remember sexuality as a site of memory. Black men and women's continued participation in sexual culture, as well as representations of black women's sex work, stands as both an experiential and theoretical critique of the pitfalls/misadventures of nationalism and nationalist parties as it relates to gender, sexuality, and work society. The participants in sexual leisure culture—consumers and performers—have shown that black orgy's transaesthetics are as important as human ethics.

Today, Vegas showgirls and burlesquers are said to perform while strippers work hard for the money. In *Bodies That Matter*, Judith Butler reminds us of some basic structures of gender performativity where "the regulatory norms of 'sex' work in a performative fashion to constitute the materiality of bodies and, more specifically, to materialize the body's sex, to materialize sexual difference in the service of the consolidation of the heterosexual imperative" (13). The aesthetics created that would have us differentiate between burlesquer and ballerina or burlesquer and stripper are not artistic aesthetics alone; they are the regulatory norms of sex working individuals into a specific gender. When we differentiate between the two art forms and privilege one over the other, it is not only a way to draw boundaries around cultural aesthetics but also to maintain a particular gender hierarchy and sexual imperialism.

The decisive boundaries that have been drawn by cultural historians and legislation, however, cannot stand firm when we understand sex-as-art as the antithesis to sex-as-work. When incorporating sex-as-art, we begin to fully comprehend strippers as not simply objects of sexual desire but another gender altogether. Further, the collaboration between the audience and dancers in such spaces potentially allows for sacredly profane communal erotics that employ rhythm as an inhuman force that sweeps away time's barrier between the living and the dead. Are such inhuman forces only at work in sacred spaces of religious institutions, or as Essex Hemphill and E. Patrick Johnson have theorized, might we find these "ceremonies" or "feel the spirit" in secular spaces organized around sexual leisure?[26] Black women's patronage of strip clubs suggests the clubs as profane sites of memory for beings still becoming funky black freaks. This is but one of the new metaphysics of political struggle.

Black Trans Narratives, Sex Work, and the Illusive Flesh

When writer and activist Janet Mock discusses her past work life, which includes clothing stores, boutiques, and fast-food establishments, she also acknowledges her sex work experience, claiming "Yeah there is the shame attached . . . and the stigma attached to being a sex worker, but there's also the other things I got from that . . . a sense of community, of sisterhood, resiliency, resources, strength . . . it was like our underground railroad."[1] Mock's sentiment about her efforts brings us full circle to black men's and women's practices around sexuality and work, but it also understands the question of freedom as one about how we inhabit our bodies and what such habitation means for how we think through these questions of work and sex. As a pivotal figure in the current era of digital media, Mock has been an activist, author, speaker, and blogger who has helped radically redefine the conversation on transgender activism and visibility as it relates to race. Mock understands her antiwork activities around gender and sexuality as divorced from necropolitics or, as C. Riley Snorton and Jin Haritaworn have named it, *trans necropolitics*.

According to Stryker, Currah, and Moore, "'Transing,' in short, is a practice that takes place within, as well as across or between, gendered spaces. It is a practice that assembles gender into contingent structures of association with other attributes of bodily being, and that allows for their reassembly" (13). However, these considerations of transing and gender are often theorized through material and physical articulations of gender authorized by medical communities with little concern for race and culture. Snorton and Haritaworn have adroitly covered the political and intellectual in their assessment of the way racialized bodies function in a trans necropolitics where the "discursive construction of the transgender body, and particularly the transgender body of color—as unnatural creates the precise moment where we as scholars, critics, and activists might apprehend a biopolitics of everyday life where the transgender body of color is the unruly body, which only in death can be transformed into the service of state power" (68). Their analysis of Tyra Hunter's death, and any future analysis of the death of Islan Nettles and the criminalization of Cece McDonald, corroborates the essay's thesis. Thus, even written and authorized mainstream narratives about being transgender by someone such as Janet Mock could use some assistance with filling in the silences and blanks produced by Western embodiment and colonial histories of empire, gender, and sexuality in political and public spheres.

In accord with Snorton and Haritaworn's truth about state power and unruly bodies, I examine how two writers, Toni Newman and Red Jordan Arobateau, record commentary and performances informed by a different nexus of embodiment and intersectional issues consistently marginalized in transgender scholarship and activism in the United States. In Arobateau's novel *The Big Change (Confessions of a Metaphysician),* the narrator's assessment of the protagonist explains gendered spaces as more metaphysical than physical, saying to readers, "You thought he should battle his narcotic habits? But actually he was engaged in a far worse battle. For his inner self to remain alive! For her to live" (*Big Change,* 13). Likewise, Toni Newman's autobiography, *I Rise: The Transformation of Toni Newman,* attends to transing as a spiritual journey when she offers, "The transformation as a black transgender was a solo journey for me and many, many others. I went deep within myself, found my spiritual identity, and rose" (211). These black writers' fabrication of the transgender body serves as a spiritual decolonization to cease the continuous separation of spirit from body that Western embodiment perpetrates and that imperialists manipulated to enslave and terrorize.

In their rough, unpolished, and explicit written narratives about sex work, these authors provide narrative representations of how unruly bodies can sometimes refuse to be transformed into the service of state power. They critically and creatively document the effect of capitalism and Western inventions of gender on the living, while astutely tending to the supernatural affect of the illusive flesh belonging to those in the afterlife. Illusive flesh, as I explain in my expansion of Robert Hayden's poetic phrase, serves as a counterphilosophy to embodiment about what the transaesthetic experience and representation of Otherly human bodies means to forms of life and being that exceed the biological. With black political traditions incapable of challenging the assumed materiality of sex and gender in the West, these discursive practices join Yoruba-influenced spirituality in the United States as black traditions willing to theorize illusive flesh as a form of metaphysical gender, less attached to the notion of a unified body.

Currently, there exist multiple types of transness: Transing has resulted in transracial, transdiscipline, transsexual, transgendered, transnational, transglobal, transmedia, transhuman, and other trans- strategies for resisting the destructive

[margin annotation: spirit/body]

[margin annotation: trans-]

transworld identity

mapping of bodies, knowledge, and cultural products. Each form of transing maintains a philosophy about identity and identity politics that may be similar to or different from the other.[2] These writers, however, depict transgender subjects and characters countering the biopolitics of everyday life with a different definition of what it means to be human, resistance to work society, and grammars and aesthetics culled from what has been theorized as transworld identity. Transworld identity was conceived in the discipline of philosophy by Alvin Plantinga during the 1970s, and the concept was later taken up in literary theory from the late 1990s to the present in regards to science fiction and postmodernist literature.[3] Plantinga's work asked, "Why, then, should we suppose that an individual is confined to one world, that you and I, for example, exist in this world and this world only" (74). Transworld identity—identity across possible worlds—assumes identity as more metaphysical than social. Hence, it displaces the unified social body or transgender identity that the state produces. This theory of transworld identity also challenges materialist approaches to creating transgender subjectivity in which contemporary theories about transgender writing traditions equate transgender texts as reflective of an underlying medical narrative. My use of *transworld identity* throughout enables me to highlight how Newman and Arobateau also confront the fetishism placed on cisgender and transgender erotic relations by dominant social paradigms upholding work society and domesticity without foreclosing on the material benefits that improve the economic realities of some transgender and transsexual subjects.

As with other chapters in *Funk the Erotic*, I am interested in figures or characters engaged in antiwork politics, subjects like Lucy Hicks Anderson, a twice-married brothel owner in the early 1900s who was tried for perjury for living as a woman for twenty-five years. Anderson's life and living, beginning in the late 1800s, predate politicized identities of transgender or transsexual. She reminds those interested in writing about transgender lives that looking within the margins of multiple communities might mean recovering a transgender subject who is not the productive citizen of transgender activism—the sex worker's life and living in nonfiction and fiction. These representations confront readers with a historical materialism similar and dissimilar to Marlon Riggs's and Roderick Ferguson's drag-queen prostitute who helps form a critique of liberal capitalism.[4] This is a life and living whose most prominent records appear in scandal sheets, police reports, blogs, and newspapers where there are no truths possible, only many fictions about cisgender and transgender lives.

The confession of Hot 97 hip-hop DJ Mister Cee in 2013 exemplifies how what could be called uses of the erotic in black America—soul and hip-hop—appear to have reached their limitations in representing black affect and bodies. Mister Cee confesses, "I know I'm still in denial because I know that I love women—any woman that's been with me knows that I love women—but occasionally I get the urge to have fellatio with a transsexual: a man that looks like a woman."[5] Mister Cee's confession, and responses to it, reveal a conundrum that transing across biopoliticized gendered spaces cannot solve, in which some black people still struggle with their facts of being, rather than the facts of blackness, and in which pathologies invalidate the material needs and self-determination of transgender individuals when they meet up with the immateriality of desire felt by cisgender folk, a desire that serves as evidence of illusive flesh's existence. These highly publicized incidents and responses to them signal the need for a funking of the erotic that can overcome transphobia and internalized transphobia. Some writers are now theorizing transattraction and transorientation for individuals attracted to transgender men or women.[6] Yet even these differentiations between cisgender and transgender attraction do not provide enough of a shift to change thinking since the same problems of embodiment remain. These are all crises created by sexual and spiritual colonization that funk's transaesthetics can manage and convert.

Mock crafted a beautiful response to the controversy surrounding Mister Cee's statement, and it demonstrates why transworld identity and attention to the spiritual matters:

> We, as a society, have not created a space for men to openly express their desire to *be* with trans women. Instead, we shame men who have this desire, from the boyfriends, cheaters and "chasers" to the "trade," clients, and pornography admirers. We tell men to keep their attraction to trans women secret, to limit it to the internet, frame it as a passing fetish or transaction. In effect, we're telling trans women that they are only deserving of secret interactions with men, further demeaning and stigmatizing trans women.[7]

As opposed to other such controversies involving gender-variant sex workers and cisgender men, Mister Cee's confession and Mock's statement moves us forward.[8]

A centering of funk within political activism directed toward transgender communities of color could better ensure the survival and well-being of black transgender individuals as well as instigate a shift in how transgender and cisgender folk engage self and others in erotic relationships. The black transgender prostitute speaks to the future of how black culture will have to engage various economic and social formations. Writers' depictions of transgender sex workers expose that it will take a critique of liberal capitalism and Western embodiment, in addition to an acknowledgment of their link to each other, to create the kind of society Mock calls for. However, before the critique of liberal capitalism and Western embodiment in these forms can be broached, I want to explain why nonfiction, fiction, and other creative forms such as pornography are essential to growing black transactivist movements and studies.

Self-Definition and Transworld

Identity and subjectivity are acts of creation whose aesthetic is logic. Being and becoming, however, require an act of creating the self shaped by transaesthetics. M. Jacqui Alexander's question, "But what are these energies or forces? What metaphysical principles do they codify?"[9] provides a way of thinking of spirituality outside of fixed binaries because energy and forces seldom adhere to one specific form. Religion may require an institution, but spirituality does not always manifest in institutions, architectural spaces, and sacred texts that require mediation or a mediator. It also comes and codifies in forms of artistic expression that can go unmediated. Black transmen and transwomen have been marginalized in mainstream transgender movements and in black political movements, while recognition of black transgender cultural production and artistic movements has focused on blues/jazz culture, documentary filmmaking, and autobiography.[10] Memoirs and fiction are a continuation of the tradition, but memoirs reflecting on what has been labeled as sex work can be as important an element of self-definition to various transgender folk as surgery has been in certain narratives. Within those products, we might discern a crucial signifying difference that both specifies a black trans movement and transes white trans movements.

Funk's ontology of being leads to a transworld identity/identification that has, like Gayle Salamon's *Assuming a Body*, theorized trans(gender) embodiments more broadly. Plantinga would postulate that "the notion of transworld identity . . . is the notion that the same object exists in more than one possible world (with the actual world treated as one of the possible worlds)" (73). Although this definition of *transworld* more readily aligns with *transgalactic*, scholars were willing to submit that the major problem with the definition of transworld identity in general was one of perception. As Plantinga explained in reference to critiques meant to dismiss transworld identity:

> The first thing to note about the objection outlined . . . is that it seems to arise out of a certain *picture* or *image*. We imagine ourselves somehow peering into another world. . . . Now perhaps this picture is useful in certain respects; in the present context, however, it breeds nothing but confusion. (77)

Plantinga's explanation of how we may or may not recognize ourselves in another world confirms the way social identity relies too much on the ocular and scopic. These markers of identity form a world-bound identity—identity that operates in a very specific temporal and geographically fixed reality. This is what transgender subjectivity based on the metaphysical opposes most of all, which is why transworld identity matters. Outside of philosophy, the concept of identity across worlds was facilitating alternative models of being and embodiment.

Black funk perfected the concept of transworld identity, if not the term itself, in ways that deserve assessment in my concerns of gender and sexuality. The concept of transworld identity originates in fields outside of race, gender, and sexuality studies, but its existence precedes its presence/naming in language. For example, Randolph's practice of sexual magic could be said to have arisen from his self-definition of being a clairvoyant and sexual magician, titles garnered from his belief in Afro-Asian concepts of being. The McKoys' articulation of their conjoined bodies as marvels is another example. The concept of transworld identity affords critics the ability to examine black transgender narrative and subjects and to navigate around the limits of identity politics and the presence of ethnocentrism in models meant to quantify or represent transgender people. Transworld identity consistently provides a new worldview when the old one is attacked or colonized. In "1492: A New World View," Sylvia Wynter demonstrates the destructiveness of world-bound identity by arguing that the way Europeans imagine the world shapes European concepts of what it means to be human and therefore Other. Wynter shows that Native Americans, Asians, and Africans did not necessarily share the belief that the world was flat, that there was nothing else out there, or that they were black, Indian, or Asian. As a result of indigenous humanism, they did possess a transworld identity, and this identity allowed violently dispersed communities to survive shifts in language, religion, displacement from land, gender conformity, and sexual terror.

In his *Introduction to Africana Philosophy,* Lewis Gordon details various forms of African humanism. Explaining that humanism was not brought into the African world from the outside, Gordon observes, "Such an error is a function of interpretations of humanism that locate its emergence in the European Renaissance and subsequent modern world. If we define humanism as a value system that places priority on the welfare, worth, and dignity of human beings, its presence in precolonial African religious and philosophical thought can easily be found" (186). Gordon devises that African humanism consists of indigenous humanism, and in accord with Gordon, philosopher Kwame Gyekye provides one of many examples in which we see Africana indigenous humanism as a school of thought that considers identity as matter of being and becoming:

> The Akan conception of the person . . . is both dualistic and interactionist. . . . [F]rom the point of view of the Akan metaphysics of the person and the world in general, all of this seems to imply that a human being is not just an assemblage of flesh and bone, that he or she is a complex being who cannot be completely explained by the same laws of physics used to explain inanimate things, and that our world cannot simply be reduced to physics. (200)

These philosophes existed throughout precolonial African societies.[11] Gordon also explains that the remaining African humanism emerged in response to imperialism and colonialism: Christian and Muslim humanism, the secular humanism of Cheikh Diop (historicist humanism), Léopold Senghor (poeticizing tradition of humanism), and Frantz Fanon (combination of historicism and poeticizing) (188–93). After Fanon, I would argue, a sonic tradition of posthumanism depicting a transworld identity surfaces in the work of black musicians.

Sun Ra's movie *Space Is the Place* demonstrates how he creates a whole new mythology for himself and potentially other black people, beginning in space and presenting black existence on earth from 1943 to the 1960s and into the future of space again, literally producing a recursive whatever of blackness that begins elsewhere and never ends. In one scene, he lectures to a classroom of black students about the myth of humanity. While the camera pans the room, viewers see young people against a wall backdrop composed of pictures of former slaves and civil rights and black power leaders juxtaposed with Sun Ra's spectacular, intergalactic funkiness that aesthetically borrows from ancient Egyptian spectacular modes of dress and veers away from black respectability and cool posing before he proclaims:

> How do you know I'm real? I'm not real. I'm just like you. You don't exist in this society. If you did exist, your people wouldn't be seeking equal rights. You're not real. If you were you'd have some status among the nations of the world. So we are both myths. I do not come to you as reality. I come to you as the myth. Because that is what black people are, myths. (Sun Ra and Smith, *Space Is the Place*)

Sun Ra deconstructs the social construction of race, but his words are also useful to questions of gender and embodiment since they highlight that ontologies of being can direct black transgender subjectivity and future movements. It is only in recognizing one's mythical status that the process of making inventive futures can begin. Black art, music, and culture, then, is not simply representation of a subject and object in the world for a celestial being. It is matter, energy, and forces to be codified into a method for creating new worlds and ways of being, and it emulates what Lewis Gordon notes as indigenous humanism and what I note as illusive flesh for its transworld being.

Illusive Flesh of Light as the Haptic Aesthetics of the Undercommon

For the past decade alone, transgender theory has interrogated the works of Sigmund Freud, Paul Schindler, and Didier Anzieu for their ideas about body materiality and ego. Theorists offer relevant foundations for thinking through gendered embodiment with little to no consideration of how white supremacy influences such embodiment. Skin ego is an extension of Freud's work on the ego, and a concept in which psychoanalytical critic Didier Anzieu theorizes subjectivity: "to be one's self is first of all to have a skin of one's own and secondly, to use it as a space in which one can experience sensations" (51). Skin ego becomes the basis of Jay Prosser's theories of transgender subjectivity and narratives in in his groundbreaking work, *Second Skins*. Prosser argues of skin's ego's importance to transgender subjectivity: "Subjectivity is not just about having a physical skin; it's about feeling one owns it: it's a matter of psychic investment of self in skin. . . . How does one function without feeling surrounded by a proper body? How does the subject survive without a skin of his or her own?" (73). However, this particular approach to individual subjectivity cannot be sufficient for descendants of the shipped.

I do not need to fully analyze why both Anzieu and Prosser cannot fully escape ethnocentrism in their rhetorics of materiality. For when Harney and Moten explore logisticality and the shipped, we learn not only of logistics' ambitions to "connect bodies, objects, affects, information, without subjects, without the formality of subjects" (92), but we also learn that the shipped were not just human capital and labor. They were "property that reproduced and realized itself" (92). They were flesh, and flesh moves and transports beings with or without human subjectivity. To begin a study of black transgender subjectivity in the skin or body ego is to accept the Western capitalist individuation and psychoanalytic methods that have literally and historically written black slaves who wanted to be free as suffering from the "horrible disease" of drapetomania.[12]

Instead, we must begin with embodiment as Gayle Salamon's *Assuming a Body* does in its development of bodily ego as a correction of Prosser's work: "The concept of the bodily ego is of particular use in thinking transgender because it shows that the body of which one has a 'felt sense' is not necessarily continuous with the physical body as it is perceived from the outside" (Salamon, 14). Although the concept of bodily ego is not of use for me here, Salamon's idea to look at embodiment has significant ramifications for black transgender bodies that may be utilizing different systems of embodiment derived from Africanisms, the experience of being the shipped, or entirely new spiritual myths. Harney and Moten's argument that "logistics somehow know that it is not true that we do not yet know what flesh can do" (93) speaks to how being shipped alters the sense of embodiment. As they theorize, we know what flesh can do, and we know that it cannot be managed. The resistance of black bodies has taught us more lessons about the transaesthetic value of flesh and not bodies.

The seemingly conflicting experiences about flesh, as opposed to skin, presented to us through the fictional characters Baby Suggs in Toni Morrison's novel *Beloved* and Nunu in Haile Gerima's film *Sankofa* reveal that through the black imaginary that writes slavery and neoslavery alike, we come face to face with a fact of blackness in Western embodiment and the human: slaves and Jim Crow black persons possessed no skin or body ego. Baby Suggs intimates to her congregation in a natural setting, "In this here place, we flesh; flesh that weeps, laughs; flesh that dances on bare feet in grass."[13] Yet Nunu's experiences of sexual violence has her proclaim, "They can never do nothing to my soul. This flesh that's all. If not because of this flesh and you know this is the thing they have on us."[14] Morrison's and Gerima's neoslave narratives capture black communal narratives about flesh. They speak of a sensory experience derived from interior movements felt on, under, and beyond the skin. Morrison's and Gerima's use of flesh instead of skin engages different definitions of Man and embodiment, and the shifting meaning of flesh in and out of slavery demonstrates that flesh has several histories and narratives, some of them human, scientific, or cultural, some of them not. Most significant, though, is that flesh has no ego. It can be collective and communal, a thing that feels, or an encasement. Whether one psychically invests in it like Baby Suggs or divests from it like Nunu depends entirely upon an interrogation of what it means to be whatever one desires to be at a particular time, rather than man or woman or black and white in the Americas forever. Black flesh is illusive.

That flesh can be illusive in this manner dictates why a black diasporic styling of identity and subjectivity away from biopower substitutes aesthetics as formative guideposts for dealing with the confines of Western embodiment. In positing the limits of Western embodiment that Sun Ra, Morrison, and Gerima grapple with in very different ways, poet Robert Hayden's illusive flesh of light suggests how we can see black funk's move away from the skin as a styling of self beyond Man that depends upon the haptic aesthetics and sensations felt somewhere other than the skin:

MONET'S WATERLILIES

Here space and time exist in light
the eye like the eye of faith believes.
The seen, the known
dissolve in iridescence, become
illusive flesh of light
that was not, was, forever is.

Hayden's poetics showcase art as entrée into another world, transworld identity, and being. Illusive flesh of light acts as both perception and haptic metaphor for a transaesthetic experience, as opposed to the aesthetic value and elements of art. He references light as spiritual energy and aesthetic element capable of touching and feeling, as well as changing perceptions of any form. Sensation makes human flesh illusive, and it too can generate an aesthetic experience. The concept of illusive flesh as a technology of the haptic provides a different theory of embodiment.

Too many reflections on human, alien, or Otherly human are based on a history where science and religion dominate and supplant other forms of knowledge—the creative arts. Sun Ra's music and Hayden's poetics do not remain an object for consumption alone; they become a life-support system for pre- and posthuman existence and transworld identity. So when Sun Ra claims, "The music that I'm playing, that's my other self playing. And that disturbs some people because they never gave that other self a chance. The natural self" (Sinclair, 23), he captures how an interior self formed using non-Western aesthetics counteracts public discourses and constructs of race or gender arranged out of human ethics. Likewise, Parliament-Funkadelic's performative spectacle of funk draws from black folkloric tradition with its presentation of interspecies and transworld perspective on race, sexuality, or gender. Labelle's hybrid blend of animal and space costumes, and other configurations of black bodies merged with nonhuman bodies, preceded what we might currently consider anthropomorphic transgendered individuals and their gendered embodiment. Outside of music, Samuel Delany's representation of consciousness and creativity as materiality and his merging of human and animal body parts with inorganic matter in *Empire Star* and *Babel-17* subvert the hierarchy of gender in transgender representation. So while there may not be an essential blackness or essential gender, given all of this evidence of words creating worlds, there can be an essential self according to transworld identity and transaesthetics.

Rising above the Knife: The Transaesthetics of Black Trans Being

Funk's transworld identity and transaesthetics do not occur only in science fiction and music. They reoccur throughout global black communities, as well as subcultures and communities arranged around gender and sexuality. Because of the considerations of embodiment and the political disenfranchisement that comes with race, black subjects have followed up on white human ethics with nonhuman aesthetics. Jackie Kay's employment of jazz and blues to unsilence the past of black LGBTQI histories insists that autobiography or biography can exist in various media and art forms. The publication of Toni Newman's *I Rise: The Transformation of Toni Newman* showcases black autobiography's potential to destabilize the overrepresentation and the notion of a coherent stable subject gained from surgery. Newman explains to her readers, "I was content as a pre-operative transsexual" (163). She continues, "I felt good about myself, and no longer had a war raging inside me. I was at peace. The decision to take the last step could wait another day" (164). Despite Newman's attention to pre- and postoperative states, her entire autobiography acts as a thesis for why her natural self needs the transaesthetics that are derivative of sex work—sex art. *I Rise* enunciates a black visual economy about the materiality of the body much like that expressed by a contemporary artist such as Wangechi Mutu. In one interview, Mutu speaks to how non-Western aesthetics of recycling materials, including the body, influences her work and that of South Asian artist Rina Banerjee:

> I know we share a sensitivity to certain cultures of production. We both understand how people in poor economies make things. . . . We're in love with this way of making things and we understand it—it's about being able to read material differently than one does in a thoroughly industrialized country. . . . It's about material landing in your realm, your sphere of operation, and you don't think, oh, this particular plastic is only used for certain things. (Mutu, 112)

Far from involving reincarnation, Mutu's vision of corporeal ecology implies the reusability of flesh, from cellular to anatomical, alongside the rebirth or reincarnation of souls. This repurposing of flesh does not exclude flesh outside of the human but remains inclusive of human social realities. Newman's autobiography proves that this same vision is present for black writers representing transgender experience with transworld identity.

Therefore, black fiction and nonfiction about transgender subjects who perform sex work should be read as markedly different from the transgender writing that Jay Prosser analyzes in *Second Skins*. Prosser explains:

> The autobiographical act for the transsexual begins even before the published autobiography—namely in the clinician's office where, in order to be diagnosed as transsexual, s/he must recount a transsexual autobiography. . . . Whether s/he publishes an autobiography or not, then, every transsexual, as a transsexual, is originally an autobiographer. (101)

I am not disputing Prosser's assessment that every transsexual is originally an autobiographer, but I do want to impugn the clinician's office as a privileged site and the primacy given to transmission of a legible discursive narrative of a transsexual autobiography.

Disputing Prosser's statement with the theories of transaesthetics and transworld identity is important for two reasons. First, these theories make it possible to address improper texts depicting improper subjects. They insist on these subjects as authorial presences that need not necessarily be written by institutional state apparatuses and therefore not written in standard English or published by corporate entities. Second, we should remember that literary genres have different histories, and these histories inform why and how autobiographical tropes of racialized subjects of an economically disenfranchised class might differ from white middle-class autobiographies. For even as we may accept that every transsexual, as an author, is originally an autobiographer, scholarship on slave narratives, oral histories, the dozens, and biomythographies in black literary tradition reminds

anyone that autobiography, authorial control, and tropes are often strategic ma-
nipulations to take into account differences of gender, class, nation, and sexuality
between authors and their audiences. Sometimes an autobiography is as much
fiction as fact, as much omission as revelation. What if the clinician's office is not
where we begin? What if the first recounting of oral autobiographies happens in
an elsewhere that does not require or need medical authorization? Is the clinician's office really the first time every transman or -woman recounts a transsexual
autobiography? What if it is in a priest's office, the police station, a lover's bed,
a daily prayer, or a song? Why this select spatial privileging of autobiography as
the construction of a stable subjectivity for that matter? These are questions that
expose the preferential treatment given to science and medicine in the discussion
of transgender studies.

Newman's *I Rise* uses narrative tropes from literary genres seldom associated
with transsexual narratives, mainly the slave narrative and black uplift autobiographies. It converses with intellectual works such as poetry by Maya Angelou, *The
Mis-Education of the Negro*, and *The Souls of Black Folk*. Yet, it also defies these
conventions with its depiction of southern religiosity, sex work, and transgender
sexual escapades. In the end, though, the autobiography accomplishes the goal
of intervening on white transsexual narratives by reconsidering the question of
wholeness from a transworld perspective. In closing her autobiography, Newman
concludes, "Fear controls the lives of too many black transsexuals. They purposely
keep themselves sheltered and protected. They never really mingle with society.
But as they change their bodies, they must also educate their minds so they can
be whole" (211). Just as she had done at the beginning of the book, Newman
ends with self-reflection on a wholeness not centered on a coherent body. She
continues, "The physical transformation may take years and cost a fortune, but
the mind cannot be neglected" (211). The publication of her autobiography as a
preoperative transsexual serves notice, but the material aesthetics of Newman's
autobiography confirm that there still remains little regard for stories about certain black transgender subjects.

A glossy cover of a dark brown–skinned Newman on the front belies the visible
aesthetics of a vanity press/self-published typesetting standard for the memoir.
Newman inserts pictures of herself at various stages of her life: as a male phy-
sique model and bodybuilder, dominatrix, and drag queen. These images are
not high-definition quality. Yet, the self-published nature of the book shows why
print continues to be relevant to capturing life at the margins. Despite the advent
of television, video, film ethnographies, and documentaries that highlight the
experience of female masculinity and black transmen as seen in *The Aggressives*
and *Still Black: A Portrait of Black Transmen*, as well as the success of Laverne
Cox, B. Scott, and Isis King in mainstream media, print materials continue to

be relevant to self-defined representations of black transmen and -women since they remain cheaper and easier to produce and circulate. Newman's autobiography recounts the life of a southern, effeminate, and smart being blossoming into a business professional, sex worker, and "black pre-operative transsexual, who discovers the power of knowledge and education" (213).

In any other narrative, the echo of uplift rhetoric could be detrimental. However, Newman tempers the rhetoric in several interesting ways. Before the official autobiography begins, she provides readers with a glossary of terms such as _transsexualism_ and _mistress_. These definitions allow Newman to foreshadow the autobiography's focus on shifts of gender, sensation and sexualities, work, and the blurred boundaries between each. In addition, ever aware of her lack of professional credentials, she uses an authenticating trope of black autobiography and provides readers with a foreword by a former Columbia professor. From there, Newman can begin her autobiography:

> I want everyone to respect transgenders as people and to understand why they transform their bodies. Many doctors have stated that there are psychological and mental reasons for this type of transformation. But my whole story is one of just trying to become one, become whole, and become who I really am. (ix)

Certainly, Newman's accounting of Tony and Terri uniting into Toni reiterates Prosser's theories about autobiography and transsexuality with one exception: "Reproduced in autobiography, transsexuality emerges as an archetypal story structured around shared tropes and fulfilling a particular narrative organization of consecutive stages: suffering and confusion; the epiphany of self-discovery; corporeal and social transformation/conversion; and finally the arrival 'home'— the reassignment" (101). Absent the reassignment, Newman's autobiography also possesses distinguishing strategies of storytelling that stem from black cultural traditions meant to authenticate a marginalized voice and elide the prism of Western embodiment. Newman's words sound similar to Sun Ra's statement about his natural self playing music.

Several moments in Newman's text demonstrate why becoming one, whole, or who one really is does not necessarily mean a final, coherent, and legible gendered subjectivity reached because of surgical intervention. First, Newman organizes her story in a narrative of myth that resists categorizing transsexuality as a disorder. The references to wholeness and oneness are spiritual rather than psychological. Newman offers, "My name is Toni Newman. I was born a male but soon realized I was a different bird, born in the wrong body. I had feminine qualities from my earliest age" (1). Newman's deliberate use of "different bird, born in the wrong body" is not bad writing or analogy, especially given the title of Newman's book. In choosing to avoid saying a woman born in a male body, while still acknowledging feminine qualities not ascribed to the male gender, Newman attempts to capture in words a "natural self" that exists before human categories of gender. The nonhuman parallel to a bird initiates her story.

Later, in discussing familial readings of feminine qualities, she explains that her mother "knew deep inside that [she] was a rare bird" (2) and that her father recognized that she was "unique and special" (3). Newman's descriptions of her family observations of her early femininity are discussed in reference to the family religious traditions. Her mother is a churchgoing woman. Her father is spiritual but not religious. She speaks of spirituality as shaping and influencing who she becomes throughout her life. At no point can readers escape spiritual diatribes such as "church brought relief" or "I thought if I surrendered myself completely to God, I could become normal and happy" (8). Even as Tony becomes Terri and thereafter Toni, her spiritual affirmation remains. Newman's first chapter, titled "The Beginning," offers a trajectory of discussion for effeminacy, homosexual desire, and Christianity in black community and family, not the medical community. She explains, "I told myself I needed to be stronger in my faith and not so weak in the flesh. . . . If I put God first, then I would be happy and my desire to dress like a woman and be with a man would go away" (13). Such consistent attention to the spiritual is why statements by Prosser such as "narrative is also a kind of second skin: the story the transsexual must weave around the body in order that this body may be 'read'" (101) do not do an equitable job of deciphering what is at stake for some black transsubjects writing their stories. Spiritual decolonization has to happen. For Newman, narrative has to be more than a second skin; it has to form and represent mythic being. Mythic being invests in artistic, creative energies and expressions, and they do not require proper bodies.

"How does one function without feeling surrounded by a proper body? How does the subject survive without a skin of his or her own?" asks Prosser (73). For Newman, sensation as illusive flesh and sex work as illusive flesh of light become major ways. Pleasure and sensations can be elicited without a proper body, and they can also make functional beings even in the most traumatic circumstances. When Newman reflects back on her younger self experiencing sexual desire, she introduces the traditional narrative trope of a woman in a man's body. Newman recounts, "I also realized by the age of ten I was attracted to men—but the attraction was not male-to-male. I longed to be the female, both in form and appearance. I believed I was a woman inside the wrong body. For me, the fantasy of being with a male was always associated with me dressing up as a female" (9). Newman cannot avoid the wrong-body trope of transsexual autobiography, but she also clarifies that she does not equate her gender with her sexual desires. The risk of doing so could easily have created an antisex or asexual element within the text, but Newman's details about early sexual experiences are positive and affirming of her true self.

Sexual encounters as aesthetic experiences take the place of the clinician's office. With each new sexual experience, Newman writes and rewrites herself through feelings of sexual pleasure. At age eleven, Newman's sexual trysts in drag with a fifteen-year-old boy neighbor provide what prayers and church were failing to do:

> Naked, we lay on the bed together, touching each other softly. We kissed. Our touches became harder, and soon our bodies were grinding into each other. I felt so free in that moment. Dressing in women's clothing *and* being with a man was ecstasy! I knew I was in the right zone. For that half hour, I felt like his girl. . . . After that encounter, dressing in women's clothing always made me feel happy and free. No matter how low I got, when I dressed up, I felt great. (italics mine; 10)

Newman's writing of this sex scene corroborates sexual desire and confirms gender outside of skin ego and mirror images. Her descriptions of sensation and movements against another body and within particular clothing items extricate the discursivity valued in the clinician's office. Moreover, Newman's depiction of sexuality exposes how sensation and feeling narrate transition outside of surgery and the body. It sets the tone for all of her other descriptions of sexual adventures. From elementary and high school to college, and from drag clubs to the professional world, Newman relishes the pleasure of sex and the affect of different performances made possible by a transitional body. Consequently, as the narrative progresses, Newman's descriptions vacillate between Nunu's and Baby Suggs's visions of flesh. At no point is Newman's narrative dependent on a skin ego rooted in a history of colonialism. Upon leaving to go to college, Newman writes, "In my mind, I was finally free. I did not have to pretend to be a manly man . . . I could be me . . . I had no examples to go by and no one famous that I wanted to be like. I read books and stuff, but none of the characters looked like me, a brown sissy boy" (22). Newman pointedly documents why race would be important in finding a transgender role model.

Newman's autobiography also speculates that performance is as much a symptom of transsexuality when she insists, "Later I would understand my fascination when I learned becoming a drag queen is the first step in the male-to-female transformation" (27). Newman's preoccupation with extravagant spending on clothing and descriptions of how women's clothing makes her feel true to self emphasize performative acts over confessional ones. Here we can add Newman's specific experience to what Perniola has already shown us in regard to sexuality and clothing. Change in clothing is important for producing new knowledge out of one's own perception and experience of the world. Throughout the college years, dressing in drag is linked not only with gender identity but with the sexual desires of many of Newman's lovers as well.[15] These sexual and performative experiences not only teach Newman to differentiate sexual desire from gender identity, but they also offer a strategic erotic subjectivity[16] that will embrace transition over an immobile state of being. The titles for specific chapters emphasize Newman's centering of erotic subjectivity and ideologies about the artistic materiality of black flesh: "The Fitness Years," "The Transformation Years," "The Mistress Years," and "The Erotic Professional Years." Such erotic subjectivity aids in navigating cisgender desire, the social categories of gender, and the perils of a Christian upbringing that may sometimes become barriers to acceptance of a complete but fluid identity. Art aesthetics with the body as canvas overcomes this barrier.

When Newman does realize that clothing and drag may no longer suffice as the method for self-representation, she is not in the clinician's office. After leaving a club in drag one night, she notices several women standing on a street corner, walks over, and asks what they are doing. One woman replies, "Girl, trying to make money so I can get me some hormones and stuff" (33). Newman's reaction of "They were transsexuals with tits, lovely bodies, and a strong feminine appearance. . . . I was in awe" (34) indicates a new awareness about the possibilities for altering the body. Drag performance might have given her a glimpse, but the prostitute's answer suggests a more radical possibility. Such street confessions are the critique of liberal capitalism and Western embodiment that may be absent in the clinician's office. From there, Newman aligns herself with the transsexual sex workers because of shared desires and an acceptance of feminine gender, but she also distances herself from them in several ways: "I was a college-educated business professional walking the streets, seeking my identity and the life I had always wanted among what society calls 'the lowest form of existence'" (106). Newman makes elitist statements that arise from what she presents as her elite educational background and "functional" family. She admits, "I admired these ladies and their looks, but the sacrifices they made to get there were too great for me" (43). Newman's decisions about whether to move forward with transitioning beyond the inorganic are as much about her desire to be more visibly female as about doing so while maintaining some semblance of the morals she had been taught. Here, Newman remains wholly invested in her class and religious upbringing.

Her invocation of sacrifices signifies a spirituality upheld by a spirit/flesh division that would make the selling of sex more immoral, and her decision to uphold the Christian morals of her family seems more important than her gendered embodiment. But this too is a split that will be rectified, as she continues, "Fifteen years later, I would make the same journey myself, giving up everything to become one of the transsexual ladies I had seen on the block . . . becoming one of those special ladies of the night would be [one of] the most significant and joyful moves I would ever make" (43). Echoing Mock's sentiment about sex work as liberating, Newman speaks not only of a conversion centered on gender reassignment but also of a conversion from spirit/flesh redemption to something else. Thus, it is not the inclination to change gender that is undoing Man alone;

rather, it is the very way class affects how that change might happen that undoes Man. Her work as a transsexual prostitute elicits such a description because sex work destabilizes work ethics and gender ideologies on its way to ignoring bourgeois assignments that assume sex should be for reproduction and occur within marriage.

Further, Newman's turn to sex work is not need based in the material sense. Newman's professional years are filled with economic security that comes from being a successful sales executive and later a college recruiter. She experiences a very active social life jam-packed with meeting new friends and having numerous lovers. Despite the stability of love, sex, and money, Newman continues to be unfulfilled by both her body and the way her lovers read her body because she exists in a static world while maintaining a transworld identity. Although she had the insurance and money to begin hormone therapy and perhaps surgery if she had chosen, her heteronormative life could not provide the strength of mind and consciousness that she intuited as important to being whole. She transitions from square life to street life easily and navigates both worlds when necessary.

Newman's depiction of existing in two worlds reveals multiple episodes that document cisgender men's attraction to transwomen as mentioned at the beginning of this chapter. Wanting to be more than the secret lover of white and black men who perceive her feminine dress as sexual performance, Newman begins to see why sex work matters. It demands of its subject a consciousness derived from affective aesthetics of being rather than the human ethics of a two-gendered world. She eventually begins working the streets and making money by being the fetishized object of heterosexual men and reveals,

> I recognized actors, musicians, politicians, and celebrities patrolling around looking for that special transsexual lady. They were attracted to the female form with male genitalia, and in their minds, they were heterosexual. Their visits to the block were strictly heterosexual. (125)

Newman makes no judgments about her exchanges with these married and unmarried men but confesses that these exchanges disprove assumptions about cisgender men and stereotypes of transgender women. Though she glosses over details, she does offer her own reflections to demonstrate her keen understanding of these experiences: "The harsh cold reality was that I was good for all types of sexual fantasies—but no more than that" (126). Although she refuses to romanticize her interactions with these johns, Newman does emphasize that when she begins doing dominatrix work, in addition to being more safe, discreet, and lucrative, this period was advantageous to her spiritual quest: "My feminine look and my female feelings were matched. My outer self reflected what I felt on the inside" (131). The chapter on Newman's mistress years contains the most pictorial images, and each photograph visually reiterates Newman's prior statement.

Newman's experience of being a street prostitute and dominatrix produces a new sensation from which to style her interior and exterior self that can be overlooked when the focus is only on labor. These are the affective modalities of challenging Western embodiment that various types of sex work confront, while also attending to the material realities of everyday living. During this period she has little to say about the clinician's office and her decision:

> I had always thought I would have my penis removed, as most transsexuals wanted. But I was learning that the post-operative stage came with uncertainties, and no guarantees. I had talked to a number of post-operative transsexuals, and none felt their expectations had been met. (131)

When we consider bodies outside of biological or sociological mandates of race and consider them as things that feel, then we grasp how sensation becomes like clothing. Monica Miller's examination of dandyism and black diasporic styling tells us how descendants of "materially deprived African captives" learned "to inhabit clothing in their own way . . . as a process of remembrance and mode of distinction (and symbolic and sometimes actual escape) from bondage in their new environment" (4). Like clothing, sensation directs black diasporic styling of illusive flesh and is especially relevant to black transsubjects and their narratives. Although performing in drag and doing bodybuilding/fitness work were certainly about visually and kinesthetically carving the body, Newman's work as a prostitute and mistress engages the intersection of visual and haptic aesthetics for the body. The props and costumes she wore as mistress were different from wearing a dress and represent a styling of the self and a functioning of self without skin. Newman adapts touch and interior movement to her spirituality and creates a new world for herself. Red Jordan Arobateau would do the same with perception.

Ghetto Heaven, Trans(ing), and Perception

"I am not the outcome or the meeting-point of numerous causal agencies which determine my bodily or psychological make-up," says Merleau-Ponty before further clarifying his theory of perception: "I cannot shut myself up within the real of science. All my knowledge of the world, even my scientific knowledge, is gained from my own particular point of view, or from some experience of the world without which the symbols of science would be meaningless" (ix). Black cultural texts articulate a similar claim about religion, spirituality, and questions of embodiment as well as science with their many conceptions of ghetto heavens. More specifically, Red Jordan Arobateau's representation of a phenomenology of perception and transworld identity for economically disenfranchised LGBTQI subjects in fiction indicates why the concept is important to reducing the risk of marginalizing race and class in transgender studies. While Spice 1 and Tupac once asked if heaven has a ghetto, it was the Family Stand's 1990 international funk hit "Ghetto Heaven" that presented us with the fluidity of what could amount to anyone's ghetto heaven.[17] The concept draws upon a long-standing critique and revision of Christianity in which the differently embodied, those unsuccessfully spiritually converted and colonized or those with antiwork ethics, make pleasure and sensation function as a strategy of decolonizing the spirit. Ghetto heaven as presented in this chapter portends to be as much about material class conditions and aspirations as it is about the wretchedness of Western embodiment.

I turn these black allusions to ghettoes and heavens to challenge Lorde's statement that pornography emphasizes sensation without feeling ("Uses of the Erotic") so that I can make legible the improper texts and bodies in the fiction of Red Jordan Arobateau. Lorde describes sensation in opposition to feeling. Sensation seems inordinately bad, without use, empty, and superficial. The theme conveyed in ghetto heaven, however, indicates that sensation can be as important as feeling mainly because it understands sensation as a unit of experience. This means that "instead of providing a simple means of delimiting sensations, if we consider it in the experience itself which evinces it, the quality is as rich and mysterious as the object, or indeed the whole spectacle perceived" (Merleau-Ponty, 5). In their joining of ghetto and heaven in various cultural iconic texts, black people have spoken and concluded that heaven and the ghetto are phenomenologies of perception rather than facticity. In turn, they are not necessarily axiological opposing sites. Ghetto heaven becomes a metaphor about sensation as a unit of experience and salvation equal to and resistant to those espoused from religious moral doctrines about heaven. The valuing of sensation as a unit of experience alongside feeling becomes all the more relevant when we consider subjects who experience the time and space of their bodies differently from the rest of the world.

Red Jordan Arobateau is a multiracial transgender author with various published short stories in edited collections (most of them out-of-print lesbian collections). He is also the author of sometimes badly written and unedited self-published novels that can further conversations about eroticism, funk, sex, and work. According to the self-penned bio:

> Red Jordan is a transsexual man born in 1943. Of mixed race heritage; White, Native, Hispanic, African American. He is looking forward to receiving social security at age 65 and is now poor, precariously housed & unemployed at [sic] still hoping for public recognition of his trashy gay-lez-bi-trans works, for which he has had only small acclaim.
>
> He is a great author who is prolific. Once you read one of these spectacular novels you will want more! And more! There are 80 titles listed in his catalogue to be exact! By [the] time the reader gets thru these erotic, adventuresome, thought

provoking, dialogue-filled mad cap portrayals of the QUEER and POOR human experience, so much time may have elapsed they will have forgotten the plot.[18]

As current and future scholars attempt to erect broader and more diverse histories of transgender and transsexual peoples and movements, Arobateau's novels featuring transgender and transsexual characters and their intersection, or lack thereof, with a more mainstream transgender movement should also garner some attention for the novels' historical importance, if not for their literary merits. Rather than focus on Arobateau's fiction about transsubjects alone, it seems more useful to explicate how the author sustained and supported the fifty-year journey from woman to man through a writing life in which transworld identity was housed in a ghetto heaven important for black transfutures beyond necropolitics. To spiritualize the transition from one gender to another emulates a use of the erotic, but to do so incorporating what might typically be written as immoral work that corrupts the erotic and literary is funking the erotic.

If transgender and transsexual history and culture depend upon what has been published, visible, legible, and authorized enough to be archived, then we might query what has been omitted as a result of the conditions of illiteracy, criminalization, or poverty. These are conditions that have made it difficult for some transgender subjects to be the absolute source, represent themselves, and write themselves into being. Recovering more black transgender narratives means making peace with improper bodies and texts. Arobateau has been a part of a black queer literary tradition for almost forty years now, beginning during the period of his life when he was recognized as a racially ambivalent lesbian writer in the late 1970s and 1980s.[19] In the journal *Sinister Wisdom*, fiction writer Ann Allen Shockley, another understudied writer of same-sex fiction, provided one of the only reviews of Arobateau's early work, stating of Arobateau's short story about a black lesbian prostitute "Susie Q": "This type of black female character, lesbian or heterosexual, has been largely ignored or glossed over in the whole of Afro-American literature by black female writers. Various reasons can be surmised for the neglect. The literary black female writers usually focus on allegorical symbolisms, women in search of a quest, or the ennobling of black women. Other writers are involved in political rhetoric, or self-serving pursuits.[20] In addition to "Susie Q," Arobateau introduced readers to black underclass characters such as Flip, Gina, and Rhonda. These were characters who held material aspirations of a better life without relying on the contingency of heteronormativity. The novels and stories presented readers with a wide array of gender variants involved in illicit criminal activity: drug dealing, boosting, and hoing.

Shockley's review of Arobateau incorporated many useful tidbits about his life, including Arobateau's psychological issues about being mixed race. Shockley revealed, "Unlike Michelle Cliff, [Arobateau] has never passed for white" (37). Other information the interview yielded: a middle-class family background, a deep devotion to a Christian father, and a conversion from atheist to Christian. Representations of queer black underclass characters appear in Arobateau's *The Bars across Heaven, Ho Stroll: A Black Lesbian Novel,* and the *Outlawz Biker* series, texts that can be classified as black queer fiction since they explicitly include issues about race, sexuality, and segregation. Written during the intersecting heights of the civil rights, sexual liberation, gay liberation, and black power movements, Arobateau's depictions of black underclass lesbian life lead to his creative representation of transsexuals. *The Big Change (Confessions of a Metaphysician)*, as well as *Black Biker* and *Tranny Biker* in the *Outlawz Biker* series, implicitly align with a black tradition of conjoining spirituality with subculture and subcultural communities. However, I limit my examination of Arobateau here to the novel *The Big Change*, written in the early 1960s but only later published in 1976.

The 2001 printed version of *The Big Change* includes a prefatory page with "Author's Notes" that reads:

> I present this novel, created circa 1962 out of those old bar-raid illegal homo days of our youth; bits and snatches of conversations we held in drunken nights. Capturing some of our early observations about transsexuals—of which nothing was known at the time by us teenage queers. A slice of The Life with its cruel gossip, street fights, lovers, dreams aspired to under the blazing eye of a hateful straight society; yet eternally within the love of God. (ii)

Given the ways in which sex work and homelessness figure into some transsexual and transgender lives, fictional representations of street life expose rather than obscure the significance of class and race in social constructions of transgender subjectivity. In Arobateau's fiction, street denizens are a group of people who may have been born into poverty or became poor as a result of being disowned from middle-class families for being queer and trans before ending up on the street. *The Big Change* includes a cast of gender-variant characters, but Arobateau's novel provides physical descriptions of characters that border on racial incongruity. We know characters are ugly or beautiful, or tall or short. One of the few times but perhaps purposeful moments when color is mentioned comes at the beginning of the novel when the narrator explains, "An Army of pale grey transvestites audit the street" (3). *The Big Change*, then, intends to be a transracial novel about transgender characters who may or may not be transracial.

Set in McCarthy-era Chicago, *The Big Change* uses disjointed flashbacks to tell the story of Sandy (a woman), Paul (a man), and April Dawn (a drag queen/ metaphysician): Paul is a boy who grows into a husband and father; Sandy is the woman and sometime prostitute oppressed by Paul's male body; and April Dawn is the drag queen who works (performs) to support Paul's family and to save up for Sandy's surgery. However, Arobateau's three distinct characters suggest that the big change exceeds a singular, strict focus on genital reconstruction surgery. The novel unfolds from the multiple perspectives of the metaphysician, Paul, Sandy, and April Dawn. Its movement between first and third person is confusing, but not unnecessary since Arobateau's novel intends that readers discern the difficulty of language (pronouns of gender) to convey a person writing about a former and future self. The novel opens with our protagonist listening to chiming church bells that symbolically remind the narrator of, and situate the reader in, a world where the passing of time is organized by specific worldviews: "Only two things remained of her old life. Ornamental; a picture of two persons framed inside a valentine wrought heart [locket]. One male . . . an adolescent. . . . The other, the woman" (2). Throughout the novel, a narrative of productivity, beauty, and function frames the lives of two people in the locket (Paul and Sandy), and the characters form the basis of Arobateau's critique of capitalism and Western embodiment. Readers soon learn that the teenage boy, Paul, was a homeless prostitute and an addict before April Dawn is born.

The early chapters detail Paul's failure at being and identifying as gay, and it includes tropes of other transsexual narratives such as disassociation with genital anatomy and dialogue about not feeling like one's true self. Because Arobateau operates in the fictional, paying attention to explicit moments when he references particular tropes means also unmasking the critique of embodiment. The narrator's discussion of transsexuality begins with a very specific history: "1952. Christine Jorgensen's case was the first widely publicized case" (12). After referencing Jorgensen's gender reassignment surgery as the first widely known transsexual success story, Arobateau fabricates a mirror scene for Paul as a way to signify the dominant gaze on an unruly body. During a beauty-school makeover, the narrator details that "his face came back to him in a mirror. . . . He watched the woman before him, quivering there in the mirror. . . . A woman on the brink of being. A newborn!" (12). Arobateau's narrator incorporates Jorgensen as an important figure in the medical history (surgery) and representation of transsexuals in the United States but then includes the mirror scene as a nod to the psychoanalytical as well. As Prosser indicates, "[T]he mirror scenes in transsexual autobiographies do not merely initiate the plot of transsexuality . . . mirror scenes also draw attention to the narrative form for this plot" (100). The mirror scene does draw attention to the narrative form for this plot, but it does not initiate the plot. Similar to authors of neoslave narratives who merged important historical facts with cultural memory to produce new knowledge about slavery and trauma, Arobateau does the same with transsexual history. He makes the obvious historical reference so that we can see where revision happens and what aesthetically dictates the revision. The narrator employs the mirror scene to transition readers from a perception of Paul as a character who feels ugly and gay to a perception of Paul as a character who feels like he exists in the wrong body.

From this point on, however, Arobateau adds Sandy as another prominent voice that can narrate portions of the novel. For Sandy, Jorgensen becomes a heroic model of what the pursuit of one's own self can be no matter what obstructions lie in the way. At one point, Sandy tells us of her deification of the woman largely written as an innovation and invention of science, "Off and on, thru these days, I remembered the Christine Jorgensen case. CJ, I coded it. That is, JC. I spelled it backwards in my diary. What an unusual Savior!" (79). Sandy displaces the medical destiny and technological othering of Jorgensen with a spiritual destiny and then creates a mythical savior for herself. Though it threatens to become an overrepresentation of *man,* Arobateau makes it a usurping of the bioeconomy attached to Jorgensen's history, and this moment is part of the metaphysician's larger goal and the real big change that had been hinted at before Christine Jorgensen or a mirror scene is introduced. Arobateau's novel intertwines gender reassignment and spiritual conversion, making them virtually inseparable. Although *The Big Change* is about a transsexual protagonist, the plot invests in a representation of transgender and transsexual beyond the rhetorics of materiality and gendered embodiment. It also serves as a conversion narrative of a subject moving from objective reason to spiritual faith to explain its being.

The full title of *The Big Change* includes the parenthetical *Confessions of a Metaphysician.* The subtitle returns us to a conversation about metaphysics, race, sexuality, and gender that the transracial author Paschal Beverly Randolph began with his work in the occult and sexual magic. Whereas Randolph included the occult, Arobateau approaches metaphysics from a different perspective. While readers will not know until the end of the novel what a metaphysician might be or what duties are entailed in such a career, the narrator confirms the meaning of it and its use as a plot device:

> I fancy you might see me as one of these metaphysicians, changing one element, which is dense, coarse, common. And refining it. Taking certain particles essential to its character, keeping them, but ridding it of the base earth. Improving. Refining. Making something of lighter weight. Gold. Better. More free. Adding height. Color.—And commitment to humankind. A soul spends its lifetime, hopefully to elevate itself to be an element of the highest possibility. (101)

Although the narrator's dialogue fits more readily with alchemy than metaphysics, dismissing Arobateau's usage of *metaphysician* would be erroneous since it in fact signals the ways in which literacy and education matter in how we interpret and read others less formally schooled in the craft of writing. Alchemy and metaphysics are both branches of philosophy linked with science, and both address questions about being and matter. In addition, readers need not know what that highest possibility is right away nor who the metaphysician might be or who she is confessing to, but the why seems obvious. The metaphysician in Arobateau's novel possesses an artistic sensibility about adapting the materiality of the body.

To address the becoming of the protagonist, the novel intends that readers understand how being transsexual involves more than completing a journey that entails and ends in physical and corporeal changes. The process will require its subject to do more than challenge social constructs of gender instilled by society; it will entail employing various methods that can counter foundations in Western embodiment that split body and mind and assume that neither ever changes. This is why the novel's first scene of recognition happens when the protagonist looks at her two past lives in the heart-shaped locket. The importance of the locket and its purpose become apparent when the protagonist says that it is one of two artifacts left from postoperative life. The locket serves as a dual metaphor that reveals the limitations of the psychoanalytic mirror and external recognition. Arobateau's narrator offers a gaze, free from transphobia, into lives in transition and beings that can be situated alongside each other. Though different subjects, Paul and Sandy were products of romanticized notions of man and woman. Whereas language would write the two out of existence, or medicine would reconstruct a new body, the heart and consciousness feel the containment of another unresolved question.

One such example comes in a depiction of one of Paul's late nights out. At a restaurant, Paul waits for food and an impromptu dance party breaks out among the protagonist, a waitress, and gay patrons. Paul's identification with the waitress—"the Queen Mother dancing in the middle of her children"—grows as "as he watches her lift her skirt and reveal a leg, thigh, and panties" of which he makes "a mental note—color, lace, material" (9). The scene serves as a confessional moment in the theatrical tradition, and it provides a temporary moment of clarity. Once the waitress is out of sight, Paul is again confronted with an image of self that he sees as ugly and wrong. At home and in bed, the narrator reveals, "Flipped over and took two Componseenes. . . . I let Paul go—stepped out of his dismal world. . . . Soon I was floating" (9). Making Christine Jorgensen a spiritual savior was one way that Arobateau could challenge Western gendered embodiment, but the uncensored representation of illicit drug use, instead of hormone therapy, is another.

Immediately after self-medicating, Paul becomes Sandy: "She saw the figure from way up high. . . . He imagines *he* is the Queen Mother. . . . And it brings many smiles to his face" (9). Drug use in the novel metaphorically offers a perceptive alteration in representation of being influenced by class contestations and gendered embodiment. The depiction of drug use becomes sensation as experience. It can either help characters dull psychic pain or help them engage the mirror of imagination rather than the mirror of recognition. Arobateau's decision to prioritize induced interior sensation over visual perception deliberately illustrates the limitations of only perceiving via one sense. Drugs prolong and extend both states. What is precipitated in this queer time is a ludic temporality[21] that the narrator remarks upon as the moment of truth when she knew perception of self as a woman was not about being gay. The mirror of imagination, the impromptu dance, and the drug use are all authorial tools invalidated by rationality. The magic of the mind offers its subject a coping mechanism to confront the social proscriptions of reason. In the novel, moments of interior movement are prompted by elements outside of moral institutions such as churches and mental hospitals. The novel's attention to its protagonist's drug use and performance career indicates that despite the possibility of surgical intervention, the process of being and becoming extends beyond rational and objective experience. Throughout the novel, drugs become an important element in dealing with the feeling that the world (gay communities and the straight world) wants to abort April Dawn.

Time and again, both Sandy's and Paul's use of drugs confirms that neither feels complete or whole, so that even as Sandy is feminine she remains incomplete, incomplete not because of anatomy, but because spiritual transcendence is absent. The representation of drug use emphasizes that the problem with embodiment is not solely about gender but the limitations of Western embodiment and its instrumentalizing of the senses as well. Though each character risks addiction, the metaphysician's confessions frame this dragging out of time through drug use and places the user in a preobjective realm that, according to Merleau-Ponty, can facilitate a better understanding of self. He explains:

> It is sometimes the adherence of the perceived object to its context, and, as it were, its viscosity, sometimes the presence in it of a positive indeterminate which prevents the spatial, temporal and numerical wholes from becoming articulated into manageable, distinct and identifiable terms. And it is this pre-objective realm that we have to explore in ourselves if we wish to understand sense experience. (14)

As Sandy and Paul continue to rely on excessive drug use, drag performances in gay clubs become another preobjective realm where exploration can be extended via queer time. The plot's pace and action throughout the novel build upon queer time by consistently juxtaposing queer street subculture with the square world of heteronormative domesticity that Paul/Sandy escaped, but this escape does not eliminate what becomes desire and longing for heteronormative domesticity.

Judith Halberstam has proposed that

> queer subcultures offer us an opportunity to redefine the binary of adolescence and adulthood that shapes so many inquiries into subcultures. Precisely because

many queers refuse and resist the heteronormative imperative of home and family, they also prolong the periods of their life devoted to sub-cultural participation.[22]

Yet, from the beginning of the novel, the rules of the street show adolescence and adulthood as another false binary. Arobateau's characters insist that sometimes, as a result of factors outside of sexuality, there is little choice in this extension. As Sandy later offers, "Gay people, they are closer to me than anything. . . . But I am not really gay. I am a woman, in a male body. I want a man. A husband. I want to live as normally as I can make it. . . . This gay life, its allnite [sic] spots, its shows . . . it is only to make do for now" (25). For Sandy, making do means replacing pill popping with another high life, the club—"The High Life—home of Chicago's own, fabulous April Dawn" (27). After several scenes depicting April Dawn as a formidable and sure presence in the nightclub venue, readers should assume that April Dawn is the confessing metaphysician. While Sandy and Paul are man and woman, April Dawn's ability to perform, to create illusions, makes her something more.

The remaining chapters juxtapose the double life of Sandy/Paul: Paul's attempted suicide, drug overdose, legal employment, and marriage in contrast with Sandy's prostitution, hormone treatments, electrolysis, office jobs, and therapy sessions. The novel contains a great deal of sex and none of it is beautiful, creative, or artistic. All of it is work:

> A so-called "straight" man, he paid me to perform a sex act with a female prostitute while he watched. . . . How I blocked out the visual scene of myself, my fine gown stripped away, naked, using it to perform sexually. . . . How I hated the men and women who came to watch me, a "freak" perform. And how my bank account grew. (62)

At various times in the novel, each character uses the word *freak* differently so that readers understand its negative and positive connotations. When queer characters use it to refer to each other, *freak* does not have a medical configuration, but as the previous excerpt demonstrates, Sandy intuits that the straight world regurgitates nineteenth-century sentiment onto transgender bodies. Sandy understands her work and does not cringe at its ugliness since its rewards will bring capital needed for surgery. She later explicates on the common ground of cisgender, heterosexual, and homosexual desire in all johns:

> I worked at a whorehouse. . . . Then another whorehouse, notoriously gay. . . . At these encounters it was necessary for a queen to . . . untuck her male organ from its hiding place . . . and give [the trick] the twisted lay of his life. . . . Usually the fleet of gayboys and transsexuals that lined the stairway of this particular house on Chicago's Southside had far wilder dreams. (67)

With Sandy's reference to Chicago's Southside, blackness enters with its ghetto heaven and good times. Despite the difference of class, Sandy's life begins to define itself through Christine Jorgensen.

Arobateau incorporates snippets of Jorgensen's real life into Sandy's story, from a tour of duty in the air force to her life in Denmark, despite the very different class position of his character. From performing and tricking, Sandy saved ten thousand dollars for the final surgery (91), and she admits, "[H]ours I have spent, telling my story in this or that office, to this Social Worker, to that Head Shrinker ... [f]rom Paul, to Sandy, to Dawn" (91). These are the autobiographical acts of transsexual autobiography that Prosser alludes to as already existing before one can even be authorized for surgery. Nevertheless, after the psychiatrists, physicians, and social workers have decided that yes, she can and should have the surgery, the hospital won't allow the operation. Sandy confirms "the official reason. It's unreligious. . . . Like a fool, I had thought the Doctor himself had the real authority" (92). Later, she proclaims, "Religion has no purpose, or business in a hospital except in the terminal cancer wards" (93). Here we see Arobateau in agreement with Sylvia Wytner's thesis that religious systems are not separate from medicine as science, and thus Arobateau confirms that embodiment must be broached from another model—art and aesthetics.

Paul and Sandy's brushes with the square world and queer communities create sensations that leave them longing for something more. As April Dawn becomes the something more, Arobateau's fictional tale diverges from Jorgensen's autobiography. Though a work of fiction, Arobateau's novel allows readers to understand that, even with medical advances, there is no way to join the split or create a coherent subject in the Western embodiment of the flesh/spirit or mind/body divide. Moreover, discerning between the voices of specific characters in the novel aesthetically attests to how difficult joining the split can be when it is not scripted by autobiographical tropes. As a performer, April Dawn has learned to avoid investing in fixed narratives, especially universal ones. April Dawn reminds readers of the difference between herself and Sandy and Paul when she explains, "Over the years, I've been losing my faith. Yet, I believe in God,—but in my own way. . . . I must be bold enough to say God has changed. . . . Everything must give over to change. Perhaps God has had a change of heart, too" (75). April Dawn's role in the novel becomes more transparent during the descriptions of Sandy and Paul's competing lives when she explains, "[T]he dreams of the metaphysician. . . . To elevate our world in love. To elevate its hospitals, its sciences, its communication into the area of love and freedom" (77). By the end of *The Big Change*, readers have figured out that the story did not intend to represent a former man or woman whose story was finalized by technology but to celebrate a character still in the process of transitioning and becoming. Arobateau's collection of fiction, poetry, and plays written during the lifelong process of transition from female to male proves that coherent stable subjectivity in narrative form is a myth of embodiment. People of color have relied upon a tradition of (un)naming rather than naming to account for fluid subjectivity.

Policing the Mythic Being of Tranny and the Monetary Purposes of Transgender

Black transgender subjects of different eras have been engaging embodiment as dictated by illusive flesh of light, as opposed to words set up by an intelligence agency. It certainly happens with vernacular culture and its myth making of the body. Thus I want to close this chapter by addressing and complicating the figurative uses of "tranny" by transgender individuals within a history of blackness and language rather than a history of gender. Based on Sun Ra's assessment "that some people or intelligence has fixed up words for people . . . some intelligence set up words, and enticed people to be part of that word. They set up civilizations, churches, educational systems, all based on words" (Sinclair, 23), I wonder then of the validity and relevance of icon RuPaul's defense for his use of *tranny* on his show *RuPaul's Drag Race*. He states, "I've been a 'tranny' for 32 years. The word tranny has never just meant transsexual."[23] The reality, however, is that RuPaul may be referencing a trans herstory unrelated to and not equivalent to white transgender history that his Logo TV network audience privileges, as exemplified by his follow-up tweet, "The absurdity! It's as if Jay Z got offended by Kanye using the word 'Nigga.'" Logo does not exist in a world of niggas, bitches, and trannies, and this controversy highlights how prioritizing terms for and between nongender-conforming folks are a type of neoliberal management of bodies and people who are already out of place and time.

While the longevity of reality television shows such as *RuPaul's Drag Race* attests to a growing interest in queer culture, its success also hinges on a legibility made possible by gay and transgender political aspirations. Tranny, on the other hand, is specifically linked within a history and culture of sex work that transgender erases. In her response to the specific transgender community who chastised RuPaul for his use of *tranny*, transgender porn star TS Madison revealed her logic for keeping and utilizing the word in her own vocabulary, stating, "I actually use *tranny* for monetary uses bitch!"[24] In expressing this sentiment, Madison highlights the capitalistic impulses behind *tranny* and *transgender*, but the difference is, as Dan Irving notes in his article "Normalized Transgressions," the latter's goal is to manufacture a productive body for the state.

> Scholars within trans studies rarely contextualize trans identities, subjectivities, and activism within historical and contemporary capitalist relations. . . . There is

a tendency within [existing] commentary to reify matters of sex/gender and to challenge state and institutional dominance over trans people by emphasizing the necessity of self-determination of sex/gender. (39)

By positing that class might matter as much as the categories of sex/gender, Irving alludes to how the rich and elite have different customs or philosophies about gender from the middle class, working class, and underclass. He examines how class may change when gender changes, and he exposes the way trans theory implicitly assumes a middle-class or rich subject when self-determination begins primarily with gender. Such thinking dismisses the way class ensures or makes sex/gender as well as allows access to technology that can legitimately unmake sex/gender. Madison's view of *tranny* incorporates an understanding about a cisgender and transgender sexuality and sexual desire that cannot and has not been productive for the state, even as it generates income for transgender persons. What *transsexual* and *transgender* mean for subjects who are not white or wealthy, as opposed to *tranny* alone, has been a debate that has been present in African Americans communities where various individuals also continue to resist the sexual identities of homosexuality and bisexuality.

As Tenika Watson, the woman who was with singer Teddy Pendergrass on the night of his debilitating car accident, once explained in an interview with the *Philadelphia Gay News,*

> You hear a lot of trans this and trans that and I don't get it. Maybe I'm old-school, but once you have the surgery, you're supposed to be a woman. Your birth certificate says female, your driver's license says female and yet in articles I read, they still refer to you as a "transwoman." And it's like, what was it all for? Why did I go through all of this if I'm not going to be considered a woman? To me, transgender means transition. Moving from one gender to another, but once you're there, that should be it if that's what you want. I don't know if girls today feel any kind of way about that, but I know I do. I don't like the term.[25]

Although some critics might consider this to be a step back, Watson's attention to transition as fluidity as opposed to the fixed identity of woman predates the current emphasis on transing in Western society. Likewise, when an interviewer keeps using the term *transgender community* in a YouTube interview with writer Red Jordan Arobateau, he replies: "You keep using a word I can't relate to because when I came out it was as a transsexual not as a transgender. . . . I like the concept a lot. It means more soldiers for the army." And when the interviewer attempts to make Arobateau compose a universal trans experience, he replies, "You gotta remember the transsexual/transgender community comes from all diverse points, you know class, college educated, lacks of . . . what attributes do we have in common, we have a sexual awareness or at least a gender awareness."[26]

The words of RuPaul, TS Madison, Red Jordan Arobateau, and Tenika Watson provide examples of how language, political affiliations, science, and technology fail to reveal what other specific forms of matter might impact gender and identity. These shared concerns over self-definition simultaneously enact a process of revision of self over time but then accept certain social categories. These contradictions reflect a transworld identity included in black cultural production. Though located in very different queer geographies—Philadelphia, San Francisco, and Hawaii—as well as age groups, Mock, Arobateau, and Watson racially identify as black. Though gender serves as the primary focus in each statement, we cannot ignore how configurations of identity based on race or class may be shaping how each person thinks about gender or how individuals are allowed to talk about gender. Their challenges to naming and being named by others are a form of unnaming practiced in racialized communities that changes with the politics of the time.[27]

Consequently, being critical of the public sphere in which past and present black trans persons have a voice maintains awareness about how self-definition must be an everyday practice. The means by which black and transracial transgender and transsexual subjects define themselves can be as important as the definition or identity itself. The problem is not identity alone as queer theory has expressed, but the world within which any identity has been created. Arobateau's fiction and Newman's autobiography confirm why transworld identity becomes the basis of self-definition. Their representations of spiritually evolving racialized transgender sex workers and their repurposing of cisgender desire support the theory that a transworld identity can be economically and psychically beneficial to marginalized transgender subjects. Conversations that begin with aesthetics of art and spirituality, instead of biological and psychoanalytical questions, matter for transgender and transsexual subjectivity throughout the African diaspora. Newman and Arobateau demonstrate how the illusive flesh and illusive flesh of light require visual and philosophic streams that extend beyond the inorganic object of "art" and into modifying or not modifying the body's anatomical sex. While the state may only be able to transform the unruly body into service of state power, in the realm of creative endeavors and personal discourses, the biopolitics of everyday human life are joined to another form of life—aesthetics of sex art as spirituality. Arobateau and Newman artistically use, rather than accept, the body/soul/spirit split of Western embodiment to make a new world.

Conclusion

Funk Studies—The B-Side

Niggers fuck. Niggers fuck, fuck, fuck.
Niggers love the word fuck . . .
When it's time to TCB
Niggers are somewhere fucking

—Last Poets, "Niggers Are Scared of Revolution"

. . . a great need existed within people of color communities
affected by Western/European colonization and cultural
hegemony for empowerment that included a space for sexual
healing and sensual liberation. The idea of a sexual cultural
center emerged as a way to address the need that I perceived.
Black Funk became that center.

—Herukhuti, *Conjuring Black Funk*

I end this study with Herukhuti's explanation of why he founded the Black Funk Center because it recaps that black people can and do create revolutionary sexual cultures that can become the foundation for centers of sexual health, well-being, and decolonization. Such centers are as important as churches, community centers, libraries, theaters, and museums. Black communities need more sexual cultural centers like Black Funk, but since sexuality and eroticism tend to be ignored, there are few political ideologies or organizations that see such centers as a part of black revolutionary movements. The Last Poets suggest that niggers are scared of revolution and that fucking is antithetical or an impediment to the business of revolution. Fortunately, freaky niggers, as this text has argued, are not scared of revolution, and they demonstrate that black sexual cultures formulate sexuality as a site of memory that can be necessary to both revolution and liberation. By examining spaces and sites where narratives and performances of the body provocatively intersect with expressions of interior movement, I have theorized how the need for such centers has already been articulated elsewhere—profane sites of memory. Reading these spaces with a methodology that incorporates the importance of aesthetics and sacred forces, as well as ethics and public spheres, brings us closer to developing communal practices of love and intimacy that can embrace all.

Black Americans are not the only people that could use such sexual centers, but the history of racialized sexual exploitation by US national policies, medical institutions, and global capitalism; the moral panics that do little to curb sexual terror; and the current pandemic of HIV/AIDS disproportionately impacting black communities require the specificity of such a radical call. As Herukhuti professes, "You have to engage in grassroots organizing in your own bedroom to change the culture" (24). More intrinsically, grassroots organizing in your own bedroom for black people, as this text has shown, will spill out of that one bedroom. In order to be self-sustaining and effective, these centers have to be organized around something more than work society, domesticated intimacy, biopolitics, and traditional race politics.

Some African American cultural producers demonstrate that intimacy and ethics in a state of sexual terrorism and sexual colonization are not necessarily compatible. Black communities have been thinking through the affective moments of identity politics and performance and the confines of civilization and work society for centuries primarily through funk's reconfiguration of "the party." Black sexual cultures become a communal, embodied, and performative satirical critique of democracy, domesticity, national consciousness, capitalism, and time. If we think of sexual liberation as linked with racial, spiritual, and class freedom, and not as a solitary singular movement about biological gender, racial genealogy, and social and psychological histories of sexuality, we understand that everything and everyone have not been liberated. Black sexual cultures offer an alternative sexual geography in which two seemingly opposite elements, the intimate or intimacy and the ecstatic and ecstasy are placed alongside each other. Intimacy is conceptualized as deep-seated interiority, while ecstasy is expressed as a state of being "beside oneself." Intimacy prioritizes humanness and human relationalities, while ecstasy accepts that there are human and nonhuman relationalities occurring in spiritual, sexual, creative, and pharmaceutical activities and expression. These sexual cultures can be about the metaphysical plane between the living and the dead, or human beings and inhuman forces. Funk studies demonstrate that we need only acknowledge these new metaphysics of struggle.

With that said, I end this book with the same words that concluded the preface: I consider this a work of funk studies, myself a funk studies scholar, and anyone reading this a superfreak.

Notes

Preface

1. See Muñoz's, *Disidentifications: Queers of Color and the Performance of Politics.*

2. In del Rio's interview with Dian Hanson, they mention the career possibilities for women in the 1960s and how those possibilities were limited to clerical or domestic worker for women of color; see del Rio and Hanson, *Fifty Years of Slightly Slutty Behavior.* Anyone further interested in the significance of del Rio should seek out the most recent work of the brilliant Juana María Rodríguez, who has taken up del Rio's performances more extensively.

3. In chapter 2, I explore the significance of Walker's ideas about porn in her short stories "Coming Apart" and "Porn."

4. See the Gamble-Huff-penned party and dance anthem "Get Up, Get Down, Get Funky, Get Loose" masterfully delivered by Teddy Pendergrass and including a bunch of background party sounds later sampled by hip-hop artists Afrika Bambaataa, Dj Maestro, AMW, Charm One, and Chilla Frauste, to name a few.

5. The definition and parameters of *funk studies* are covered in the introduction.

Introduction

1. Listen to Davis's song "F.U.N.K."

2. Listen to Parliament's "Prelude."

3. Lee Edelman and Michael Warner have proclaimed the death of queer theory, Kenneth Warren has issued a book-length statement about the end of African American literature, and Jasbir Puar has proclaimed the demise of intersectionality.

4. Royster's definition of *post-soul eccentricity* allows her to reflect on how soul as a cultural aesthetic reflects Christian influences and polices and privileges heteromasculinity and heterosexuality (9).

5. During TV One's *Unsung* episode 11 of season 3 about Parliament, George Clinton references funk in this way, and the BBC's documentary *The Definitive History of UK Dance Music* about disco includes an interview with Nile Rodgers of Chic in which he mentions that the phrase *freak out* repeated in "Le Freak" had initially been *fuck off*. Likewise, in season 5, episode 2 of TV One's *Unsung* series, in an episode about percussionist Sheila E., she mentions that her debut on Prince's "Erotic City" caused concern because some stations and listeners couldn't be sure if they were singing "*funk* until the dawn" or "*fuck* until the dawn."

6. Thompson, *Flash of the Spirit,* 66.

7. Walcott, "Outside in Black Studies," 95.

8. Wynter, "Unsettling the Coloniality," 281.

9. In Harney and Moten's *The Undercommons,* the authors explain how important feeling is for political projects and black social life and insist upon intimacy as a point of origin for resistance. They equate hapticality with love and assert it is "the interiority of sentiment, that feel that what is to come is here" (98).

10. Castronovo, "Aesthetics," 10.

11. Stevenson, "Twelve Conceptions of Imagination," 238.

12. Foucault, *History of Sexuality,* 57–58.

13. Ibid., 103.

14. Foucault defines *ars erotica* as "truth . . . drawn from pleasure itself," and *scientia sexualis* is delineated as "geared to a form of knowledge-power"; ibid., 58.

15. Grosz, *Time Travels,* 158.

16. For a demonstrable critique of this issue, see Rocha's "Scientia Sexualis versus Ars Erotica" and Scott Lauria Morgensen's discussion of sexuality, queerness, and settler colonialism in *Spaces Between Us.*

17. De Veaux, *Warrior Poet,* 227.

18. "Uses of the Erotic" contains a statement that not only remarks upon the metaphysical androgyny of eros, but that also reinforces ideologies that gender the spiritual and psychic: "The erotic is a resource within each of us that lies in a deeply female and spiritual plane" (53). Consequently, this leads feminist politics to make the erroneous differentiation of eros as feminine and pornographic as masculine, even as gender has been reassessed as a social construct.

19. See Mbembe's "Necropolitics," which critiques Foucault's biopower and examines how sovereignty is ultimately expressed in the "power and capacity to dictate who may live and who must die" (11) or "politics as the work of death" (16).

20. In an examination of race and US film, Wilderson's *Red, White, and Black* demonstrates that black ontology has produced a grammar of suffering (5).

21. Stryker, Currah, and Moore, "Introduction," 13.

22. Jones, "Mediated Sensorium," 6.

23. Quashie, *Sovereignty of Quiet,* 4.

24. Newman, "An Evening with Hal Bennett," 357.

25. Nussbaum, *Sex and Social Justice,* 276.

26. Kempadoo, *Sexing the Caribbean,* 42. Kempadoo has used Caribbean history and experience to single-handedly redirect anthropological and sociological debates about

contemporary sex work, prostitution, and human trafficking in her entire opus comprised of edited collections such as *Global Sex Workers* (1998), *Sun, Sex, and Gold* (1999), *Trafficking and Prostitution Reconsidered* (2005). Wekker's examination of mati work as disruptive of hetero-/homosexual identity binaries may not be initially broached as about sex work, but Wekker's disruption of scholarly research methods around gender and sexuality (sex with Juliette), as well as her positioning of matism as doing a particular kind of work, as sexuality on the move, addresses both the sexual and asexual sex industries highlighted throughout this book.

27. Given that state institutions such as prisons and juvenile detention centers serve as a form of neoslavery, and welfare agencies, adoption agencies, and orphanages seldom seek out or attend to the consent of the rescued children it trades via narratives of proper family and love, we might also speak of these arms of democracy as being involved in human trafficking issues.

28. Nash's The *Black Body in Ecstasy* and Allen's ¡*Venceremos?* are two examples.

29. Stevenson, "Twelve Conceptions of Imagination," 249.

30. Brooks's *Unequal Desires* and Franks's *G-Strings and Sympathy* are the most notable works to do so, and I engage these works chapter 6. Also see Colosi's essay "'Just Get Pissed and Enjoy Yourself.'"

31. See Prosser's discussion of transsexual autobiography in *Second Skins*, 103–4.

32. In "Playing for Keeps," Robin Kelly briefly turns his attention away from his primary interest of African American youth play centered on sporting activities and attends to a gendered reading of sex work and wage labor, finding that one of his subjects locates pleasure within her labor choices (222).

33. Moten writes in "The Case of Blackness": "How can we fathom a social life that tends toward death, that enacts a kind of being-toward-death, and which, because of such tendency and enactment, maintains a terribly beautiful vitality? Deeper still, what are we to make of the fact of a sociality that emerges when lived experience is distinguished from fact, in the fact of life that is implied in the very phenomenological gesture/analysis within which Fanon asserts black social life as, in all but the most minor ways, impossible?" (188).

34. Wynter, "Unsettling the Coloniality," 287.

35. Cohen, "Deviance as Resistance," 29.

36. Wynter, "Unsettling the Coloniality," 279, 318.

37. See Weheliye's *Habeas Viscus*.

Chapter 1. Sexual Magic and Funky Black Freaks in Nineteenth-Century Black Literature

1. James Brown, "Get Up (I Feel Like Being a) Sex Machine": "Get up / Get on up / Stay on the scene / Like a sex machine"; Whodini, "Freaks Come Out at Night": "And you could just about find a freak anywhere / But then again, you could know someone all their life / But might not know they're a freak unless you see them at night"; Lil Wayne's "A Milli" and "Steady Mobbin'" transitions away from freak with the question, "Okay you're a goon, but what's a goon to a goblin?" In each case, what might be read as alien or unnatural is refigured by black funk aesthetics.

2. Collins, *Black Sexual Politics*, 121.

3. Davis, "'Don't Let Nobody Bother Yo' Principle,'" 104.

4. Ibid., 105–6.

5. In addition to Foucault's well-known work, Paul Ludwig's *Eros and Polis* reads numerous Greek plays to demonstrate how "three separable strands can be discerned in Greek political discourse on eros: (1) political pederasty, (2) civic friendship or homonoia, and (3) the city as an object of eros" (19). Just as Ileana Rodríguez writes against the city as object of eros and civic friendship, I demonstrate throughout how funk has countered the way Greek politic discourse of eros has been assimilated into cultures influenced by societies originating outside of Greece.

6. In addition to Kempadoo's work and Spillers's "Mama's Baby, Papa's Maybe," Frances M. Shaver's "Sex Work Research" and, despite the title, Hardy, Kingston, and Sanders's edited collection *New Sociologies of Sex Work* offer some atypical perspectives in the social sciences.

7. In Blumberg's *Freaks of Nature*, Blumberg mentions father/son zoologists/teratologists Etienne Geoffroy Saint-Hilaire and Isidore Saint-Hilaire. He directly quotes and translates this statement from *Histoire générale et particulière des anomalies de l'organisation chez l'homme et les animaux* (27).

8. See Garland-Thomson's *Extraordinary Bodies*, 56.

9. Thompson, *Flash of the Spirit*, 42.

10. Blumberg, *Freaks of Nature*, 17.

11. In addition to Garland-Thomson's *Extraordinary Bodies*, and Blumberg's *Freaks of Nature*, see also Rachel Adams's *Sideshow U.S.A.: Freaks and the American Cultural Imagination*, Robert Bogdan's *Freak Show: Presenting Human Oddities for Amusement and Profit*, Nadja Durbach's *Spectacle of Deformity*, Garland-Thomson's *Freakery: Cultural Spectacles of the Extraordinary Body*, Jack Hunter's *Freak Babylon: An Illustrated History of Teratology and Freakshows*, and Michael Mitchell's *Monsters: Human Freaks in America's Gilded*.

12. "I was a turtle before I was a human being," says Grandmother Eagleton of Gayl Jones's novel *The Healing*, a novel that makes a connection between the freak shows and sideshows featuring marvels and monsters and the big-tent revivals of faith healing, snake-oil salesman, and charlatans. It is not the spectacle alone that Jones visits, but the process of making interior anomalies (neuro and psychic) spectable, a process vitally important to a tradition of funky erotixxx. Grandmother Eagleton, known for her physical anomalies, speaks these words to her granddaughter, protagonist Harlan, who will later join a sideshow exhibiting her healing abilities.

13. Reid-Pharr, *Conjugal Union*, 5.

14. Randolph, *Eulis!*, 9.

15. Listen to Jackson's "Don't Stop 'Til You Get Enough."

16. Randolph, *Eulis!*, 61.

17. Randolph, *Ansairetic Mystery*, 317.

18. In his autobiography, Randolph admits that his mother was a bigamist who never divorced her first husband, making Randolph a love child (10). Randolph claims his family

heritage as that of the Randolphs in the Virginia area, but Deveney suggests that Randon is Randolph's actual surname. I am going with Randolph's account.

19. Randolph, *Dealings with the Dead*, 101.

20. Randolph, *His Curious Life*, 18.

21. Ibid., 4.

22. Ibid., 68.

23. Randolph, "Letter."

24. Randolph, *Eulis!*, 5–6.

25. Ibid., 9.

26. Ibid., 28.

27. Ibid., 2.

28. "Unsettling the Coloniality," 273.

29. Because Randolph was a medium, and his particular occupation dealt with the dead, the senses or sensorium associated with this work would be beyond the scope of biological life. We would need to think of energy and forces as shaping sensory abilities as he does.

30. Randolph, *Sexual Magic*, 18.

31. Ibid., 20.

32. Ibid., 22.

33. Ibid., 27.

34. Words such as *duty* and *moral* are examples of Randolph's moralizing, but I would argue that his discussion of these things are not pathological because his triplicate being refuses the binaries that produce sexuality as pathology.

35. *Oxford English Dictionary Online*, http://www.oed.com/.

36. Anti–free love zealots, puritanical antisocialists, moral crusaders, and later Anthony Comstock and the Comstock Act threatened the livelihood and life of critics and artists who took up sexuality as their themes. In Randolph's *His Curious Life*, he reveals his run-ins with the law, specifically a policeman named French. French reported to the police that Randolph was a smut-peddler, specifically of free-love literature. The police obtained a search warrant for Randolph's residence, and during the search they found copies of Randolph's books and "The Golden Letter," an essay for physicians about preventing conception by free will. Randolph was arrested, but after a judge read the literature and decided it was not obscene, he was set free (67).

37. Randolph, *Eulis!*, 18.

38. There were clearly limits to the advocating of sexual pleasure and release in mainstream and occult sexuality. As was the case with most free-love doctrines and writings on sexuality, masturbation, referred to as *onanism* at the time, was an evil that depleted vital energy that could later lead to health and reproductive problems that would contaminate gene pools. A number of writings, including Randolph's, discouraged the practice of autoeroticism.

39. Randolph's spiritual approach differs from those in feminist science studies such as Alice Dreger's *Hermaphrodites and the Medical Invention of Sex* and Felicity Nussbaum's *Torrid Zones* and *The Limits of the Human*.

40. These are the two most notable women who participated, either by coercion or choice, in freak shows away from their home nations.

41. The adjective *spectable* can mean spectacle or worthy of being seen or contemplated (*Oxford English Dictionary Online,* http://www.oed.com/). *Spectable,* however, implies that the perception determining whether one is worthy of being seen comes from within rather than from outside. *Respectable,* as one of its definition states, alludes to being spectable again. Grandmother Eagleton (of Gayl Jones's novel *The Healing*) makes us aware of what the cost of being human in the New World means: the interior spectable gets overlooked in the spectacle of exteriority.

42. Pancoast, "Biographical Sketch," 43.

43. Dreger, *One of Us,* 43–44.

44. Andrews, *To Tell a Free Story,* xi.

45. Quashie, *Sovereignty of Quiet,* 24.

46. Garland-Thomson, *Extraordinary Bodies,* 57.

47. Martell, *Millie-Christine,* 109.

48. See Martell's *Millie-Christine.*

Chapter 2. In Search of Our Mama's Porn

1. I have already referenced the work of Alice Walker and Audre Lorde, but we might also add bell hooks to this tradition.

2. One episode of the television show *Girlfriends,* "Porn to Write," depicted Lynn and Maya working for a porn publisher during dire financial straits for the characters (season 5, episode 10, 2004).

3. Coleman, interview with author, December 22, 2005.

4. *Players* 1, no. 5 (July 1974): 94.

5. "Makin' It," *Players* 1, no. 5 (July 1974): 42.

6. "Conversin'," *Players* 1, no. 5 (July 1974): 26.

7. Ibid., 26.

8. "Conversin'," *Players* 1, no. 8 (January 1975): 27.

9. Coleman, interview with author, December 22, 2005.

10. DeCosta-Willis, "Letting Go with Love," 63.

11. Ibid., 67.

12. Dunn, "Our Own Erotica," 31.

13. This term defines how science, technology, engineering, and mathematics are being intertwined with a twenty-first-century nationalism and nationalist identity, and STEM serve as the basis of the United States' evolving project of democracy.

14. "Shit That Siri Says" is an online tumblr blog filled with racist and sexist language. There have also been controversies about sexually explicit content in mods, program code alternations that create hidden mini-games in video games, such as *Grand Theft Auto: San Andreas* and *Sims 2.* The 2009 flash game *Ching-Chong Beautiful* has an Asian character speaking broken English. The video game *The Stanley Parable* had a visual gag of a global Southern boy being set afire, and video game *Deus Ex: Human Revolution*'s Letitia is a black homeless woman. These examples provide evidence of why scholars in digital

humanities must continue to interrogate not just formulations of gender and sexuality in their analysis, but concerns about eros, aesthetics, and funk as well.

15. See David J. Leonard's "Not a Hater, Just Keepin' It Real: The Importance of Race- and Gender-Based Game Studies," *Games and Culture* 1, no. 1 (January 2006): 83–88; Nina Huntemann's documentary *Game Over: Gender, Race, and Violence in Video Games* (Media Education Foundation, 2000); and Yi Mou and Wei Peng's "Gender and Racial Stereotypes in Popular Video Games" in *Handbook of Research on Effective Electronic Gaming in Education,* ed. Richard E. Ferdig (Hershey, PA: IGI Global, 2009), 922–937. Anita Sarkeesian, founder of the video blog *Feminist Frequency,* initiated a Kickstarter fund to create a web series about sexism in video games, as discussed in an article by John Walker, "Tropes vs. Women in Video Games vs. the Internet" (http://www.rockpapershotgun .com/2012/06/13/tropes-vs-women-in-video-games-vs-the-internet/). The web show *Game/Show* from PBS Digital Studios discusses the relationship between video games and modern life, including race (www.youtube.com/user/pbsgameshow).

16. Julie Bosman, "Discreetly Digital, Erotic Novel Sets American Women Abuzz," *New York Times,* March 9, 2012, http://www.nytimes.com/2012/03/10/business/media/ an-erotic-novel-50-shades-of-grey-goes-viral-with-women.html?pagewanted=all&_r=0.

17. Johnson, "Zane, Inc," 17.

18. The worldwide domination of Black Twitter, as well as the Ebonics ingenuity utilized in the creation of numerous Internet memes, are contemporary expression black eroticism and play with technology.

19. Spears, "Directness in the Use of African American English."

20. Zane, *Sex Chronicles,* 9.

21. In "On the Issue of Black English," Toni Cade Bambara signifies and sanctifies when she wrote an entire essay on African American vernacular English (AAVE) or Ebonics in black English. She still remains one of the few to get away with it.

22. Taylor, "Libertine or Prude?"

23. Ibid.

24. Moreover, new technology affects that writing. Zane confirms that she has become aware of the discursive disciplining of bodies on the page when she acknowledges her initial hesitancy before she made the strategic move from the Internet and paper self-publishing to being published by Simon and Schuster: "I have all the benefits of being the editor of an imprint. If I'd done an imprint deal instead of a distribution agreement, I'd have to get [Simon and Schuster's] approval, and I wanted the final word on everything" (Johnson, "Zane, Inc.," 17). She was initially concerned about having to tone down the sexual explicitness of her writing, but the freak stroll of a cybermetropolis serves as the spatial territory where Zane's tenure begins before mainstream publishers and bookstores hungry for a profit placed Zane's Strebor Books under their conglomerate umbrella.

25. Reading Group Guide, http://books.simonandschuster.com/Zanes-Addicted/ Zane/9781476748047/reading_group_guide.

26. Floyd, "Inside the Secret World of Sex Parties," *Essence* 37, no. 8 (December 2006): 192–98.

Chapter 3. "Make Ya Holler You've Had Enough"

1. Bambara, "On the Issue of Roles," 103.

2. Ibid., 110.

3. Rick James was arrested in 1991 on charges of torturing, drugging, and kidnapping a twenty-one-year-old woman, Mary Sauger, and twenty-four-year-old Frances Alley, while he was supposedly under the influence of crack cocaine.

4. See Lisa Thompson's *Beyond the Black Lady* and Hazel Carby's *Reconstructing Womanhood*.

5. Ileana Rodríguez covers this romanticization in her work, but in the 1960s the Black Panther Party (BPP) had projected similar models with romantic narratives about George Jackson and Angela Davis, as well as Kathleen Cleaver and Eldridge Cleaver.

6. McClintock, "Maid to Order," 95.

7. In the urban documentary *Gangstress*, Stephanie "Mama" Mayhem is credited with creating and defining the term *gangstress*. Other female hustlers and significant popular figures such as Mary J. Blige, Lil' Kim, and Vanessa del Rio offer definitions as well.

8. See Patricia Hill Collins's discussion of Missy Elliott's "Get Ur Freak On" in *Black Sexual Politics*.

9. See Nelson's "Domestic Harlem"; Smith's "Chester Himes's *The Third Generation.*"

10. From prostitutes and pimps to transsexual and gay hustlers, Himes's uses of the detective genre to explore the black underclass made him a wealthy man and popular writer. Coffin Ed Johnson and Gravedigger Jones appear in *A Rage in Harlem* (1968; a.k.a. *La Reine des Pommes*), *The Crazy Kill* (1959), *The Real Cool Killers* (1959), *All Shot Up* (1960), *The Big Gold Dream* (1960), *Cotton Comes to Harlem* (1965), *The Heat's On* (1966; a.k.a. *Come Back, Charleston Blue*), *Blind Man with a Pistol* (1969; a.k.a. *Hot Day, Hot Night*). Himes's short story "Tang" is very much a part of Himes's career critique of domesticity, black male victimization, and female complicity. The female protagonist and title namesake "Tang" is a prostitute. Himes names her after the shortened version of the black funk slang for women's genitalia—*pootie tang* or *poon tang* (*puntain*) to draw on the slang's inference to women's nonreproductive sexual anatomy as product, magic, and marvel. In the story, Himes reflects on the impossibility of work society, domesticity, and revolution existing side by side in his depiction of a secret revolution whose sexual guerrillas could be a pimp and a ho. Turning the racial realism of black revolutionary representations on its head, Himes underscores the use of eroticism within revolutionary fantasies.

11. In Bill Thompson's *Sadomasochism*, he suggests BDSM as a practice of the "prerogative" of "high status" and "middle" class (136–37).

12. Simone de Beauvoir's *Must We Burn Sade?* analyzes de Sade's familial upbringing, as well as societal claims to him as savior and monster.

13. This is because edgeplay can involve physical or mental harm, all of which can be subjective and based on factors of race, gender, or other physical stereotypes. Likewise, given the legislation criminalizing those infected with HIV, one could be arrested for bloodplay or barebacking.

14. McClintock, "Maid to Order," 112.

15. See David Bell and Jon Binne's *The Sexual Citizen*

16. See *Loving v. Virginia*, 388 U.S. 1 (June 12, 1967), http://law2.umkc.edu/faculty/projects/ftrials/conlaw/loving.html, as well as Botham's *Almighty God Created the Races. The Loving Story* (HBO Documentary Films, 2011) and Newbeck's *Virginia Hasn't Always Been for Lovers* discusses how Mildred Jeter was more outspoken and seemed more intelligent than Richard (18). While both discuss *Loving's* partnership of a race team with two black friends, each ignores how intertwined racing and moonshine or illegal stills were well into the 1960s in dry counties in Virginia.

17. Thomas, *Sexual Demon of Colonial Power*, 23.

18. Amy Kaplan sees this as relevant to how we can understand domesticity as inseparable from imperialism and nation building: *Domestic* in this sense is related to the imperial project of civilizing, and the conditions of domesticity often become the markers that distinguish civilization from savagery. Through the process of domestication, the home contains within itself those wild or foreign elements that must be tamed. . . . If domesticity plays a role in imagining the nation as home, then women, positioned as the center of home, play a major role in defining the contours of the nation.

19. In *Mutha' Is Half a Word*, I asserted that in some black female communities, a cultural id, the Queen B (?) figure, exists for black women's culture. Queen B (?) consistently seeks to unname and unmake the social construction and category of black woman and black womanhood through black folklore and the strategy of trickster-troping so that black women can develop unrestricted efforts to pursue pleasure.

20. Walcott, "Novels of Hal Bennett: Part I," 37.

21. Royster, *Sounding Like a No-No*, 100.

22. Ibid., 100.

23. In *Our Living Manhood*, Rolland Murray deftly demonstrates how the black power movement's "pursuit of phallic integrity" created its own critical deconstruction and critics of such strategies. Murray contends of Joe that "his pursuit of the phallus through the erotic creates a politics that perpetually reverts back to the *merely* carnal, the *merely* erotic" (emphasis added, 68). Murray's reading underscores that Bennett was far from being an advocate for black nationalist masculinities.

24. See Foucault's *Birth of the Clinic* and *Madness and Civilization*.

25. Breton, *Manifestoes of Surrealism*, 26.

Chapter 4. Marvelous Stank Matter

1. Banks's book in organization and content emphasizes market, labor, and economy. Chapter 3 "The Man Shortage" and chapter 4 "The Market" are only two examples. The entire book exemplifies my concept of marriage as an antierotic sex industry.

2. Writer Christian Hoard of *Rolling Stone* interviewed Janelle Monáe in his "Artist of the Week," and Monáe playfully revealed a little about her sexual preferences. Monáe is quoted as saying, "The lesbian community has tried to claim me," she says. "But I only date androids. Nothing like an android—they don't cheat on you." http://www.rollingstone.com/music/news/artist-of-the-week-janelle-monae-20100630#ixzz2uTPnCElQ.

3. Baraka, "Abbey Lincoln: Straight Ahead."

4. Cooper, *Noises in the Blood*, 161.

5. See Banks's discussion about man-sharing in chapter 4 of *Is Marriage for White People?*

6. Davis, "Regulating Polygamy," 1959.

7. See Foucault's essay "Nietzsche, Genealogy, History" and Nietzsche's *On the Genealogy of Morals*. Jack Halberstam's talk for the Center for 21st Century Studies at the University of Wisconsin–Milwaukee, "No Church in the Wild: Anarchy, Failure and Chaos," uses Jay-Z and Kanye West to examine gender anarchy in hip-hop; https://www.youtube.com/watch?v=b5apvL6WJB0.

8. Davis, "Don't Let Nobody Bother Yo' Principle," 103.

9. Gordon, *Introduction to Africana Philosophy*, 193.

10. Vincent, *Funk*, 260.

11. Noble, "Abbey Lincoln on Love, Marriage, and Polygamy/Polyamory."

12. Ahmed, *Queer Phenomenology*, 159.

13. Ibid., 160.

14. Corbin, *Foul and the Fragrant*, 6.

15. Gopinath, *Impossible Desires*, 6.

16. Zedde's other novels, *Hungry for It*, *Every Dark Desire*, *Dangerous Pleasures*, *A Taste of Sin*, *Return to Me*, and *Desire at Dawn* also adopt this pattern.

17. Corbin, *Foul and the Fragrant*, 185.

18. Lorde used the scent of memory, her mother's, to begin an examination of the connection between her own same-sex desire and her mother's subjectivity.

19. Corbin, *Foul and the Fragrant*, 185.

20. Ibid., 6.

21. Ibid., 7.

22. Walcott, "The Poor Cousins of Modernity."

23. Thomas, *Hip-Hop Revolution*; Price, *Maroon Societies*, 1–2, n. 1.

24. Thomas draws from two works by Daniel O. Sayers: "Diasporan Exiles in the Great Dismal Swamp, 1630–1860," *Transforming Anthropology* 14, no. 1 (2006): 10–20, and "The Underground Railroad Reconsidered," *Western Journal of Black Studies* 28, no. 3 (Fall 2004): 435–43.

25. Gopinath, *Impossible Desires*, 4.

26. Ibid., 11.

27. Dale Carpenter's *Flagrant Conduct* confirms the role whiteness plays in various aspects of the *Lawrence v. Texas* case that establishes gay sexual citizenry in the United States. His findings corroborate that when one is white and male, which is why the *Lawrence v. Texas* case mattered, one can escape criminalization and project criminalization as well. Robert Eubanks, a lover of John Lawrence, called the police on Tyron Garner in a fit of jealousy. His call relied upon the criminal pathologization of black men in the United States. All of this means that a queer liberal subject anywhere outside of the United States brings with it foundations that are not applicable to the creation of sexual identity and its corresponding politics.

Chapter 5. Sexuality as a Site of Memory and the Metaphysical Dilemma of Being a Colored Girl

1. Alexander, *Pedagogies of Crossing,* 300.

2. "Women in Theater: Lynn Nottage," CUNY TV, https://www.youtube.com/watch?v=j1–1eEY_c4E; Nottage, "La Jolla Playhouse Artist's Statement."

3. In "Shiny Jewels," a short documentary featuring Shine L. Houston talking to Shine Louise Houston about making porn where she discusses how porn can be feminist and humanist. Available at https://www.youtube.com/watch?v=VdfZ8cUIy_w (published April 18, 2013).

4. At various times in Reed's novel *Mumbo Jumbo,* characters face the consequences of not being mindful of the ancestors.

5. Writers such as Erna Brodber, Toni Cade Bambara, Alice Walker, Gloria Naylor, Nalo Hopkinson, and Phyllis Alesia Perry have been especially innovative in their exploration of ancestral lives.

6. Maffesoli, "Orgy," 6861.

7. The archives are filled with treatises and statements assessing and validating the aesthetics of black art, and literally making it work as something "more" than simple pleasure: for example, W. E. B. Du Bois, Richard Wright, Addison Gayle, Amiri Baraka, Paule Marshall, and Toni Morrison.

8. Interview with Jacki Lyden, NPR, February 7, 2009, http://www.npr.org/templates/transcript/transcript.php?storyId=100348726.

9. See Nottage, *Intimate Apparel,* pp. 33 and 59.

10. Bernstein's *Temporarily Yours* defines *bounded authenticity* "as the sale and purchase of authentic emotional and physical connection" (103).

11. McKittrick, *Demonic Grounds,* xviii.

12. Pick, "New Queer Cinema and Lesbian Films."

13. Pink and White Productions website, http://pinkwhite.biz/.

14. See Delany, *Times Square Red, Times Square Blue;* James, *Shaming the Devil;* and Muñoz, *Cruising Utopia.*

15. Snorton, "Transfiguring Masculinities in Black Women's Studies."

16. Gordon explains, "Complex personhood means that even those who haunt our dominant institutions and their systems of value are haunted too by things they sometimes have names for and sometimes do not" (5).

17. Gordon insists that "[g]host is primarily a symptom of what is missing" (63), and with the understanding that gender or sexuality can exist outside Western designs of the phallus or lesbian phallus, I offer the term *phallic ghosting* to attend to the ways in which objects rendered as sexual alone have been deployed as spiritual elsewhere. In alignment with Randolph, I propose this a sacred-profane remembrance of sex that continues in the afterlife.

Chapter 6. From the Freaks of Freaknik to the Freaks of Magic City

1. Written by Black Women's Blueprint, an organization dedicated to social justice, the letter was circulated and signed by several organizations and prominent black feminist leaders. "An Open Letter from Black Women to the SlutWalk" (September 23, 2011) was later picked

up and posted by other media sites; http://www.blackwomensblueprint.org/2011/09/23/an
-open-letter-from-black-women-to-the-slutwalk/.

2. Halberstam's *Queer Art of Failure* explains this phrase as "alternative ways of knowing and being that are not unduly optimistic, but nor are they mired in nihilistic critical
dead ends" (24).

3. The translation suggests it might actually be "misadventures of national consciousness," and Fanon reminds us that "[n]ational consciousness, instead of being the all-
embracing crystallization of the innermost hopes of the whole people, instead of being
the immediate and most obvious result of the mobilization of the people, will be in any
case only an empty shell, a crude and fragile travesty of what it might have been" (109).

4. "This Is My Art: Ernie Barnes," *Here's the Story,* https://www.youtube.com/watch?v=rljRJ8Z
-VKE/; see also "Ernie Barnes: An Athletic Artist," *New York Times,* May 7, 1984.

5. "SlutWalks v. Ho Strolls," Crunktastic, Crunk Feminist Collective, http://www.crunk
feministcollective.com/ 2011/05/23/slutwalks-v-ho-strolls/.

6. Suggs, "Street Party Became Its Own Undoing."

7. During the BBC documentary *The Definitive History of UK Dance Music,* Nile Rodgers says of the freak dance, "The Freak was actually the closest thing to having sex without
. . . going all the way." While also insisting that their song was about not being able to get
into Studio 54, "fuck off" became "freak out." http://www.chictribute.com/video/sidor/
ledance.html/.

8. Elliott, "Oral History of Freaknik."

9. Mardi Gras, a carnivalesque tradition combining various spiritual rites, takes place
both within and outside of the United States.

10. Elliott, "Oral History of Freaknik."

11. Ibid.

12. McKittrick's "On Plantations, Prisons, and a Black Sense of Place" theorizes a black
sense of place as alternative mapping practices (949).

13. There were LA screenings of the film in 2011, but, as of this printing, the final fin-
ished film is expected to be distributed and released in December 2014.

14. Long before Grosz's "Bodies-Cities" and *Time Travels,* Prince's funk machination
"Erotic City (Make Love Not War Erotic City Come Alive)" demonstrated the connection
between bodies and cities organized by time, direction, aesthetics: "All my purple life /
I've been looking for a dame / That would wanna be my wife / . . . / If we cannot make
babies / Maybe we can make some time / Thoughts of pretty you and me / Erotic City
come alive." Prince's lyrics detail what Grosz sees as an unthinkable form of interiority
and matter without materiality.

15. Siobhan Brooks in her book *Unequal Desires* relies upon these histories to introduce
her examination of race and erotic capital.

16. For great discussions of this concern, read Mohanty's *Feminism without Borders,*
Alexander's *Pedagogies of Crossing,* and Ferguson's *Reorder of Things.*

17. See *Black, Brown, and Beige,* 261–62.

18. Andil Gosine's "Politics and Passion" challenges conventional practices in ethnographic research in works such as John and Jean Comaroff's *Ethnography and the Historical
Imagination* and Martin Cortazzi's "Narrative Analysis in Ethnography."

19. See Jones, "Performance and Ethnography."

20. This is the statement choreographer Oth'than Burnside makes regarding the dance happening in the video that she choreographs.

21. Clark, "Performing the Memory of Difference in Afro-Caribbean Dance," 190–91.

22. According to Clark, Dunham's less traditional methods went against the advice of her mentor Melville Herskovits (193).

23. A student of the Dunham technique, Sarah Anindo Marshall, once explained of the technique, "You have to be able to switch from [the] pulled-up posture of a ballet dancer to the weighted movements of African dance within a step. . . . If you can do Dunham, you can do any technique"; Simpson, "Dancing in Radical Time," *Pasatiempo*, June 4, 2010, 20. https://sarweb.org/media/files/pasa_dunham_article.pdf.

24. Of course, there have been exceptions to this rule with various street art forms getting their due.

25. Weinrub mentions this aspect of the shows in clips of the film that were circulating from 2011–12 on various websites, including http://thedefinition.org/post/15902741393/shake-downmovie-shakedownworldwide and http://jezebel.com/5749449/the-best-documentary-about-black-lesbian-strip-clubs-youll-see-today.

26. Essex Hemphill's poem "American Hero" and E. Patrick Johnson's article "Feeling the Spirit in the Dark: Expanding Notions of the Sacred in African-American Gay Community" (*Callaloo* 21, no. 2 (Spring 1998): 399–416) offer some ways in which these leisure spaces can become sites of communal meeting.

Chapter 7. Black Trans Narratives, Sex Work, and the Illusive Flesh

1. Mock, "On Sex Work and Redefining Realness," https://www.youtube.com/watch?v=Xd55yq4LMC8

2. Roen's "Transgender Theory and Embodiment" discusses how ethnocentrism pervades transgender theory in the United States in terms of approach and constructions of transgender subjectivity.

3. See Ronen's *Possible Worlds in Literary Theory* and Kusnir's "Reality, Imagination and Possible Worlds."

4. According to Ferguson, the drag-queen prostitute "stands for black culture as it has engaged various economic and social formations" where her racial difference is joined to her sexuality, gender, and class (*Aberrations in Black*, 3).

5. Audio of Mister Cee's confession is available on Hot 97's website: http://www.hot97.com/news/dj-mister-cee/dj-mister-cees-final-mix-on-hot-97-audio.

6. Thomas Matt's "I'm Attracted to Trans Women" on Salon.com discusses transattraction (http://www.salon.com/2013/10/22/im_attracted_to_trans_women/), and anonymous persons have established an online resource and support site for men attracted to ("with an orientation for") transwomen called TransOriented (http://transoriented.com).

7. Mock, "How Society Shames Men Dating Trans Women."

8. In the cases of Eddie Murphy, Teddy Pendergrass, and LL Cool J, none of these stars ever confirmed rumors about their desires.

9. Alexander, *Pedagogies of Crossing*, 303.

10. Matt Richardson, Kai Green, and Kortney Ryan Ziegler have addressed these cultural forms, and even as the real and true are privileged in political forums, each of these critics demonstrates how important myth making and storytelling continue to be for black political movements.

11. When discussing Western philosophy, Placide Tempels argues of Western metaphysics: "Christian thought in the West . . . has defined this reality common to all beings, or, as one should perhaps say, being as such; 'the reality that is,' 'anything that exists,' 'what is.' Its metaphysics has most generally been based upon a static conception of being" (50).

12. In his 1851 "Report on Diseases and Peculiarities of the Negro Race," Samuel Cartwright defines *drapetomania* as a disease that "induces the negro to run away from service, is as much a disease of the mind as any other species of mental alienation" (34).

13. Morrison, *Beloved*, 88–89.

14. *Sankofa*, written and directed by Haile Gerima.

15. Newman has several relationships with men that are specifically attracted to transwomen, as well as men who read her as gay and express discomfort with her desire to identify as trans. Newman reveals that fraternity life provides her with a lover during her college years (39).

16. Gill defines *erotic subjectivity* in "Chatting Back an Epidemic."

17. I say funk because of its sampling of Coke Escovedo's "I Wouldn't Change a Thing" and because the liminality of what constitutes ghetto heaven in song-hustling, reconsideration of work leisure. Additionally, lyrics of the song use the same refrain, "I need a little ghetto heaven," but with each bridge ghetto heaven changes: brandy, drugs, love, and sex.

18. Red Jordan Arobateau website, http://www.redjordanarobateau.com/bio.html.

19. See Arobateau's interview with Ann Allen Shockley, "A Different Kind of Black Lesbian Writer"; see also Arobateau's "Nobody's People" (an essay from his *Stories from the Dance of Life*) in *Daughters of Africa: An International Anthology of Words and Writings by Women of African Descent from the Ancient Egyptian to the Present*, ed. Margaret Busby (London: Cape, 1992), 593–603.

20. Shockley, "A Different Kind of Black Lesbian Writer," 40.

21. Halberstam, *In a Queer Time and Place*, 5.

22. Ibid., 161.

23. "#TransvestiteHerstoryLesson" (tweet), May 24, 2014.

24. TS Madison, "A Community Divide" (YouTube post), May 27, 2014, https://www.youtube.com/watch?v=b09LGSCLprs.

25. Watson remains one of the few transwomen who has been able to offer her own account of her star-scandal. See Suzi Nash, "Tenika Watson: Living beyond Pendergrass' Tragedy," *PGN: Philadelphia Gay News*, April 21, 2011, http://www.epgn.com/arts-culture/portraits/3405-12875676-tenika-watson-living-beyond-pendergrass-tragedy/.

26. "Clocked: An Oral History: Online Interview." http://clockedmovie.blogspot.com/2007/02/red-jordan-arobateau.html.

27. See Stallings, *Mutha' Is Half a Word*, 38–39.

Bibliography

Abdur-Rahman, Aliyyah I. *Against the Closet: Black Political Longing and the Erotics of Race*. Durham, NC: Duke University Press, 2012.

Ahmed, Sara. *Queer Phenomenology: Orientations, Objects, Others*. Durham, NC: Duke University Press, 2006.

Alexander, M. Jacqui. *Pedagogies of Crossing: Meditations of Feminism, Sexual Politics, Memory, and the Sacred*. Durham, NC: Duke University Press, 2005.

Allen, Jafari S. *¡Venceremos? The Erotics of Black Self-Making in Cuba*. Durham, NC: Duke University Press, 2011.

Andrews, William L. *To Tell a Free Story: The First Century of Afro-American Autobiography, 1760–1865*. Urbana: University of Illinois Press, 1988.

Anzieu, Didier. *The Skin Ego*. New Haven, CT: Yale University Press, 1989.

Arobateau, Red Jordan. *The Big Change (Confessions of a Metaphysician)*. Oakland, CA: Red Jordan Press, 2001, 1976.

Badu, Erykah. "I Want You." *Worldwide Underground*. Motown Records, 2003.

Bakhtin, Mikhail. *Rabelais and His World*. Translated by Hélène Iswolsky. Bloomington: Indiana University Press, 1984.

Baldwin, James. "Freaks and the American Ideal of Manhood." *Playboy*, January 1985, 150–51, 192, 256–60.

Bambara, Toni Cade, "On the Issue of Black English." *Confrontation* 1, no. 3 (1974): 103–17.

———, ed. "On the Issue of Roles." In *The Black Woman: An Anthology*, 101–11. New York: Signet, 1970.

———. "Salvation Is the Issue." In *Black Women Writers (1950–1980): A Critical Evaluation*, edited by Mari Evans, 41–47. New York: Anchor/Doubleday, 1984.

———. "What It Is I Think I'm Doing Anyhow." In *The Writer on Her Work: Contemporary Women Reflect on Their Art and Their Situation*, edited by Janet Sternburg, 153–78. New York: W. W. Norton, 1980.

Banks, Ralph Richard. *Is Marriage for White People? How the African American Marriage Decline Affects Everyone*. New York: Dutton, 2011.

Barad, Karan. "Queer Causation and the Ethics of Mattering." In *Queering the Non/ Human,* edited by Noreen Giffney and Myra J. Hird, 311–39. Burlington, VT: Ashgate Press, 2008.

Baraka, Amiri. "Abbey Lincoln: Straight Ahead." *JazzTimes,* January/February 2001. http:// jazztimes.com/articles/20621-abbey-lincoln-straight-ahead.

Bataille, Georges. *Erotism: Death and Sensuality.* Translated by Mary Dalwood. New York: Marion Boyars, 1998.

Battle, Juan, and Sandra L. Barnes, eds. *Black Sexualities: Probing Powers, Passions, Practices, and Policies.* New Brunswick, NJ: Rutgers University Press, 2010.

Baudrillard, Jean. *The Transparency of Evil: Essays on Extreme Phenomena.* Translated by James Benedict. London: Verso, 1993.

Beaney, Michael. *Imagination and Creativity.* Milton Keynes, UK: Open University, 2010.

Beauvoir, Simone de. *Must We Burn Sade?* Translated by Annette Michelson. London: P. Nevill, 1953.

Bell, David, and Jon Binnie. *The Sexual Citizen: Queer Politics and Beyond.* Malden, MA: Polity Press, 2000.

Bell, Kevin. "Assuming the Position: Fugitivity and Futurity in the Work of Chester Himes." *Modern Fiction Studies* 51, no. 4, special issue: "Paris, Capital of the Black Atlantic" (Winter 2005): 846–72.

Bennett, Hal. *Lord of Dark Places.* London: Calder and Boyars, 1970, 1971; New York: Turtle Point Press, 1997.

———. *A Wilderness of Vines.* New York: Doubleday, 1966.

Bernstein, Elizabeth. *Temporarily Yours: Intimacy, Authenticity, and the Commerce of Sex.* Chicago: University of Chicago Press, 2007.

Biggers, Sanford. *Sweet Funk: An Introspective.* New York: Brooklyn Art Museum, 2011.

Blair, Cynthia M. *I've Got to Make My Livin': Black Women's Sex Work in Turn-of-the-Century Chicago.* Chicago: University of Chicago Press, 2010.

Blumberg, Mark S. *Freaks of Nature: What Anomalies Tell Us about Development and Evolution.* New York: Oxford University Press, 2009.

Boggs, James. *The American Revolution: Pages from a Negro Worker's Notebook.* New York: Modern Reader, 1968.

Bolden, Tony, ed. "Theorizing the Funk: An Introduction." In *The Funk Era and Beyond: New Perspectives on Black Popular Culture,* 13–33. New York: Palgrave Macmillan, 2008.

———. "Groove Theory: A Vamp on the Epistemology of Funk." *American Studies* 52, no. 4 (2013): 9–34.

Botham, Fay. *Almighty God Created the Races: Christianity, Interracial Marriage, and American Law.* Chapel Hill: University of North Carolina Press, 2009.

Botting, Fred, and Scott Wilson, eds. *The Bataille Reader.* Oxford: Blackwell, 1997.

Breton, André. *Manifestoes of Surrealism.* Translated by Richard Seaver and Helen R. Lane. Ann Arbor: University of Michigan Press, 1972.

Brody, Jennifer DeVere. *Punctuation: Art, Politics, and Play.* Durham, NC: Duke University Press, 2008.

Brooks, Siobhan. *Unequal Desires: Race and Erotic Capital in the Stripping Industry.* Albany: State University of New York Press, 2010.

Brown, James. "Get Up (I Feel Like Being a Sex Machine)." *Sex Machine.* Starday and King Records, 1970.

Butler, Judith. *Bodies That Matter: On the Discursive Limits of "Sex."* New York: Routledge, 1993.

Butler, Octavia E. *Fledgling.* New York: Grand Central Publishing, 2007.

Cable, Umayyah. "Let's Talk about Pornography: An Interview with Shine Louise Houston." *Feministe* (blog), April 7, 2009. http://www.feministe.us/blog/archives/2009/04/07/lets-talk-about-pornography-an-interview-with-shine-louise-houston/.

Carby, Hazel V. *Reconstructing Womanhood: The Emergence of the Afro-American Woman Novelist.* New York: Oxford University Press, 1987.

Carpenter, Dale. *Flagrant Conduct: The Story of* Lawrence v. Texas. New York: W. W. Norton, 2012.

Carter, Angela. "Polemical Preface: Pornography in the Service of Women." In *Feminism and Pornography,* edited by Drucilla Cornell, 527–40. New York: Oxford University Press, 2000.

Cartwright, Samuel. "Report on Diseases and Peculiarities of the Negro Race." In *Health, Disease, and Illness: Concepts in Medicine,* edited by Arthur L. Caplan, James J. McCartney, and Dominic A. Sisti, 28–39. Washington, DC: Georgetown University Press, 2004.

Castronovo, Russ. "Aesthetics." In *Keywords for American Cultural Studies,* edited by Bruce Burgett and Glenn Hendler, 10–12. New York: New York University Press, 2007.

Churchill, Ward. *Pacifism as Pathology: Reflections on the Role of Armed Struggle in North America.* Oakland, CA: AK Press, 2007.

Clark, John R. "Formal Straining: Recent Criticism of Satire." College English 32 no. 4 (January 1971): 498–505.

Clark, VèVè. "Performing the Memory of Difference in Afro-Caribbean Dance: Katherine Dunham's Choreography, 1938–87." In *History and Memory in African-American Culture,* edited by Geneviève Fabre and Robert O'Meally, 188–204. New York: Oxford University Press, 1994.

Cohen, Cathy. "Deviance as Resistance: A New Research Agenda for the Study of Black Politics." *Du Bois Review* 1, no. 1 (March 2004): 27–45.

Collins, Patricia Hill. *Black Sexual Politics: African Americans, Gender, and the New Racism.* New York: Routledge, 2004.

Colosi, Rachela. "'Just Get Pissed and Enjoy Yourself': Understanding Lap-Dancing as 'Anti-Work.'" In *New Sociologies of Sex Work,* edited by Kate Hardy, Sarah Kingston, and Teela Sanders, 181–96. Burlington, VT: Ashgate, 2010.

Comaroff, John, and Jean Comaroff. *Ethnography and the Historical Imagination.* Boulder, CO: Westview Press, 1992.

Cooper, Carolyn. *Noises in the Blood: Orality, Gender, and the "Vulgar" Body of Jamaican Popular Culture.* London: Macmillan, 1993.

Corbin, Alain. *The Foul and the Fragrant: Odor and the French Social Imagination.* Cambridge, MA: Harvard University Press, 1986.

Cortazzi, Martin. "Narrative Analysis in Ethnography." In *Handbook of Ethnography,* edited by Paul Atkinson, Amanda Coffey, Sara Delamont, John Lofland, and Lyn Lofland, 384–94. Thousand Oaks, CA: Sage Publications, 2001.

Danielsen, Anne. *Presence and Pleasure: The Funk Grooves of James Brown and Parliament.* Middleton, CT: Wesleyan University Press, 2006.

Davis, Adrienne D. "'Don't Let Nobody Bother Yo' Principle': The Sexual Economy of American Slavery." In *Sister Circle: Black Women and Work,* edited by Sharon Harley and the Black Women and Work Collective, 103–27. New Brunswick, NJ: Rutgers University Press, 2002.

———. "Regulating Polygamy: Intimacy, Default Rules, and Bargaining for Equality." *Columbia Law Review* 110, no. 8 (December 2010): 1955–2046.

Davis, Betty. "F.U.N.K." *Nasty Girl.* Light in the Attic Records, 2009. Island Records, 1975.

———. "Your Mama Wants Ya Back." *They Say I'm Different.* Light in the Attic Records, 2009. Just Sunshine Records, 1974.

DeCosta-Willis, Miriam. "Letting Go with Love." In *Wild Women Don't Wear No Blues: Black Women Writers on Love, Men, and Sex,* edited by Marita Golden, 57–71. New York: Anchor, 1994.

———. "Looking toward Arbutus: Remembering Frank." In *Father Songs: Testimonies by African-American Sons and Daughters,* edited by Gloria Wade-Gayles, 205–16. Boston: Beacon Press, 1997.

DeCosta-Willis, Miriam, Reginald Martin, and Roseann P. Bell, eds. *Erotique Noire: Black Erotica.* New York: Anchor Books, 1992.

DeFrantz, Thomas F. "The Black Beat Made Visible: Hip Hop Dance and Body Power." In *Of the Presence of the Body: Essays on Dance and Performance Theory,* edited by André Lepecki, 64–81. Middletown, CT: Wesleyan University Press, 2004.

Delany, Samuel R. *Times Square Red, Times Square Blue.* New York: New York University Press, 1999.

Deleuze, Gilles. *Masochism: An Interpretation of Coldness and Cruelty.* Translated by Jean McNeil. New York: G. Braziller, 1971.

del Rio, Vanessa, and Dian Hanson. *Fifty Years of Slightly Slutty Behavior.* Los Angeles: Taschen, 2010.

Desmond, Jane. "Terra Incognita: Mapping New Territory in Dance and 'Cultural Studies.'" *Dance Research Journal* 32, no. 1 (Summer 2000): 43–53.

De Veaux, Alexis. *Warrior Poet: A Biography of Audre Lorde.* New York: W. W. Norton, 2004.

Deveney, John P. *Paschal Beverly Randolph: A Nineteenth-Century Black American Spiritualist, Rosicrucian, and Sex Magician.* Albany: State University of New York Press, 1997.

Dewey, John. *Art as Experience.* New York: Perigee Books, 1980, 1934.

Dimock, Wai Chee. "Deep Time: American Literature and World History." In *Transatlantic Literary Studies: A Reader,* edited by Susan Manning and Andrew Taylor, 160–66. Edinburgh: Edinburgh University Press, 2007.

Dreger, Alice Domurat. *Hermaphrodites and the Medical Invention of Sex.* Cambridge, MA: Harvard University Press, 1998.

———. *One of Us: Conjoined Twins and the Future of Normal.* Cambridge, MA: Harvard University Press, 2004.

Duggan, Lisa. *Sex Wars: Sexual Dissent and Political Culture.* New York: Routledge, 2006.

Dunham, Katherine. "Notes on the Dance: With Special Reference to the Island of Haiti." In *Black, Brown, and Beige: Surrealist Writings from Africa and the Diaspora*, edited by Franklin Rosemont and Robin D. G. Kelley, 261–62. Austin: University of Texas Press, 2009.

Dunn, James L. "Our Own Erotica." *American Visions* 12 no. 5 (October/November 1997): 31.

Durbach, Nadja. *Spectacle of Deformity: Freak Shows and Modern British Culture*. Berkeley: University of California Press, 2010.

Easton, Dossie, and Catherine A. Liszt. *The Ethical Slut: A Guide to Infinite Sexual Possibilities*, 1st ed. Gardena, CA: Greenery Press, 1997.

Edwards, Erica R. *Charisma and the Fictions of Black Leadership*. Minneapolis: University of Minnesota, 2012.

Elliot, Angel. "The Oral History of Freaknik." *Complex Magazine Online*, April 12, 2013. http://www.complex.com/pop-culture/2013/04/the-oral-history-of-freaknik/.

Ellison, Ralph. "Change the Joke, Slip the Yoke," In *Shadow and Act*, 45–59. New York: Vintage Books, 1972, 1964.

Emens, Elizabeth F. "Monogamy's Law: Compulsory Monogamy and Polyamorous Existence." *New York University Review of Law and Social Change* 29, no. 2 (February 2004): 277–376.

Ensslin, Astrid. *Canonizing Hypertext: Explorations and Constructions*. New York: Continuum, 2007.

Eshun, Kodwo. *More Brilliant Than the Sun: Adventures in Sonic Fiction*. London: Quartet Books, 1998.

Evans, Mari, ed. *Black Women Writers: Arguments and Interviews*. London: Pluto Press, 1985.

Fanon, Frantz. *The Wretched of the Earth*. Translated by Constance Farrington. New York: Grove Press, 1966.

Ferguson, Roderick A. *Aberrations in Black: Toward a Queer of Color Critique*. Minneapolis: University of Minnesota Press, 2004.

———. *The Reorder of Things: The University and Its Pedagogies of Minority Difference*. Minneapolis: University of Minnesota Press, 2012.

Fleetwood, Nicole R. *Troubling Vision: Performance, Visuality, and Blackness*. Chicago: University of Chicago Press, 2011.

Foucault, Michel. *The Birth of the Clinic: An Archaeology of Medical Perception*. New York: Vintage Books, 1975.

———. *The History of Sexuality: Volume 1: An Introduction*. Translated by Robert Hurley. New York: Vintage, 1990.

———. *Madness and Civilization: A History of Insanity in the Age of Reason*. New York: Vintage Books, 1988.

———. "Nietzche, Genealogy, History." In *The Foucault Reader*, edited by Paul Rabinow, 76–101. New York: Pantheon, 1984.

———. "What Is an Author?" In *The Foucault Reader*, edited by Paul Rabinow, 101–20. New York: Pantheon, 1984.

Franks, Katherine. *G-Strings and Sympathy: Strip Club Regulars and Male Desire.* Durham, NC: Duke University Press, 2002.

Frappier-Mazur, Lucienne. *Writing the Orgy: Power and Parody in Sade.* Translated by Gillian C Gill. Philadelphia: University of Pennsylvania Press, 1996.

Freeman, Elizabeth. *Time Binds: Queer Temporalities, Queer Histories.* Durham, NC: Duke University Press, 2010.

Freilla, Omar. "¡Ola, Hermano! A Black Latino Feminist Organizes Men." In *African Americans Doing Feminism: Putting Theory into Everyday Practice,* edited by Aaronette M. White, 73–82. Albany: State University of New York Press, 2010.

Frost, Linda, ed. *Conjoined Twins in Black and White: The Lives of Millie-Christine McKoy and Daisy and Violet Hilton.* Madison: University of Wisconsin Press, 2009.

Fullwood, Sam. "Before Zane Was a Star." *Black Issues Book Review* 6, no. 5 (September 2004): 19.

Garland-Thomson, Rosemarie. *Extraordinary Bodies: Figuring Physical Disability in American Culture and Literature.* New York: Columbia University Press, 1997.

———. *Staring: How We Look.* New York: Oxford University Press, 2009.

Gerima, Haile. *Sankofa.* Washington, DC: Mypheduh Films, 2003.

Gertzman, Jay A. *Bookleggers and Smuthounds: The Trade in Erotica, 1920–1940.* Philadelphia: University of Pennsylvania Press, 1999.

Gifford, Justin. *Pimping Fictions: African American Crime Literature and the Untold Story of Black Pulp Publishing.* Philadelphia: Temple University Press, 2013.

Gill, Lyndon. "Chatting Back an Epidemic: Caribbean Gay Men, HIV/AIDS, and the Uses of Erotic Subjectivity." *GLQ: A Journal of Lesbian and Gay Studies* 18, no. 2–3 (2012): 277–95.

Gomez, Jewelle. "Piece of Time." In *Erotique Noire: Black Erotica,* edited by Miriam DeCosta-Willis, Reginald Martin, and Roseann P. Bell, 387–91. New York: Anchor Books, 1992.

Gopinath, Gayatri. *Impossible Desires: Queer Diasporas and South Asian Public Cultures.* Durham, NC: Duke University Press, 2005.

Gordon, Avery F. *Ghostly Matters: Haunting and the Sociological Imagination.* Minneapolis: University of Minnesota Press, 1997.

Gordon, Lewis R. *An Introduction to Africana Philosophy.* New York: Cambridge University Press, 2008.

Gosine, Andil. "Politics and Passion: An Interview with Gloria Wekker." *Caribbean Review of Gender Studies: A Journal of Caribbean Perspectives of Gender and Feminism* 3 (2009). https://sta.uwi.edu/crgs/november2009/journals/CRGS%20Wekker.pdf.

Gottschild, Brenda Dixon. *The Black Dancing Body: A Geography from Coon to Cool.* New York: Palgrave Macmillan, 2003.

Grewal, Inderpal, and Caren Kaplan. "Global Identities: Theorizing Transnational Studies of Sexuality." *GLQ: A Journal of Lesbian and Gay Studies* 7, no. 4 (2001): 663–79.

Grosz, Elizabeth. "Bodies-Cities." In *Sexuality and Space,* edited by Beatriz Colomina, 241–54. Princeton Architectural Press, 1992.

———. *Time Travels: Feminism, Nature, Power.* Durham, NC: Duke University Press, 2005.

Guignery, Vanessa, and Ryan Roberts, eds. *Conversations with Samuel R. Delany.* Jacksonville, MS: University of Mississippi, 2009.

Gyekye, Kwame. "Akan Concept of a Person." In *African Philosophy: An Introduction,* edited by Richard A. Wright, 199–213. Lanham, London: University Press of America, 1984.

Halberstam, Judith. *In a Queer Time and Place: Transgender Bodies, Subcultural Lives.* New York: New York University Press, 2005.

———. *The Queer Art of Failure.* Durham, NC: Duke University Press, 2011.

Hammonds, Evelynn. "Toward a Genealogy of Black Female Sexuality: The Problematic of Silence." In *Feminist Genealogies, Colonial Legacies, Democratic Futures,* edited by M. Jacqui Alexander and Chandra Talpade Mohanty, 170–82. New York: Routledge, 1997.

Hardy, Kate, Sarah Kingston, and Teela Sanders, eds. *New Sociologies of Sex Work.* Burlington, VT: Ashgate, 2010.

Harney, Stefano, and Fred Moten. *The Undercommons: Fugitive Planning and Black Study.* Wivenhoe, England/Port Watson, NY: Minor Compositions, 2013.

Hayden, Robert. "Monet's Waterlilies." In *Collected Poems,* edited by Frederick Glaysher, 101. New York: Liveright, 1985.

Herukhuti. *Conjuring Black Funk: Notes on Culture, Sexuality, and Spirituality.* New York: Vintage Entity Press, 2007.

Himes, Chester. *Pinktoes.* New York: Dell, 1961, 1968.

———. *My Life of Absurdity: The Autobiography of Chester Himes,* vol. 2. New York: Thunder's Mouth Press, 1976.

———. "Tang." In *The Collected Stories of Chester Himes,* 407–11. New York: Thunder's Mouth Press, 1990.

Holland, Sharon P. *The Erotic Life of Racism.* Durham, NC: Duke University Press, 2012.

Holmes, Linda Janet, and Cheryl A. Wall, eds. *Savoring the Salt: The Legacy of Toni Cade Bambara.* Philadelphia: Temple University Press, 2008.

Houston, Shine Louise. *The Crash Pad.* San Francisco, CA: Blowfish Video, 2005.

———. *Superfreak.* San Francisco, CA: Blowfish Video, 2006.

Irving, Dan. "Normalized Transgressions: Legitimizing the Transsexual Body as Productive." *Radical History Review* 100 (Winter 2008): 38–59.

Iton, Richard. *In Search of the Black Fantastic: Politics and Popular Culture in the Post–Civil Rights Era.* New York: Oxford University Press, 2008.

Jackson, Michael. "Don't Stop 'Til You Get Enough." *Off the Wall.* Epic Records, 1979.

James, G. Winston. *Shaming the Devil: Collected Short Stories.* Hollywood, FL: Top Pen Press, 2009.

Jenkins, Artemus. *P.O.P. Power of Pussy.* 2013. http://artemusjenkins.com/home-2/portfolio -1/#!prettyPhoto[portfolio]/0/.

Johnson, Kalyn. "Zane, Inc." *Black Issues Book Review* 6, no. 5 (September 2004): 17–20.

Jones, Caroline A., ed. "The Mediated Sensorium." In *Sensorium: Embodied Experience, Technology, and Contemporary Art,* 5–49. Cambridge, MA: MIT Press/The MIT List Visual Arts Center, 2006.

Jones, Gayl. *The Healing.* Boston, MA: Beacon Press, 1998.

Jones, Omi Osun Olomo. "Performance and Ethnography, Performing Ethnography, Performance Ethnography." In *The Sage Handbook of Performance Studies,* edited by D. Soyini Madison and Judith Hamera, 339–47. Thousand Oaks, CA: Sage Publications, 2006.

Juffer, Jane. *At Home with Pornography: Women, Sex, and Everyday Life*. New York: New York University Press, 1998.

Kahn, Chaka. "Sweet Thing." *Rufus featuring Chaka Kahn*. ABC Records, 1975.

Kaplan, Amy. "Manifest Domesticity." *American Literature* 70, no. 3, *No More Separate Spheres!* (September 1998): 581–606.

Karenga, Maulana. "Black Art: Mute Matter Given Force and Function." In *Norton Anthology of African American Literature*, 1st ed., edited by Henry L. Gates and Nellie Y. McKay, 2086–90. New York: W. W. Norton, 1997.

Keeling, Kara. *The Witch's Flight: The Cinematic, the Black Femme, and the Image of Common Sense*. Durham, NC: Duke University Press, 2007.

Kelly, Robin D. G. "Playing for Keeps: Pleasure and Profit in the Postindustrial Playground." In *The House That Race Built: Black Americans, U.S. Terrain*, edited by Wahneema Lubiano, 195–231. New York: Pantheon Books, 1997.

Kempadoo, Kamala. *Sexing the Caribbean: Gender, Race, and Sexual Labor*. New York: Routledge, 2004.

———, ed. *Sun, Sex, and Gold: Tourism and Sex Work in the Caribbean*. Lanham, MD: Rowman and Littlefield, 1999.

———, ed. *Trafficking and Prostitution Reconsidered: New Perspectives on Migration, Sex Work, and Human Rights*. Boulder, CO: Paradigm Publishers, 2005.

Kempadoo, Kamala, and Jo Doezema, eds. *Global Sex Workers: Rights, Resistance, and Redefinition*. New York: Routledge, 1998.

Knight, Charles A. *The Literature of Satire*. New York: Cambridge University Press, 2004.

Kusnir, Jaoslav. "Reality, Imagination and Possible Worlds in American Postmodern Fiction." *South Bohemian Anglo-American Studies* 1, Dreams, Imagination and Reality in Literature issue (2007): 34–41.

Lancaster, Roger N. *Sex Panic and the Punitive State*. Berkeley: University of California Press, 2011.

Lee, Shayne. *Erotic Revolutionaries: Black Women, Sexuality, and Popular Culture*. Lanham, MD: Hamilton Books, 2010.

Lil Wayne. "A Milli." *Tha Carter III*. Cash Money Records, 2008.

———. "We Be Steady Mobbin." *We Are Young Money*. Young Money Records, 2009.

Lim, Bliss Cua. *Translating Time: Cinema, the Fantastic, and Temporal Critique*. Durham, NC: Duke University Press, 2009.

Lo, Malinda. "Shine Louise Houston Will Turn You On." *Curve Magazine* 16, no. 1 (April 2006). http://backup.curvemag.com/Detailed/711.html.

Long, Alecia P. *The Great Southern Babylon: Sex, Race, and Respectability in New Orleans, 1865–1920*. Baton Rouge: Louisiana State University Press, 2004.

Lorde, Audre. "Uses of the Erotic: The Erotic as Power." In *Sister Outsider: Essays and Speeches*, 53–59. Berkeley, CA: Crossing Press, 2007.

———. *The Cancer Journals*. Argyle, NY: Aunt Lute Books, 1980.

Lorde, Audre, and Susan Leigh Star. "Sadomasochism: Not about Condemnation: An Interview with Audre Lorde." In *A Burst of Light: Essays by Audre Lorde*, 11–16. Ann Arbor, MI: Firebrand Press, 1988.

Loren, Arielle. "Black Feminist Pornography: Reshaping the Future of Adult Entertainment." *Clutch Magazine Online.* http://www.clutchmagonline.com/2011/04/black-feminist -pornography-reshaping-the-future-of-adult-entertainment/.

Lowe, Scottie. "The State of Black Erotica." *ChickenBones: A Journal for Literary and Artistic African-American Themes.* http://www.nathanielturner.com/stateofblackerotica.htm.

Ludwig, Paul W. *Eros and Polis: Desire and Community in Greek Political Theory.* New York: Cambridge University Press, 2002.

Lune, Sadie. "Interview: Shine Louise Houston." *Bend Over Magazine* 4 (2010): 18–30.

Maffesoli, Michel. "Orgy: An Overview." In *Encyclopedia of Religion,* 2nd ed., edited by Lindsay Jones, 6860–63. Detroit: Macmillan Reference USA, 2005.

Margolies, Edward, and Michel Fabre. *The Several Lives of Chester Himes.* Jackson: University Press of Mississippi, 1997.

Martell, Joanne. *Millie-Christine: Fearfully and Wonderfully Made.* Winston-Salem, NC: John F. Blair, 2000.

Maultsby, Portia K. "Funk." In *African American Music: An Introduction,* edited by Mellonee V. Burnim and Portia K. Maultsby, 293–315. New York: Routledge, 2006.

Mbembe, Achille. "Necropolitics." Translated by Libby Meintjes. *Public Culture* 15, no. 1 (2003): 11–40.

McClintock, Anne. "Maid to Order: Commercial Fetishism and Gender Power." *Social Text* 37, A special section edited by Anne McClintock explores the sex trade (Winter 1993): 87–116.

McKittrick, Katherine. *Demonic Grounds: Black Women and the Cartographies of Struggle.* Minneapolis: University of Minnesota Press, 2006.

———. "On Plantations, Prisons, and a Black Sense of Place." *Journal of Social and Cultural Geography* 12, no. 8 (2011): 947–63.

McKoy, Millie and Christine. *The History of the Carolina Twins: Told in "Their Own Peculiar Way" by "One of Them."* Buffalo, NY: Buffalo Courier Printing House, [18—?]. Chapel Hill: University Library, University of North Carolina, *Documenting the American South* Collection. http://docsouth.unc.edu/neh/millie-christine/menu.html.

Merleau-Ponty, Maurice. *Phenomenology of Perception.* Translated by Colin Smith. New York: Routledge, 1989.

Meyers, Marian. "African American Women and Violence: Gender, Race, and Class in the News." *Critical Studies in Media Communication* 21, no. 2 (June 2004): 95–118.

Miller, Denene, Lynya Floyd, and Akiba Solomon. "Inside the Secret World of Sex Parties." *Essence* 37, no. 8 (December 2006): 192–98.

Miller, Henry D. *Theorizing Black Theatre: Art versus Protest in Critical Writings, 1898–1965.* Jefferson, NC: McFarland, 2011.

Miller, Monica L. *Slaves to Fashion: Black Dandyism and the Styling of Black Diasporic Identity.* Durham, NC: Duke University Press, 2009.

Miller-Young, Mireille. "Interventions: The Deviant and Defiant Art of Black Women Porn Directors." In *The Feminist Porn Book: The Politics of Producing Pleasure,* edited by Tristan Taormino, Celine Parreñas Shimizu, Constance Penley, and Mireille Miller-Young, 105–20. New York: Feminist Press/City University of New York, 2013.

———. *A Taste for Brown Sugar: Black Women in Pornography.* Durham, NC: Duke University Press, 2014.

Ménil, René. "Introduction to the Marvelous." In *Black, Brown, and Beige: Surrealists Writings from Africa and the Diaspora,* edited by Franklin Rosemont and Robin D. G. Kelley, 82. Austin: University of Texas Press, 2009.

Mitchell, Michele. *Righteous Propagation: African Americans and the Politics of Racial Destiny after Reconstruction.* Chapel Hill: University of North Carolina Press, 2004.

Mock, Janet. "How Society Shames Men Dating Trans Women and How This Affects Our Lives." Janet Mock website. http://janetmock.com/2013/09/12/men-who-date-attracted-to -trans-women-stigma/.

———. "My Experiences as a Young Trans Woman Engaged in Survival Sex Work." Janet Mock website. http://janetmock.com/2014/01/30/janet-mock-sex-work-experiences/.

Mohanty, Chandra Talpade. *Feminism without Borders: Decolonizing Theory, Practicing Solidarity.* Durham, NC: Duke University Press, 2003.

Morant, Kesha M. "Language in Action: Funk Music as the Critical Voice of a Post–Civil Rights Movement Counterculture." *Journal of Black Studies* 42, no. 1 (2011): 71–82.

Morgensen, Scott Lauria. *Spaces between Us: Queer Settler Colonialism and Indigenous Decolonization.* Minneapolis: University of Minnesota Press, 2011.

Morrison, Toni. *Beloved.* New York: Alfred A. Knopf, 2006.

———. *The Bluest Eye.* New York: Holt, Rinehart and Winston, 1970.

———. "Rootedness: The Ancestor as Foundation." In *Norton Anthology of African American Literature,* 1st ed., edited by Henry Louis Gates Jr. and Nellie Y. McKay, 2286–90. New York: W. W. Norton, 1997.

———. "The Site of Memory." In *Inventing the Truth: The Art and Craft of Memoir,* edited by William Zinsser, 183–200. New York: Houghton Mifflin, 1995.

Moten, Fred. "The Case of Blackness." *Criticism* 50, no. 2 (Spring 2008): 177–218.

Muñoz, José Esteban. *Cruising Utopia: The Then and There of Queer Futurity.* New York: New York University Press, 2009.

———. *Disidentifications: Queers of Color and the Performance of Politics.* Minneapolis: University of Minnesota Press, 1999.

Murray, Rolland. *Our Living Manhood: Literature, Black Power, and Masculine Ideology.* Philadelphia: University of Pennsylvania Press, 2007.

Mutu, Wangechi. *Wangechi Mutu: A Fantastic Journey.* Edited by Trevor Schoonmaker. Durham, NC: Nasher Museum of Art, Duke University, 2013.

Nagle, Jill, ed. *Whores and Other Feminists.* New York: Routledge, 1997.

Nash, Jennifer C. "From Lavender to Purple: Privacy, Black Women, and Feminist Legal Theory." *Cardozo Women's Law Journal* 11 (2005): 303–30.

———. *The Black Body in Ecstasy: Reading Race, Reading Pornography.* Durham, NC: Duke University Press, 2014.

Nelson, Raymond. "Domestic Harlem: The Detective Fiction of Chester Himes." *Virginia Quarterly Review* 48 (Spring 1972): 260–76.

Newbeck, Phyl. *Virginia Hasn't Always Been for Lovers: Interracial Marriage Bans and the Case of Richard and Mildred Loving.* Carbondale: Southern Illinois University Press, 2004.

Newman, Katharine. "An Evening with Hal Bennett: An Interview." *Black American Literature Forum* 21, no. 4 (Winter 1987): 358–78.

Newman, Toni. *I Rise: The Transformation of Toni Newman.* Los Angeles: CreateSpace, 2011.

Nguyen, Tan Hoang. *A View from the Bottom: Asian American Masculinity and Sexual Representation.* Durham, NC: Duke University Press, 2014.

Noble, Gil. "Abbey Lincoln on Love, Marriage, and Polygamy/Polyamory." On *Like It Is,* WABC-TV, 1979. http://www.youtube.com/watch?v=ZokBQsC4AdA.

Nora, Pierre. "Between Memory and History: Les Lieux de Mémoire." *Representations* 26, Special Issue: Memory and Counter-Memory (1989): 7–24.

Nottage, Lynn. *Intimate Apparel.* New York: Theatre Communications Group, 2006.

———. "La Jolla Playhouse Artist's Statement: Lynn Nottage on *Ruined.*" http://www.lajollaplayhouse.org/KBYG/Ruined/pg4.html.

———. *Ruined.* New York: Dramatists Play Service, 2010.

Nussbaum, Felicity A. *The Limits of the Human: Fictions of Anomaly, Race, and Gender in the Long Eighteenth Century.* New York: Cambridge University Press, 2003.

———. *Torrid Zones: Maternity, Sexuality, and Empire in Eighteenth-Century English Narratives.* Baltimore: Johns Hopkins University Press, 1995.

Nussbaum, Martha C. *Sex and Social Justice.* New York: Oxford University Press, 1999.

Oakley, Annie, ed. *Working Sex: Sex Workers Write about a Changing Industry.* Emeryville, CA: Seal Press, 2007.

Pancoast, William. "Biographical Sketch: The Carolina Twins." *Photographic Review of Medicine and Surgery: A Bi-Monthly Illustration of Interesting Cases,* edited by F. F. Maury and L. A. Duhring. Vol. 1, no. 5: 43–57. Philadelphia: J. B. Lippincott, 1870–71.

Parliament. "Prelude." *The Clones of Dr. Funkenstein.* Casablanca Records, 1976.

Partridge, Burgo. *A History of Orgies.* New York: Bonanza Books, 1960.

Perniola, Mario. *The Sex Appeal of the Inorganic: Philosophies of Desire in the Modern World.* Translated by Massimo Verdicchio. New York: Continuum, 2004.

Phelan, Peggy. *Unmarked: The Politics of Performance.* New York: Routledge, 1993.

Phillips, Layli, ed. *The Womanist Reader.* New York: Routledge, 2006.

Pick, Anat. "New Queer Cinema and Lesbian Films." In *New Queer Cinema: A Critical Reader,* edited by Michele Aaron, 103–19. New Brunswick, NJ: Rutgers University Press, 2004.

Platinga, Alfred. "Transworld Identity or Worldbound Individuals." In *Essays in the Metaphysics of Modality,* edited by Matthew Davidson, 72–90. New York: Oxford University Press, 2003.

Povinelli, Elizabeth A. *The Empire of Love: Toward a Theory of Intimacy, Genealogy, and Carnality.* Durham, NC: Duke University Press, 2006.

Prashad, Vijay. *Everybody Was Kung Fu Fighting: Afro-Asian Connections and the Myth of Cultural Purity.* Boston: Beacon Press, 2001.

Price, Richard, ed. *Maroon Societies: Rebel Slave Communities in the Americas,* 3rd ed. Baltimore: Johns Hopkins University Press, 1996.

Prince. "Computer Blue." *Purple Rain.* Warner Bros., 1984.

———. "Erotic City (Make Love Not War)." *The Hits/The B-Sides.* Warner Bros., 1989.

Prosser, Jay. *Second Skins: The Body Narratives of Transsexuality.* New York: Columbia University Press, 1998.

Quashie, Kevin. *Black Women, Identity, and Cultural Theory: (Un)Becoming the Subject.* New Brunswick, NJ: Rutgers University Press, 2004.

———. *The Sovereignty of Quiet: Beyond Resistance in Black Culture.* New Brunswick, NJ: Rutgers University Press, 2012.

Raiskin, Judith. "The Art of History: An Interview with Michelle Cliff." *Kenyon Review* 15, no. 1 (Winter 1993): 57–71.

Randolph, Paschal Beverly. *After Death; or, Disembodied Man.* Toledo, OH: Randolph, 1886. http://www.archive.org/details/AfterDeathTheDisembodimentOfMan.

———. *The Ansairetic Mystery: A New Revelation Concerning Sex.* Toledo, OH: Liberal Printing House (unpublished print of *Toledo Sun*).

———. *Dealings with the Dead: The Human Soul, Its Migrations and Its Transmigrations.* Utica, NY: M. J. Randolph, 1861–62. http://purl.dlib.indiana.edu/iudl/wright2/wright2–1992.

———. *Eulis! The History of Love.* Toledo, OH: Randolph, 1874.

———. "Letter from P. B. Randolph." *New Orleans Tribune,* December 2, 1864.

———. *Paschal B. Randolph, His Curious Life, Works, and Career,* 2nd ed. Boston: Randolph, 1874.

———. *Sexual Magic.* Translated by Robert North. New York: Magickal Childe, 1988.

Reid-Pharr, Robert. *Conjugal Union: The Body, the House, and the Black American.* New York: Oxford University Press, 1999.

Reiss, Benjamin. *The Showman and the Slave: Race, Death, and Memory in Barnum's America.* Cambridge, MA: Harvard University Press, 2001.

Rocha, Leon Antonio. "Scientia Sexualis versus Ars Erotica: Foucault, van Gulik, Needham." *Studies in History and Philosophy of Biological and Biomedical Sciences* 42, no. 3 (September 2011): 328–43.

Rodríguez, Ileana. *Women, Guerrillas, and Love: Understanding War in Central America.* Minneapolis: University of Minnesota Press, 1996.

Rodríguez, Juana María. *Sexual Futures, Queer Gestures, and Other Latina Longings.* New York: New York University Press, 2014.

Roen, Katrina. "Transgender Theory and Embodiment: The Risk of Racial Marginalisation." *Journal of Gender Studies* 10, no. 3 (2001): 253–63.

Rogers, J. A. *Sex and Race: Vol. 2: The New World.* New York: Helga M. Rogers, 1942.

———. *Sex and Race: Vol. 3: Why White and Black Mix in Spite of Opposition.*

Ronen, Ruth. *Possible Worlds in Literary Theory.* New York: Cambridge University Press, 1994.

Royster, Francesca T. *Sounding Like a No-No: Queer Sounds and Eccentric Acts in the Post-Soul Era.* Ann Arbor: University of Michigan Press, 2013.

Rubin, Gayle. "Thinking Sex: Notes for a Radical Theory of the Politics of Sexuality." In *Pleasure and Danger: Exploring Female Sexuality,* edited by Carole S. Vance, 267–319. New York: Routledge/Kegan Paul, 1984.

———. "The Traffic in Women: Notes on the 'Political Economy' of Sex." In *Toward an Anthropology of Women,* edited by Rayna R. Reiter, 157–210. New York: Monthly Review Press, 1975.

Ruffles, Tom. *Ghost Images: Cinema of the Afterlife.* Jefferson, NC: McFarland, 2004.

Russell, Heather. "Man-Stealing, Man-Swapping, and Man-Sharing: Wifeys and Mateys in Tanya Stephens's Lyrics" In *Caribbean Erotic: Poetry, Prose, and Essays,* edited by Opal Palmer Adisa and Donna Aza Weir-Soley, 276–92. Leeds, UK: Peepal Tree Press, 2010.

Salamon, Gayle. *Assuming a Body: Transgender and Rhetorics of Materiality.* New York: Columbia University Press, 2010.

Sexton, Jared. "The Social Life of Social Death: On Afro-Pessimism and Black Optimism." *InTensions* 5.0 (Fall/Winter 2011). www.yorku.ca/intent/issue5/articles/jaredsexton.php.

Shange, Ntozake. *Sassafrass, Cypress, and Indigo.* New York: St. Martin's Press, 1982.

Sharpe, Jenny. *Ghosts of Slavery: A Literary Archaeology of Black Women's Lives.* Minneapolis: University of Minnesota Press, 2003.

Shaver, Frances M. "Sex Work Research: Methodological and Ethical Challenges." *Journal of Interpersonal Violence* 20, no. 3 (March 2005): 296–319.

Shockley, Ann Allen. "A Different Kind of Black Lesbian Writer." *Sinister Wisdom* 21 (1982): 35–39.

Sinclair, John, ed. *Sun Ra: Interviews and Essays.* London: Headpress, 2010.

Smith, Sandra Wilson. "Chester Himes's *The Third Generation*: A Dystopic Domestic Novel." *Southern Literary Journal* 41, no. 2 (Spring 2009): 38–52.

Snorton, C. Riley. *Nobody Is Supposed to Know: Black Sexuality on the Down Low.* Minneapolis: University of Minnesota Press, 2014.

———. "Transfiguring Masculinities in Black Women's Studies." *Feminist Wire,* May 18, 2011. http://thefeministwire.com/2011/05/transfiguring-masculinities-in-black-womens-studies/.

Snorton, C. Riley, and Jin Haritaworn. "Trans Necropolitics: A Transnational Reflection on Violence, Death, and the Trans of Color Afterlife" In *Transgender Studies Reader 2,* edited by Susan Stryker and Aren Z. Aizura, 66–76. New York: Routledge, 2013.

Snow, C. P. *The Two Cultures.* Cambridge: Cambridge University Press, 1993.

Spears, Arthur K. "Directness in the Use of African American English." In *Sociocultural and Historical Contexts of African American English,* edited by Sonja L. Lanehart, 239–59. Philadelphia: John Benjamins, 2001.

Spillers, Hortense J. "Interstices: A Small Drama of Words." In *Black, White, and in Color: Essays on American Literature and Culture,* 152–75. Chicago: University of Chicago Press, 2003.

———. "Mama's Baby, Papa's Maybe: An American Grammar Book." In *Black, White, and in Color: Essays on American Literature and Culture,* 203–29. Chicago: University of Chicago Press, 2003.

Springer, Claudia. "Black Women Filmmakers." *Jump Cut* 29 (1984): 34–37.

Stallings, L. H. *Mutha' Is Half a Word: Intersections of Folklore, Vernacular, Myth, and Queerness in Black Female Culture.* Columbus: Ohio State University Press, 2007.

Stein, Michael Carl. *The Ethnography of an Adult Bookstore: Private Scenes, Public Places.* Lewiston, NY: Edwin Mellen Press, 1990.

Stevenson, Leslie. "Twelve Conceptions of Imagination." *British Journal of Aesthetics* 43, no. 3 (July 2003): 238–59.

Stryker, Susan, Paisley Currah, and Lisa Jean Moore. "Introduction: Trans-, Trans, or Transgender?" *WSQ: Women's Studies Quarterly* 36, no. 3–4 (2008): 11–22.

Suggs, Ernie. "Whatever Happened to . . . Freaknik? Street Party Became Its Own Undoing." *Atlanta Journal-Constitution,* April 14, 2008.

Sullivan, Mecca Jamilah. "A Strange People." In *All about Skin: Short Fiction by Women of Color,* edited by Jina Ortiz and Rochelle Spencer, 232–44. Madison: University of Wisconsin Press, 2014.

Sun Ra and Joshua Smith. *Space Is the Place.* Directed by John Coney. New York: Rhapsody Films, 1993.

Tate, Claudia, ed. *Black Women Writers at Work.* New York: Continuum, 1983.

Taylor, Charles. "Libertine or Prude?" *Salon.com,* September 4, 2002. http://www.salon.com/sex/feature/2002/09/04/zane.

Tempels, Placide. *Bantu Philosophy.* New York: Continuum, 1983.

Terborg-Penn, Rosalyn. "Migration and Trans-Racial/National Identity Re-Formation: Becoming African Diaspora Women." *Black Women, Gender, and Families* 5, no. 2 (Fall 2011); 4–24.

Thomas, Greg. "The Erotics of 'Under/Development' in Walter Rodney: On Sexual or Body Politics and Political Economics—for 'Guerilla Intellectualism.'" *CLR James Journal* 16, no. 1 (Spring 2010): 149–67.

———. *Hip-Hop Revolution in the Flesh: Power, Knowledge, and Pleasure in Lil' Kim's Lyricism.* New York: Palgrave Macmillan, 2009.

———. "On Psycho-Sexual Racism and Pan-African Revolt: Fanon and Chester Himes." *Human Architecture: Journal of the Sociology of Self-Knowledge* 5, no. 3 (2007): 219–30.

———. *The Sexual Demon of Colonial Power: Pan-African Embodiment and Erotic Schemes of Empire.* Bloomington: Indiana University Press, 2007.

Thompson, Bill. *Sadomasochism: Painful Perversion or Pleasurable Play?* London: Cassell, 1994.

Thompson, Krista A. "Performing Visibility: Freaknic and the Spatial Politics of Sexuality, Race, and Class in Atlanta." *TDR: The Drama Review: A Journal of Performance Studies* 51, no. 4 (2007): 24–46.

Thompson, Lisa B. *Beyond the Black Lady: Sexuality and the New African American Middle Class.* Urbana: University of Illinois Press, 2012.

Thompson, Robert Farris. *Flash of the Spirit: African and Afro-American Art and Philosophy.* New York: Vintage Books, 1984, 1983.

———. *African Art in Motion: Icon and Act in the Collection of Katherine Coryton White.* Los Angeles: University of California Press, 1974.

Tinsley, Omise'eke Natasha. *Thiefing Sugar: Eroticism between Women in Caribbean Literature.* Durham, NC: Duke University Press, 2010.

Toepfer, Karl Eric. *Theatre, Aristocracy, and Pornocracy: The Orgy Calculus.* New York: PAJ, 1991.

Traina, Cristina L. H. *Erotic Attunement: Parenthood and the Ethics of Sensuality between Unequals.* Chicago: University of Chicago Press, 2011.

Tweedy, Ann E. "Polyamory as a Sexual Orientation." *University of Cincinnati Law Review* 79, no. 4 (Summer 2011): 1461–1516, 2011.

Valdes, Francisco. "Afterword and Prologue: Queer Legal Theory." *California Law Review* 83, no. 1 (January 1995): 344–78.

———. "Coming Out and Stepping Up: Queer Legal Theory and Connectivity." *National Journal of Sexual Orientation Law* 1, no. 1 (1995): 1–42.

Vincent, Rickey. *Funk: The Music, the People, and the Rhythm of the One.* New York: St. Martin's Griffin, 1996.

Walcott, Rinaldo. "The Poor Cousins of Modernity." *TVO,* August 10, 2011. http://www .youtube.com/ watch?v=2kcNmFgHiH8.

———. "Outside in Black Studies: Reading from a Queer Place in the Diaspora." In *Black Queer Studies: A Critical Anthology,* edited by E. Patrick Johnson and Mae G. Henderson, 90–105. Durham, NC: Duke University Press, 2005.

———. "Reconstructing Manhood; or, The Drag of Black Masculinity." *Small Axe* 13, no. 1 (2009): 75–89.

Walcott, Ronald. "The Novels of Hal Bennett: Part I." *Black World,* June 1974, 37.

Walker, Alice. "Coming Apart." In *Womanist Reader,* edited by Layli Phillips, 3–11. New York: Routledge, 2006.

———. "Porn." In *You Can't Keep a Good Woman Down,* 77–84. New York: Harcourt Brace Jovanovich, 1981.

Wallace, Maurice O. *Constructing the Black Masculine: Identity and Ideality in African American Men's Literature and Culture, 1775–1995.* Durham, NC: Duke University Press, 2002.

Warner, Michael, and Lauren Berlant. "Sex in Public." *Critical Inquiry* 24, no. 2 (Winter 1998): 547–66.

Warren, Kenneth W. "Does African-American Literature Exist?" *Chronicle of Higher Education,* February 24, 2011. http://chronicle.com/article/Does-African-American/126483/.

Weeks, Kathi. *The Problem with Work: Feminism, Marxism, Antiwork Politics, and Postwork Imaginaries.* Durham, NC: Duke University Press, 2011.

Weheliye, Alexander G. "After Man." *American Literary History* 20, no. 1–2 (Spring/Summer 2008): 321–36.

———. *Habeas Viscus: Racializing Assemblages, Biopolitics, and Black Feminist Theories of the Human.* Durham, NC: Duke University Press, 2014.

Weinraub, Leilah, director. *Shakedown.* 2014.

Weiss, Margot. *Techniques of Pleasure: BDSM and the Circuits of Sexuality.* Durham, NC: Duke University Press, 2011.

Weiss, Paul. *Being and Other Realities.* Chicago: Open Court, 1995.

Wekker, Gloria. *The Politics of Passion: Women's Sexual Culture in the Afro-Surinamese Diaspora.* New York: Columbia University Press, 2006.

White, Hayden. "The Value of Narrativity in the Representation of Reality." *Critical Inquiry* 7, no. 1 (Autumn 1980): 5–27.

Whodini. "Freaks Come Out at Night." *Escape.* Jive Records, 1984.

Wilderson, Fred. *Red, White, and Black: Cinema and the Structure of U.S. Antagonisms.* Durham, NC: Duke University Press, 2010.

Williams, John A. "Negro in Literature Today." *Ebony Magazine,* September 1963, 73–76.

Williams, Linda, ed. *Porn Studies.* Durham, NC: Duke University Press, 2004.

Willis, Susan. "Eruptions of Funk: Historicizing Toni Morrison." *Black American Literature Forum* 16, no. 1 (Spring 1982): 34–42.

Wolfe, Cary. *What Is Posthumanism?* Minneapolis: University of Minnesota Press, 2010.

Wyatt, Gail Elizabeth. *Stolen Women: Reclaiming Our Sexuality, Taking Back Our Lives.* New York: John Wiley, 1997.

Wynter, Sylvia. "1492: A New World View." In *Race, Discourse, and the Origin of the Americas: A New World View,* edited by Vera Lawrence Hyatt and Rex Nettleford, 5–57. Washington, DC: Smithsonian Institution Press, 1995.

———. "Beyond Miranda's Meanings: Un/silencing the 'Demonic Ground' of Caliban's 'Woman.'" In *Out of the Kumbla: Caribbean Women and Literature,* edited by Carol Boyce Davies and Elaine Savory Fido, 355–72. Trenton, NJ: Africa World Press, 1990.

———. "Towards the Sociogenic Principle: Fanon, Identity, the Puzzle of Conscious Experience, and What It Is Like to Be 'Black.'" In *National Identities and Sociopolitical Changes in Latin America,* edited by Mercedes F. Durán-Cogan and Antonio Gómez-Moriana, 30–67. New York: Routledge, 2001.

———. "Unsettling the Coloniality of Being/Power/Truth/Freedom: Towards the Human, After Man, Its Overrepresentation—An Argument." *New Centennial Review* 3, no. 3 (Fall 2003): 257–337.

Zane. *Addicted.* New York: Atria Books, 2003.

———. *The Sex Chronicles: Shattering the Myth.* New York: Atria Books, 2003.

Zedde, Fiona. *Bliss.* New York: Kensington, 2005.

Index

L. H. STALLINGS is Associate Professor of Women's Studies at the University of Maryland–College Park.

THE NEW BLACK STUDIES SERIES